# THE RACIAL CRISIS IN AMERICAN HIGHER EDUCATION

Revised Edition

SUNY series

FRONTIERS IN EDUCATION

*Philip G. Altbach, Editor*

The Frontiers in Education Series draws upon a range of disciplines and approaches in the analysis of contemporary educational issues and concerns. Books in this series help to reinterpret established fields of scholarship in education by encouraging the latest synthesis and research. A special focus highlights educational policy issues from a multidisciplinary perspective. The series is published in cooperation with the School of Education, Boston College. A complete listing of books in the series can be found at the end of this volume.

# THE RACIAL CRISIS IN AMERICAN HIGHER EDUCATION

Revised Edition

CONTINUING CHALLENGES FOR
THE TWENTY-FIRST CENTURY

Edited by
WILLIAM A. SMITH
PHILIP G. ALTBACH
AND KOFI LOMOTEY

STATE UNIVERSITY OF NEW YORK PRESS

Published by
State University of New York Press, Albany

For information, address the State University of New York Press,
90 State Street, Suite 700, Albany, NY 12207

Production by Cathleen Collins
Marketing by Fran Keneston

**Library of Congress Cataloging-in-Publication Data**

The racial crisis in American higher education : continuing challenges for the
twenty-first century / edited by William A. Smith, Philip G. Altbach, and Kofi
Lomotey.—Rev. ed.
     p. cm. — (SUNY series, frontiers in education)
    Includes bibliographical references.
    ISBN 0-7914-5235-2 (alk. paper) — ISBN 0-7914-5236-0 (pbk. : alk. paper)
    1. Minorities—Education (Higher)—United States. 2. College integration—United
States. 3. Universities and colleges—United States—Case studies. 4. United States—
Race relations—Case studies. I. Smith, William A., 1964–  II. Altbach, Philip G.
III. Lomotey, Kofi. IV. Series.

    LC3731.R255 2002
    378.1'9829—dc21                      2001031124

10  9  8  7  6  5  4  3  2  1

# Contents

v

# Foreword

My knowledge of the racial crisis in higher education extends over a half century—from 1944 into the twenty-first century. I spent my undergraduate years at Morehouse College before pursuing graduate study in sociology at Atlanta University, where I earned my Master of Arts degree in 1949. I earned my Doctor of Philosophy degree in sociology at Syracuse University in 1957. Eventually, I became chair of the Department of Sociology and vice president for student affairs at Syracuse University and then Charles William Eliot Professor of Education at Harvard University. It is tempting to reflect upon my own experiences as a teacher, learner, and administrator in higher education in this foreword, but I will resist the temptation and instead mention a few concepts from my earlier work that will help readers better understand the rich material included in this volume.

The most important idea to remember is the resiliency of Black people and people of color in general. It is easy to declare "ain't it awful" about the circumstances of people of color and overlook their marvelous survival strategies. Probably one of the best examples of resilience among Blacks is their struggle to obtain an education. In his history of the Reconstruction period, W. E. B. DuBois said, "The eagerness to learn among American [Black people] was exceptional . . ." (DuBois 1935, 637). The struggle did not end in the Reconstruction period, but intensified as Black people entered the twentieth century. Due in large part to this eagerness and the political work of the Black community around issues of education, the number of Black college graduates has risen from 2,304 in 1898, according to W. E. B. DuBois, to 2,806,000 according to the National Center for Educational Statistics (1999, 18). Although one-sixth of all Blacks over twenty-five years of age have completed college today, the number mentioned above is an impressive increase of more than 1,200 percent during the twentieth century.

Discussions of higher education statistics such as those in this volume lead directly into the matter of social power and critical mass. A diversified learning community is beneficial for dominant as well as subdominant people. On predominantly White college campuses, small populations of color sometimes feel overwhelmed, as reported in several chapters in this collection. When the number of students of color is relatively large, their needs receive more attention; and White students must learn to negotiate with the less powerful who are large enough in numbers to veto "business as usual" if it does not accommodate their special needs and interests.

When the number of students of color is quite small, the probability that a White student will have the privilege of interacting with a student from a racial or cultural group unlike his or her own is minimal. Thus, a critical mass of students of color (at least one-fifth of the student body) is essential, if all students are to receive the blessings of a multicultural campus experience. Harvard has learned this lesson well and, for the past several years, has enrolled a first-year class in the College in which one-third of the students identify themselves as "minorities."

Much attention has been focused on intergroup relations at predominantly White colleges and universities; to its credit, this book also mentions learning derived from predominantly Black colleges that may not only help Black students but also enrich all institutions of higher education. Several authors in this book analyze schools whose student bodies are predominantly Black, Latino, or Asian.

I consider "inclusiveness" a generalized principle that has emerged from the minority experience and especially the Black experience in higher education that could benefit all colleges and universities. In earlier times, Black colleges demonstrated the benefit of a diversified faculty before other schools recognized it. The faculty for many Black colleges today is one-quarter to one-half Brown or White. Moreover, advocates of Black colleges and universities understand that an able faculty is a more important attribute in the creation of a good school. A good faculty is essential since Black colleges tend to accept students with a wide range of scores on achievement tests. Such students need faculty who are sensitive and dedicated teachers who accept them as they are before attempting to influence them to change behavior that may be inappropriate in the college environment.

Most Black colleges have student bodies that are more diversified in terms of their socioeconomic characteristics than those found in similarly situated White colleges. And Black colleges today are quite diversified in terms of the religious affiliation of their students, ranging from Protestant, Catholic, and Muslim and from fundamentalists and Pentecostal to mainline congregations.

In summary, I identify Black institutions of higher education as institutions that seek to maintain a "double culture" that helps their students develop a "double consciousness" by affirming who they are while understanding how others view them, and that teach their students how to achieve a "double victory"—a victory for the formerly oppressed and the former oppressor, a victory for the educated and uneducated, a victory for the high and mighty and the meek and lowly.

While William A. Smith, Philip G. Altbach, and Kofi Lomotey provide a useful service in recruiting a multiracial and multicultural group of wonderful scholars to muse upon the meaning of the linkage between race and higher education, they do more than make a contribution to research on these topics. They also make a contribution to the politics of higher education. Several of the authors in this volume stimulate questions about whom the author is attempting to influence and the purpose to which the analysis is dedicated. These are political questions that each reader should ask himself or herself.

For example, in discussions about standards in higher education, it is appropriate to question whose standards should be enforced in schools of good learning—the standards of the poor or the affluent, the standards of the majority or minorities, the standards of fast learners or slow learners? From a phenomenological perspective, the standards of each category are valid. The political question is: How may the differences between disparate but valid standards be negotiated to the benefit of the total society?

In those articles discussing the gap between Black and White populations in achievement, one should ask: For whom is the gap troublesome? Also, why does there seem to be less concern about that gap between high achieving Asian American students and White U.S.A.-born students who tend to lag behind them on some performance scales? And why are some scholars concerned that Black and Latino students may lag behind White students on achievement tests but are not disturbed that White students tend to lag behind Black students in self-esteem scores? And then, of course, the issue of who has the highest Justice Quotient (JQ) raises a valuable question. Justice and self-esteem should be cultivated during education and should also be classified as meaningful educational outcomes.

While the questions mentioned above are important, probably more important in the politics of higher education is this question: Who has the power and authority to place these issues on the nation's higher education agenda? These questions are prompted, in part, by the findings of William Bowen and Derek Bok on the long-term consequences of considering race in college and university admissions. Despite the fact that "the average combined SAT score for White applicants . . . was 186 points higher than the corresponding SAT average for black applicants" in some predominantly White selective colleges (Bowen and Bok 1998, 20), the Black students "overwhelmingly expressed satisfaction with their undergraduate education at these schools" (Bowen and Bok 1998, 194). Bowen and Bok concluded that "attentive advising, counseling and the simple provisions of encouragement and support made some differences in the lives of many of these [Black] students [at selective schools]" (1998, 205).

We know, based on contributions in this book, that Black students tend to receive this kind of care and concern in predominantly Black colleges. However, the data analyzed by Bowen and Bok indicate that care and concern can be kindly given by all schools to all sorts and conditions of students. Therefore, there is no excuse for not having a diversified student body.

I conclude this foreword to *The Racial Crisis in American Higher Education* with a discussion on the politics of higher education because scholars concerned with research findings pay too little attention to the ways in which their data and the data of other researchers are used.

The Civil Rights Act of 1964 required the Commissioner of Education to survey "the lack of availability of equal educational opportunities for individuals by reason of race, color, religion or national origin in public educational institutions at all levels in the United States." The main author of this study was James Coleman. Cornelius Riordan claims that "Coleman reformulated the concept of equality of educational opportunity" by focusing on "the extent of equality in educational outcomes across various racial and socioeconomic groups" (1997, 114), rather than focusing on educational inputs.

Actually, Coleman found that "the achievement of minority pupils depends more on the schools they attend than does the achievement of majority pupils," and that "for the most disadvantaged children . . . improvements in school quality will make the most difference in achievement" (1966, 22). For White children, Coleman found that "school-to-school variation in achievement appears to be not a consequence of effects of school variations at all, but of variations in family background" (1966, 296). Taking all of the results together, Coleman seemed to have forgotten about his findings for minority students and offered this as his main conclusion: "that schools bring little influence to bear on a [student's] achievement that is independent of his background and general social context" (1966, 325).

This conclusion, therefore, was a political one about equality of educational opportunity because it left out of the final statement any codicil about minorities and focused only on findings about White people, the majority population.

In dealing with the racial crisis on United States campuses, we must insist that researchers tell the truth, the whole truth, and nothing but the truth, rather than offering a partial truth that could lead to misunderstanding, faulty policy making, great harm, and the absence of help for racially and ethnically diverse members of society.

### References

Bowen, William G., and Derek Bok. 1998. *The shape of the river*. Princeton, NJ: Princeton University Press.

Coleman, James S., et al. 1966. *Equality of educational opportunity.* Washington, DC: U.S. Government Printing Office.

DuBois, W. E. B. 1935. *Black reconstruction in America, 1860–1880.* New York: Atheneum (published in 1969).

National Center of Educational Statistics. 1999. *Digest of educational statistics.* Washington, DC: U.S. Department of Education.

Powell, Gloria. 1973. Self-concept in White and Black children. In *Racism and mental health,* edited by Charles Willie et al., 299–318. Pittsburgh, PA: University of Pittsburgh Press.

# Acknowledgments

In preparing this book we had the pleasure of working with and being supported by a wonderful group of people. Their support made this project infinitely easier. We would like to briefly acknowledge some key people. We are indebted to Lavina Fielding Anderson for assisting us in editing, proofreading, and indexing the manuscript. Priscilla Ross of SUNY Press has been a constant supporter for this book. Routledge Press allowed us to reprint one of the chapters. William A. Smith wishes to thank Dr. Lascelles Anderson and the Center for Urban Educational Research and Development at the University of Illinois at Chicago which provided support during the initial stages of preparing this volume. He would also like to thank the Department of Education, Culture, and Society at the University of Utah for creating the best environment to think, debate, and develop ideas around social justice. Also, Dr. Phillip J. Bowman has been an incredibly critical colleague throughout the years. Most importantly, he would like to acknowledge his wife, Dr. Paula Smith, his three sons, Kenon, Kubasa, and Maulana Kasim, his daughter, Abena, and his mother, Gwen Smith, for their love and compassion. Kofi Lomotey would like to acknowledge his wife, Nahuja, and his three offspring, Shawnjua, Juba, and Mbeja, for their everlasting love, support, and encouragement. We are grateful to the Center for International Higher Education at Boston College for its financial support for editing and indexing this work. We are also beholden to the Center for the Study of Race and Diversity in Higher Education at the University of Utah for its financial contributions. This book is part of its research program. The Center's work is supported by the Ford Foundation.

# Introduction

## PHILIP G. ALTBACH, KOFI LOMOTEY, AND WILLIAM A. SMITH

In 1991 two of us (Altbach and Lomotey) published the first edition of *The Racial Crisis in American Higher Education*. When we started working on the book in 1989, race-based campus conflict was much in the news. The scenarios were similar. A hate speech, a racist poster, or some other race-related campus incident stimulated protests and debate. Meetings were organized, protest marches took place, and controversy ensued. In more than a few cases, antiracist demonstrations organized by student groups, often with broad campus support, led to conflicts with university administrators and occasionally arrests.

While the number of campus racial incidents was small, the pattern of increased racial tensions was clear. Campus administrators, in most cases, were unable to deal constructively with the situations that arose. The general reaction was to minimize the incidents. Most universities did little if anything to address the campus racial tensions that the incidents reflected. Many administrators made the mistake of exacerbating campus tensions by summoning police or resorting to disciplinary measures before such measures were absolutely necessary. Academicians, politicians, and the general public strongly felt that race relations in U.S. higher education were deteriorating.

Our goal in *The Racial Crisis* edition was to highlight the issue of race on campus and especially to critically analyze both the underlying issues and the campus situation at the time. To do this, we commissioned essays by key researchers and observers of the campus racial scene. Our book succeeded in bringing together analyses of both background issues, such as demographic trends, and case studies of campuses that had experienced racial tension and unrest.

We were surprised at the time that there was so little analysis and discussion available on the topic of race in higher education. Indeed, one of our goals was to stimulate research and debate on campus race relations, yet the issue remains underresearched. *The Racial Crisis* edition remains to this day one of few full-scale discussions of the topic.

Much has happened since the end of the 1980s. While data are hard to find, campus racial tensions have, to some extent, become less severe. The numbers of incidents have declined, and race is a *somewhat* less divisive issue on most campuses. At the same time, the location of racism has moved. E-mail and the Internet now seem to be a major source of racist messages and sentiments. Universities have had to consider how to maintain civility on the Internet, a matter of considerable complexity, with free speech and legal consequences.

Yet, as this book shows, there are still challenges. The issues have, to some extent, changed. If race relations among students have improved, the issue of race has moved to the arena of policy and the courts, where matters have become much more complex. *The Racial Crisis* edition was published at a time when affirmative action was widely accepted. Public opinion still largely supported it. University policies, legislative mandates, and executive authority were generally sympathetic to affirmative action. With hindsight, it is possible to see that public opinion was gradually changing and becoming less supportive. The end of the 1990s saw a variety of court decisions, voter initiatives, and election results antithetical to affirmative action; and the policy climate dramatically changed. For these reasons, we are more concerned here with the policy climate and with the legal and administrative aspects of race issues in higher education than we were in the first edition.

We are convinced that race remains a salient issue in U.S. higher education. The issues are much more complicated and nuanced but just as important. While there seems to be less direct overt strife on campus, the gains made in ensuring access to underrepresented racial and ethnic groups are deeply threatened in the current climate. Further, the racial and ethnic mosaic on campus has also shifted. The number of students "of color" has increased significantly; furthermore, their complexion has changed. Asian American students now constitute a larger percent of the student population nationally. In some parts of the country, Latina/o students are now the major racial group, and in some California schools, they represent a majority. The number of African Americans has increased in higher education. However, problems of persistence, access to some fields and disciplines, and related issues continue.

This volume provides an overview of the racial situation at the beginning of the twenty-first century. It is our hope that the analyses presented here will provide the catalyst for both thought and action. We are convinced that race remains a central issue of higher education—and of U.S. society.

The book is organized in a fashion similar to the first volume. In the first volume we considered student and historical issues in Part I. In this volume, we consider historical and contemporary issues first, to set the tone. Anderson broadly considers the issue of race in the larger U.S. society to set the scene for a more specific discussion of race in higher education, which follows in the essay by Altbach, Lomotey, and Rivers. Solmon, Solmon, and Schiff provide a discussion of the changing demographic scene in U.S. higher education. Teddlie and Freeman explicate an interesting framework for an insightful documentation of desegregation in U.S. higher education during the twentieth century. Together those chapters set the scene for the subsequent detailed discussions of specific aspects of the racial crisis in U.S. higher education.

We next discuss student issues. Bowman and Smith describe students and race on campus in general. They highlight the growing racial complexity and climate that is emerging within our twentiy-first century historically White colleges and universities. Hurtado focuses exclusively on Latina/o students, the fastest growing student population in U.S. higher education. Chang and Kiang provide an interesting assessment of the state of Asian American higher education. Lastly, Feagin, Vera, and Imani consider the concepts of educational choice, institutional reputation, and collective memory.

The third part of this volume (like the second part of Volume I) is devoted to faculty and administrative issues. Allen, Epps, Guillory, Suh, Bonous-Hammarth, and Stassen consider the status of college and university faculty by race and gender. Scheurich and Young reflect on the issue of racism as it is practiced by white faculty in U.S. colleges and universities. Villalpando and Delgado Bernal also add an important and new dimension to our discussion with an assessment of critical race theory as it impacts the status of faculty of color. Tierney and Chung provide a timely assessment of current affirmative action issues and their effect on higher education. Their contribution is particularly important in light of recent affirmative action developments in higher education.

# PART I

# Historical and Contemporary Background

# CHAPTER 1

# Race in American Higher Education

*Historical Perspectives on Current Conditions*

## JAMES D. ANDERSON

The racial crisis in American higher education stretches from the founding of the nation's first university, Harvard, in 1636 to the passage of California's Proposition 209 in 1997 and into our present. The origins and development of American higher education paralleled the evolution of a national system of racially qualified slavery and its attendant ideologies of racism and class subordination. In the seventeenth and eighteenth centuries, the intellectual and political leaders in Europe and America, as part and parcel of their domination over American Indian and African peoples, constructed themselves as the possessors of superior intelligence and as the creators of the highest forms of human civilizations. The subordination of Native Americans and Africans was rationalized and justified in terms of their innate inferiority (Adams 1995; Berkhofer 1978; Smedley 1993). Similar arguments were used against Mexicans in the late 1840s and against Chinese in the 1850s and beyond (Horsman 1981; McClain 1994).

The Scottish philosopher David Hume was among the first to articulate, in 1748, a hierarchy of race and intelligence. "I am apt to suspect," he said, "the negroes, and in general all the other species of men (for there are four or five different kinds) to be naturally inferior to the Whites. There never was a civilized nation of any other complexion than White, nor even any individual eminent either in action or speculation. No ingenious manufactures amongst them, no arts, no science" (Horsman 1981, 48). The works of such European scholars were widely read by American intellectuals and politicians. By the early nineteenth century such leading American "scientists" as Samuel Morton, Josiah Nott, and Louis Agassiz propounded pseudo-scientific theories that promoted the idea of African, Asian, and Indian intellectual inferiority (Horsman 1981, 48). There was a common assumption that Indians were doomed to inevitable extinction because of innate inferiority, that they

3

were succumbing to a superior Anglo-Saxon race, and that this was for the good of America and the world.

Similarly, by the early 1840s, few Anglo-Americans were willing to acknowledge that Mexicans had anything to commend them as a race. Sam Houston, two-term president of Texas, consistently thought of the conflict in his region as one between a glorious Anglo-Saxon race and inferior Mexican rabble (Horsman 1981, 191, 213). Hinton Helper, a chief Republican polemicist against slavery, wrote of the Chinese he saw on the Pacific Coast in 1852 that they were "semibarbarians" having no more business to be in California than "flocks of blackbirds have in a wheat field." "No inferior race of men can exist in these United States without becoming subordinate to the will of the Anglo-Americans," said Helper. "It is so with the Negroes in the South; it is so with the Irish in the North; it is so with the Indians in New England; and it will be so with the Chinese in California" (qtd. in Saxton 1971, 19). Racism was imbedded in the nation's foundations, affecting its major institutions, including the institutions of higher education.

Although the concept of race has changed dramatically over the course of three centuries, in vital respects, there has been an enduring sameness about scholarly works promoting the idea of race inferiority (Powell 1992; Feagin and Vera 1995). From the works of David Hume in the mid-eighteenth century to the works of Arthur Jensen, William Shockly, Hans Eysenck, Phillippe Rushton, Richard Herrnstein, and Charles Murray in the late twentieth century, there has been a constant assault on the intellectual capacity of people of color. Belief in the intellectual inferiority of people of color has pervaded the national culture for nearly three centuries (Goldberg 1993). More important, the translation of such beliefs into law and institutional practice has impeded the pursuit of higher education by members of ethnic groups of color. The dominant racial ideologies running throughout the past three centuries testify eloquently to the flexibility with which European and American perceptions integrated color, the myth of intellectual inferiority, and the practice of racial subordination into an elaborate legal and social rationale to deny many students of color opportunities for higher education (Orfield and Ashkinaze 1991).

American higher education virtually excluded African American students until after the Civil War. From the founding of Harvard College in 1636 to the 1830s, no American institution of higher education opened its doors to African American students. A powerful structure of racial exclusion was constructed in slave states by state governments and legal mandates and in the free states by practices of institutionalized racism.

Oberlin College constituted the important exception to this tradition of racial exclusion. Founded in 1833, the college began accepting African American students in 1835. During the 1840s and 1850s, African Americans comprised from 4 to 5 percent of Oberlin's total enrollment. A few other colleges, such as Antioch, followed Oberlin's example and admitted a few African American students during the antebellum period. Still, until after the Civil War, African American participation in American higher education was almost imperceptible. Historians of Black education estimate that, during the first 230 years of American higher education (1636–1866), the nation's colleges and universities graduated a total of from fifteen to twenty-eight African American students (Sollors, Titcomb, and Underwood 1993, 1–9).

The years between the beginning of the Civil War and World War I were an era of tremendous growth in American higher education. Institutions of higher learning multiplied in numbers that had no precedent. The new millionaires—Johns Hopkins, Andrew Carnegie, Leland Stanford, John D. Rockefeller, James B. Duke, and Matthew Vassar—generously supported institutions of higher learning. But higher education spread over the land primarily through institutions financed by public taxes. The typical American college or university tended to be public, popular, tied to the interests of local communities, and governed by boards of trustees drawn from the community. The era was symbolized by the land-grant colleges which expanded rapidly to occupy a large place in American higher education. In 1882, twenty years after the enactment of the Morrill Act, the total land-grant enrollment was only 2,243. By 1916, land-grant colleges enrolled some 135,000 students, one-third of all the nation's students in higher education. Land-grant universities, coupled with a growing system of state colleges, marked the emergence of a distinctive style of American higher education—publicly supported institutions of higher learning serving the educational, cultural, economic, and political interests of various local and state constituencies. In post–Civil War America, federal and state governments assumed the responsibility that in antebellum times had been borne by private wealth (Anderson 1996, 33–37).

African American higher education took a different path. The transformation of American higher education from a private, elite system to a more public, democratic one paralleled the triumph of White supremacy in the southern states and the emergence of institutionalized racism in northern states. State governments in the South successfully resisted the education of African Americans in general and were particularly opposed to secondary and higher education for African American students. Even many of the so-called progressive southern Whites who advocated formal education for African American children, proposed a special form and content of "Negro Education," a curriculum designed to meet their perceptions of the "peculiar" aptitudes and needs of a "race" of manual laborers. If African Americans, like Whites, were to be educated at public expense, southern White public officials all but universally held that education for African Americans must be not only separate but subordinate. This meant, above all else, limiting education for African Americans as much as possible to elementary schooling (Anderson 1988, 79–109).

Institutionalized racism in the North, though different in law and social practice, achieved similar results. African Americans in the North during the nineteenth and twentieth centuries were virtually denied access to public institutions of higher education. However, unlike the legally mandated barriers that characterized state systems of higher education in the South, the racial barriers in northern systems of public higher education were achieved through a complex process of institutionalized discrimination (Anderson 1993, 151–75). This process was based on an elaborate rationale that fused racism and meritocracy. Since institutionalized racism was a matter of social practice and not a matter of law, its defense and rationale became deeply entrenched in the cultural values and social norms of northern society. While southern institutions of public higher education barred African Americans as a matter of law, northern institutions barred them as a matter of educationally and socially rationalized practices. In both regions the results were similar; the legal and institutional systems of racial discrimination precluded significant opportunities for higher education.

From the Reconstruction era through World War II, African American students were largely enrolled in private Black colleges and universities, established and maintained for the most part by northern mission societies. (See also Altbach, Lomotey, and Rivers; Teddlie and Freeman, this volume.) The American Missionary Association was most prominent in this work. Its colleges and universities for African American students included Fisk University, Talladega College, Tougaloo College, and Dilliard University. The Freedmen's Aid Society of the Methodist Episcopal Church founded such institutions of higher learning as Clark College, Bennett College, Claflin College, Morgan College, Rust College, and Meharry Medical College. The American Baptist Home Mission Society maintained Morehouse College, Spelman College, Virginia Union University, Benedict College, and Shaw University. The Presbyterian Board of Missions for the Freedmen founded Johnson C. Smith University, Stillman College, and Knoxville College. The major nondenominational missionary institutions of higher learning were Atlanta University, Howard University, and Leland University (Anderson 1988, 238–78).

African American religious philanthropy also established a significant number of Black colleges and universities. Paving the way among Black religious mission societies was the African Methodist Episcopal (AME) church. Its colleges and universities included Allen University, Morris Brown College, and Wilberforce College. Lesser known AME schools were Paul Quinn College, Edward Waters College, Kittrell College, and Shorter College. The college work sustained by the African Methodist Episcopal Zion church was confined to Livingstone College. The Colored Methodist Episcopal church owned and operated four colleges for African American students: Lane, Texas, Paine, and Miles colleges. The bulk of higher education fostered by Black Baptist denominations was carried on under the auspices of the American

Baptist Home Mission Society. Still, Black Baptist denominations established and maintained their own colleges for African American students. Some of them were Arkansas Baptist College, Selma University, and Virginia College and Seminary.

Private missionary colleges figured heavily in the overall scheme of higher education for African Americans because they were virtually excluded by various states from the general development and expansion of publicly supported higher education. African Americans would become only marginal participants in publicly supported higher education during the post–Civil War era. During the late nineteenth and early twentieth centuries, the vast majority of African Americans lived in southern states. These states effectively resisted tax-supported higher education for African Americans from the Reconstruction era until after the *Gaines* decision in 1938. Then they created extremely marginalized systems of public higher education for African Americans.

Prior to 1900, seventeen states mandated racially segregated education; but other than the feeble efforts put forth to meet the terms of the 1890 Morrill-McComas Act, only Virginia, Alabama, North Carolina, and Maryland made any efforts to establish tax-supported institutions for African Americans. Still, even in these four states, tax-supported "higher education" for African Americans was limited to normal school education, despite the fact that in some instances these institutions were called universities. More important, fourteen of the seventeen southern states simply refused to establish land-grant colleges for African American students until it was required by Congressional mandate to receive the 1890 Morrill-McComas funds. Within a decade of the passage of the Morrill-McComas Act in 1890, the seventeen southern states acceded to the "nondiscrimination" provisions of the statute by agreeing to designate or establish land-grant colleges for African Americans. But these institutions, like the state normal schools established before them, were colleges in name only. They also were restricted by the states to function primarily as pre-collegiate teacher training institutes. Not one of them met the land-grant requirement to teach agriculture, mechanic arts, and liberal education on a collegiate level. Consequently, since more than 90 percent of African Americans lived in southern states, the vast majority entered the twentieth century residing in states with virtually no publicly supported institutions of higher education for Black students.

By World War I, this pattern of racial discrimination in public higher education had not changed significantly. A major government document produced in 1916 emphasized the inadequate level of Black higher education in the seventeen southern states. Thomas Jesse Jones of the federal Bureau of Education (Department of the Interior) conducted a thorough survey of higher education for Blacks in the southern states. There were sixteen Black land-grant "colleges" and seven state-controlled "colleges" for Blacks in the South in 1916. Jones found that these twenty-three public colleges were colleges in name only. Whereas the White land-grant colleges enrolled one-third of the nation's White college students in 1916, the sixteen Black land-grant colleges had virtually no students enrolled in college-level curricula; the sole exception was Florida Agricultural and Mechanical College. The seven Black state-controlled "colleges" reported no college students. Thus, in 1916, of the twenty-three Black public colleges in seventeen southern states, only one was making a serious effort to become a legitimate college. Yet even this effort was soon repressed (Anderson 1988, 238–41).

Nathan Young, President of Florida A&M, had quietly developed the institution's academic programs to the verge of accreditation and to the point where, according to the U.S. Bureau of Education, the institution would soon become "an excellent state college for Blacks." White trustees of Florida A&M who had sympathized with what they thought was Young's program expressed fear and reservations about his efforts to provide Black students with a college education. It might lead to "social equality," one trustee explained. "To be educated like a White man begets a desire to be like a White man." Capitalizing on White fears of college-bred African Americans, Cary Hardee, Democratic nominee for governor, seized upon this issue in his 1922 campaign. He portrayed Black higher education as a symbol of all the forces that threatened the rural White South and demanded that A&M be reorganized around vocational and industrial education. Young's resignation was one consequence of Hardee's victory at the polls in 1922. His successor was a professor of mechanical arts and vocational studies who had never earned an academic degree.

Other efforts to repress the development of Black higher education characterized the era. In 1904, Governor James K. Vardaman of Mississippi closed Holly Springs Normal School for Blacks, arguing that education was "ruining our Negroes." "They're demanding equality," Vardaman exclaimed. In 1919, Alabama State Teachers College and Alabama A&M were placed under the governance of Alabama's State Board of Education. The board promptly restricted both institutions to junior college status, which meant that the state maintained no institutions in which Blacks could secure a four-year college education. Alabama State College was not restored to a four-year degree-granting institution until 1931 and Alabama A&M did not become a college again until 1940 (Sansing 1990, 79; McMillen 1989, 72–108).

During much of the period from 1900 to 1950, therefore, especially up until the 1930s, most of the students enrolled in African American public "colleges" were enrolled at the elementary and secondary level, with a few in junior college courses. In 1916, for instance, of the 7,513 students enrolled in the twenty-three African American public colleges, 4,061 or 54 percent were classified as elementary level students; 3,400 or 45 percent were considered secondary or high school level students; and the additional 74 were distributed between the categories of "unclassified" and "collegiate." Hence, fully 99 percent of the students attending African American public colleges during the teens era were enrolled below the collegiate level.

This pattern continued until 1938 when the *Gaines* decision forced southern states to make some improvements in public higher education for African Americans to comply with the separate but equal principle of *Plessy*. Until 1938, Alabama, for example, maintained one public college for African Americans and no graduate and professional schools while maintaining seven public colleges for Whites including several graduate and professional schools. Mississippi supported only one college for African Americans, Alcorn, a land-grant college; but it supported six colleges for Whites, including two graduate schools. South Carolina supported one college for African American and six for Whites. Louisiana had a state-supported land-grant college for African Americans and four state-supported institutions of higher education for Whites. In 1930, African Americans were 35.7 percent of the total population in Alabama, 36.9 percent in Louisiana, 50.2 percent in Mississippi, and 45.6 percent in South Carolina. Thus, the four states with the largest proportions of African American citizens supported four public institutions of higher education for them while maintaining twenty-three public colleges for Whites. Moreover, none of these states provided graduate and professional educational opportunities for African Americans.

Because state after state repressed the development of publicly supported Black colleges and universities, higher education opportunities for African American students existed primarily in a system of private liberal arts colleges. During the first two decades of the twentieth century, 99 percent of African Americans enrolled in college were in private schools. This pattern of postsecondary enrollment stood in marked contrast to the national pattern in which significant proportions of students were enrolled in publicly supported colleges. This structure of African American higher education, with some improvement, persisted into the Great Depression. By 1930, approximately 75 percent of African American college students were enrolled in private institutions. Hence, African Americans were forced to rely heavily on the private sector for support of Black colleges and universities.

The founding of the United Negro College Fund (UNCF) in 1944 underscored the need for an organized effort to secure funds from private sources. African Americans were faced with the prospects of securing adequate resources for private colleges and universities or being dependent on extremely underdeveloped systems of public higher education. They pressed forward on two fronts. Through the UNCF they enlisted the support of corporate philanthropy and thousands of individuals to develop private colleges and universities. They also continued to press for equality in public higher education, the system that had become the mainstream of American higher education.

The *Brown v. the Board of Education* decision was handed down in 1954. It formed the legal basis for enabling African American students to seek admission to all-White colleges and universities in southern states. However, except for spectacularly successful attempts by individuals here and there, racial exclusion remained a pervasive practice in traditionally White institutions of higher education. Indeed, segregation and exclusion existed both in the North and in the South. Even in northern White universities where African Americans were admitted on a very limited basis, segregation existed within the campuses. A 1946 post–World War II government document emphasized that racial discrimination in the dormitories, honorary societies, fraternities and sororities, on athletic teams, and at social functions struck at the personal dignity of students of color. Still, the basic pattern of racial discrimination in American higher education remained intact until it was confronted by the modern civil rights movement. Until the 1970s, historically Black colleges and universities (HBCUs) were essentially the only institutions to provide higher education for African American students. In 1968, as Walter R. Allen and Joseph O. Jewell document, 80 percent of all African Americans who were awarded undergraduate degrees graduated from HBCUs (1995, 85).

Between the late 1960s and the 1970s, the African American presence on northern university campuses altered significantly, a trend that was true for students of color in general. By 1968 almost half of the nation's colleges and universities were making some efforts to recruit and provide financial assistance to students of color. The social forces that set such changes in motion began mainly with the civil rights movement, which protested all forms of racial subordination and discrimination against ethnic groups. Beginning in the mid-1950s, African Americans organized a grassroots struggle to protest state-enforced policies and practices of ethnic and racial subordination. These state policies included legally mandated, ethnically segregated schooling; political disfranchisement (i.e., various mechanisms to deny ethnic citizens of color the right to vote and run for political office); and many forms of civil and political inequality. U.S. institutions of higher education reflected the general societal practices of discrimination and exclusion against citizens of color and consequently were confronted with rebellions on campuses across the nation. By 1968 some sixty-five African American student organizations existed in traditionally White colleges. Similar organizations were also formed by Mexican American, Puerto Rican, and Asian American students.

As the civil rights movement gained momentum and broadened to include various ethnic groups of color, government and educational institutions were faced with the choice of increasing social unrest or changing long-standing policies and practices that had kept groups of color from all but token representation in dominant U.S. educational, political, economic, and social institutions. Eventually the federal government took the initiative to dismantle laws, policies, and mechanisms that barred ethnic groups of color from meaningful participation in American society. In 1964, President Lyndon Johnson signed into law the Civil Rights Act empowering the federal government to enforce equal protection under the law for all citizens. The following year he signed into law a Voting Rights Act with real teeth, meaning that it empowered federal officials to eliminate various forms of political disfranchisement against ethnic voters of color and candidates for political office. Almost immediately African American voter registration levels and election turnouts began to rise rapidly throughout the South. Many African Americans were elected to political office; and their increased political participation, together with the vanguard leadership of the civil rights movement, provided new voices for social justice in all aspects of American life.

In the mid-1960s, as groups of color pressed their demands for social justice and the federal government took greater initiative in demanding equality for all citizens, U.S. institutions of higher education began to open their doors to students of color. President Johnson's opinions helped set the tone and intent of the new policies. In June 1965, speaking to an audience of students of color at Howard University, an institution primarily for African American students, Johnson gave a working definition of fairness for groups of color after many decades of state and federal efforts to subordinate them: "You do not take a person who, for years, has been hobbled by chains and liberate him, bring him up to the starting line in a race and then say, 'you are free to compete with all others,' and still justly believe that you have been completely fair." To be fair, said Johnson, the nation must take affirmative steps to include groups of color in its dominant social institutions. The Presidential executive order and the various institutional policies that derived from this position came to be known as "affirmative action" (Bowen and Bok 1998, 6).

By the end of the 1960s, virtually all leading U.S. institutions of higher education had initiated policies and programs to include more students of color in undergraduate and graduate and professional education. The nation's traditionally White institutions of higher education moved away from virtual exclusionary practices to special educational opportunities, designed to attract limited enrollments of students of color. Special educational opportunities programs recruited highly talented students of color. For example, between 1961 and 1973, African American enrollment at Harvard increased about tenfold, from one hundred to one thousand (Weinberg 1977, 333).

Yet Harvard's admission office noted in 1973 that between 75 and 80 percent of the institution's African American students could not be categorized as disadvantaged. A study of 159 traditionally White colleges in 1968 found that 75 had no special programs for "high risk" students with substandard academic preparation. Of the 84 institutions with some kind of program or special effort to recruit disadvantaged students, no more than 6 or 8 were working with students who were unquestionably high risks (Weinberg 1977, 333–34).

The new policies and programs designed to increase the enrollment of students of color gradually included grants and scholarships to help finance the cost of higher education, as well as academic support programs aimed at helping them to adjust to campus life and thereby to increase their rates of retention and graduation. A whole new philosophy of cultural diversity developed around these changes. Leaders in American higher education stressed the importance of having students from diverse ethnic, cultural, and social backgrounds; this perspective defined diversity as important to national and international interests. Both the growing diversity of U.S. society and an increasingly globalized economy and political world made it evident that going to college only with students from your own culture was out of step with national and international changes. The advantages of being able to understand how others think and function, the ability to bridge racial and ethnic differences, and especially the skills and knowledge to lead groups composed of individuals from different cultures and languages were emphasized as both noble and practical reasons to increase the representation of students of color in the nation's colleges and universities (Bowen and Bok 1998, 53–73).

In addition, the higher education of students of color would enable them to offer their skills and services to traditionally underserved populations of color and give well-trained political leadership to constituencies of color. Diversity, it was said, enriched the educational experience by affording students the opportunity to learn from experiences, beliefs, and perspectives different from their own; promoted personal growth by challenging stereotyped preconceptions; strengthened communities by fostering mutual respect and teamwork; and enhanced the nation's economic competitiveness by making effective use of the talents and abilities of citizens from all ethnic backgrounds.

These efforts soon bore fruit. From the beginning of the civil rights movement to the present day, the numbers and percentages of students of color enrolled in and graduating from U.S. colleges has grown tremendously. To be sure, the vast majority of students of color has not reached parity with White students. However, much has changed since the 1960s. For example, from 1960 to 1995, the percentage of African Americans ages twenty-five to twenty-nine who had graduated from college increased from 5.4 percent to 15.4 percent. In U.S. law schools the percentage of African Americans grew from barely 1 percent in 1960 to 7.5 percent in 1995. Similarly, the percentage of African American medical students climbed from 2.2 percent in 1964 to 8.1 percent in 1995. Latina/o students experienced similar growth rates, and the increases for Asian American students were even higher. (See Chang and Kiang; Hurtado, this volume.)

To fully understand the increased participation of students of color in American higher education, it helps to begin with high school completion rates and then proceed to analyze college participation rates. The most recent high school completion rates for White, African Americans, and Latina/os ages eighteen-to-twenty-four nationwide are based on the U.S. Census Bureau's

1996 Current Population Survey (CPS). These data report students who earned either a high school diploma or an equivalency such as the General Education Development (GED) certificate. (CPS does not report the rates for Asian Americans or American Indians because the survey sample is too small to provide reliable estimates.) In 1996, the high school completion rates for the ethnic majority, Whites, was 82.3 percent. African Americans in this age group completed high school at a rate of 75.3 percent and Latina/os at a rate of 57.5 percent. African Americans achieved a gain in high school completion rates of nearly 8 percentage points from 1976 to 1996, but gains prior to 1990 accounted for all of this progress. The 1996 rate of 75.3 is nearly two percentage points below the 1990 rate, indicating some decline in the African American rate of high school completion. High school completion rates for Latina/os varied greatly during the past twenty years, and the 57.5 percent rate for 1996 is slightly more than 2 percentage points below the 1986 rate of 59.9 percent. The rates of high school completion provide a general indication of the rate at which students of color have access to higher education. (See also Hurtado; Teddlie and Freeman, this volume.)

Other indicators are the percentage of high school graduates qualified for college and the extent to which they aspire to attain a bachelor's degree, plan to attend college, actually take steps toward admission, and are accepted at a four-year college. Asian American high school graduates are most likely to qualify for admission to a four-year college (72.7 percent), followed by Whites (68.2 percent), Latina/os (53 percent), African Americans (46.9 percent), and American Indians and Alaskan Natives (44.8 percent). The 1992 Asian American high school graduates also expected to attain a bachelor's degree at a higher rate (89.9 percent) than Whites (83.4 percent), African Americans (82.7 percent), Latina/os (78.3 percent), and American Indians and Alaskan Natives (81.3 percent). The different ethnic groups were accepted at four-year colleges at varying rates, ranging from a high of 75.1 percent for Asian Americans to a low of 42.6 percent for American Indians and Alaskan Natives.

Students of color have made steady increases in college enrollment—by 61.3 percent from 1986 to 1996, including an increase of 22.2 percent since 1991. From 1986 to 1996, the college enrollment of African Americans has increased by 38.6 percent, Asian Americans by 83.8 percent, and Latina/os by 86.4 percent. In 1996, African Americans made up 12.5 percent of the U.S. general population and 11 percent of all college students. Latina/os constituted 11 percent of the total population and 8.7 percent of all undergraduate students. Asian Americans comprised 3.7 percent of the U.S. total population and 5.8 percent of the undergraduate student population. These levels of college participation by students of color represent significant increases over the past ten years. Since 1986, the enrollment of African students in undergraduate colleges has increased 35.8 percent, that of Latina/os 89.3 percent,

and that of Asian Americans 81.5 percent. The number of American Indians
enrolled in higher education remains small. They accounted for less than 1
percent of all U.S. higher education students in 1996.

Getting accepted to college, of course, is only the first step toward the
primary goal of attaining a college degree. The graduation rates by ethnicity
differ significantly from one group to another. In 1996, Asian Americans
graduated from college at a rate of 64 percent, Whites 59 percent, Latina/os
45 percent, African Americans 38 percent, and American Indians 37 percent.
The bachelor's degree completion rates determine the number and quality of
students of color qualified for admission to graduate and professional schools.

Significant increases in enrollment of students of color have also occurred at the graduate and professional levels. In 1996, African Americans
made up 7.2 percent of the total U.S. graduate student population. Latina/os
comprised 4.2 percent of the total, and Asian Americans constituted 4.5 percent of all graduate students. In 1996, African Americans accounted for 7
percent of all students in professional schools, Latina/os 4.7, and Asian
Americans 10.4. The enrollment of African American students in graduate
school increased by 74.3 percent from 1986 to 1996; for Latina/os the change
was 57.9 percent and 83.7 percent for Asian Americans. The increases in
enrollment in professional schools were similar except for Asian Americans
where the increase from 1986 to 1996 was a remarkable 185.4 percent.

A record number of Americans of color earned doctorates from U.S.
universities in 1996, continuing a decade-long rise. African American, Latina/o,
Asian American, and American Indian students received 3,542 Ph.D.s in 1996,
up from 3,517 in 1995 and up 73 percent since 1986. In 1996, African
American received 4.7 percent of doctoral degrees awarded to U.S. citizens;
Latina/os earned 3.4 percent and Asian Americans accounted for 4.0 percent
of all doctorates awarded to U.S. citizens. The percentage of doctoral degrees
earned in different academic fields varies from one ethnic group to another.
In 1996, African American students received only 1.4 percent of all doctorates awarded to U.S. citizens in the physical sciences, 2.3 percent in engineering, 3.1 percent in the life sciences, 4.8 percent in the social sciences, 2.7
percent in the humanities, and 10 percent in education. Asian American students received 6.1 percent of all U.S. doctorates in the physical sciences, 10.7
percent in engineering, 5.3 percent in the life sciences, 3.3 percent in the
social sciences, 2.3 percent in humanities, and 1.4 percent in education. The
pattern for Latina/o students was most similar to that for African American
students: 2.4 percent in the physical sciences, 2.6 percent in engineering, 2.9
percent in the life sciences, 4.3 percent in the social sciences, 3.3 percent in
humanities, and 4.1 percent in education. (See also Teddlie and Freeman;
Solomon, Solomon, and Schiff, this volume.)

Three decades ago, affirmative action programs in American higher education had many critics. These individuals were particularly critical of efforts

by America's most highly selective universities to recruit and enroll students of color. Critics assumed that students of color, specifically African American and Latina/o students, were ill prepared to deal with the rigorous academic curricula in the nation's best universities. After three decades, we now have clear data on this topic. Two of the most respected figures in American higher education, William G. Bowen and Derek Bok, examined how students of color have performed academically in comparison to their White classmates. Bowen, former president of Princeton University, and Bok, former president of Harvard University, examined the academic performance of the 1976 and 1989 entering cohorts of students of color at some of America's most prestigious colleges, including Princeton, Stanford, Swarthmore, Yale, Barnard, Columbia, Duke, Northwestern, Vanderbilt, and Washington University.

The overall graduation rate for the 1989 African American matriculants at these selective institutions was very high by any standard: 75 percent graduated from the college they first entered within six years and at least 4 percent transferred and graduated from some other college within this same time frame, bringing the overall six-year graduation rate to 79 percent. The fact that these are six-year graduation rates understates the final graduation rate because a significant percentage of African American B.A. recipients nationally earn their degrees more than six years after matriculation. Latina/o students at the same schools had an overall graduation rate of 90 percent, Asian Americans 96.2 percent, Whites 93.7, and Native Americans 81 percent (Bowen and Bok 1998, 55–57).

In a survey of the 1976 entering cohort, Bowen and Bok found that 51 percent of the graduates completed an advanced degree of some kind; this percentage, in fact, surpasses the rate at which White graduates of these selective schools earn advanced degrees. The graduates of color of these selective schools went on to have successful careers and to form the backbone of the emergent African American and Latina/o middle classes and the expanding Asian American middle class. Hence, the affirmative action policies of the 1960s did not fail; indeed, they worked all too well and the thirty-year success of students of color has created a strong backlash against such programs.

The opposition to affirmative action was generated in part by the fierce competition for admission to the most highly selective U.S. colleges and universities. It is important to emphasize that most U.S. colleges and universities are not selective in the sense that they do not receive enough qualified applicants to pick and choose among them. Between 70 to 80 percent of U.S. undergraduate colleges accept all qualified applicants and thus do not give preference to any group defined by ethnicity or any other criterion. About 20 to 30 percent of U.S. colleges receive enough qualified applicants to select on a competitive basis. These institutions have become the focal point for the current debate over the admission and support of students of color. This is so primarily because Whites compete strongly to get their children into the most highly selective colleges. Consequently, they feel that affirmative action programs to recruit and retain students of color deprive their children of privileges and opportunities. They favor a system based on "strict merit," meaning essentially that selective institutions should give preference to individuals with the highest grade point averages and standardized tests scores. Such standards, of course, would favor the children of the dominant class since income is highly correlated to performance on standardized tests and grade point averages. More important, majority students have much greater access to the best elementary and secondary schools and therefore are much more likely to have superior academic profiles. As the competition to enter America's leading colleges and professional schools has intensified over the past two decades, the opposition to affirmative action has become more determined and more successful. Today America is moving toward laws and policies that threaten to dismantle the programs that opened the doors of mainstream higher education to students of color. (See also Teddlie and Freeman; Chang and Kiang, this volume.)

Recent assaults on affirmative action programs by the University of California Board of Regents and the Texas Fifth Circuit Court of Appeals (*Hopwood v. Texas*) have called into question long-standing policies for recruiting and supporting students of color. The California Board of Regents in 1995 approved a ban on affirmative action in admissions, announcing that the nine universities in the University of California system (including Berkeley and UCLA) could no longer take ethnicity into account in admitting students. Its implementation was phased in during the 1996–97 academic year for graduate and professional schools and for undergraduates in 1997–98. California voters endorsed a similar initiative, Proposition 209, in 1996. This law bans affirmative action in public hiring, contracting, and education.

In Texas, a sweeping 1996 ruling by the Fifth Circuit Court of Appeals in *Hopwood v. Texas* upheld a charge that affirmative action constituted "reverse discrimination." The Texas Attorney General has interpreted the ruling as banning affirmative action in admissions, scholarships, and outreach programs aimed at recruiting students of color.

More recently, the state of Washington followed California in passing an anti-affirmative action referendum that bars "preferential treatment to any group on the basis of race, sex, color, ethnicity or national origin in the operation of public employment, public education or public contracting." The language of its Resolution I-200 echoes that of California's Proposition 209. Public university officials in Washington have suspended the state's thirty-year practice of affirmative action in its admissions and financial aid policies. These include programs encouraging women to go into engineering and students of color into science and mathematics.

In the Midwest, four Michigan legislators announced in April 1997 that they planned to instigate a lawsuit against the University of Michigan for unlawfully discriminating against White applicants. Statistics and guidelines from the University of Michigan's admissions office, they said, showed that its affirmative action policies favored students of color over White students with higher grade point averages and standardized test scores. The legislators have stated that other policies of the university, including those governing decisions on scholarships, grants, employment, and government contracts, will also be targets of the lawsuit. Their aim is consistent with those in California and Texas, to end affirmative action in higher education. Such politics resulted in the case of *Gratz v. Bollinger* which charged the University of Michigan's officials in the College of Literature, Science, and the Arts with violating Title VI of the Civil Rights Act, as well as the equal protection clause of the Fourteenth Amendment, by using race as a factor in decisions on admission. On December 13, 2000, Judge Patrick Duggan's decision upheld the integrity of Michigan's admissions policy.

The U.S. House Judiciary Constitution Subcommittee in July 1997 approved legislation that would end federal affirmative action policies and programs. Senators Mitch McConnell (R-Kentucky) and Orrin Hatch (R-Utah) sponsored a Senate version of the bill. It is uncertain if, or when, the anti-affirmative action bills will be voted on by the current Congress. Given the fact that former President Clinton would veto any strong anti-affirmative action bill, the Republican leadership are more likely to pursue their anti-affirmative action legislation under the current Republican president. However, if enacted, the bills would effectively end higher education grant and fellowship programs that target underrepresented students of color and women.

Early reports, while not conclusive, indicate that both the legislative/legal changes and their attendant campus racial climate could have a significant impact on the recruitment, admission, and retention of underrepresented graduate and professional students of color. Nearly two hundred African American students applied to the University of California-San Diego's medical school for the fall semester of 1997, the first semester after the new ban on affirmative action. None was admitted. The acceptance of Latina/o students to the medical school dropped to less than a third of those for the fall semester 1996. Plummeting enrollment at the University of California and Texas law schools also evidences the early impact of the bans on affirmative action.

Furthermore, acceptances have also declined sharply, indicating that the legal bans on affirmative action have engendered a climate of despair and alienation. The University of California at Berkeley announced in June 1997 that only one of the seventeen African American students admitted for the fall 1997 entering class of 270 decided to attend. None of the fourteen African American applicants admitted during the 1996–97 academic year actually enrolled in the fall of 1997. The only African American law student who enrolled in the fall of 1997 had been admitted in the 1995–96 academic year but had deferred his enrollment until fall 1997. Two other African American students who deferred their enrollment decided not to attend. Both UCLA and Berkeley reported substantial drops in the numbers of new African American and Latina/o law students as well. Berkeley's law school enrollment dropped from twenty African American and twenty-eight Latina/o law students in the fall 1996 entering class to one African American and eighteen Latina/o students in the entering class of fall 1997. UCLA's law school saw declines from nineteen African American students to ten and from forty-five Latina/o students to forty-one. Enrollments of color at the University of Texas at Austin law school went from thirty-one African American and forty-two Latina/o students in the entering class of fall 1996 to three African American and twenty Latina/o students in the class entering in fall 1997. The fact that Berkeley, UCLA, and Texas are ranked among the top five public law schools and among the top twenty overall underscores the centrality of their policies and results on nationwide efforts to recruit and retain students historically underrepresented in graduate and professional education.

The central question is what would happen to the current and future enrollment of students of color in the most highly selective U.S. colleges if officials decided or were compelled to admit applicants only on the basis of grades and test scores? In a careful estimate of the adoption of ethnic-neutral admission standards, Bowen and Bok conclude that African American enrollment at academically selective colleges would fall by between 50 and 70 percent. Latina/o students would experience similar results. Such policies would have little impact on the enrollment of Asian American students. It seems safe to say that the elimination of affirmative action policies would probably take African American and Latina/o enrollments at selective colleges most of the way back to the early 1960s levels, before such institutions began to make serious efforts to recruit students of color (Bowen and Bok 1998, 39, 50).

Hence, America is at a crossroads regarding the higher education of its students of color and, by extension, the very health of its society. In about three decades, citizens of color will constitute 40 percent of all U.S. citizens and a majority of both the school population and work force. We cannot afford to turn the clock back to the 1960s. Rather, it is critical to look ahead to our society's needs in the twenty-first century. The wise direction is not only to sustain representation of groups of color in U.S. higher education but also to improve it in many areas.

U.S. President Bill Clinton launched a long-overdue discussion on the problems of ethnicity in U.S. society. In his words: "We must resolve the barriers that divide us if our nation is to fulfill its promise in the next century." Nothing divided the nation more in the twentieth century than racial and ethnic conflict over issues of civil, political, and educational equality. Current efforts to dismantle affirmative action in college and university admissions and financial aid decisions demonstrate that ethnic conflict continues to be a central problem in American education and in the society at large. If our nation is serious about achieving ethnic diversity in its economic, political, and social institutions and seeks to fulfill its promise in the next century, American colleges and universities must do an even better job in recruiting, retaining, and graduating more students of color.

Approximately 75 million or 28 percent of the U.S. total population of 267 million (using the current population survey of 1997) are members of groups of color. The major groups are African Americans (33 million or 12.5 percent), Latina/os (30 million or 11 percent), Asian Americans (10 million or 3.7 percent), and Native Americans and Alaskan Natives (2 million or 1 percent). Currently, African Americans are the largest ethnic group in the United States, making up 44 percent of all groups of color; they are followed by Latina/os (40 percent), Asian Americans (13.3 percent), and American Indians (3 percent). However, population experts project that Latina/os will soon become the largest ethnic group in the United States. By 2030, approximately 40 percent of all Americans will be members of groups of color; and by 2050, approximately 50 percent of American K-12 and college-age students will be members of such groups (U.S. Department of Commerce). Hence the higher education of students of color is not only important to the progress of communities of color but equally important to the long-term needs and prosperity of the nation.

Today there is much debate about the nation's policies and regulations on higher education for students of color, particularly African Americans, Latina/os, and Native Americans who account for more than 85 percent of all U.S. students of color. In about three decades, institutions in the United States have gone from actively resisting the higher education of students of color to actively supporting it, to a backlash, or active resistance against the long-standing policies and practices that enabled students of color to gain greater representation in U.S. colleges. The majority of U.S. citizens and some powerful political leaders and special-interest groups are convinced that students of color enjoy an unfair preference in college admissions, especially admissions to the more selective U.S. colleges and universities.

This state of affairs gives a tragic irony to the continuing racial crisis in American higher education. As recently as 1968, students of color in America could look back on 332 years of racial segregation and exclusion from American colleges and universities. Many citizens—in fact, the majority— now believe that political and educational reforms during the past three decades have erased over three centuries of racial discrimination. Moreover, the widespread belief that current policies give unfair advantages to students of color and have made them preferred groups to be admitted to academically selective institutions hearkens back to the late nineteenth century when the White backlash fell on the last vestiges of civil rights gained during the Reconstruction era. As the U.S. Supreme Court struck down the civil rights

cases of 1883, which were based on the public-accommodations section of
the 1875 Civil Rights Act, Justice Joseph J. Bradley remarked that it was time
for African Americans to take the rank of mere citizens and cease being "the
special favorite of the laws" (Kluger 1975, 65–66).

In reality African Americans were moving into a period of oppression
that historians would recognize as their "nadir." That Justice Bradley could
view African Americans in the late nineteenth century as being the "special
favorite of the laws" boggles the mind, but this stance is no less amazing than
the late twentieth-century assertion that African Americans enjoy a privileged
position in American higher education. Both examples underscore the great
gulf between the reality in which African Americans live and work and the
perceptions of the dominant society. How America bridges this gulf in the
new century will ultimately determine how we resolve the racial crisis in
higher education and the society at large.

## References

Adams, David Wallace. 1995. *Education for extinction: American Indians and the
boarding school experience, 1875–1928.* Lawrence: University Press of Kansas.

Allen, Walter R., and Joseph O. Jewell. 1995. African American education since *An
American Dilemma. Daedalus: Journal of the American Academy of Arts and
Sciences* (winter): 77–100.

Anderson, James D. 1988. *The education of Blacks in the South, 1860–1935.* Chapel
Hill: University of North Carolina Press.

———. 1993. Race, meritocracy, and the American academy during the immediate
post–World War II era. *History of Education Quarterly*, 33, no. 2 (summer): 152–
75.

———. 1996. The evolution of historically Black colleges and universities. In *Mind
on freedom: Celebrating the history and culture of America's Black colleges and
universities,* edited by Spencer Crew and Lonnie G. Branch, 33–45. Washington,
DC: Smithsonian Institute.

Berkhofer, Robert F., Jr. 1978. *The White man's Indians.* New York: Alfred A. Knopf.

Bowen, William G., and Derek Bok. 1998. *The shape of the river: Long-term consequences of considering race in college and university admissions.* Princeton, NJ:
Princeton University Press.

Feagin, Joe R., and Hernan Vera. 1995. *White racism: The basics.* New York: Routledge.

Goldberg, David Theo. 1993. *Racist culture: Philosophy and the politics of meaning.*
Cambridge, MA: Blackwell.

Horsman, Reginald. 1981. *Race and manifest destiny: The origins of American racial Anglo-Saxonism.* Cambridge: Harvard University Press.

Kluger, Richard. 1975. *Simple justice: The history of Brown v. the Board of Education and Black America's struggle for equality.* New York: Vintage Books.

McClain, Charles J. 1994. *In search of equality: The Chinese struggle against discrimination in nineteenth-century America.* Berkeley: University of California Press.

McMillen, Neil R. 1989. *Dark journey: Black Mississippians in the age of Jim Crow.* Urbana: University of Illinois Press.

Orfield, Gary, and Carole Ashkinaze. 1991. *The closing door: Conservative policy and Black opportunity.* Chicago: University of Chicago Press.

Powell, Thomas. 1992. *The persistence of racism in America.* New York: University Press of America.

Sansing, David G. 1990. *Making haste slowly: The troubled history of higher education in Mississippi.* Jackson: University Press of Mississippi.

Saxton, Alexander. 1971. *The indispensable enemy: Labor and the anti-Chinese movement in California.* Berkeley: University of California Press.

Smedley, Audrey. 1993. *Race in North America: Origin and evolution of a worldview.* Boulder, CO: Westview Press.

Sollors, Werner, Caldwell Titcomb, and Thomas A. Underwood. 1993. *Blacks at Harvard: A documentary history of African-American experience at Harvard and Radcliff.* New York: New York University Press.

U.S. Department of Commerce, Bureau of the Census. 1998. *Current population reports: Population projections of the United States, by age, sex, race, and Hispanic origin, 1993 to 2050 and U.S. population estimates, by age, sex, race, and Hispanic origin: 1990 to 1994.* PPL-21. Washington, DC: U.S. Government Printing Office.

Weinberg, Meyer. 1977. *A chance to learn: A history of race and education in the United States.* New York: Cambridge University Press.

# CHAPTER 2

# Race in Higher Education

*The Continuing Crisis*

PHILIP G. ALTBACH, KOFI LOMOTEY,
AND SHARIBA RIVERS

Race remains one of the most volatile and divisive issues in U.S. higher education and has been a flashpoint of crisis since the civil rights movement of the 1960s. In the 1980s, the issue of race became the impetus for campus unrest; and in the 1990s, the battleground shifted to the policy arenas of affirmative action, admissions, and others. The racial situation manifests itself in many ways, from incidents on campus to policy decisions concerning affirmative action, to debates on multicultural content in the curriculum. In this chapter, we focus attention on the multifaceted, complex, and contentious elements of the present racial situation on campus. We look not only at campus conditions but also at broader societal trends and policies during the Reagan and Bush years, as well as at the policy context in the 1990s.

The impact of Supreme Court decisions on affirmative action, the actions of state court, and voter initiatives in California and other states relating to a range of race-related issues on campus race and ethnic policies has been immense. The university is no ivory tower; it is deeply affected by society. We must understand campus race relations, not only because the potential for continued turmoil exists, but also because we can learn a great deal about the nature of contemporary higher education through an examination of this central issue. Most important, the higher education community has a responsibility to constructively deal with one of the United States's most perplexing and difficult social issues.

What do the racial incidents that have taken place on campus mean for the broader context of U.S. higher education and for campus race relations? It is clear that there is an undercurrent of racial animosity among students in the United States. This feeling is perhaps related to a resurgence of ethnic identity that has characterized the campuses and much of society as well.

Young people seem to value ethnic self-identification now more than in the recent past. On the other hand, college students generally are liberal on racial questions and supportive of providing assistance to groups that need special help. Yet when such programs are perceived to affect the opportunities and perquisites of middle-class White college students, attitudes seem to become less liberal. In 1996, for example, 54 percent of all college freshmen favored abolishing affirmative action in college admissions (Sax, Astin, Korn, and Mahoney 1996). At the same time, 63 percent favored prohibiting "hate speech" on campus, and only 12 percent felt that racial discrimination is no longer a problem in the United States.

More recent statistics show that 21 percent of students believe that racial discrimination is no longer a problem. Although these numbers indicate an increase in students who have not perceived racial discrimination, it is still a relatively small number. The fact that discrimination persists on college campuses is indicated by 61.8 percent of the student population's belief that colleges should prohibit racist and sexist speech. Additionally, articles are still being written about hate crimes being committed on a daily basis (Fleischer 1999).

Racial incidents have to some extent polarized the campuses on which they have occurred. Race has become a key point of debate, creating a residue of bitterness and disillusionment. Racial incidents have perplexed campus administrators and faculty. Confident of their own good will and enlightened attitudes, these leaders have been unpleasantly surprised by these crises. How, they think, can such things happen on campuses devoted to intellectual inquiry and supportive of civil rights and other liberal campaigns? Administrators and faculty feel betrayed and resentful at the "ingratitude" of underrepresented students. At many universities, even where White students have started racial incidents, it is the reactions of underrepresented students that often engender administrative sanctions. These incidents have created confusion in the academic community. An example of the confusion is the most recent type of campus racial tension—the use of the Internet for transmitting racial slurs and other racist messages.

Campus race relations concern not only the underrepresented groups but also everyone involved in the academic enterprise. First, racial issues have great potential for precipitating campus disruption. More important, racial issues pervade the entire university—from debates about the curriculum to relations in dormitories, from intercollegiate sports to key decisions on admissions. Affirmative action regulations are directly linked to concerns about the presence of underrepresented groups on the faculties of colleges and universities. Indeed, since the 1970s, racial questions have come to play an unprecedented role in U.S. higher education, although the volatility of the issue declined somewhat in the mid-1990s. Despite this decline, the importance of the topic has not diminished. The issues may have changed to some extent and the arena of debate shifted as well, but race remains a central issue.

It sometimes appears that few on campus realize the impact of racial issues. Many academic administrators and the faculty, for the most part, see racial issues in isolation, as individual crises to be dealt with on an ad hoc basis, rather than as a nexus of issues requiring careful analysis. Most people in positions of authority seem to feel that racial questions are peripheral to the academic enterprise—that they are individual problems brought to center stage by small groups, unnecessary distractions from the real business of higher education. Many, in and out of academic life, are convinced that racial issues were "dealt with" in the 1960s and that underrepresented students should be satisfied with the policies put into place at that time. On the other hand, many, especially African American observers, have argued that race has been historically ignored as a central issue in U.S. education and society (Woodson 1993).

Policy makers in the universities and in government feel that they should not have to be concerned with racial issues, and their reactions often reflect a basic unwillingness to take such matters seriously or to consider their broader implications. Recent court decisions have strengthened this view by deemphasizing race as a salient factor in academic policy and, in some cases, forbidding race from being taken into consideration in admissions and other areas. Other developments, including voter initiatives in California and elsewhere and political decisions at The City University of New York, have also had the effect of eliminating race as a central issue in higher education decision making.

## Demographics

The campus racial situation is the result of developments in the number of underrepresented students and faculty in U.S. colleges and universities. Many of the programs started since the 1970s were aimed at increasing the number of underrepresented students—particularly African Americans—in higher education. Much controversy has surrounded the admission of underrepresented students and the recruitment and retention of underrepresented faculty. In the decades from the 1960s through the early 1990s, U.S. colleges and universities were subject to political and judicial pressure to increase racial diversity on campus. The basic demographics of the U.S. population as well as demands for access to higher education have contributed to the growth in numbers of underrepresented students. Many colleges and universities, sensing these trends, committed themselves to increasing the number of underrepresented students on their campuses and to improving services for these students. These efforts have met with some success over the past several decades.

The problems of representation in both the student population and the academic profession are multifaceted. Departments and programs have in many instances resisted the rigorous enforcement of affirmative action guide-lines—both for women and for racial groups. Most academics may be in favor of equal access to the academic profession, but they are less than enthusiastic about preferential hiring quotas or pressure to hire staff from different groups. There has also been a serious problem of an appropriate "pool" of candidates from various fields. The number of African American doctoral recipients in mathematics, for example, is extraordinarily small and is declining. In 1996, only 8 of the 488 Ph.D.'s awarded in mathematics were earned by African Americans. This trend can also be seen in other areas such as physics (12 African American Ph.D.'s out of 898) and engineering (59 out of 2,591) (National Research Council 1998, 41). (See also Solomon, Solomon, and Schiff; Anderson, this volume.)

The racial composition of U.S. higher education is complex. Although the enrollment of underrepresented groups has slowly begun to increase, the gap between White student enrollment and that of other groups has not yet closed (U.S. Department of Education 1996). During the 1970s, the numbers of underrepresented students in the undergraduate student population increased significantly. By the 1980s, however, the growth rate for most groups had slowed significantly. In 1985, 87.3 percent of the student population was White, while 8.1 percent was African American, 2.1 percent was Asian American, and 1.6 percent was Hispanic. In the 1993–94 school year, total enrollment for these underrepresented groups increased by 4.9 percent, while there has been no change in enrollment rates for Whites. However, the gap in real numbers is still large. Between fall 1991 and fall 1994, the percentage change for whites was –5.2 percent; however, real numbers indicate that total enrollment for White students ranged between 1,335,000 and 1,448,000 over the four years (U.S. Department of Education 1996). Members of underrepresented groups are still just that in higher education—underrepresented. (See also Anderson, this volume.)

These groups are not evenly distributed through the academic system. Asian Americans overall are overrepresented in the student population in terms of their numbers in the general population, although there are significant variations within the Asian American population (Hsia 1988). Japanese, South Asian, and Chinese Americans participate in higher education in extremely high proportions. In fact, their enrollment rates are higher than that of Whites. Some of the newer immigrant groups, however, such as Laotians and Viet-namese, remain underrepresented. In addition, Asian American enrollments are skewed with regard to fields of study. The large bulk of Asian American enrollments are in fields such as engineering and the sciences. Relatively few Asian Americans major in the humanities or social sciences. Asian Americans now constitute a significant portion of students at many of the nation's most prestigious and selective schools, and this too has caused some controversy. At the University of California, there have been charges that university officials discriminate against Asian Americans so that their proportions in California's most selective institutions will not rise too high (*Asian Americans at Berkeley* 1989). After lengthy political controversy and a statewide affirmative action referendum that supported an end to affirmative action, the Board of Regents of the University of California voted in 1995 to eliminate racial preferences in university hiring and admissions.

Overall, there are fewer African Americans in the high-prestige sector of U.S. higher education. Their numbers tend to be concentrated in less selective public colleges, community colleges, and of course in the historically Black institutions. Urban African American males are especially underrepresented. While the African American middle class has expanded dramatically in recent years, with rates of college attendance as high as, if not higher than, comparable populations in the majority population, in some fields (such as engineering and computer science), African Americans and Hispanics are still dramatically underrepresented. These groups seem to have a relatively high dropout rate, and fewer go on to graduate or professional education. And the trajectory of progress, particularly in predominantly White institutions, seems to be slowing at the same time that the proportion of underrepresented groups in the U.S. population is increasing.

Historically Black colleges and universities (HBCUs) are more than 90 percent African American in their student populations, and most of the degrees awarded to African Americans come from HBCUs. In a recent article published in *Black Issues in Higher Education* (Bennefield 1999), it was noted that, of the top ten schools awarding baccalaureate degrees to African Americans, almost all were historically Black institutions. The top school for the number of baccalaureate degrees awarded to African American students was Howard University.

The inclusion of a significant number of underrepresented students on campus has had implications for academic institutions—implications that are not fully understood. In the early period of active recruitment for diversity, academic institutions failed to provide adequate support services for these new students; not surprisingly, dropout rates were extraordinarily high. Later, it was recognized that these students required special assistance to overcome the disadvantages of often inferior secondary school preparation and to cope with an unfamiliar and frequently hostile environment. The provision of such services has proved costly in terms of financial and staff resources, engendering some resentment from White students.

In a way, the success of academic institutions in increasing the enrollment of underrepresented students and in serving these student populations has contributed to the growing number of racial incidents over the past several years. Underrepresented students on campuses have become more visible and the programs to serve them have attracted attention as well. The fact remains that it is always easy to express liberal opinions on issues that are distant from everyday realities. It is more difficult to combine liberal attitudes and behavior when theoretical issues have a concrete reality on campus. Both White racism and African American separatism may, in part, be reflections of this situation.

Nevertheless, with an increasing number of colleges being restricted from using race-based criteria for admissions and financial aid decisions, other alternatives have been sought. Some campuses, such as Ohio State University, have publicized their commitment to diversity in spite of rulings such as *Hopwood v. Texas* (1996), California's Proposition 209 (1996), and Washington State's Initiative 200 (1998). Diversity efforts have been implemented in a variety of other ways. For example, the University of Wisconsin is using its private, nonprofit organizations to raise money for scholarships that will be targeted for use by underrepresented students. The university has also asked for funding to enhance its precollege programs as a means of attracting students from underrepresented groups (Selingo 1999).

## The Dilemma: Reagan/Bush and Beyond

Race relations in the United States are affected by government policy, and the racial crisis on campus is very much a part of the legacy of the Reagan and Bush administrations—the policies and the atmosphere of the federal government during those twelve years (1980–92). There are several key aspects of this legacy. One is the sense of a lack of caring about racial issues in particular and social problems in general. The "Willie Horton" messages in George Bush's 1992 presidential campaign advertisements were very much a part of this pattern. The lack of rigorous enforcement of civil rights laws, the "taming" of the U.S. Civil Rights Commission, and official opposition to new antibias initiatives are all part of the political and social atmosphere. (See also Teddlie and Freeman, this volume.) The nature of appointments made by the Reagan and Bush administrations to government posts, including the Supreme Court, sent important messages; and the more conservative court has had a significant impact on court decisions relating to campus policies concerning racism. Not only were specific policies put into place and budgetary priorities implemented, but an overall tone was reflected in statements by administration officials. Lack of concern for the problems of underrepresented groups, exhibited in high places, tends to trickle down. For example, many campus administrators, never terribly enthusiastic about affirmative action goals, put issues of racial equality on the back burner during the Reagan/Bush era—where they have remained to this day, in many cases.

Specific governmental policies not only signaled a mood change in Washington, but also directly affected underrepresented students on campus. Government funds for virtually every program dealing with education were reduced in response to the double pressures of Reagan's military buildup and the growing budget deficit. Student loan programs were cut back and administrative and financial restrictions relating to them were increased. As a result, access to higher education was made more difficult. Enforcement of antibias and affirmative action policies was significantly weakened—so much so that both civil rights organizations and liberals in Congress vociferously complained. In general, funding for research in the hard sciences was protected better than that of programs to serve underrepresented students on campus.

The ethos and atmosphere created were just as important as the specific policies implemented. In the end, few government programs were actually canceled, although many were underfunded. The value of individual initiative was stressed, while social responsibility was ignored. President Reagan's statements questioning whether there were any homeless people in the United States illustrate the mentality of the era and its orientation toward social problems. Public statements by officials directly concerned with education and with law enforcement, including former Education Secretary William Bennett and former Attorney General Edwin Meese, buttressed both the style and the substance of the approach. The combination of policy decisions and public pronouncements by government officials set a powerful tone for the national debate on issues of social policy, including race relations.

The racial and ethnic legacy of the post-Reagan-Bush era is more complex. The Clinton administration's posture toward race relations in general and government policy in particular was in sharp contrast with that of its predecessor. The administration was more sympathetic to the concerns of racial and ethnic minorities. At the same time, solving the nation's racial and ethnic problems was not a top priority of the administration, especially since the Republicans took control of Congress. Indeed, the overall political atmosphere in the nation is fairly conservative and in general unsympathetic to the needs of the poor or underrepresented. The courts have been notably conservative in their approaches to racial issues, including affirmative action. Decisions at the state and federal levels, such as the 1996 Texas *Hopwood* action overturning race-based admissions at the University of Texas Law School and Initiative 200 (1998), which bars the use of racial preferences in admissions decisions in Washington state, have affected specific university practices and enrollment figures, as well as the overall climate regarding racial issues on campus (Ma 1999).

Efforts to cut public spending, demands from other sectors, such as health care and prisons, and efforts to balance the federal budget, have created significant financial problems for higher education. Even in the period of prosperity of the late 1990s public higher education did not, in most states, fully benefit from budgetary surpluses and the generally healthy economy. There were some exceptions, such as California, where higher education saw substantial budgetary increases; but at the same time, Proposition 209 ended affirmative action in student admissions at the University of California.

## The Impact on Higher Education

Those in positions of academic leadership found themselves strapped for resources to support programs for underrepresented groups. They also found that civil rights laws relating to affirmative action were not being rigorously enforced. In this environment, it was easy to ignore campus-based racial issues. Students also noted the change in national policy and direction. A vague White middle-class resentment against special programs for under-represented groups in higher education and against affirmative action in general could now be openly expressed. The mean-spiritedness expressed in Washington during the Reagan-Bush years was transferred to the campus. While it would be an exaggeration to blame the rise in the number of campus racial incidents entirely on the legacy of the Reagan and Bush administrations, there is little doubt that White students were affected by the changing national atmosphere regarding race relations. The legacy of that period has shaped the campus debate about race relations as well as both national and university policies affecting race.

An interesting aspect of this issue in higher education concerns desegregation in colleges and universities, largely in the South. In several southern cities—including Jackson, Mississippi, and Baton Rouge, Louisiana—predominantly White and historically African American colleges and universities operate side by side. Much controversy has arisen because of this seeming paradox, culminating in numerous state and federal court cases down through the years. Suggested measures to end this segregation have included merging schools. But such suggestions, though implemented in some cities, have been met with angry opposition. For example, in 1994, at least two thousand students marched from Jackson State University—a predominantly African American school—to the state capital, protesting a plan to close one historically African American school in the state and make it a part of a predominantly White school (Lomotey and Teddlie 1996; Teddlie and Lomotey 1997). (See also Teddlie and Freeman, this volume.)

## Implications for Faculty

The racial and social class composition of the academic profession puts it at some disadvantage in dealing with students from different racial and cultural backgrounds since the professorate is overwhelmingly White, male, and middle class. Also, most faculty members have not shown much concern about the situation. Professors are more likely to be focused on their own careers. The attitudes of the faculty, on racial matters as well as on politics, tend to be more liberal than those of the general population in the United

States, but at the same time the professorate is rather conservative on matters relating to change in the university (Ladd and Lipset 1975). Thus, faculty have resisted structural and curricular changes aimed at reducing racial tensions on campus. As Edward Shils (1982) has pointed out, the faith of the professorate in the "academic ethic" and the historical traditions of the university insulate the institution from rapid change.

Where racial tensions have flared into academic crisis, the faculty has been unable to avoid involvement. Students have frequently demanded changes in the curriculum, the strengthening of ethnic studies programs, and the like. The faculty has had to deliberate on these issues and has had a responsibility, on most campuses, for implementing such academic changes. Campus crises are disruptive for the faculty in many ways. Crisis management is often costly, not only in financial and human terms, but also for the reputation of the institution. In general, the academic profession has tried to avoid involvement with campus racial strife. The faculty has been less than enthusiastic about student demands for expanded ethnic studies programs and more multicultural courses in the curriculum. (See also Chang and Kiang, this volume.)

## Some Implications for Students

The student community is also very much a part of the campus racial equation. Many White students in colleges and universities do not grasp the seriousness of the situation, nor do they recognize the feelings and reactions of underrepresented students. Although student attitude surveys continue to show that White students remain liberal in their attitudes about race relations, an undercurrent of resentment against affirmative action and other special programs for underrepresented populations shows a certain callousness on the part of many White students about race relations.

Racial and ethnic identity has become a more central part of campus culture, and many students focus more on racial identity, becoming in some cases somewhat isolated in homogenous communities. Underrepresented students retreat into their own groups, creating "communities within communities," for many reasons—including the absence of cultural fit, professors from their ethnic group, and of positive faculty and peer interaction. A desire for social familiarity in the sometimes impersonal environment of the university is understandable. Further, the tensions evident in such events as the Los Angeles riots, the O. J. Simpson verdict, the James Byrd case, and other polarizing incidents cannot but have an impact on campus. Clearly, the campus simply reflects the social distance and tensions of the broader society.

Those most affected by racial problems are, of course, the underrepresented student communities in U.S. higher education. The bulk of overt campus racism has been directed against African American students. Organized campus protests relating to race have focused on opposing racist incidents and on ensuring that African Americans are not subjected to racial incidents on campus or in other ways made to feel unwelcome. In recent demonstrations, significant solidarity among underrepresented student groups in terms of goals and demands is evident, but there are, nonetheless, differences in the communities. Underrepresented students are concerned about a number of campus issues.

Asian American students have been more concerned about perceived patterns of discrimination in admissions rather than overt racial prejudice, although several recent incidents have heightened their awareness of racism. On a small number of campuses where there are large numbers of Asian Americans, there have been demands for the establishment of Asian American studies programs and similar initiatives. Chicano students have sought to expand the presence of Hispanic culture on campus and to increase the number of Hispanic students in colleges and universities. A key issue on which all of these communities agree is the need for multicultural and ethnic studies in the curriculum. Students have dealt with this issue on two fronts: demanding the expansion of ethnic studies programs such as African American studies and Asian American studies and calling for the integration of their cultural perspectives into the entire curriculum. These demands have aroused a good deal of opposition from faculty, who oppose tampering with the traditional curriculum, and from administrators, who cite the increased costs from the creation of new specializations and courses.

In many instances, underrepresented students have reacted to racism on campus or demanded that the university take action to meet their demands. In contrast to the volatile 1960s, the activism of the 1980s was, in general, free of violence and remarkably subdued in its rhetoric. Recent administrative reaction has also been more measured than in earlier periods, although on occasion police have been called onto the campus and disciplinary procedures have been invoked. In a number of cases, university administrators have responded to campus racial problems with ill-advised and sometimes heavy-handed measures that have exacerbated the situation. For example, the refusal of Stanford's president to meet with students informally, albeit on short notice, led to the calling in of local police and to arrests; a major confrontation was narrowly averted only when campus administrators reversed themselves and agreed to meet with the students. At the University of Massachusetts at Amherst, protracted demonstrations in 1997 demanding increased numbers of underrepresented students and faculty on campus and more financial aid for underrepresented students resulted in a commitment by the university administration to boost the numbers. After several decades of racial incidents and demonstrations, university and college administrators remain divided on how to deal with crisis.

In the late 1990s, while the overall number of racial incidents on campus seemed to have declined slightly, tensions remain and incidents occur. The ubiquitous Internet has been the scene of a number of racist incidents, including the dissemination of racist messages, slogans, and insults aimed at individual underrepresented students.

## Some Curricular Implications

The racial situation on campus has important academic implications. The establishment of ethnic studies programs is a result of the student struggles of the 1960s and later years (Astin 1975). In general, these programs and departments have not been lavishly supported and have been relegated to the periphery of the institution.

Nevertheless, through political pressure and activist movements, the number of African American studies programs and departments grew dramatically during the 1960s and early 1970s, although more recently there has been some consolidation and decline in the number of African American studies programs. In the 1980s, courses and programs devoted to Hispanic, Asian American, and more general ethnic studies were established and are still expanding. As recently as 1993, students, community members, and a faculty member at the University of California at Los Angeles went on a hunger strike to demand the creation of a Chicano studies department. Asian American students have lobbied, often successfully, to include courses in the curriculum focusing on the Asian American experience. (See Chang and Kiang, this volume.) During the 1995–96 academic year, students at Columbia University went on a hunger strike to demand the establishment of an ethnic studies department. The conflict escalated, with 150 students occupying the administration building and with the arrests of 22 students. The detailed discussion of the even more widespread development of women's studies programs, which preceded these ethnic studies programs, is beyond the scope of this chapter. Despite lukewarm academic support, these programs are now fairly well institutionalized and are perhaps the most important legacy of the campus unrest of the 1960s and the rise of racial consciousness in U.S. higher education.

Ethnic studies programs are, of course, not without their problems. For a period during the vocationally oriented 1970s, they lost significant support from students. To some extent, they have been labeled as low-status programs catering only to members of underrepresented groups, and there is widespread agreement among faculty and administrators that these programs are not central to the mission of the university. At Oberlin College (Lomotey 1990), for example, a White faculty member had this to say:

> I think that there is a kind of sense in which it [Black studies] is a marginal program. And I am not sure that all members of the faculty accept intellectually and curricularly the need for Black studies although they recognize it is a sort of social and political necessity, but not necessarily an intellectual or academic curricular one. (Lomotey 1990, xiv)

On the same topic, another White faculty member at Oberlin made the statement:

> I have a sneaking suspicion that there are more than a few faculty members and academic disciplines—take your pick— chemistry, Latin, history—who might not fully accept black studies. . . . I don't think that is a mark against black studies. But there is a certain degree of snobbery in the traditional academic disciplines about anything that is new. In part because universities have left significant control over faculty appointments in the hands of "mainstream" departments and disciplines, ethnic studies departments have only limited autonomy; and during periods of fiscal constraints, they often fall prey to budget cutbacks or cancellations. (Lomotey 1990, 29)

Since 1987, debate has taken place in many colleges and universities concerning the nature of the liberal arts curriculum and the role of ethnic studies in it. The struggle over the curriculum at Stanford in the late 1990s was widely reported in the media. When former U.S. Secretary of Education William Bennett went to Stanford to speak against "watering down" the traditional liberal arts curriculum, a national debate ensued. Traditionalists at Stanford argued that the established "canon" of accepted (and entirely Western) scholarship constituted the appropriate core of studies for undergraduates. Proponents of change favored the inclusion of material that reflected a wider cultural and racial experience, arguing that U.S. culture is not solely Eurocentric and that to understand both an increasingly complex and interdependent world and a more multicultural nation it is necessary to significantly expand the curriculum. After more than a year of acrimonious debate by the Stanford faculty, one required Western civilization course was supplemented by a "culture, ideas, and values" (CIV) component.

The Stanford debate, thanks in part to Bennett, received wide national attention, but the scenario was mirrored at many universities around the country, with the usual result being some expansion in the curricular horizons for undergraduates. These events have helped shape the debate concerning the nature of the curriculum because they go to the heart of conceptions of knowledge. While students have not played a major role in the curriculum debate, groups representing underrepresented students and feminist groups have from time to time supported multicultural curricular initiatives. Academic traditionalists— including those who led the fairly successful struggle for the primacy of the liberal arts curriculum—were never supportive of ethnic studies (Bloom 1987).

## The Backlash

The question naturally arises: Why have there been so many reported incidents of racial confrontation in U.S. colleges and universities? And why at some of the nation's most prestigious institutions?

There is little doubt that the legacy of the Reagan and Bush administrations has provided the political and rhetorical background. Recent and often successful anti-affirmative action initiatives in Washington and in a number of states have added to the national mood. The idea that racial intolerance is acceptable in society naturally trickles down to the campus level. Academic institutions are caught in the contradictory situation of having made a commitment to serve all students and to provide special assistance to students from underrepresented groups, but then finding that they have neither the fiscal nor the political support to implement workable programs. The problem is partly fiscal—special programs for students are expensive. Another problem is the lack of staff, particularly teaching faculty, who are themselves from underrepresented backgrounds and who can serve as role models. Underrepresented students are sometimes unable to keep up with their peers who usually have better academic preparation in high school. It is difficult for them to obtain the additional assistance that they need. This breeds frustration. Problems with cultural fit are also relevant when considering the discomfort students from underrepresented groups feel at these institutions. (See also Anderson; Teddlie and Freeman; Hurtado, this volume.)

In the less political atmosphere of the 1980s and 1990s, students had less ideological or moral commitment to racial harmony than was the case in earlier decades, when the spirit of the civil rights movement and of a moral commitment to the struggle for racial equality in the United States had an impact on campuses. More recently, the "me generation" was overwhelmingly concerned with careers and with personal matters, and less about social issues (Levine 1980). This lack of an ideological and moral "anchor" for good race relations had some impact on White students.

In many of the incidents of racial intolerance that have stimulated campus crises, the original event was relatively trivial. The perpetrator—typically a White student, often from a fraternity—had little idea of the reaction an event such as defacing a poster or making a racially biased remark would precipitate. Such happenings generally go unnoticed in today's racially and ethnically charged campus environment. The perpetrators, in general, "meant no harm." In the well-publicized series of events at Dartmouth College, conservative student groups sought to make ideological points relating to South

Africa, affirmative action, or other issues. Their campaigns became racially oriented, going far beyond the original intention. In 1993 an anonymous caller told five African American students at Salisbury State University, "Nigger, on October 30 we are coming to get you." Crosses were burned at Oberlin College, and on the same campus someone wrote a message on the Muslim Student Association's door vilifying Muslims. Such incidents seem to have abated somewhat, although it is possible that they are simply less widely reported in the media. More recently (1999), there was a bombing at Florida A&M University that was suspected as being racially motivated.

At many U.S. colleges and universities, underrepresented students have often demanded and received separate dormitories. Two examples are found at Stanford and Oberlin. Some argue that such arrangements lessen the level of informal interaction among racial groups. However, there is no evidence that a high level of such interaction occurs on campuses where separate dormitories do not exist. In 1993, the *Chronicle of Higher Education* reported that Cornell University had reviewed its policy of allowing members of special groups to live in program houses. It appears that this separation seems to provide a certain level of positive self-esteem for these students and also a less pressured environment. Drawing again on the Oberlin data, a staff person there addressed the importance of Oberlin's Afrikan Heritage House— its dormitory for African American students:

> Highly important. Not all black students choose to live in the House but many do. I think it contributes to a culturally enriching environment for the black students. It's a place where they can be away from the majority culture for a while if they want to have that family atmosphere.... When [African American] parents bring their students to campus, they are bringing their students to a predominantly White campus. It is important for parents to see that there is a place, a refuge, a camaraderie. Again this family atmosphere they can be a part of if they so choose. Certainly not all black students choose to live there. But it is important that it is there as a choice. (Lomotey 1990, 23)

The students at Oberlin all had something to say about Afrikan Heritage House. One student explained:

> I think it is important for people to have a place to feel comfortable—to go back home and relax and not always be on guard. Some people are comfortable with themselves no matter where they are ... come in a completely White dorm and still know who they are, feel comfortable. Not many of us today have reached that level of self-confidence and level of self-assuredness about themselves, and so I feel for us as young Black Americans growing [up] here in this country, places like Afrikan Heritage House and a family home are necessary. If not for political [reasons], at least for that family. I think Afrikan Heritage House appeals to black students for different reasons. I think most often the

reasons would be I feel very comfortable there. I don't need to put on any airs. I want to be myself. Also to learn about other people. (Lomotey 1990, 24)

White students and faculty may be resentful of what they perceive as special advantages given to underrepresented students and faculty. Variable admissions standards designed to permit more underrepresented students to be admitted are widely discussed on campus by White students. They feel that underrepresented students with lesser qualifications are being accepted while many Whites, with higher test scores and better high school records, are denied entry. White students may also resent the special programs provided to underrepresented students—programs that are costly and use scarce resources. White faculty members feel that faculty from underrepresented groups receive preferential treatment in the hiring process because the institution is trying to meet a hiring quota.

Yet, in Texas, the Higher Education Coordinating Board barred race as a consideration in granting student financial assistance. This decision came after the U.S. Court of Appeals for the Fifth Circuit (which includes Louisiana, Texas, and Mississippi) ruled that the University of Texas could not use race as a factor in making law school admissions decisions.

## An Overview of Student Activism after the 1970s

During the 1980s, the bulk of student activism was related, in one way or another, to racial issues. The most important flashpoint of activism was related to South Africa and its former apartheid policies. Hundreds of campuses saw demonstrations demanding university divestment of stocks of companies doing business in South Africa. In some cases, these protest movements were successful. In others, academic institutions made token changes; and in still others, the movements did not gain much support (Altbach 1997, xiii–xxxix).

A second focus of campus activism was in reaction to racial incidents or expressions. African American students sometimes protested these incidents to express their outrage and to direct campus attention to racial problems. More than two hundred such incidents received attention in the press between 1986 and 1988—and very likely many more were not widely reported. A final, less widespread, stimulus for activism during the 1980s was the demand for reform to diversify the curriculum.

During the 1990s, the call for curriculum reform increased. Activism over issues like the environment and U.S. intervention in Central America took a back seat to the rallying cry of marginalized groups who decided it was time to "bring the margin to the center." Ethnic studies programs and departments began to make new strides (although not nearly enough) in scholarly contributions. In the late 1990s, there were reportedly more than seven hundred ethnic studies programs and departments on campuses across the United States.

In spite of the curriculum gains at institutions of higher education, the racial climate still seems to be deteriorating. The campus racial situation tells us something about the society. If the most educated community in the United States—those in institutions of higher learning—is experiencing racial problems, then there is cause for worry about the rest of society.

## Recommendations

Various solutions to these challenges have been half-heartedly attempted—many of the "Band-Aid" variety. Very few have introduced lasting changes in approaches to educating African American and other underrepresented students. If we expect to successfully educate our college-age students from undergraduate through graduate or professional school, we must support them and find ways of ensuring that success. The faculty needs to be especially concerned about campus relations. At the most basic level, the schooling process is diminished by racial tensions and conflicts. Attention is deflected from teaching and learning. The campus atmosphere may be poisoned by racial conflict.

Many higher education institutions have put efforts into recruiting and retaining students from underrepresented groups. Colleges, such as Oberlin, that have a historical commitment to African American students should be used as models for "what works," and even Oberlin has not been entirely immune from the conservative societal trends discussed in this chapter. At the end of the nineteenth century, Oberlin graduated half of all African American graduates of predominantly White colleges and universities. Oberlin's African American enrollment and retention rates, which are far ahead of the national average, attest to the fact that other predominantly White institutions could also achieve better results. Lomotey's case study data from Oberlin College indicate a shared perception that an organizational commitment exists at such institutions with regard to African American students. That is, a commitment to the presence of African American students is prominent in the attitudes, behaviors, and characteristics of individuals in each of the constituencies of the college community.

The concept of a critical mass has significance for the retention of African American and other underrepresented students. These students provide support for each other, and the situation also encourages the continuation of support services provided for these students. Research shows that African American students are more likely to persist when there is a critical mass of African American students on the campus (Lomotey 1990). On predominantly White campuses, a critical mass is important for several reasons. The presence of a reasonable number of "same-race" peers provides role models and academic, social, and cultural support for these students—critical ingredients for a successful college experience.

## Final Observations

U.S. higher education faces some dilemmas dealing with race issues. The policy of in loco parentis was virtually abandoned in the aftermath of the turmoil of the 1960s, and students are viewed as adults who should be able to take care of themselves. There are now few rules governing student life. At the same time, universities are considered responsible for helping to shape the racial attitudes and social values of students and are widely criticized for racial incidents that take place. Universities cannot solve society's problems nor can they compensate for government policies that have contributed to racial tensions. Yet they are expected to provide a model for other societal institutions through their programs and the general atmosphere on campus. Ideally, universities are meritocractic institutions where judgments about individual performance are supposed to be made solely on the basis of qualifications and merit. Universities are key "sorting" institutions in society, providing credentials based putatively on merit for many key positions. But there are pressures to take the status of an underrepresented student or faculty member into account. Affirmative action programs and special admissions criteria vitiate pure meritocratic ideals, as do considerations of sports and social class background.

It is not surprising that tensions and conflicts in society are transferred to the campus. Yet the crises of the past few years relating to intergroup relations, the curriculum, the academic profession, and the mission of higher education vis-à-vis underrepresented individuals have proven disruptive and difficult. In the context of fiscal difficulties and a mission that stresses traditional teaching and research rather than solving complex social problems, the academic community has succeeded to a surprising degree in accommodating the multifaceted challenges of contemporary racial issues.

The academic community has sought, with some success, solutions to racial problems, and there is a significant consciousness on campus concerning race questions. After much debate, changes have been made in the curriculum to reflect a wider cross-cultural experience. Ethnic studies programs have been established and institutionalized. Resources have been found to support these underrepresented students. After some initial missteps in reacting to the tensions, many administrators seem committed to solving intergroup problems on campus and creating a positive campus climate.

However, the efforts must not stop there. With this in mind, colleges and universities (as well as elementary and secondary schools) should put forth

the committed effort of righting the wrongs. New paradigms, ways of thinking, and attitudes will take the educational system a very long way. In the
words of John Stanfield, "Until we engage in radical efforts to criticize and
revise the paradigms . . . to create and legitimate new ones, the more secondary traditions of critiquing racialized ethnic theories, methods . . . and patterns of knowledge dissemination will remain grossly incomplete" (Stanfield
1994, 183).

## References

Altbach, Philip G. 1997. *Student politics in America.* New Brunswick, NJ: Transaction
Books.

*Asian Americans at Berkeley: A report to the chancellor.* 1989. Berkeley: University
of California.

Astin, Alexander, et al. 1975. *The power of protest.* San Francisco: Jossey-Bass.

Bennefield, Robin M. 1999. Top of the Top 100. *Black Issues in Higher Education* 16,
no. 5 (August 19): 97–101.

Bloom, Allan. 1987. *The closing of the American mind.* New York: Simon and Schuster.

Fleischer, Jeff. 1999. Hate wave? *Black Issues in Higher Education* 16, no. 11 (August
5): 14–15.

Hsia, Jayjia 1988. *Asian Americans in higher education and work.* Hillside, NJ:
Lawrence Erlbaum.

Ladd, Everett Carll, Jr., and Seymour Martin Lipset. 1975. *The divided academy:
Professors and politics.* New York: McGraw-Hill.

Levine, Arthur. 1980. *When dreams and heroes died: A portrait of today's college
student.* San Francisco: Jossey-Bass.

Lomotey, Kofi. 1990. Culture and its artifacts in higher education: Their impact on the
enrollment and retention of African-American students. Paper presented at the
annual meeting of the American Educational Research Association, April, Boston.

Lomotey, Kofi, and Charles Teddlie, eds. 1996. *Readings on equal education, Vol. 13:
Forty years after the Brown decision: Implications of school desegregation for
U.S. education.* New York: AMS Press.

Ma, Kenneth. 1999. University of Washington expects fewer Black freshmen. *Chronicle
of Higher Education* (May 28): A33.

National Research Council. 1998. *Status report on minorities in higher education,
1998.* Washington, DC: National Research Council.

Sax, Linda J., Alexander Astin, William S. Korn, and Kathryn M. Mahoney. 1996. *The American freshman: National norms for 1996.* Los Angeles: Higher Education Research Institute, University of California at Los Angeles.

Selingo, Jeffrey. 1999. Affirmative action without numerical goals. *Chronicle of Higher Education* (May 28): A34.

Shils, Edward. 1982. *The academic ethic.* Chicago: University of Chicago Press.

Stanfield, John H., II. 1994. Ethnic modeling. In *Handbook of qualitative research,* edited by N. K. Denzin and Yvonna S. Lincoln, 175–87. Thousands Oaks, CA: Sage.

Teddlie, Charles, and Kofi Lomotey, eds. 1997. *Readings on equal education, Vol. 14: Forty years after the Brown decision: Social and cultural effects on school desegregation.* New York: AMS Press.

U.S. Department of Education, National Center for Education Statistics. 1996. *Digest of Education Statistics, 1996.* Washington, DC: National Center for Education Statistics.

Woodson, Carter G. 1993. *Miseducation of the Negro.* Trenton, NJ: Africa World Press.

# CHAPTER 3

# The Changing Demographics

*Problems and Opportunities*

LEWIS C. SOLMON, MATTHEW S. SOLMON,
AND TAMARA W. SCHIFF

In 1991, we contributed a chapter on racial demographics to *The Racial Crisis in American Higher Education.* The most important implication of that timing is that the U.S. Census Bureau had not yet published its detailed demographic data from the 1990 census. Many of the data points discussed in the 1991 paper were based on the 1980 census and some updates from the early 1980s. This chapter utilizes the 1990 census as well as subsequent data from the current population survey series and other sources, though, once again, information from the most recent (2000) census is not available at this writing. In addition, the world has changed profoundly in the last decade: the end of Communism and the true globalization of the world economy; the progression from the postindustrial age to the information technology age; and, in the United States, from a severe recession to the longest period of sustained economic growth in our lifetimes. Each of these changes alters our perspectives on the role and importance of higher education in America and, in particular, on the prospects for those who do or do not benefit from higher education in the future.

Before discussing the future trends for students and faculty of color in American higher education, and the policies they imply, it is important to understand the overall current and future demographics of our nation. Population trends affect the demand for higher education—that is, the number of people seeking to enroll and the supply of faculty available to various postsecondary institutions. A college-going population which is more ethnically and racially diverse than in the past will have different needs than previous generations of higher education participants.

## The Number of Traditional College-Age Students

The number of undergraduates each year is the number of people born about eighteen years earlier who are still alive, plus net immigration of people of the same age, adjusted for the number of students who persist through high school and then enter college. Using information from the 1980 and 1990 censuses as well as from 1997 resident population estimates (U.S. Bureau 1980, tab. 43; 1998a, tab. 22), we developed our initial projection of the number of eighteen-year-olds (the modal age of college entrants) by looking at individuals in each specific year from "under one" to nineteen. Ignoring the possibility that some individuals will die before they turn eighteen and, for the moment, immigrants, we assumed that these age cohorts will translate directly into eighteen-year-olds in the future. For example, in 1991 we assumed that all those who were listed as seventeen in the 1980 census would become eighteen in 1981; those who were sixteen in 1980 would be eighteen in 1982 and so on until those under age one would be eighteen in 1998. (See Figure 3.1.) We now extend those figures to 2015 by using the 1997 population estimates. Those listed there as under one in 1997 will be eighteen in 2015.

The postwar baby boom (1946–64) led to an unprecedented expansion in American higher education seventeen to nineteen years later. In the late 1950s, the number of births began to decline; however, the expected decline in college enrollments did not occur as expected precisely eighteen years later. Except for 1969–70, births declined steadily from 1964 through 1975 but then started to rise as baby boomers began to have babies. This growth continued until 1989–90 when the number of births finally reached the levels of the early 1960s. Births have declined each year in the 1990s.

Rapid growth in the number of eighteen-year-olds ceased in the mid-1970s; yet between that time and approximately 1982, the number of eighteen-year-olds stayed relatively constant. After 1982, however, their number declined until the mid-1990s. Based on 1980 census data, we predicted a steady decline in the number of eighteen-year-olds between 1979 and 1986, a slight increase from 1986 to 1989, and a decline from 1989 to 1992. Between 1979 and 1992, we projected that the number of American eighteen-year-olds would fall from 4,451,724 to 3,109,095—30 percent below the high point in 1979 (U.S. Bureau 1980, tab. 43).

As a result of these birth trends, college enrollments declined between the 1970s and the 1990s, but not as early or as sharply as birth figures alone would indicate. Not only are a higher share of the age cohorts enrolled in college, but also more older people are enrolled.

Between 1992 and 1997, we thought the number of eighteen-year-olds in the United States would increase very slightly, from 3,109,095 to 3,269,557,

# Figure 3.1. Eighteen Year Olds

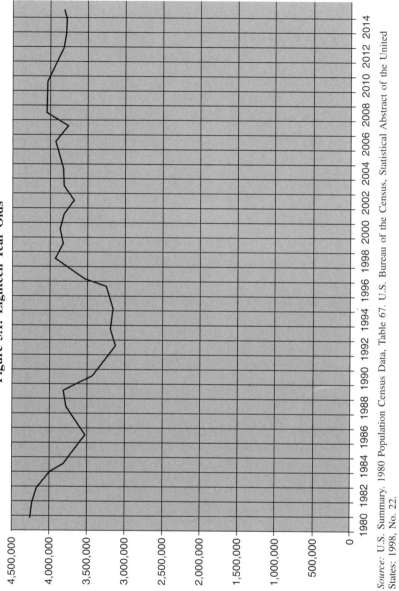

*Source:* U.S. Summary. 1980 Population Census Data, Table 67. U.S. Bureau of the Census, Statistical Abstract of the United States: 1998, No. 22.

## Table 3.1
### Eighteen Year Olds by Race/Ethnicity Based on Live Births Eighteen Years Earlier

| | National Total | Y2/Y1 | White Total | Y2/Y1 | Blacks Total | Y2/Y1 | American Indian Total | Y2/Y1 |
|---|---|---|---|---|---|---|---|---|
| 1979 | 4,451,724 | | 3,587,991 | | 600,008 | | 334,102 | |
| 1980 | 4,251,779 | 0.9551 | 3,417,053 | 0.9524 | 589,101 | 0.9818 | 319,622 | 0.9567 |
| 1981 | 4,223,848 | 0.9934 | 3,380,772 | 0.9894 | 600,169 | 1.0188 | 324,585 | 1.0155 |
| 1982 | 4,180,875 | 0.9898 | 3,343,837 | 0.9891 | 600,439 | 1.0004 | 316,742 | 0.9758 |
| 1983 | 4,059,898 | 0.9711 | 3,232,449 | 0.9667 | 595,146 | 0.9912 | 311,277 | 0.9827 |
| 1984 | 3,782,784 | 0.9317 | 2,992,789 | 0.9259 | 567,872 | 0.9542 | 297,613 | 0.9561 |
| 1985 | 3,643,189 | 0.0631 | 2,889,432 | 0.9655 | 537,569 | 0.9466 | 289,555 | 0.9729 |
| 1986 | 3,518,982 | 0.9659 | 2,786,155 | 0.9643 | 517,587 | 0.9628 | 285,634 | 0.9865 |
| 1987 | 2,580,644 | 0.7333 | 2,846,168 | 1.0215 | 513,788 | 0.9927 | 292,372 | 1.0236 |
| 1988 | 3,716,530 | 1.4402 | 2,946,378 | 1.0352 | 536,456 | 1.0441 | 309,824 | 1.0597 |
| 1989 | 3,760,120 | 1.0117 | 2,968,127 | 1.0074 | 549,963 | 1.0252 | 319,936 | 1.0326 |
| 1990 | 3,395,998 | 0.9032 | 2,658,627 | 0.8957 | 506,709 | 0.9214 | 301,298 | 0.9417 |
| 1991 | 3,273,052 | 0.9638 | 2,539,701 | 0.9553 | 498,320 | 0.9834 | 305,492 | 1.0139 |
| 1992 | 3,109,095 | 0.9499 | 2,410,344 | 0.9491 | 467,645 | 0.9384 | 299,199 | 0.9794 |
| 1993 | 3,162,691 | 1.0172 | 2,456,167 | 1.0190 | 468,080 | 1.0009 | 311,256 | 1.0403 |
| 1994 | 3,141,748 | 0.9934 | 2,428,232 | 0.9886 | 469,947 | 1.0040 | 317,896 | 1.0213 |
| 1995 | 3,179,441 | 1.0120 | 2,460,551 | 1.0133 | 470,660 | 1.0015 | 324,066 | 1.0194 |
| 1996 | 3,223,816 | 1.0140 | 2,497,249 | 1.0149 | 477,708 | 1.0150 | 324,950 | 1.0027 |
| 1997 | 3,269,557 | 1.0142 | 2,528,598 | 1.0126 | 486,890 | 1.0192 | 328,216 | 1.0101 |
| 1998 | 3,533,692 | 1.0808 | 2,719,445 | 1.0755 | 530,964 | 1.0905 | 368,045 | 1.1213 |

Source: U.S. Bureau of the Census, U.S. Summary, 1980 Population Census Data, Table 67.

**Table 3.1**
*Continued*

| | National Total | Y2/Y1 | White Total | Y2/Y1 | Blacks Total | Y2/Y1 | American Indian Total | Y2/Y1 | Asian, PI Total | Y2/Y1 | Hispanic Total | Y2/Y1 |
|---|---|---|---|---|---|---|---|---|---|---|---|---|
| 1997 | 3,679,000 | | 2,469,000 | | 548,000 | | 33,000 | | 125,000 | | 503,000 | |
| 1998 | 3,915,000 | 1.0641 | 2,630,000 | 1.0652 | 585,000 | 1.0675 | 38,000 | 1.1515 | 139,000 | 1.1120 | 522,000 | 1.0378 |
| 1999 | 3,815,000 | 0.9745 | 2,565,000 | 0.9753 | 557,000 | 0.9521 | 39,000 | 1.0263 | 142,000 | 1.0216 | 513,000 | 0.9828 |
| 2000 | 3,870,000 | 1.0144 | 2,606,000 | 1.0160 | 575,000 | 1.0323 | 40,000 | 1.0256 | 146,000 | 1.0282 | 503,000 | 0.9805 |
| 2001 | 3,829,000 | 0.9894 | 2,578,000 | 0.9893 | 558,000 | 0.9704 | 42,000 | 1.0500 | 149,000 | 1.0205 | 502,000 | 0.9980 |
| 2002 | 3,725,000 | 0.9728 | 2,512,000 | 0.9744 | 539,000 | 0.9659 | 41,000 | 0.9762 | 145,000 | 0.9732 | 488,000 | 0.9721 |
| 2003 | 3,799,000 | 1.0199 | 2,564,000 | 1.0207 | 558,000 | 1.0353 | 40,000 | 0.9756 | 143,000 | 0.9862 | 494,000 | 1.0123 |
| 2004 | 3,813,000 | 1.0037 | 2,571,000 | 1.0027 | 556,000 | 0.9964 | 39,000 | 0.9750 | 138,000 | 0.9650 | 509,000 | 1.0304 |
| 2005 | 3,873,000 | 1.0157 | 2,594,000 | 1.0089 | 580,000 | 1.0432 | 40,000 | 1.0256 | 138,000 | 1.0000 | 521,000 | 1.0236 |
| 2006 | 3,912,000 | 1.0101 | 2,587,000 | 0.9973 | 599,000 | 1.0328 | 40,000 | 1.0000 | 143,000 | 1.0362 | 542,000 | 1.0403 |
| 2007 | 3,732,000 | 0.9540 | 2,464,000 | 0.9525 | 575,000 | 0.9599 | 38,000 | 0.9500 | 134,000 | 0.9371 | 521,000 | 0.9613 |
| 2008 | 4,029,000 | 1.0796 | 2,656,000 | 1.0779 | 606,000 | 1.0539 | 40,000 | 1.0526 | 145,000 | 1.0821 | 584,000 | 1.1209 |
| 2009 | 4,043,000 | 1.0035 | 2,625,000 | 0.9883 | 598,000 | 0.9868 | 36,000 | 0.9000 | 160,000 | 1.1034 | 625,000 | 1.0702 |
| 2010 | 4,022,000 | 0.9948 | 2,568,000 | 0.9783 | 597,000 | 0.9983 | 36,000 | 1.0000 | 154,000 | 1.0250 | 657,000 | 1.0512 |
| 2011 | 3,947,000 | 0.9814 | 2,505,000 | 0.9755 | 590,000 | 0.9883 | 35,000 | 0.9722 | 159,000 | 0.9695 | 658,000 | 1.0015 |
| 2012 | 3,838,000 | 0.9724 | 2,432,000 | 0.9709 | 554,000 | 0.9390 | 34,000 | 0.9714 | 160,000 | 1.0063 | 658,000 | 1.0000 |
| 2013 | 3,795,000 | 0.9888 | 2,408,000 | 0.9901 | 530,000 | 0.9567 | 32,000 | 0.9412 | 159,000 | 0.9938 | 666,000 | 1.0122 |
| 2014 | 3,773,000 | 0.9942 | 2,392,000 | 0.9934 | 513,000 | 0.9679 | 32,000 | 1.0000 | 162,000 | 1.0189 | 674,000 | 1.0120 |
| 2015 | 3,797,000 | 1.0064 | 2,390,000 | 0.9992 | 517,000 | 1.0078 | 33,000 | 1.0313 | 166,000 | 1.0247 | 690,000 | 1.0237 |

*Source:* U.S. Bureau of the Census, the Official Statistics, *Statistical Abstract of the United States: 1998*, No. 22.

then accelerate after 1997 with the increase resulting in an eighteen-year-old population of 3,533,692 in 1998 (Table 3.1). At the end of the period covered in our earlier paper, 1998, we projected the number of eighteen-year-olds at 20 percent less than the number in 1979. In fact, our predictions for the 1998 eighteen-year-old population were 381,000 below the actual number; we were off by 8.6 percent of the 1979 figure. Part of the difference came from immigration, particularly from Asia and Central America.

The number of eighteen-year-olds in 1998 was larger than that of any year since 1983; but rather than seeing any consistent rise or fall over the next two decades, we expect to see year-to-year fluctuations between 3.9 and 3.7 million until 2015, except for 2008–2010, when there should be over 4 million eighteen-year-olds. In 2015, we expect 240,000 fewer White eighteen-year-olds, 68,000 fewer Black eighteen-year-olds, and 168,000 more Hispanic[1] eighteen-year-olds than in 1998. This projection is based on live births eighteen years earlier and does not allow for changes in immigration, birth rates, etc. In 1997 there were 125,000 eighteen-year-old Asians[2] and 166,000 Asians under age one; in 2015 the eighteen-year-old population will include both more Asians and more Hispanics (U.S. Bureau 1998a, tab. 22).

The composition of the student-age population has also changed and will continue to change in important ways. In 1980, Americans under eighteen were 74 percent White, 15 percent Black/non-Hispanic, 9 percent Hispanic, and 2 percent Asian/Pacific Islander. By 1997, these proportions changed to 66 percent, 15 percent, 15 percent, and 4 percent respectively. Broken down by race, we expected to see a nationwide drop in eighteen-year-olds of over 868,000 Whites, a drop of 69,000 Blacks, and an increase of almost 34,000 Hispanic by 1998. We overestimated Whites by 89,000 (2.5 percent), underestimating Blacks by 54,000 (9 percent) and Hispanics by 154,000 (46 percent). By the year 2018, we estimated these proportions of the under-eighteen population: 55 percent White, 16 percent Black, 22 percent Hispanic, and 6 percent Asian/Pacific Islander (Forum 1998, tab. POP3).

Although birth rates are the most important predictor of the age cohort and subsequent college enrollments, immigration is also extremely important. As long as the U.S. standard of living remains superior to that of many other countries, significant numbers of foreigners will seek entry through legal or illegal means. Our population's racial and ethnic composition is directly impacted by immigration laws, resources and resolve to enforce these laws, and international political and economic conditions.

---

1. People of Hispanic origin were those who indicated that their origin was Mexican, Puerto Rican, Cuban, Central or South American, or some other Hispanic origin. It should be noted that people of Hispanic origin might be of any race.

2. In this paper, "Asians" include people who identified themselves as Pacific Islander, Chinese, Filipino, Japanese, Asian Indian, Korean, Vietnamese, or other Asian.

**Table 3.2**
**Number and Percentage of Eighteen Year Olds**
**by Race/Ethnicity, 1998 and 2015**

| 18 Year Olds | Total | White | Black | Asian | Hispanic |
|---|---|---|---|---|---|
| 1998 | 3,915,000 | 2,630,000 | 585,000 | 139,000 | 522,000 |
| 2015 | 3,797,000 | 2,390,000 | 517,000 | 166,000 | 690,000 |
| | | | | | |
| 1998 | | 67.18% | 14.94% | 3.55% | 13.33% |
| 2015 | | 62.94% | 13.62% | 4.37% | 18.17% |

*Source:* U.S. Bureau of the Census, the Official Statistics, *Statistical Abstract of the United States: 1998,* No. 22

Based upon U.S. births eighteen years earlier, in 1998 the eighteen-year-old population was 67.2 percent White, 14.9 percent Black, 3.6 percent Asian, and 13.3 percent Hispanic. We project these percentages for 2015 at 62.9 percent, 13.6 percent, 4.4 percent, and 18.2 percent respectively. (See Table 3.2.) However, immigration is likely to enhance the shares of non-Whites, particularly if immigration continues roughly the current pattern. Between 700,000 and 900,000 immigrants entered the United States each year from 1994 to 1997, over two-thirds from Asia, the Caribbean, or Central America. (See Table 3.3.) About 20 percent of all immigrants are under fifteen; over one-quarter are of childbearing age or younger. These figures refer only to legal immigrants, and virtually all illegal immigrants are non-White. Therefore, immigrants, both legal and illegal, and their children will increase the

**Table 3.3**
**Immigration into the United States by Country of Origin, 1994–1997**

| Immigrants by Country of Origin | 1994 | 1995 | 1996 | 1997 |
|---|---|---|---|---|
| All countries | 804,416 | 720,461 | 915,900 | 798,378 |
| North America | 272,226 | 231,526 | 340,540 | 307,488 |
| Canada | 16,068 | 12,932 | 15,825 | 11,609 |
| | | | | |
| North America less Canada (basically Caribbean and Central America) | 256,158 | 218,594 | 324,715 | 295,879 |
| % Caribbean and Central America | 31.84% | 30.34% | 35.45% | 37.06% |
| | | | | |
| Asia | 292,589 | 267,931 | 307,807 | 265,786 |
| % Asian | 36.37% | 37.19% | 33.61% | 33.29% |
| | | | | |
| Total Asia, Caribbean, and Central America | 68.22% | 67.53% | 69.06% | 70.35% |

*Source:* U.S. Department of Justice, Immigration and Naturalization Service, Office of Policy and Planning, Legal Immigration, Fiscal Year 1997. January 1999.

share of non-White college-age people even beyond what would be expected from the birth rate data (U.S. Dept. of Justice 1999).

## Patterns of High School Completion

Next we ask what proportion of these potential college-entering cohorts will actually graduate from high school. According to the U.S. Bureau of the Census (1985), 67.6 percent of eighteen-year-olds had completed high school in October 1985; 81.5 percent of nineteen-year-olds had graduated from high school. By October 1997, 74.2 percent of all eighteen- and nineteen-year-olds had graduated from high school while another 8.1 percent received GEDs for a total of 82.3 percent (U.S. Dept. of Education 1999, tab. 4). The increase in the nineteen-year-old graduation rate has grown very slightly in twelve years, probably representing a ceiling.

Historically, in 1869–70, only about 2 percent of seventeen-year-olds graduated from high school; this figure reached 29 percent in 1929–30, but stood at 50.8 percent by 1939–40 (U.S. Bureau of the Census, 1961). In 1968–69, it peaked at over 77 percent. Beginning in 1973, the proportion of seventeen-year-olds graduating from high school declined steadily to 71.8 percent in approximately 1980, increased slightly to 73.4 percent in 1991–92, then dipped to 69.7 percent in 1996–97 (U.S. Dept. of Education 1998, tab. 101).

For all eighteen- and nineteen-year-olds, the high school graduation rate was 73.4 percent in 1974 and 74.6 percent in 1985. Today it is most useful to look at high school graduation rates for eighteen- to twenty-four-year-olds as more people are graduating later. Indeed in 1997, only 25.4 percent of high school graduates between eighteen and twenty-four were eighteen or nineteen years old. There are dramatic differences in high school completion rates according to race and ethnic origin. The high school graduation rate for people eighteen to twenty-four for all races was 80.7 percent in 1974, 81.6 percent in 1984, and 85.9 percent in 1997 (76.7 percent diplomas and the remainder GED). For Whites, the rate increased from 82.7 percent to 83.0 percent, then to 90.5 percent. (See Table 3.4.) Black completion rates rose

**Table 3.4**
**Percentage of Distribution of High School Graduates: 1997**

|  | All High School Graduates (18–24 year olds) | High School Graduates Enrolled in College (16–24 year olds) |
|---|---|---|
| Total U.S. | 85.9 | 67.0 |
| White | 90.5 | 67.5 |
| Black | 82.0 | 59.6 |
| Hispanic | 66.7 | 65.5 |

*Source:* U.S. Dept. of Education, Dropout Rates in the United States, Table 4. *Digest of Educational Statistics 1998,* Table 183.

markedly from 67.1 percent to 74.7 percent in 1984 and to 82 percent in 1997. Hispanic rates rose from 55.9 percent to 60.1 percent to 66.7 percent (U.S. Bureau of the Census 1985; U.S. Dept. of Education 1999, tab. 4). In short, a significant and increasing proportion of non-Whites graduate from high school—though substantially below Whites' rates; however, completion often occurs after age eighteen or nineteen.

High school dropouts, particularly youth of color, have been one of our most urgent social issues recently. Discussion has focused on the economic and social costs of dropping out. The rate has become a measurable target for politicians, corporate leaders, and educators. Because of this increased attention, we predicted a decade ago that high school graduation rates for students of color would rise. They did. However, an easy way to increase graduation rates is to lower standards, and that appears to have happened in many places. Increased high school graduation rates, coupled with the demographic shifts, emphasize that the college pool will become increasingly dominated by currently underrepresented groups and that they will often be less well prepared than earlier cohorts.

Our 1991 paper said little about Asian students, due to data limitations. This population, the largest recent component of immigrants, has a low high school dropout rate and a high rate of college matriculation. If we had included them, our conclusion about the increasing dominance of people of color in American higher education would be magnified, but our conclusion about their lack of preparation would be tempered. However, recent Asian immigrants may now more closely resemble other groups of color. They too are disadvantaged compared to Whites in their high school preparation for college. (See also Chang and Kiang, this volume.)

## Rates of Progression into College

The next issue is how many high school graduates actually progress into college. Factors influencing the relationship between birth rates and college enrollments fall into two basic categories. The first is economics and the labor market; the second is the public school system.

The increased number of matriculating eighteen-year-olds during the early- and mid-1970s resulted from the postwar baby boom. As a result, some argued, the comparative oversupply of college graduates entering the labor market meant that less-skilled workers would become relatively scarce, demand for them would increase, and more would skip college in favor of immediate jobs (Freeman 1976, 535–69).

It is true that the number of jobs traditionally held by college graduates before the baby boom did not grow as quickly as the number of graduates during the 1960s and 1970s. Nevertheless, the rate of return (the earnings difference between a college graduate and a high school graduate, adjusted for the incremental costs of attending college which include foregone earnings), did not decline (O'Neil and Sepielli 1985). Furthermore, unemployment rates have always been lower for college graduates. These economic factors, plus the reasons beyond economics that people have for attending college, supported an increasing demand for higher education. During the 1980s and particularly the 1990s, the demand for highly educated workers grew dramatically and increasingly outpaced supply, especially in mathematics, the sciences, and anything remotely related to computers and the Internet. Simultaneously, much manufacturing has moved offshore to take advantage of lower wages abroad for unskilled labor. Even the manufacturing that remains demands high-tech skills. Thus, the earnings premium for college vs. high school education is now at an all-time high, leading to a predictable demand for higher education.

The second influence on the correlation between birth rates and subsequent college enrollments is the standards and activities of the K-12 educational systems. That its standards have plummeted is universally known, as evidenced by international test score comparisons, the growth of general vs. college-bound curricula, social promotion, and the huge remediation programs in colleges. Moreover, the larger pool of college-eligible students joined the system of higher education that expanded to accommodate baby boom students; faced with lower enrollments after the boom, these schools had to admit greater proportions of a smaller high school graduating class simply to survive, including many who would not previously have qualified.

As a result, students entering or even leaving college may not know any more than a high school graduate of a couple of generations ago; a college diploma has lost its former status; and truly capable students seek to distinguish themselves by attending more selective colleges with higher standards. Thus, while the total number of eighteen-year-olds entering college is declining, the more elite institutions get greater numbers of applicants.

Of eighteen- to twenty-one-year-old high school graduates, 33.5 percent were in college in 1975, 43.8 percent in 1996. For Whites, the increase was from 34.6 to 45.3 percent, for Blacks from 24.9 to 31.3 percent, and for Hispanics a slight decline from 24.4 to 23.1 percent (U.S. Bureau 1998b, tab. 298). College enrollments in October for individuals ages sixteen to twenty-four who graduated from high school during the preceding twelve months show an overall increase from 50.7 percent in 1975 to 65 percent in 1996 and to 67 percent in 1997. For Whites, the percentages in the three years were 51.2, 65.8, and 67.5; for Blacks 41.9, 55.3, and 59.6. Figures for Hispanics fell from 52.6 percent to 50.7 percent between 1975 and 1996, but rose to 65.5 percent the next year. The small sample size causes large sampling errors for Hispanics. The wider the age span, the higher the share in college (U.S. Dept. of Education 1998, tab. 183).

Recently, college enrollment rates have risen for all groups, yet matriculation rates for Black and Hispanic high school graduates have stayed below that of Whites. Economic patterns are clearly one reason. Poverty pressures many Black and Hispanic youth to drop out of high school and find a job. Even those who complete high school may feel the need to work rather than attend college. Opportunities for students of color to attend college decrease as college costs increase and need-based financial aid declines. In-state tuition at both public and private four-year colleges rose by about 228 percent between 1985 and 1996 (U.S. Bureau 1998a, tab. 312), while virtually no form of student aid has kept pace. (See Table 3.5.) The number of Pell Grant recipients grew by 130 percent and the average award by 123 percent. The average Supplementary Education Opportunity Grant increased by 107 percent and the number of recipients by 174 percent. For College Work Study, average annual earnings grew by 124 percent and the number of recipients declined by 5 percent. The average loan amount grew by about 150 percent for both Perkins loans and Federal Family Education Loans; the number of

**Table 3.5**
**Tuition and Fees of Four-year Colleges and**
**Student Financial Assistance, 1985 and 1996**

|  | *1985* | *1996* | *% Change* |
|---|---|---|---|
| Tuition of Four-Year College: |  |  |  |
| Public | $ 1,386 | $ 3,151 | 227.3% |
| Private | $ 6,843 | $ 15,605 | 228.0% |
| Voluntary Support/Student | $ 516 | $ 1,003 | 194.4% |
| Pell Grants: |  |  |  |
| # of Recipients | 2,813,000 | 3,660,000 | 130.1% |
| Average Award | $ 1,279 | $ 1,574 | 123.1% |
| Supplemental Education |  |  |  |
| Opportunity Grants: |  |  |  |
| # of Recipients | 686,000 | 1,191,000 | 173.6% |
| Average Grant | $ 598 | $ 640 | 107.0% |
| College Work-Study: |  |  |  |
| # of Recipients | 728,400 | 691,000 | 94.9% |
| Average Annual Earning | $ 901 | $ 1,123 | 124.6% |
| Perkins Loans: |  |  |  |
| # of Recipients | 700,900 | 674,000 | 96.2% |
| Average Loan | $ 1,003 | $ 1,516 | 151.1% |
| Federal Family Education Loans: |  |  |  |
| # of Loans | 3,833,000 | 5,531,000 | 144.3% |
| Average Loan | $ 2,374 | $ 3,748 | 157.9% |

*Source:* U.S. Bureau of the Census, the Official Statistics, *Statistical Abstract of the United States: 1998,* Tables No. 310, 312, and 313.

Perkins loans declined although FFE loans grew by 158 percent (U.S. Bureau 1998a, tab. 310). Only private support per student grew at a rate close to tuition growth, but voluntary support is a small fraction of total aid (U.S. Bureau 1998a, tab. 313).

As student loan balances build up, so does pressure to drop out and start working to pay them off. This dynamic is particularly true for members of low-income groups who are less willing to incur large debts. We see little reason to expect reversals in these trends of declining financial aid. Ironically, as private rates of return to college education rise, there is less economic rationale for subsidizing such education in general. However, even though there is a clear payoff, students of color encounter cash flow problems and lack of access to capital, keeping many from college's benefits.

Arguments that the truly needy still have access to college funds ignore the evidence of declining aid and the comparatively low enrollment of Black high school graduates. Part of the problem is that Black and Hispanic graduates may have access to funds for tuition and even perhaps incidental expenses, but these funds rarely cover the earnings foregone by choosing college over even the most menial jobs. For many, deferring income is a luxury they cannot afford when they see parents and younger siblings living in poverty. Thus, even if these high school graduates of color qualify for college admittance and funding, their need to support their families takes precedence over their desire to enter college. More optimistically, teenage pregnancy rates in communities of color have fallen in the 1990s; perhaps students who might otherwise have dropped out either to work or to look after their children will enter college (Rumberger 1983; National Committee on Vital 1999, tab. B).

Clearly, policy makers must look beyond simply providing out-of-pocket college costs to qualified people of color. Unless the financial aid packages of poor students compensate for the opportunity costs of attending college, many will still feel that they must join the labor force. Students' need to work is a primary factor explaining enrollment by institutional type; community colleges are often the only choice for students who must earn more than any scholarship program currently provides. Yet such a compensatory program does not exist, nor does it seem likely to soon.

In addition to economic constraints, the quality of education that students of color receive in high school also affects their college admission. In 1976 progression to college rates for Whites, Blacks, and Hispanics ages sixteen to twenty-four were 48.9, 41.9, and 52.6 percent respectively. By 1997, 67.5 percent of White high school graduates entered college, compared to 65.5 percent of Hispanic graduates and 59.6 percent of Blacks (U.S. Dept. of Education 1998, tab. 183). At the same time, pressure has mounted to reduce dropout rates, track students of color into college preparatory programs, and increase graduation rates. This emphasis may explain the recent catching up in progression-to-college rates of students of color. Another reason for the improved matriculation rates is affirmative action efforts by many colleges; but this movement seems to be weakening. In some states, most notably California, voters have made affirmative action at the public college level illegal.

Despite the decline in the total population of eighteen- to nineteen-year-olds, their numbers in college have risen from 2.8 million in 1975 to 3 million in 1996. However, the cohort of eighteen- to twenty-four-year-olds in college has grown even more, from 6.8 million to 8 million. Thus, the traditional-age group now comprises a smaller share of those enrolled in college. (See Table 3.6.) In 1980, a third of the total 8.7 million eighteen- to nineteen-year-olds were in college, 31 percent of them full-time. In 1996, 47 percent of the 6.4 million eighteen- to nineteen-year-olds were in college, with 39 percent full-time (U.S. Dept. of Education 1998, tab. 174). The percentage of the population in college is the product of the high school graduation rate and the progression rate of high school graduates into college. Perhaps these figures reflect the longer time it takes to graduate from both high school and college. Or some students do not immediately enter college, perhaps needing to work and save money.

The pattern of high school graduation rates for Whites, Blacks, and Hispanics is more diverse than that of their progression into college. When these two ratios are combined, the percentage of the population in college is substantially higher for Whites than for Blacks and Hispanics, who graduate

**Table 3.6**

**Total Fall Enrollment of Eighteen-and Nineteen-Year-Olds in Institutions of Higher Education, 1970–2008**

| Year | # of 18 and 19 Year Olds | Change (Y2/Y1) | # of 18–24 Year Olds | Change (Y2/Y1) | # 18–19/ # 18–24 |
|------|--------------------------|----------------|----------------------|----------------|------------------|
| 1970 | 2,600,000 | | 5,937,000 | | **43.8** |
| 1975 | 2,786,000 | 1.0715 | 6,782,000 | 1.1423 | **41.1** |
| 1980 | 2,901,000 | 1.0413 | 7,314,000 | 1.0784 | **39.7** |
| 1990 | 2,950,000 | 1.0169 | 7,855,000 | 1.0740 | **37.6** |
| 1993 | 2,840,000 | 0.9627 | 8,084,000 | 1.0292 | **35.1** |
| 1994 | 2,787,000 | 0.9813 | 7,993,000 | 0.9887 | **34.9** |
| 1995 | 2,894,000 | 1.0384 | 8,010,000 | 1.0021 | **36.1** |
| 1996 | 3,004,000 | 1.0380 | 7,963,000 | 0.9941 | **37.7** |
| 1997* | 3,089,000 | 1.0283 | 7,871,000 | 0.9884 | 39.2 |
| 1998* | 3,247,000 | 1.0511 | 8,082,000 | 1.0268 | 40.2 |
| 1999* | 3,347,000 | 1.0308 | 8,275,000 | 1.0239 | 40.4 |
| 2000* | 3,390,000 | 1.0128 | 8,451,000 | 1.0213 | 40.1 |
| 2008* | 3,842,000 | 1.1333 | 9,605,000 | 1.1366 | 40.0 |

*Source:* U.S. Dept. of Education, *Digest of Education Statistics 1998,* Table 174.

from high school and progress to college at lower rates. As a result of the increasing proportion of non-Whites under eighteen, the potential number of students of color at all educational levels is increasing. Between 1984 and 1996, students of color in higher education rose from 17 percent to 26 percent (U.S. Dept. of Education 1998, tab. 210). In addition to increasing immigration, the enrollment of foreign students in U.S. colleges increased by 18.3 percent between 1990 and 1997 (U.S. Bureau 1998, tab. 304).

Until 1983, the share of eighteen- to nineteen-year-old Blacks in higher education was greater than the share of Hispanics; however, after 1983, the two groups had approximately equal shares. The proportion of eighteen- to nineteen-year-old White college attenders rose from 34.4 percent in 1974 to 42.9 in 1985. The proportion for Blacks was 23.2 percent in 1974, 27 percent in 1981, but 24 percent in 1985. For Hispanics, the 1974 share was slightly under 24 percent. After reaching an all-time high of almost 27 percent in 1976, the Hispanic share fell to 22.3 percent in 1985. Combining high school graduation rates of people ages eighteen to twenty-four with progression rates of those sixteen to twenty-four, we find that the proportion of all races in college in 1997 is 57.6 percent—of Whites about 60 percent, Blacks 48.9, and Hispanics 43.7 (U.S. Dept. of Education 1998, tab. 183; 1999, tab. 4). These numbers are higher than earlier because the traditional college-going population has increased and because the nontraditional older population has increased. (See also Teddlie and Freeman, this volume.)

It appears that the primary bottleneck keeping Blacks and Hispanics ages eighteen to nineteen out of college is their relatively low rate of high school completion, but race differences in high school completion are smaller now than in the past. Since Blacks and Hispanics are more likely to graduate from high school after age eighteen or nineteen, they enter college at increased rates in their twenties. The data clearly reveal that any effort to increase "on time" graduation rates for Blacks and Hispanics would be beneficial. However, maintaining or raising graduation standards—rather than lowering them to improve the statistics—is crucial. Higher completion rates without lowering standards suggests the improved likelihood of success in college and the labor market, in contrast to those who drop out.

We raised several questions about implementing a policy of demanding high performance for high school graduation and college admission. First, can high school educators insist on appropriate graduation requirements even if the short-term results are higher dropout rates and lower graduation rates for students of color? They have not done so until recently, but many states have begun requiring that students pass proficiency tests to graduate. If affirmative action falters, in theory all students will have to meet the same admissions standards.

Second, even if this long-term view prevails, are the socioeconomic circumstances of many impoverished people of color such that higher standards *will* result in more graduates fully prepared for college? Is the crisis purely educational, or is academic performance simply one manifestation of deeper social problems such as teenage pregnancy, gangs, drugs, and family disintegration? Some schools are underfunded, and the quality and motivation of teachers is lower than in previous generations. But can any level of funding and teacher ability compensate for the dismal circumstances facing many youth of color? If these problems can be successfully attacked, the representation of students of color in our institutions of higher education can and will increase.

A decade ago, we argued that if high schools emphasized college preparation, then rates of progression to college for people of color would likely increase over the next decade or so. Progression rates did indeed increase, but more likely because of lower standards in both high schools and colleges. Total undergraduate enrollment increased by 17.1 percent from 1980 to 1996, peaking in 1992 at 12.5 million students, then dropping to 12,259,400 in 1996. White non-Hispanic enrollment increased by only 3 percent from 1980 to 1996: 8.5 million in 1980, a high in 1990 of 9.5 million, and a decline to 8.7 million in 1996 (U.S. Bureau 1998a, tab. 303).

Enrollment of undergraduates of color increased 83 percent over the same sixteen years—a steady rise from 1.8 million to 3.3 million by 1996. Most of this growth came from a 146 percent increase in Hispanic enrollment and a 186.8 percent increase in Asian students. (See Hurtado; Chang and Kiang, this volume.) The much smaller, but still noteworthy increases for Black/non-Hispanic and American Indians were 32.8 percent and 57.8 respectively. These data give us hope for the future (U.S. Dept. of Education 1998, tab. 207).

## College Choice

As with high school graduation progression rates into college, first-time enrollment figures have fluctuated over the past two decades. Between 1970 and 1981, the fifty states and the District of Columbia together experienced a 25.8 percent increase in first-time enrollments in their institutions of higher education (American Council 1987, tabs. 92–93). From 1981 to 1984, this trend was reversed, with first-time enrollments declining by 9.2 percent. Twice as many states had declining first-time enrollments than increases. (See Table 3.7.) Except for the Rocky Mountain and Far West states, the decline was greater for private than public instituions. Since 1984, the figures have continued to fluctuate, exceeding the 1984 total only in 1988 (by nearly 1 percent) and falling to the lowest figures since 1971 in 1994. From 1993 to 1996, first-time enrollments increased by 1.5 percent, with enrollment decreasing in almost half the states over that time (U.S. Dept. of Education 1998, tab. 182).

**Table 3.7**
**Percentage of Change in First-Time Enrollments**

|  | 1981–1984 | 1993–1996 |
|---|---|---|
| Alaska |  | −27.7% |
| South Dakota | −19.8% | −13.8% |
| Michigan |  | −12.4% |
| Alabama |  | −12.3% |
| Illinois | 30.4% | −5.4% |
| Colorado | −16.1% | 1.3% |
| New Jersey | −20.4% | 2.1% |
| South Carolina | −16.3% | 2.2% |
| Nebraska | −22.7% | 7.5% |
| California | 21.8% | 10.7% |
| Montana |  | 13.3% |
| Minnesota |  | 17.3% |
| Nevada | 84.0% | 35.2% |

*Source:* American Council on Education (ACE), *Fact Book on Higher Education* (1987), Tables 92–93; U.S. Dept. of Education, *Digest of Education Statistics 1998,* Table 182.

Stability nationally, however, does not necessarily mean that particular states or regions are also stable.

Total enrollment declined slightly from 1993 to 1996—about 4,300 students out of the over 14.3 million enrolled. Throughout the 1990s, most first-time enrollment fluctuations have occurred in public schools. Since total college enrollments grew by approximately 17 percent between 1980 and 1996, the decline in first-time enrollments was more than made up for by returning students and students who continued beyond the traditional time period (U.S. Dept. of Education 1998, tabs. 181, 207).

The National Center for Education Statistics (NCES) calculated the percentage of students of color by state who were enrolled in institutions of higher education in the fall of 1984 (total enrollment less nonresident aliens). They found that, overall, 17.4 percent were students of color—26.1 percent in 1996. (See Table 3.8.) The highest percentage was 70.7 percent in Hawaii with a low of 1.4 percent in Maine in 1984; in 1996, the percentages for the same states were 70.6 and 4 percent. Every state (except Hawaii) increased its percentage of students of color with California experiencing the greatest increase—19.1 percent (U.S. Dept. of Education 1998, tab. 210).

The differential distribution of people of color from state to state accounts in part for the wide variations among states of people of color in higher education. Also relevant is whether racial/ethnic groups are represented in colleges in the same proportion as the overall college-age population. For example, California and Texas have seen dramatic changes since the mid-1980s. In 1984 in California, although the college-age population was 72.3 percent White, only 68.0 percent of undergraduate enrollments in 1984–

## Table 3.8
## Percentage of Minorities Enrolled in Institutions of Higher Education

| State | 1984 | 1996 | Change |
|---|---|---|---|
| Hawaii | 70.7 | 70.6 | –0.1 |
| California | 29.6 | 48.7 | 19.1 |
| District of Columbia | 39.3 | 45.7 | 6.4 |
| New Mexico | 33.5 | 43.7 | 10.2 |
| Texas | 25.4 | 37.3 | 11.9 |
| Florida | 21.3 | 32.7 | 11.4 |
| Mississippi | 30.1 | 32.7 | 2.6 |
| Louisiana | 26.7 | 32.6 | 5.9 |
| Maryland | 21.5 | 32.2 | 10.7 |
| New York | 20.8 | 31.7 | 10.9 |
| Georgia | 21.5 | 30.8 | 9.3 |
| New Jersey | 18.2 | 29.5 | 11.3 |
| Illinois | 19.4 | 28.3 | 8.9 |
| Alabama | 22.8 | 26.9 | 4.1 |
| South Carolina | 22.2 | 26.1 | 3.9 |
| Arizona | 17.0 | 25.5 | 8.5 |
| North Carolina | 20.6 | 24.8 | 4.2 |
| Virginia | 17.3 | 24.8 | 7.5 |
| Nevada | 12.3 | 23.0 | 10.7 |
| Oklahoma | 12.7 | 21.0 | 8.3 |
| Alaska | 14.9 | 19.4 | 4.5 |
| Delaware | 12.6 | 19.4 | 6.8 |
| Arkansas | 16.8 | 18.5 | 1.7 |
| Colorado | 10.8 | 18.2 | 7.4 |
| Tennessee | 15.8 | 18.2 | 2.4 |
| Washington | 9.8 | 18.1 | 8.3 |
| Massachusetts | 8.0 | 17.7 | 9.7 |
| Connecticut | 8.3 | 17.5 | 9.2 |
| Michigan | 12.7 | 17.5 | 4.8 |
| Pennsylvania | 9.4 | 14.2 | 4.8 |
| Ohio | 10.1 | 14.0 | 3.9 |
| Missouri | 10.5 | 13.8 | 3.3 |
| Oregon | 7.3 | 13.0 | 5.7 |
| Rhode Island | 5.9 | 13.0 | 7.1 |
| Kansas | 8.7 | 12.6 | 3.9 |
| Montana | 6.3 | 11.2 | 4.9 |
| Indiana | 8.2 | 11.1 | 2.9 |
| Wisconsin | 6.3 | 9.6 | 3.3 |
| Kentucky | 8.8 | 9.5 | 0.7 |
| Minnesota | 3.9 | 8.9 | 5.0 |
| South Dakota | 7.6 | 8.8 | 1.2 |
| North Dakota | 5.2 | 8.2 | 3.0 |
| Wyoming | 4.0 | 8.0 | 4.0 |
| Nebraska | 5.1 | 7.9 | 2.8 |
| Iowa | 4.3 | 7.7 | 3.4 |
| Utah | 5.2 | 6.8 | 1.6 |
| Idaho | 4.7 | 6.5 | 1.8 |
| West Virginia | 5.2 | 6.2 | 1.0 |
| New Hampshire | 2.7 | 5.0 | 2.3 |
| Vermont | 2.1 | 4.5 | 2.4 |
| Maine | 1.4 | 4.0 | 2.6 |
| **United States** | **17.4** | **26.1** | **8.7** |

*Source:* U.S. Dept. of Education, *Digest of Education Statistics 1987,* Table 133; 1998, Table 210.

85 were White. (See Table 3.9.) Similarly, in Texas, while 76.1 percent of the college-age population was White, 71.9 percent of undergraduate enrollments were White. In California, Blacks made up 8.5 percent of the college-age population, but only 6.7 percent of actual enrollments. The comparable figures for Texas were 13.1 and 8.9 percent.

While both Whites and Blacks were somewhat underrepresented in undergraduate enrollments in California and Texas in 1984, the underrepresentation of Hispanics was substantially larger. In California, although 22.6 percent of the college-age population was Hispanic in 1984–85, they accounted for only 10.4 percent of enrollments. In Texas, the comparable figures were 21.9 percent and 13.1 percent. In both California and Texas, American Indian enrollments were at least equal to their proportion in the college-age population. But Asians inverted this pattern. In California, although 5.1 percent of the college-age population was Asian, they accounted for 10.2 percent of college enrollments. In Texas, the figures were 0.8 of 1 percent of the college-age population but 2.1 percent of enrollments.

By 1996 in California, the White college-age population fell to 39.8 percent of the total but accounted for 51.3 percent of higher education enrollments in 1996. Similarly, in Texas in 1996, 47.4 percent of the college-age population and 62.7 percent of enrollments were White. In California, Blacks made up 7.2 percent of the college-age population and 8 percent of enrollments. The comparable figures for Texas were 13 percent and 10.2 percent (U.S. Dept. of Education 1998, tab. 210).

In 1996, Whites in both states and Blacks in California are overrepresented in their state's enrollments, but the percentage of Hispanic underrepresentation is the same as in 1984. In California, 40 percent of the college-age population but only 21.3 percent of enrollments were Hispanic; in Texas, the comparable figures were 36.2 percent and 21.8 percent. In both states, American Indian enrollments were at least equal to the proportion of American Indians in the college-age population, and Asians continued to be overrepresented. The underrepresentation of Hispanics (and to some extent Blacks) explains the growing clamor for affirmative action in higher education during the 1980s and 1990s. However the declining proportion of Whites explains the affirmative action backlash, even though Whites are overrepresented compared to their share of the college-age population.

Another reason that different states have different ratios of students of color in their institutions of higher education is that students, particularly White students, often attend out-of-state schools. Blacks and Hispanics are more likely to be members of low socioeconomic status (SES) groups and are also most likely to attend colleges close to home. In 1996, 84 percent of freshmen attended college in their home state. Alaska (50 percent) and Connecticut, New Hampshire, and Vermont (56–58 percent) retained the smallest shares of their residents while California, Mississippi, North Carolina, Texas, Utah, and Wash-

## Table 3.9
### Comparison of the College Age Population and College Enrollment by Race/Ethnicity in California and Texas, 1984 and 1996

| | 1984 | | | 1996 | | | | |
| --- | --- | --- | --- | --- | --- | --- | --- | --- |
| | % College Age | % Enrollment, U.S. Citizens, All Higher Ed | Enrollment /Population | % College Age | % Enrollment, U.S. Citizens, All Higher Ed | Enrollment /Population | Change in Population | Change in Enrollment |
| *California* | | | | | | | | |
| White Non-Hispanic | 72.3% | 68.0% | 94.1% | 39.8% | 53.1% | 133.4% | 55.0% | 78.1% |
| Black Non-Hispanic | 8.5% | 6.7% | 78.8% | 7.2% | 8.0% | 111.1% | 84.7% | 119.4% |
| Hispanic | 22.6% | 10.4% | 46.0% | 40.0% | 21.3% | 53.3% | 177.0% | 204.8% |
| American Indian | 0.9% | 1.3% | 144.4% | 1.1% | 1.2% | 109.1% | 122.2% | 92.3% |
| Asian | 5.1% | 10.2% | 200.0% | 11.9% | 18.2% | 152.9% | 233.3% | 178.4% |
| *Texas* | | | | | | | | |
| White Non-Hispanic | 76.1% | 71.9% | 94.5% | 47.4% | 62.7% | 132.3% | 62.3% | 87.2% |
| Black Non-Hispanic | 13.1% | 8.9% | 67.9% | 13.0% | 10.2% | 78.5% | 99.2% | 114.6% |
| Hispanic | 21.9% | 13.1% | 59.8% | 36.2% | 21.8% | 60.2% | 165.3% | 166.4% |
| American Indian | 0.3% | 0.3% | 100.0% | 0.5% | 0.6% | 120.0% | 166.7% | 200.0% |
| Asian | 0.8% | 2.1% | 262.5% | 2.8% | 4.0% | 142.9% | 350.0% | 190.5% |

*Source*: U.S. Department of Labor, Bureau of Labor Statistics, Office of Employment and Unemployment Statistics. Current Population Survey, 1984 and 1996.

ington retained the highest (92–94 percent) (U.S. Dept. of Education 1998, tab. 203). Many factors influence migration decisions including family income and the quality and pervasiveness of in-state schools.

Institutions, especially private schools, compete for highly qualified students of color, often across state lines. However, public institutions that receive state funding are pressured to satisfy the enrollment demand within the state before looking elsewhere, since out-of-state students may be viewed as receiving an unwarranted subsidy.

An important question on college choice is how students sort themselves into various types of institutions. Groups of color attending highly selective private institutions have historically had the smallest rates. These rates probably rose somewhat recently with increases in need-based financial aid and affirmative action (U.S. Bureau of the Census 1998, tab. 303). Whether this pattern will continue as affirmative action wanes remains to be seen. Since the college's quality affects income and career success (Dale and Krueger 1999), it is important to increase the representation of qualified students of color in these colleges; but if their high school preparation improves, their access to selective institutions should also increase.

In general, all races, but particularly Hispanics, are most likely to matriculate first in public two-year colleges; Hispanics make up 11.9 percent of enrollments at two-year colleges vs. 6 percent at four-year institutions (U.S. Dept. of Education 1998, tab. 206). (See Table 3.10.) The completion

**Table 3.10**
**Percentage of Change of College Enrollment, by Race/Ethnicity, in Two- and Four-Year Institutions, 1988–1996**

| Two Year | 1988 | 1996 | % Change | % Minority | % Minority |
|---|---|---|---|---|---|
| Total | 5,240,100 | 5,497,400 | 4.9 | 1988 | 1996 |
| White, non-Hispanic | 3,954,300 | 3,742,800 | −5.35 | | |
| Minority total | 1,218,600 | 1,654,000 | 35.7 | 23.3% | 30.1% |
| Black, non-Hispanic | 524,300 | 629,300 | 20.0 | | |
| Hispanic | 424,200 | 644,200 | 51.9 | | |
| American Indian | 54,900 | 65,600 | 19.5 | | |
| Asian | 215,200 | 314,900 | 46.3 | | |
| Four Year | 1988 | 1996 | % Change | | |
| Total | 8,579,400 | 8,802,800 | 2.6 | | |
| White, non-Hispanic | 6,768,700 | 6,483,200 | −4.2 | | |
| Minority total | 1,486,300 | 1,946,200 | 30.9 | 17.3% | 22.1% |
| Black, non-Hispanic | 722,800 | 870,200 | 20.4 | | |
| Hispanic | 358,300 | 508,100 | 41.8 | | |
| American Indian | 47,900 | 67,200 | 40.3 | | |
| Asian | 357,300 | 500,700 | 40.1 | | |

*Source:* U.S. Census Bureau, Statistical Abstract of the United States, Table No. 303.

through the baccalaureate of such students is very low. Indeed, less than 10 percent of two-year students transferred to a four-year institution in the mid-1980s. Of all first-time enrollees in public two-year colleges in 1989–90, 17.5 percent had an associate of arts (A.A.) degree by 1994, but only 6.3 percent had bachelor's degrees (U.S. Dept. of Education 1997, tab. 310). Thus, four-year institutions could increase their enrollments by encouraging two-year college students to transfer after receiving their A.A. degree, but a high proportion (48.6 percent) drop out before completing even their A.A. Thus, increasing these students' persistence and subsequent transfers is important, particularly because two-year colleges enroll disproportionate numbers of students of color: 30.8 percent in 1996 contrasted to 23.1 percent for four-year schools.

Are students in two-year colleges, particularly those in vocational programs, interested in more than an A.A. degree? Although some academicians view any college experience short of a bachelor's degree as failure, a better perspective may be to see some college attendance as a greater achievement than none. In fact, a bachelor's degree may not be the objective of some high school graduates.

Except for Asians, private universities generally attract few students of color. In 1997, non-Hispanic Whites comprised 66.5 percent of eighteen- to twenty-four-year-olds in the United States. Although underrepresented in both public and private institutions (compared to their 33.5 percent share of eighteen- to twenty-four-year-olds), students of color made up a smaller share in private schools (21.5 percent) than in public institutions (26.4 percent) (U.S. Dept. of Education 1998, tab. 206). Both types of institutions have experienced almost identical patterns of increases for students of color and decreases for Whites since 1980. Private schools usually require higher tuition costs, often living far from home, and sometimes higher admissions standards. Historically, with a large pool of middle-class Whites to choose from, private institutions could afford to be rather complacent in recruiting students of color; but the declining share of Whites in the college-age cohort over the next several decades will force a reconsideration. These schools will also need to obtain more financial aid for applicants of color, something they have been quite successful at in recent years.

Much of the interinstitutional competition for students over the next decade will be for students of color. However, for any given pool, such competition is a zero-sum game. It would be much more fruitful to enlarge the pool. The military and job market, both of which are becoming increasingly attractive, will continue to compete for students. They are particularly successful with low-SES high school graduates, because they offer job-related training without making the recruit forego a full-time income.

## The Future of the Faculty

The supply of people for various careers, including academic careers, depends on the number of individuals who are willing and able to persist through various degree levels. Their academic and career choices result from adequate preparation early in their education, their ability to finance lengthy schooling, rates of return to careers in college teaching compared to other fields, and the values and attitudes of students and society toward higher education. By graduate school, the share of students of color is even smaller than their share in college. Those with graduate degrees are often wooed into the business sector, leaving few in academe. The financial incentive for any quality Ph.D. to take an academic position is weaker when jobs in the private sector are available; moreover, there is intense competition for the limited number of candidates of color who are being recruited by both businesses and higher education. As a result, higher education has difficulty meeting its faculty affirmative action and diversity goals.

In 1976, there were 1.7 million students of color in higher education compared to 9.1 million White non-Hispanics. By 1996, these numbers increased to 3.6 million and 10.2 million respectively (U.S. Dept. of Education 1998, tab. 206). In other words, the share of people of color doubled from 18.7 percent to 36 percent. As the number of non-White students in higher education increases, most colleges and universities are committed to increasing their faculty of color. Such efforts reflect both their commitment to expand opportunities for students of color with similar-race role models and also their belief that the multiracial perspectives of such role models will enhance the interests, motivation, and success of students of color.

This situation is almost but not exactly as true today as it was a decade ago. California's Proposition 209 (1996) prohibits all state instrumentalities—including the University of California, the California state college system, and California community colleges—from discriminating against or giving preferential treatment to any individual or group in public employment, public education, or public contracting on the basis of race, sex, color, ethnicity, or national origin. Similar initiatives have followed in other states, signaling a backlash against affirmative action.

Although the search for faculty of color often results in bidding wars, such efforts may raise starting salaries for some faculty of color; however, they do not expand the total pool of faculty of color. Most institutions find it very difficult to identify new Ph.D.'s of color to hire. Some conclude that if a particular institution does not hire many faculty of color, it simply is not trying hard enough, but this conclusion is not supported by data on Ph.D. production over the last fifteen or so years. Because only a non-White *American* faculty member "counts" as an affirmative action hire, this discussion will focus on

U.S. citizens rather than on permanent or temporary residents who are citizens of other countries.

Our examination looks at Ph.D's awarded in 1974, 1987, and 1997, the most recent year for which data are available. In 1974, Ph.D.'s glutted the employment market in most fields because the hiring boom of the late 1950s and 1960s had peaked several years earlier and most of those hires were many years from retirement. By 1987, institutions, aware of their pending retirements, were hiring before current faculty retired, rather than waiting for shortages to reappear. With the end of compulsory retirement policies in 1986 (Hammond and Morgan 1991), many professors continued to teach beyond their expected retirement ages, keeping the retirement rate low. Many colleges and universities have encouraged retirements, enabling them to replace high-priced senior faculty with less expensive juniors. But hiring has been slower than expected, and many highly qualified Ph.D's have been forced to take nonacademic jobs. In addition, over the last thirty years, the prestige of academe has faded somewhat while the business sector has offered increasingly attractive opportunities.

In 1974, 26,827 Ph.D.'s were awarded to U.S. citizens. This total fell to 22,863 by 1987 but rose to 27,668 in 1997. Between the first two years, the number of Ph.D.'s awarded to permanent resident aliens dipped from 1,853 to 1,570, but rose to 2,915 by 1997. Noncitizens with temporary visas were the only group who earned more Ph.D.'s (from 3,447 in 1974 to 5,593 in 1987 to 8,475 in 1997). Of course, not all new doctoral recipients expect to work in colleges and universities. In 1974, 55.6 percent of new U.S. Ph.D.'s expected to hold a job in an institution of higher education; this proportion fell to 44.3 percent by 1987 and to 39.6 percent in 1997. The number anticipating a postdoctoral appointment in 1974 was 13.2 percent, 22 percent in 1987, and 20.9 percent in 1997 (National Research 1974, 1987; National Opinion 1999, appen. tab. A-4). (See also Teddlie and Freeman; Anderson, this volume.)

The range of new Ph.D.'s available to academe lies somewhere between a low estimate (those who hold academic jobs when they receive their doctorates) and a high one (a combination of those anticipating jobs in higher education plus those with postdoctoral fellowships—assuming that these fellows will move into academic jobs). This high estimate shows that the proportion of new Ph.D.'s available to academe fell from 69 percent in 1974 to 66 percent in 1987 and to 55.7 percent in 1997. The low estimate shows that the number of new Ph.D.'s available for academe fell from 14,916 in 1974 to 10,228 in 1987 (68.6 percent of 1974) and in 1997 rose to 10,957 (7 percent above the 1987 level). Using our higher estimate, the number of new Ph.D.'s available for academe was 18,457 in 1974, 15,158 in 1987, and 15,411 in 1997 (National Research 1974, 1987; National Opinion 1999, appen. tab. A-4).

Even though the total pool of Ph.D.'s available for academe shrank between 1974 and 1997, opportunities to appoint faculty of color might have increased had the proportion of U.S. citizens of color receiving doctorates risen commensurately with the ethnic distribution of the population. Instead, the proportion of White citizens receiving Ph.D.'s between 1974 and 1987 increased from 87.4 percent to 89 percent, then dropped to 83.2 percent by 1997 (National Research 1974, 1987; National Opinion 1999, appen. tab. A-4). That is, doctoral recipients of color comprised a larger share in 1997 than previously.

The comparatively few Ph.D. recipients of color is striking even though the number of Ph.D.'s in some groups rose between 1974 and 1987 and Ph.D.'s for all groups increased from 1987 to 1997. The percentage growth in the number of Ph.D.'s was smallest for Whites between 1987 and 1997, when Asian Americans and Blacks each comprised 4.8 percent of Ph.D. recipients, with Hispanics receiving 2.1 percent (National Opinion 1999, appen. tab. A-4). (See Table 3.11.) These figures are low, and we have not subtracted the proportion who will take jobs outside of academe. Such a reduction would lower the numbers dramatically in the physical sciences, including computer science and engineering. (See Table 3.12).

## Table 3.11
## Number of Doctorates Received by U.S. Citizens

|  | 1974 | 1987 | 1996 | % Change 1987–97 |
|---|---|---|---|---|
| Total U.S. | 26,827 | 22,863 | 27,668 | 21.0 |
| American Indian | 129 | 116 | 166 | 43.1 |
| Asian American | 293 | 540 | 1,328 | 145.9 |
| Black | 846 | 765 | 1,335 | 74.5 |
| White | 23,442 | 20,358 | 23,021 | 13.1 |
| Puerto Rican | 60 | 180 | 312 | 73.3 |
| Mexican American | 195 | 174 | 290 | 66.7 |
|  |  | Change | Change |  |
| Total U.S. |  | −3,964 | 4,805 |  |
| American Indian |  | −13 | 50 |  |
| Asian American |  | 247 | 788 |  |
| Black |  | −81 | 570 |  |
| White |  | −3,084 | 2,663 |  |
| Puerto Rican |  | 120 | 132 |  |
| Mexican American |  | −21 | 116 |  |

Source: National Research Council, *Doctorate Recipients from United States Universities,* 1974 and 1987. National Opinion Research Center, *Summary Report: 1997, Doctorate Recipients from United States Universities,* Appendix Table A-4, 1999.

## Table 3.12
### Percentage of Distribution of Doctorate Recipients of U.S. Citizens by Race/Ethnicity, 1987 and 1997

| | % of U.S. Citizen Recipients | |
|---|---|---|
| | *1987* | *1997* |
| Total U.S. | 100.0 | 100.0 |
| American Indian | 0.5 | 0.6 |
| Asian American | 2.4 | 4.8 |
| Black | 3.3 | 4.8 |
| White | 89.0 | 83.2 |
| Puerto Rican | 0.8 | 1.1 |
| Mexican American | 0.8 | 1.0 |

*Source:* National Opinion Research Center, *Summary Report: 1997, Doctorate Recipients from United States Universities,* Appendix Table A-4, 1999.

To spell out the obvious, colleges and universities do not hire "a" Ph.D. but rather Ph.D.'s in specific fields. Therefore, the most relevant data in affirmative action hiring policies are the numbers of Ph.D.'s awarded to various ethnic groups in particular fields. For present purposes, we group disciplines into seven categories: physical sciences, engineering, life sciences, social sciences, humanities, education, and other professional fields. (See Table 3.13.) Whatever the number of Ph.D.'s awarded to a particular ethnic group in, for example, the physical sciences, they must still be distributed among physics, chemistry, mathematics, computer science, etc. Thus, the number of new Ph.D.'s available to any specific department is even smaller than the numbers presented here.

The 166 doctorates awarded to American Indians in 1997 reflect growth compared to 1974 (129) and 1987 (116). Yet the number of American Indians with new Ph.D.'s in the physical sciences is 13, in engineering 16, in the life sciences 20, in the humanities 24, in social sciences 30, and in education 51 (National Research 1974, 1987; National Opinion 1999, appen. tab. A-4). American Indians received the fewest Ph.D.'s in 1997 of any ethnic group. No more than a few institutions at best can succeed in hiring one.

Asian Americans received 1,328 doctorates in 1997, more than four times the figure for 1974. They received the bulk of their degrees in the physical and life sciences and engineering, with fewer in the social sciences, humanities, and education. Attempts to increase representation of Asian Americans in engineering departments and the physical and life sciences have significant prospects of success at this time, but such hires are not a pressing need in most institutions. It is also noteworthy that in virtually every field, the doctorates

**Table 3.13**
**Number of Doctorates Awarded**

| | Total U.S. | American Indian | Asian American | Black | White | Puerto Rican | Mexican American | Other Hispanic |
|---|---|---|---|---|---|---|---|---|
| **1997** | | | | | | | | |
| Physical Sciences | 3,592 | 13 | 257 | 59 | 3,031 | 35 | 23 | 42 |
| Engineering | 2,707 | 16 | 294 | 83 | 2,138 | 23 | 17 | 42 |
| Life Sciences | 5,139 | 20 | 324 | 165 | 4,319 | 50 | 47 | 77 |
| Social Sciences | 5,062 | 30 | 188 | 254 | 4,220 | 71 | 70 | 90 |
| Humanities | 4,158 | 24 | 114 | 136 | 3,571 | 52 | 35 | 85 |
| Education | 5,415 | 51 | 100 | 529 | 4,397 | 70 | 87 | 88 |
| Professional/Other | 1,596 | 11 | 51 | 108 | 1,346 | 10 | 10 | 21 |
| **1987** | | | | | | | | |
| Physical Sciences | 3,087 | 10 | 104 | 29 | 2,789 | 33 | 12 | 19 |
| Engineering | 1,555 | 8 | 135 | 12 | 1,323 | 4 | 6 | 14 |
| Life Sciences | 4,207 | 16 | 145 | 78 | 3,807 | 28 | 15 | 34 |
| Social Sciences | 4,344 | 22 | 75 | 136 | 3,888 | 21 | 44 | 81 |
| Humanities | 2,721 | 11 | 25 | 73 | 2,463 | 31 | 18 | 47 |
| Education | 5,464 | 41 | 41 | 379 | 4,743 | 53 | 72 | 61 |
| Professional/Other | 1,440 | 8 | 15 | 58 | 1,323 | 10 | 7 | 8 |

**Table 3.13**
*(Continued)*

| | Total U.S. | American Indian | Asian American | Black | White | Puerto Rican | Mexican American | Other Hispanic |
|---|---|---|---|---|---|---|---|---|
| **1974** | | | | | | | | |
| Physical Sciences | 3,648 | 15 | 61 | 46 | 3,258 | 6 | 13 | * |
| Engineering | 1,797 | 7 | 64 | 16 | 1,571 | 7 | 7 | * |
| Life Sciences | 3,675 | 15 | 51 | 69 | 3,282 | 6 | 22 | * |
| Social Sciences | 5,231 | 19 | 35 | 107 | 4,665 | 12 | 27 | * |
| Humanities | 4,587 | 19 | 28 | 75 | 4,055 | 17 | 42 | * |
| Education | 6,707 | 46 | 43 | 501 | 5,556 | 11 | 78 | * |
| Professional/Other | 1,180 | 8 | 11 | 32 | 1,031 | 1 | 6 | * |
| **Change 1987–97** | | | | | | | | |
| Physical Sciences | 505 | 3 | 153 | 30 | 242 | 2 | 11 | 23 |
| Engineering | 1,152 | 8 | 159 | 71 | 815 | 19 | 11 | 28 |
| Life Sciences | 932 | 4 | 179 | 87 | 512 | 22 | 32 | 43 |
| Social Sciences | 718 | 8 | 113 | 118 | 332 | 50 | 26 | 9 |
| Humanities | 1,437 | 13 | 89 | 63 | 1,108 | 21 | 17 | 38 |
| Education | –49 | 10 | 59 | 150 | –346 | 17 | 15 | 27 |
| Professional/Other | 156 | 3 | 36 | 50 | 23 | 0 | 3 | 13 |
| **Change 1974–87** | | | | | | | | |
| Physical Sciences | –561 | –5 | 43 | –17 | –469 | 27 | –1 | * |
| Engineering | –242 | 1 | 71 | –4 | –248 | –3 | –1 | * |
| Life Sciences | 532 | 1 | 94 | 9 | 525 | 22 | –7 | * |
| Social Sciences | –887 | 3 | 40 | 29 | –777 | 9 | 17 | * |
| Humanities | –1,866 | –8 | –3 | –2 | –1,592 | 14 | –24 | * |
| Education | –1,243 | –5 | –2 | –122 | –813 | 42 | –6 | * |
| Professional/Other | 260 | 0 | 4 | 26 | 292 | 9 | 1 | * |

*Source*: National Research Council, *Doctorate Recipients from United States Universities*, 1974 and 1987. National Opinion Research Center, *Summary Report: 1997, Doctorate Recipients from United States Universities*, Appendix Table A-4, 1999.

awarded to Asians who are permanent residents in the United States, and especially to Asians studying here on temporary visas, far exceed those awarded to Asian Americans (National Research 1974, 1987; National Opinion 1999, appen. tab. A-4).

American Blacks received 1,335 doctorates in 1997, almost double the figure for 1987. More doctorates were awarded to American Blacks in education than in any other field (40 percent of all Ph.D.'s). Blacks received only 59 Ph.D.'s in the physical sciences in 1997, 83 in engineering, 136 in the social sciences, and 165 in the life sciences. The concentration of Black Ph.D.'s in education is a long-standing tradition; but it underscores that the availability of new Black Ph.D.'s in other fields is small.

As Table 3.13 shows, the number of Puerto Ricans and Mexican Americans receiving doctorates grew from 255 to 602 between 1974 and 1997. However, other than in education (157) and the social sciences (141), Hispanics received fewer than 100 degrees in any field (National Research 1974, 1987; National Opinion 1999, appen. tab. A-4). Few departments, in short, can increase their numbers of Hispanic faculty.

**Conclusions and Recommendations**

This chapter traces the demographic trends that higher education will face beyond the turn of the century. Based on the age distribution of the already-born U.S. population and the ethnicities and national origins of likely immigration, it is clear that eighteen-year-olds who will be considering higher education in the first decades of the twenty-first century will continue to grow more ethnically diverse. The number of candidates of color entering the potential faculty pipeline is now growing—a change from 1987. If we extrapolate current characteristics of people of color, we could conclude that the typical eighteen-year-old college entrant might be less well prepared for college than earlier; if so, the pool of Ph.D.'s of color will shrink.

However, we choose to take a more optimistic view. School reform efforts are apparently having a positive impact. Technology is entering many classrooms, apparently enhancing learning, particularly of lower-achieving students. The quality of new teachers, although still poor, seems to be rising a bit, especially with new pay scales based on accomplishments and new career development possibilities. Perhaps most importantly, traditional public schools are facing competition from charter and voucher schools, many of which serve currently underserved students of color. Thus, there is hope that all students will begin to achieve at levels closer to those of suburban students and that the achievement level will rise for all.

To what extent can we extrapolate from the past in predicting the progress of people of color? Efforts are now underway to help underprepared poor children and children of color increase their academic achievement. Certainly a great deal of money has been spent on such efforts in the K-12 system in recent years. Optimistically, by 2010, when people of color comprise a greater share of those considering college, they will be better prepared and will more closely resemble their White peers than has been the case to date. On the other hand, if a greater share of eighteen-year-olds retains the characteristics of today's people of color, the higher education system must continue to make substantial adjustments. We said much of this ten years ago; and despite quite a bit of churning, not much solid change for good has occurred in our K-12 system.

Required adjustments will include changing recruiting policies (perhaps including higher standards for admission) and increasing the availability of financial aid, which has declined relative to need. The U.S. Department of Education reported that Black enrollment plateaued during the 1980s after great growth from the mid-1960s to the mid-1970s. Commenting on this report, Patricia Smith, director of Legislative Analysis for the American Council on Education, said: "The concern is not so much that the number is down (26,000 below the peak of 1.1 million in 1980), but that we're not making great progress toward increasing it" (qtd. in "Minorities" 1988). It is encouraging that Black enrollment increased to 1.5 million in 1996 and is probably higher now (U.S. Dept. of Education, 1997 tab. 206). But is that all there is? If more people of color get to higher education but drop out or do not learn much, we cannot be satisfied.

In 1990 we projected that college-level remediation would require a larger proportion of resources. This has occurred, especially in large state colleges. It will continue until our K–12 system improves or until colleges drastically limit admissions to the truly qualified. We also said that colleges must do better advising in order to retain students through graduation. However, the budget crunches of the past decade have often cut rather than expanded such services. We also urged greater concern with the transfer function of two-year colleges. However, there are fewer transfers today than a decade ago.

The next twenty years—like the past twenty—could be considered a time of crisis in higher education, or they could be considered an opportunity. It is probably fair to say that so far the crises have outweighed the successes. It is tempting to blame other institutions besides higher education: families, social services agencies, and particularly secondary schools. However, no matter what improvements are made in these areas, responsibility for higher education is the job of this country's colleges and universities. Meeting the needs of a changing student body will remain a major challenge.

Table 3.14 presents the racial ethnic composition of full-time instructional faculty in higher education in 1995. Combining all ranks, we see that Asian faculty (5 percent) are overrepresented compared to Asian students (3 percent) while all other people of color are underrepresented. The prospects

## Table 3.14
### Full-time Instructional Faculty in Higher Education, by Race/Ethnicity and Academic Rank: Fall 1995

| | Total | White, non-Hispanic | | Black, non-Hispanic | | Hispanic | | Asian or Pacific Islander | | American Indian/Alaskan Native | | Nonresident Alien | | Race/Ethnicity Unknown | |
|---|---|---|---|---|---|---|---|---|---|---|---|---|---|---|---|
| | Number | Number | Percent | Number | Percent | Number | Percent | Number | Percent | Number | Percent | Number | Percent | Number | Percent |
| Total, all ranks | 550,822 | 468,518 | 85.1% | 26,835 | 4.9% | 12,942 | 2.3% | 27,572 | 5.0% | 2,156 | 0.4% | 10,853 | 2.0% | 1,946 | 0.4% |
| Professors | 159,333 | 142,819 | 89.6% | 4,768 | 3.0% | 2,470 | 1.6% | 7,643 | 4.8% | 373 | 0.2% | 975 | 0.6% | 285 | 0.2% |
| Associate professors | 125,082 | 108,953 | 87.1% | 5,634 | 4.5% | 2,607 | 2.1% | 6,119 | 4.9% | 350 | 0.3% | 1,179 | 0.9% | 240 | 0.2% |
| Assistant professors | 129,682 | 104,037 | 80.2% | 8,011 | 6.2% | 3,736 | 2.9% | 8,459 | 6.5% | 519 | 0.4% | 4,311 | 3.3% | 609 | 0.5% |
| Instructors | 66,708 | 55,211 | 82.8% | 4,857 | 7.3% | 2,530 | 3.8% | 2,323 | 3.5% | 513 | 0.8% | 848 | 1.3% | 426 | 0.6% |
| Lecturers | 12,874 | 10,533 | 81.8% | 798 | 6.2% | 429 | 3.3% | 557 | 4.3% | 54 | 0.4% | 426 | 3.3% | 77 | 0.6% |
| Other faculty | 57,143 | 46,965 | 82.2% | 2,767 | 4.8% | 1,170 | 2.0% | 2,471 | 4.3% | 347 | 0.6% | 3,114 | 5.4% | 309 | 0.5% |

Source: U.S. Dept. of Education, Digest of Education Statistics 1998, Table 226.

of hiring new American Indian, Black, and Hispanic faculty are dismal. If every non-White doctorate recipient entered academe (surely improbable, given the push for diverse hires in the government and private sectors), there are not enough for each baccalaureate-level institution in this country to hire even one. And ideally, a department's goal should not be to hire only one faculty member of color but rather to hire a critical mass from the one or more groups most relevant to its particular student population. Once we account for the disproportionate number of doctorates awarded to people of color in education and the social sciences, it is almost futile for other disciplines to spend much time and money searching for candidates. In 1995 there were 2,244 four-year institutions in the United States and 1,462 two-year colleges (U.S. Bureau 1998, tab. 306). If the 26,835 Black faculty were divided equally among the four-year institutions, there would be a dozen in each. However, this figure includes Black faculty in traditionally Black colleges and two-year colleges who are not really available for four-year schools. In large institutions, even a dozen hires would have almost no impact. Virtually the same pattern is apparent for Hispanic and Asian faculty, numbering 13,000 and 27,500 respectively (U.S. Dept. of Education 1998, tab. 226).

Given these slim chances, then, should colleges and universities ignore pleas for hiring faculty of color? Clearly, no; these institutions must play a major role in rectifying higher education's ethnic imbalance among both students and faculty. However, merely trying harder to hire from the available pool is bound to prove futile. Moreover, colleges and universities must analyze the short- and long-term cost effectiveness of spending increasingly scarce resources to buy faculty of color away from other institutions compared to attracting and retaining students of color who will increase the available pool in a few years.

We can no longer look at hiring faculty of color as an absolute good. Budget constraints and personnel limitations force us to ask how much effort is worthwhile to recruit faculty of color. Given the discouraging results after decades of efforts to increase the share of faculty of color, we must ask:

1. How much more valuable are faculty of color for students of color? That is, do students of color learn more or better from faculty of color?

2. Do otherwise similar institutions with more faculty of color attract and retain more students of color?

3. Would students of color be better off with more financial aid or more counselors than with more faculty of color if a choice was necessary?

The problem cannot be solved quickly because it requires long-term solutions. The non-White proportion of our citizens is rising dramatically, and we must make certain that non-White youth complete high school. Many of those who choose to attend college will require counseling and remediation to overcome inferior preparation, stimulating and relevant curricula, and adequate financial aid, or too many will drop out. As the extensive literature on college retention shows, students of color need financial aid, opportunities to live on campus, and involvement in academic and extracurricular life—all important factors that increase the prospects of graduation (Astin 1975; Ekstrom et al. 1983).

Once a student of color graduates from college, the opportunity costs of going further are immense, especially given the nonacademic sectors' efforts to employ him or her. The difficulty of postponing immediate income from a job to pursue further study is magnified for the least wealthy college graduates whose families depend on their earnings. In addition to generous fellowship support for students of color who decide to go on, graduate programs will have to work hard to attract students of color, provide stipends to compensate for some of the earnings lost from the workplace, and make credible commitments of involvement in the scholarly work of leading faculty. Efforts to make academic salaries competitive with salaries in other sectors are absolutely crucial.

Such an approach will take time. We cannot expect the pool of new Ph.D.'s of color to expand rapidly in the next several years; despite recent large percentage gains, their absolute numbers have not increased much in a decade. However, colleges and universities must continue to provide not only opportunities but incentives so that bright people of color will choose academe for their career.

## References

American Council on Education (ACE). 1987. *Fact book on higher education.* London: Collier MacMillan.

Astin, Alexander W. 1975. *Preventing students from dropping out.* San Francisco: Jossey-Bass.

Dale, S. B., and A. B. Krueger. 1999. Estimating the payroll to attending a more selective college: An application of selection on observables and unobservables. *National Bureau of Economic Research,* No. W7322.

Ekstrom, R., M. Goertz, J. Pollack, and D. Rock. 1983. Who drops out of high school and why? *Teachers College Record* 87, no. 3: 356–73.

Forum on Child and Family Statistics. 1998. *America's children: Key national indicators of well-being.* Washington, DC: U.S. Government Printing Office.

Freeman, R. B. 1976. *The overeducated American.* New York: Academic Press.

Hammond, Brett, and Harriet Morgan, eds. 1991. *Ending mandatory retirement for tenured faculty: The consequences for higher education.* Washington, DC: National Academy Press.

Minorities' share of college enrollments edges up. 1988. *Chronicle of Higher Education* (March 9): A33–36.

National Opinion Research Center. 1999. *Summary report: 1997, Doctorate recipients from United States universities.* Chicago: National Opinion Research Center.

National Research Council. 1974. *Doctorate recipients from United States Universities.* Washington, DC: U.S. Government Printing Office.

———. 1987. *Doctorate recipients from United States Universities.* Washington, DC: U.S. Government Printing Office.

National Committee on Vital and Health Statistics. 1999, April 29. *National Vital Statistics Report,* 47, no. 18.

O'Neil, D., and P. Sepielli. 1985. *Education in the United States: 1940–83.* Washington, DC: U.S. Government Printing Office.

Rumberger, R. W. 1983. Dropping out of high school: The influence of race, sex, and family background. *American Educational Research Journal* 20, no. 2: 199–200.

U.S. Bureau of the Census. 1961. *General Population Characteristics: U.S. Summary.* Washington, DC: U.S. Government Printing Office.

———. 1980. *General Population Characteristics: U.S. Summary.* Washington, DC: U.S. Government Printing Office.

———. 1985. School enrollment—social and economic characteristics of students: October, 1985. *Current Population Reports,* ser. P-20, no. 409. Washington, DC: U.S. Government Printing Office.

———. 1998a. *Current population survey: March 1997.* Washington, DC: U.S. Government Printing Office.

———. 1998b. *Statistical Abstract of the United States.* Washington, DC: U.S. Government Printing Office.

U.S. Department of Education. National Center for Education Statistics. 1987. *Digest of education statistics.* Washington, DC: U.S. Government Printing Office.

———. 1997. *Digest of education statistics.* Washington, DC: U.S. Government Printing Office.

———. 1998. *Digest of education statistics.* Washington, DC: U.S. Government Printing Office.

———. 1999. *Dropout rates in the United States*, NCES 1999-082, by Phillip Kaufman, Steve Klein, and Mary Frase. See full report at http://nces.ed.gov/pubsearch/pubsinfo.asp?pubid=1999082

U.S. Department of Justice, Immigration, and Naturalization Service, Office of Policy and Planning. 1999, January. *Legal immigration, fiscal year 1997.*

# CHAPTER 4

# Twentieth-Century Desegregation in U.S. Higher Education

*A Review of Five Distinct Historical Eras*

## CHARLES TEDDLIE AND JOHN A. FREEMAN

It is hard to argue against the proposition that the United States has made vast improvements in educational equity when contrasted with our society a hundred years ago. We have progressed from the remnants of slavery, to a dual society predicated on the false assumption that separate can be equal, to the post-*Brown v. the Board of Education of Topeka, Kansas* (347 US 483 [1954]) era of desegregation and federal activism that has given legal authority to the tenets of equal education. However, progress toward educational equity was strenuously opposed during the twentieth century, and continued progress in the twenty-first century is not guaranteed.

If the general battle for racial equality was fought and won in the twentieth century, then why have we not yet declared a victory on higher education desegregation? The answer to that question can be found in higher education enrollments in the thirty-five years after *Brown*. Not until 1964, with the passage of the Civil Rights Act, did the federal government make a determined effort to enforce higher education desegregation. From that year to the mid-1970s, African American enrollment in higher education increased dramatically; however, since then, it has largely stagnated. If we accept the concept that equal higher educational opportunity has not yet been achieved in the United States, then we must ask ourselves, Why not, and if not, how can we reach this goal in the next century?

This chapter will examine the history of higher education desegregation in the United States by comparing five distinct eras (Teddlie and Freeman 1996) and college enrollment data during each, in their sociopolitical context. It also identifies remaining obstacles to equality of opportunity in higher education and methods for addressing them.

## 1933–53: Initial Strategies for Desegregating U.S. Higher Education

The year 1933 marks the beginning of higher education desegregation during the twentieth century. The National Association for the Advancement of Colored People (NAACP) filed the first lawsuit on behalf of an African American student denied admission to a college due to race: *Hocutt v. Wilson* (Superior Court, Durham County, North Carolina, filed 16 March 1933; answered 24 March 1933; dismissed). From 1896 when the Supreme Court had announced its verdict in *Plessy v. Ferguson* (163 US 538 [1896]), state-sanctioned segregation in education had been the law of the land. The separate-but-equal doctrine contained in *Plessy* permitted states to deny African American students admission to all-White universities. The fact that it took thirty-seven years for a case to be filed contesting this practice is remarkable.

*Hocutt* was the beginning of an orchestrated NAACP strategy to attack state-sanctioned segregation through the courts. This strategy was devised by Nathan Margold in 1930, when the Garland Fund hired him to direct the legal campaign. Originally, it had three basic elements: (1) to file numerous taxpayers' lawsuits designed to win equality in elementary schools by creating an economic burden that would force states to abandon segregation, (2) to launch an immediate attack on the inequality and unconstitutionality of segregation, and (3) to begin segregation lawsuits against graduate/professional schools (Hill and Greenberg 1955).

As mentioned, this effort was funded by a trust established by Charles Garland in 1922. When the Great Depression depleted this trust, the NAACP reorganized its strategy, created the Legal Defense and Education Fund to raise funds and direct the legal campaign, and appointed Charles Hamilton Houston, a renowned African American legal scholar as its director. Houston refocused the campaign on the third element: attacking segregation in graduate/professional schools. Many states were legally vulnerable on this point since they had failed to provide separate facilities. To Houston, such situations represented a prima facie case of inequality according to *Plessy* (Hill and Greenberg 1955).

Although the North Carolina superior court dismissed *Hocutt* when the plaintiff failed to provide valid transcripts, three years later, the Maryland's Court of Appeals heard *Pearson v. Murray* (169 Md. 478, 182 Atl. 590 [1936]), based on the plaintiff's contention that he was denied admission to the University of Maryland Law School due to race. The state of Maryland did not provide a separate African American law school; the NAACP argued that since no "separate, equal" law school existed, the University of Maryland had to admit the plaintiff.

Although *Murray* did not reach the U.S. Supreme Court, the Maryland Court of Appeals addressed two critical questions related to *Plessy*. The first concerned equality. Like many states, Maryland granted out-of-state tuition scholarships to Black students as a cost-effective means of satisfying *Plesssy,* while avoiding the creation of separate law schools. The court ruled that this policy was inadequate to prove equality of financial burden, because the student still had to pay the costs of living away from home. The second question dealt with the proper remedy; because Maryland had only one law school, the court held that the student had to be admitted (Hill and Greenberg 1955).

Two years after *Murray,* the NAACP filed *Missouri ex rel. Gaines v. Canada* (305 US 337 [1938]) on behalf of Lloyd Gaines, who was denied admission to the University of Missouri Law School even though the state had no separate African American law school. This case was the first NAACP lawsuit to reach the U.S. Supreme Court, which agreed with the *Murray* ruling and ordered that Gaines be admitted. This ruling continued to recognize the validity of "separate-but-substantially equal," an illusory term to communicate that separate institutions did not have to be equal in every sense. However, since Missouri did not provide a separate law school, admitting Gaines to the "White" law school did not contradict *Plessy.*

The second higher education desegregation case reached the Supreme Court in 1948 when it heard *Sipuel v. Board of Regents of the University of Oklahoma* (332 US 631 [1948]). The University of Oklahoma Law School denied Ada Lois Sipuel, an African American student, admission because of her race. Citing *Gaines,* the Supreme Court ruled that Sipuel should be admitted to the all-White law school based upon the equal protection clause of the Fourteenth Amendment and that she had the right to an education at the same time as any other individual in the state, thus preventing the state from delaying her admission until a separate law school could be hurriedly created.

In the case of *Sweatt v. Painter* (339 US 629 [1950]), an African American student sought admission to the University of Texas Law School, and a lower state court ordered that Texas establish a law school for African Americans. The law school was quickly set up in the basement of an African American college, and two African American attorneys were hired as the faculty. The school was woefully inadequate, and Sweatt again sued the state. *Sweatt* represented a different problem for the Supreme Court. The *Gaines* and *Sipuel* decisions relied on the constitutionality of separate-but-equal. However, in *Sweatt,* the plaintiff argued that the schools were not equal and that he should therefore be allowed to attend the University of Texas Law School. After hearing the arguments, the Court determined that the African American law school was not equal to that of the University of Texas; therefore, Sweatt had the right to be admitted to the University of Texas Law School.

On the same day, the Supreme Court also decided *McLaurin v. Oklahoma State Regents for Higher Education* (339 US 637 [1950]). The plaintiff had been admitted to the University of Oklahoma as a doctoral student in the

College of Education, based upon the *Sipuel* ruling. After being admitted, he was required to sit and study in designated sections of the university. The Court ruled that, once a state chooses not to establish a separate-but-substantially-equal school for African Americans, it cannot segregate them within the all-White school. The particular importance of *Sweatt* and *McLaurin* lies in the fact that they addressed the equality issue of *Plessy* in terms of the effects on students and their educational opportunities, rather than on equality of revenues. These cases served as the foundation upon which *Brown* was built.

## 1954–63: The Impact of the *Brown* Decision on the Desegregation of U.S. Higher Education

The *Brown* case, decided four years after *Sweatt* and *McLaurin,* obliged the Supreme Court to address the ultimate question: Is racial segregation in public schools unconstitutional per se? (Blaustein and Ferguson 1962). The Court referred to the previous higher education cases where the entire learning process was weighed in determining equality. This process required balancing tangible, as well as intangible factors, such as benefits of association with fellow students and the prestige and traditions of the educational institutions in question.

Since the Fourteenth Amendment requires equality, it follows that "in the field of public education the doctrine of separate but equal has no place" (Hill and Greenberg 1955, 120). With these words, Chief Justice Earl Warren overruled *Plessy* and declared the separate-but-equal doctrine unconstitutional. However, it took two additional years before *Brown* was applied to higher education. In the case of *Florida, ex rel. Hawkins v. Board of Control* (350 US 413 [1956]), several African American students sought admission to the University of Florida Law School. Since Florida had already created an African American law school at Florida A&M University, Hawkins and the other students were denied admission to the University of Florida based on *Plessy.* The original lawsuit was filed four years before *Brown,* but the case did not reach the Supreme Court until after the *Brown* decision. The Court ordered the Florida Supreme Court decision vacated and remanded the case to be reconsidered in light of *Brown.* As a result, the Florida Supreme Court unanimously agreed that its state universities must admit all qualified applicants. However, the University of Florida urged a delay in admitting Hawkins to its law school, arguing that Chief Justice Warren had delayed desegregation of K-12 schools due to "social complexities." On this principle, five of the seven Florida Supreme Court judges decided that there was no duty to admit Hawkins at any particular time.

In 1956 the Supreme Court clarified its decision in *Hawkins* by stating that the "social complexities" of desegregating K-12 schools did not exist in graduate programs. The case was again remanded to the Florida courts with clear instructions to immediately admit the plaintiffs to the University of Florida Law School. With this decision, *Hawkins* succeeded in extending the *Brown* decision to higher education.

Open resistance to higher education desegregation continued throughout the 1950s and early 1960s. Incidents of opposition to desegregation occurred at several universities, including the University of Alabama (1956), the University of Georgia (1961), and the University of Mississippi (1962). When the army secured James Meredith's enrollment at the University of Mississippi, the era of "mob violence" against higher education desegregation ended (Sansing 1989; Synnott 1989). Although the *Brown* and *Hawkins* decisions ended segregation in public education, several southern states focused on delaying desegregation. The passage of the 1964 Civil Rights Act finally resulted in significant progress in the desegregation of higher education.

Information about African American enrollment in higher education until 1954 is important at this point as a benchmark for data presented later. Estimates of African American enrollment in higher education from the late 1800s and early 1900s are very rare, but the following estimates are among the most accurate:

- According to data first published by W. E. B. DuBois (1989), there were 2,304 "Negro college graduates" up to 1899 in the United States. Of this total, 83 percent were from "Negro colleges" and the remaining 17 percent were from White colleges.
- Anderson (1989) estimated that in 1900 there were 3,880 African American college/professional students enrolled in the southern states and the District of Columbia, 56 percent in "Negro colleges." These figures increased to 13,860 by academic year 1926–27 and to 28,269 by 1935. Anderson did not report the number of African Americans enrolled outside the southern states and the District of Columbia, but it was limited.
- Bowles and DeCosta (1989) estimated that there were 63,000 African American undergraduates enrolled in African American colleges in 1954, with another 45,000 enrolled in northern colleges, for a total of 108,000. These numbers increased dramatically over the next twenty years.

## 1964–73: The Impact of the 1964 Civil Rights Act on the Desegregation of U.S. Higher Education

In 1964, approximately 300,000 African Americans were enrolled in higher education institutions in the United States, compared to 4.7 million Whites (U.S. Dept. of Education 1987). According to Williams (1991), the federal government recognized this inequity and enacted the 1964 Civil Rights Act to give African Americans greater opportunities to attend institutions of higher education. To overcome de facto segregation, Title VI of the Civil Rights Act specifically prohibited spending federal funds in higher education institutions that discriminated on the basis of "race, color or national origin" (Blaustein and Zangrando 1968; Trent 1991).

In 1964 African Americans constituted only about 6 percent of the total number of students attending institutions of higher education; by 1974 that percentage had increased to 8.4 percent (U.S Dept. of Education 1976). More dramatically, the absolute number of African Americans enrolled in higher education increased more than 200 percent (from 300,000 to more than 900,000). While enrollment at historically Black colleges and universities (HBCUs) also increased during that time, most of the gains in African American enrollment came at predominantly White institutions.

While the *Brown* decision and the resultant 1964 Civil Rights Act produced impressive gains in African American enrollment, they also presented potential threats to HBCUs in three areas: (1) potential loss of enrollment, (2) potential mergers with predominantly White schools, and (3) the potential closing of HBCUs due to their inability to compete in the larger marketplace. Additionally, as part of the challenge to the separate-but-equal doctrine of *Plessy,* the NAACP argued that the education received in HBCUs was not equal to that received in predominantly White institutions due to the inequity in financial support. While the legal strategy was successful, it had two unfortunate side effects: damaging the credibility of HBCUs and pitting NAACP and HBCU supporters against each other (Preer 1982; Trent 1991).

## 1974–84: The *Adams* and *Bakke* Cases and Their Effects on U.S. Higher Education Desegregation

The *Adams* cases encompassed several separate court decisions.[1] These NAACP cases were brought to assure that the U.S. Department of Education (USDE) (initially the Department of Health, Education, and Welfare [DHEW]) would force compliance with Title VI. There is strong evidence that the presidencies of Nixon/Ford (1968–76) and Reagan/Bush (1980–92) adopted a policy of "nonenforcement of desegregation laws and policies" (Dentler

---

1. *Adams v. Richardson,* 356 F.Supp. 92 (D.C.C. 1973); *Adams v. Weinberger,* 391 F.Supp. 269 (D.C.C. 1975); *Adams v. Califano,* 430 F.Supp. 118 (D.C.C. 1977); *Adams v. Bell,* Civil Action No. 70-3095 (D.C.C. 1982).

1991; Trent 1991; Williams 1991). The initial *Adams* suit sought to change Nixon's desegregation policy by requiring that the DHEW institute enforcement proceedings in documented cases of noncompliance, conduct additional reviews, monitor compliance, and respond to state plans for higher education desegregation.

By the mid-1970s, the governors of ten states received DHEW letters requiring them to submit desegregation plans to the federal government (Williams 1991). In 1981, this department (now USDE) notified an additional eight states of their Title VI noncompliance. In 1977, the *Adams v. Califano* case finally established guidelines for the desegregation of higher education. These guidelines required that: the proportion of African American and White high school graduates entering institutions of higher education will be equal; there will be an annual increase in the proportion of African Americans in predominantly White institutions; and there will be an increase in the proportion of White students attending HBCUs (Williams 1991).

The *Adams* litigation ended in 1990, with *Women's Equity Action League v. Cavazos* (906 F.2d 742 [D.C.C. 1990]). With the dismissal of this case went the guidelines for achieving higher education desegregation. Those states under court order to bring about an end to dual systems of higher education were no longer under federal obligation to do so. States continuing to use plans designed to increase African American enrollment have received conflicting messages from recent court decisions against affirmative action. (See the *Podberesky* and *Hopwood* cases below.)

*The University of California Regents v. Bakke* (438 US 265 [1978]) case also occurred at the beginning of this period. Allan Bakke, a White applicant, claimed that he was denied access to the University of California (Davis) Medical School solely on the basis of race. The medical school had "set aside" sixteen places for minorities and had therefore denied Whites access to those places. He sought relief under the equal protection clause of Title VI. A divided Supreme Court decided in Bakke's favor (Trent 1991), introducing the term "reverse discrimination" into the civil rights lexicon.

Immediately following the *Bakke* decision, the number of African Americans enrolled in higher education declined. Some analysts believe that *Bakke* contributed to that decline, but it is more likely that *Bakke* was a manifestation of a larger issue: the continued resistance of institutions and individuals to affirmative action components of Title VI compliance. Trent (1991) concluded that the mediating effects of *Bakke* (threats of similar suits and a more conservative judiciary) combined to produce a chilling effect on minority access.

While the first decade after the 1964 Civil Rights Act was characterized by large increases in African American enrollment, the second decade (1974–84) was not. As indicated in Table 4.1, the number of African American students enrolled in higher education remained relatively constant from the mid-1970s through the mid-1980s. Since White enrollment in higher education increased during this period, the proportion of African American students declined from 9.4 percent in 1976–78 to 8.8 percent in 1982–84 (U.S. Dept. of Education 1987).

Several authors considered this trend particularly disturbing since the proportion of African American high school graduates increased during this same time period (Garibaldi 1991a; Willie 1991). Between 1974 and 1984, the number of African American students who graduated from high school increased by 39 percent and the high school completion rate increased by 7.6 percent. (See

**Table 4.1**
**Enrollment in Higher Education by Type of Institution**
**and Ethnicity (White, Black) for Selected Years, 1976–84**

| Year/ Ethnicity | Total Enrollment | Four-Year Institution | Two-Year Institution | % Two-Year Institution |
|---|---|---|---|---|
| 1976 Total | 10,970 | 7,090 | 3,880 | 35.4% |
| White | 9,061 | 5,984 | 3,077 | 34.0% |
| Black | 1,032 | 603 | 429 | 41.6% |
| % Black | 9.4% | 8.5% | 11.1% | NA |
| 1980 Total | 12,038 | 7,548 | 4,490 | 37.3% |
| White | 9,791 | 6,259 | 3,532 | 36.1% |
| Black | 1,101 | 633 | 468 | 42.5% |
| % Black | 9.1% | 8.4% | 10.4% | NA |
| 1984 Total | 12,235 | 7,708 | 4,527 | 37.0% |
| White | 9,815 | 6,301 | 3,514 | 35.8% |
| Black | 1,076 | 617 | 459 | 42.9% |
| % Black | 8.8% | 8.0% | 10.1% | NA |
| % Change 1976–84 Total | 11.5% | 8.7% | 16.7% | 1.6% |
| % Change 1976–84 White | 8.3% | 5.3% | 14.2% | 1.8% |
| % Change 1976–84 Black | 4.3% | 2.3% | 7.0% | 1.3% |

*Note:* Enrollment numbers are indicated in thousands. The White/Black numbers do not equal the totals because other ethnicities are excluded.
NA = Not Applicable.
*Sources:* U.S. Department of Education 1994; Carter and Wilson 1995.

Table 4.2.) During the same time period, the rate of high school graduates enrolled in college declined from 34 percent in 1976 to 27 percent in 1984. Garibaldi (1991a) described these trends (Tables 4.1 and 4.2) as follows:

> Thus, rather than capitalizing on the increasing size of the age cohort and the higher numbers graduating from high school, college participation rates of today's generation of African American youth have regressed significantly in . . . proportional representation on college campuses. (94)

Trent (1991) concluded that the only regional college/university group that succeeded both in increasing its enrollment and in decreasing its segregation index (Becker 1978) during this period was the traditionally White

**Table 4.2**

**High School Completion Rates and College Progression Rates by Ethnicity (White, Black) for Selected Years, 1974–84**

| Year/ Ethnicity | High School Graduates | Completion Rate (%) | # Enrolled in College | Progression Rate (%) |
|---|---|---|---|---|
| 1974 | 20,725 | 80.7% | 6,316 | 30.5% |
| White | 18,318 | 82.7% | 5,589 | 30.5% |
| Black | 2,083 | 67.1% | 555 | 26.6% |
| 1976 | 21,677 | 80.5% | 7,181 | 33.1% |
| White | 19,045 | 82.4% | 6,276 | 33.0% |
| Black | 2,239 | 67.5% | 749 | 33.5% |
| 1980 | 23,413 | 80.9% | 7,400 | 31.6% |
| White | 20,214 | 82.6% | 6,423 | 31.8% |
| Black | 2,592 | 69.7% | 715 | 27.6% |
| 1984 | 22,870 | 81.6% | 7,591 | 33.2% |
| White | 19,373 | 83.0% | 6,256 | 33.7% |
| Black | 2,885 | 74.7% | 786 | 27.2% |
| Change 1974–84 Total | 2,145 | 0.9% | 1,275 | 2.7% |
| Change 1974–84 White | 1,055 | 0.3% | 667 | 3.2% |
| Change 1974–84 Black | 802 | 7.6% | 231 | 0.6% |

*Note:* Enrollment numbers are indicated in thousands. The White/Black numbers do not equal the totals because other ethnicities are excluded.
*Source:* Carter and Wilson 1995.

public colleges in the South. This was the major group of colleges identified in the *Adams* litigation, so some tangible success for the *Adams* cases can be inferred from these data.

Despite occasional victories in federal courts, there is a general consensus that Title VI compliance was severely curtailed during the Reagan years (Dentler 1991; Trent 1991; Williams 1991). The Office of Civil Rights at the USDE and the Department of Justice's Civil Rights Division virtually shut down their desegregation activities. (See also Altbach, Lomotey, and Rivers, this volume.) Dentler (1991) describes desegregation during this period:

> With the advent of the Reagan administration . . . a quarter of a century of slow, often disenchanting, and uneven movement toward compliance with *Brown* drew to a close. . . . There were, in other words, just a few brief years—a decade at most (1966 to 1976)—during which the far-reaching policy of *Brown* had a direct impact on the learning opportunities of African American students. (34–35)

## 1985–99: Mixed Messages Concerning Progress in the Desegregation of U.S. Higher Education

A new trend developed in African American higher education enrollment figures after 1985. As indicated in Table 4.3, total higher education enrollment increased by more than 16 percent from 1986 to 1997, while African American enrollment increased by more than 43 percent during that same period of time. While not as dramatic as the increases in African American enrollment during the 1964–73 period, these recent increases have reversed the 1974–84 decline. Moreover, these increases since 1985 have been especially pronounced in four-year institutions where the percentage of African Americans increased 46 percent, compared to an overall 13.7 percent increase in total enrollment at those institutions during this period.

An especially encouraging trend since 1985 has been the increase in the percentage of the total higher education enrollment that is African American—from 8.7 percent in 1986 to 10.7 percent in 1997. This change reverses the decline of the previous decade (from 9.4 percent in 1976 to 8.8 percent in 1984). Thus, the trend in the percentage of the total higher education enrollment that is African American has been curvilinear over the past two decades, with a peak in 1976–78 at 9.4 percent, a valley in 1986–88 at 8.7 percent, and a peak again in 1997 at 10.7 percent.

The 1997 data are especially encouraging because they represent the highest enrollment and percentage of total enrollment figures that African Americans have ever had for higher education institutions in general and for four-year institutions. These recent gains in African American percentages of total higher education enrollment are across the board, not limited to certain

**Table 4.3**
**Enrollment in Higher Education by Type of Institution**
**and Ethnicity (White, Black) for Selected Years, 1986–97**

| Year/ Ethnicity | Total Enrollment | Four-Year Institution | Two-Year Institution | % Two-Year Institution |
|---|---|---|---|---|
| 1986 Total | 12,504 | 7,824 | 4,680 | 37.4% |
| White | 9,921 | 6,337 | 3,584 | 36.1% |
| Black | 1,082 | 615 | 467 | 43.2% |
| % Black | 8.7% | 7.9% | 10.0% | NA |
| 1990 Total | 13,820 | 8,579 | 5,240 | 37.9% |
| White | 10,723 | 6,769 | 3,954 | 36.9% |
| Black | 1,247 | 723 | 524 | 42.0% |
| % Black | 9.0% | 8.4% | 10.0% | NA |
| 1997 Total | 14,502 | 8,897 | 5,606 | 38.7% |
| White | 10,266 | 6,496 | 3,770 | 36.7% |
| Black | 1,551 | 896 | 655 | 42.2% |
| % Black | 10.5% | 9.9% | 11.4% | NA |
| % Change 1986–97 Total | 16.0% | 13.7% | 19.8% | 1.3% |
| % Change 1986–97 White | 3.5% | 2.5% | 5.2% | 0.6% |
| % Change 1986–97 Black | 43.3% | 45.7% | 40.3% | −1.0% |

*Note:* Enrollment numbers are indicated in thousands. The White/Black numbers do not equal the totals because other ethnicities are excluded. (See Table 4.4)
NA = Not Applicable.
*Sources:* U.S. Department of Education 1994; Wilds and Wilson 1998; Wilds 2000.

types of institutions. These recent data also indicate that Garibaldi's (1991a) conclusion that African Americans were not "capitalizing on the increasing size of the age cohort and the higher numbers graduating from high school" may no longer be relevant (94).

Data from Table 4.4 appear to confirm this cautiously optimistic assessment. The percentage of African American high school graduates enrolled in college increased from a low of 26.1 percent in 1985 to just below 40 percent in 1997. Interestingly, the changes in the overall trends for Whites and African Americans in both high school completion rates and rates of high school graduates enrolled in college are very similar for the 1985–97 period. These

**Table 4.4**

**High School Completion Rates and College Progression Rates
by Ethnicity (White, Black) for Selected Years, 1985–97**

| Year/ Ethnicity | High School Graduates | Completion Rate (%) | # Enrolled in College | Progression Rate (%) |
|---|---|---|---|---|
| 1985 Total | 22,349 | 82.4% | 7,537 | 33.7% |
| White | 18,916 | 83.6% | 6,500 | 34.4% |
| Black | 2,810 | 75.6% | 734 | 26.1% |
| 1990 Total | 20,311 | 82.3% | 7,964 | 39.1% |
| White | 16,823 | 82.5% | 6,635 | 39.4% |
| Black | 2,710 | 77.0% | 894 | 33.0% |
| 1997 Total | 20,338 | 81.4% | 9,204 | 45.2% |
| White | 16,557 | 82.7% | 7,495 | 45.3% |
| Black | 2,726 | 74.7% | 1,085 | 39.8% |
| Change 1985–97 Total | −2,011 | −1.0% | 1,667 | 11.5% |
| Change 1985–97 White | −2,359 | −0.9% | 995 | 10.9% |
| Change 1985–97 Black | −84 | −0.9% | 351 | 13.7% |

*Note:* Enrollment numbers are indicated in thousands. The White/Black numbers do not equal the totals because other ethnicities are excluded.
*Source:* Wilds 2000.

1985–97 data indicate that if students can get through high school, it is more likely that they will proceed on to college. That was not the case for African American students in 1974–84 when a 7.6 percent increase in high school completion rate translated into a negligible increase (0.6 percent) in the high school graduates enrolled-in-college rate.

Other noticeable trends since 1985 include the following:

- The percentage of African Americans (74.7 percent in 1997) who graduate from high school is still less than that of White Americans (82.7 percent) and the gap did not decrease over the 1985–97 period. (See Table 4.4.)
- The percentage of African American high school graduates that enroll in colleges or universities is still less than that for White Americans and the gap did not decrease over the 1985–97 period. Thus, the guideline established in the 1977 *Adams v. Califano* case—that the propor-

tion of African American and White high school graduates entering institutions of higher education will be equal—has yet to be realized.

- While segregation indices are not available for recent years, it is likely that the current level of segregation is equal to or lower than that measured in 1984. While the federal government has continued to downplay higher education desegregation, affirmative action programs based at least partially on a "moral imperative" persist at many predominantly White institutions.
- The remaining Title VI compliance cases are being settled without the closure or merger of institutions.
- "Reverse discrimination" cases have been relatively rare since the *Bakke* decision. Nevertheless, resentment of affirmative action programs persists at higher education institutions and at the national political level. Since the Republican victories in the 1994 congressional elections, the affirmative action debate has grown more confrontational, with some legislators calling for a reappraisal of all affirmative action programs. While the Clinton administration has had a more positive stance toward affirmative action in higher education than the Nixon and Reagan presidencies, the overall role of the federal government in desegregating higher education has become increasingly disjointed. (See also Altbach, Lomotey, and Rivers, this volume.)

## A Closer Examination of Trends in HBCU Enrollment

As noted in Table 4.5, the number of African Americans attending HBCUs increased 26.8 percent during the 1986–97 period. This percentage of increase is somewhat lower than the overall increase of 43.3 percent in the number of African American students enrolled in all higher education institutions during this period of time. (See Table 4.3.)

Despite this disparity in growth rates, several authors have concluded that HBCUs have continued to enroll their share of African American students throughout the entire thirty-five-year period from the passage of the 1964 Civil Rights Act. In fact, some analysts have concluded that HBCUs graduate a disproportionate share of African American students due to a more positive campus culture or ethos (Davis 1991; Garibaldi 1991a; Myers 1989). (See also Anderson, this volume.)

Garibaldi (1991b) has also contended that HBCUs enroll and graduate a larger proportion of African American students who might not be eligible to enroll at other schools due to low ACT/SAT scores or other factors (Garibaldi 1991b). For many of these students with low college entrance test scores, the choice for higher education often comes down to two-year institutions or HBCUs, if there are any within the student's geographical area. These

**Table 4.5**
**Enrollment at HBCUs by Ethnicity for Selected Years,**
**Fall 1986 to Fall 1997**

| Year | Enrollment | Black | White | Other | % Black |
|------|-----------|-------|-------|-------|---------|
| 1986 | 213,114 | 176,610 | 22,784 | 13,720 | 82.9% |
| 1987 | 217,670 | 182,020 | 23,227 | 12,423 | 83.6% |
| 1988 | 230,758 | 192,848 | 25,767 | 12,143 | 83.6% |
| 1989 | 238,946 | 199,974 | 26,962 | 12,010 | 83.7% |
| 1990 | 248,697 | 207,547 | 29,601 | 11,549 | 83.5% |
| 1991 | 258,509 | 213,904 | 31,085 | 13,520 | 82.7% |
| 1992 | 277,261 | 224,946 | 36,203 | 16,112 | 81.1% |
| 1993 | 284,247 | 230,078 | 37,375 | 16,794 | 80.9% |
| 1994 | 280,915 | 229,046 | 36,045 | 15,824 | 81.5% |
| 1995 | 284,951 | 230,279 | 38,936 | 15,736 | 80.8% |
| 1996 | 277,974 | 225,886 | 37,013 | 15,075 | 81.3% |
| 1997 | 273,752 | 223,895 | 35,224 | 14,633 | 81.8% |
| % Change 1986–97 | 28.5% | 26.8% | 54.6% | 6.7% | −1.1% |

*Note:* The numbers in "Other" were determined by subtracting the number of Black and White students from the total number of students.
*Source:* Wilds 2000.

two-year institutions are often dead ends for students wishing to complete a bachelor's degree. Using this logic, it may be concluded that HBCUs graduate a disproportionate number of African American undergraduate students who have academic or economic disadvantages and little access to other institutions of higher education. Beyond these definitional considerations, however, there have been some changes in graduation rates at other institutions that have affected the role of HBCUs.

According to American Council on Education (ACE) data for 1983–84 through 1996–97 (Wilds and Wilson 1998; Wilds 2000), the percentage of bachelor's degrees awarded to African Americans by HBCUs remained consistently between 27 percent and 29 percent of the total awarded by all institutions. Thus, HBCUs have kept pace with the general increases in African American undergraduate enrollment and graduation rates over this time period. At the graduate level, however, the number of master's degrees awarded by HBCUs remained about the same from 1984–85 through 1991–92 (at around 2,500 per year). However, the number began to increase substantially from 1992–93 through 1996–97 (to more than 4,200). During the same time period, the total number of master's degrees awarded to African Americans from all institutions increased from around 14,000 in 1985 to more than 28,000 in 1997. Accordingly, the percentage of master's degrees awarded to

African Americans by HBCUs declined from 18 percent to 15 percent of the total awarded by all institutions during that time period. A decline was also reported in the percentage of first-professional degrees awarded to African Americans by HBCUs during this same time period (Wilds and Wilson 1998; Wilds 2000).

The role of HBCUs in producing African American students with advanced degrees appears to be diminishing as the absolute number of such students in all institutions continues to rise modestly, while the number produced by HBCUs stays about the same. Unless states begin to place more graduate and professional programs at HBCUs or increase those institutions' capacity to produce graduates within existing programs, the role of HBCUs in this academic arena will continue to slowly decline.

## Overall Trends in African American Enrollment, 1964–99

The overall trends in African American enrollment in higher education since 1964 can be broken down into three periods:

1. The 1964–73 period, marked by a 200+ percent increase in the number of African American students enrolled in higher education as Title VI regulations were first enforced.

2. The 1974–84 period, in which African American participation in higher education stagnated in terms of absolute numbers and declined in terms of percentage of total enrollment, due to such factors as increasing costs, declining student aid, the failure to vigorously enforce Title VI regulations, and concern over reverse discrimination.

3. The 1985–97 period, characterized by a 48 percent increase in African American enrollment in higher education that was fueled by an increase in the percentage of African American high school graduates enrolling in college. (See Table 4.6.)

There has been a curvilinear trend in the percentage of the total higher education enrollment that is African American over the past two decades, with high percentages being registered in 1976 and 1997 and a low percentage occurring in 1986. Data simply comparing the 1974 higher education enrollment with 1997 enrollment tends to obscure this curvilinear trend. (See Table 4.6.)

Looking at just these two data points (1974, 1997), one might conclude that African Americans have experienced concurrent, moderate increases in both high school completion rate (7.6 percent) and in percentage of high school graduates enrolled in college (13.2 percent) over the past two decades. One might conclude that, as the high school graduation rate increased, so linearly also did the percentage of high school graduates enrolled in college.

**Table 4.6**
**High School Completion Rates and College Progression Rates**
**by Ethnicity (White, Black), for 1974 and 1997 Only**

| Year/ Ethnicity | High School Graduates | Completion Rate (%) | # Enrolled in College | Progression Rate (%) |
|---|---|---|---|---|
| 1974 Total | 20,725 | 80.7% | 6,316 | 30.5% |
| White | 18,318 | 82.7% | 5,589 | 30.5% |
| Black | 2,083 | 67.1% | 555 | 26.6% |
| 1997 Total | 20,338 | 81.4% | 9,204 | 45.2% |
| White | 16,557 | 82.7% | 7,495 | 45.3% |
| Black | 2,726 | 74.7% | 1,085 | 39.8% |
| Change 1974–97 Total | −387 | 0.7% | 2,888 | 14.7% |
| Change 1974–97 White | −1,761 | −0.0% | 1,906 | 14.8% |
| Change 1974–97 Black | 643 | 7.6% | 530 | 13.2% |

*Note:* Enrollment numbers are indicated in thousands. The White/Black numbers do not equal the totals because other ethnicities are excluded.
*Sources:* U.S. Department of Education 1994; Wilds and Wilson 1998; Wilds 2000.

This interpretation would fail to capture two conflicting trends noted above: (1) an increase in African American high school completion rates that was not accompanied by an increase in the percentage of high school graduates enrolled in college (1974–84), and (2) a decline in the African American high school completion rate that was interestingly accompanied by an increase in the percentage of high school graduates enrolled in college (1985–97).

We discussed above various reasons for the 1974–84 trends, but thus far few analysts have attempted to explain the most recent trends in African American high school completion rates and college participation rates. It appears that more African American high school students are now "valuing the importance" of a college degree, as contrasted to the trend in the mid-1980s. This reversal may be partly due to the fact that the first wave of African Americans who gained access to higher education under Title VI now have children who are of college age, and research indicates that the educational level of parents is a good predictor of their children's scholastic attainment. It could be that these college-educated African American parents are better able to convince their children of the importance of a college education due to its importance in their own lives. Certainly, college-educated African Americans have greater personal awareness of college/university systems and requirements than most of their parents. They can now pass this information on to their children, making them more knowledgeable consumers of higher education services and demystifying the experience for them.

Due to demographic trends, some colleges may be more actively recruiting African Americans (and other minorities) as the pool of White high school graduates declines. Competitive market forces have led to a "corporate revolution" in the management of U.S. colleges and universities, as the 3,300 institutions of higher education attempt to find their "market niche" (Best 1989; Trow 1989). Thus, many institutions of higher education have altered their entrance requirements and are casting recruiting nets more widely to attract students that were previously underserved. These market trends toward greater recruitment of African American students may explain part of the upturn in their total enrollment over the past ten years. It could be that market forces, rather than a moral imperative, will be the primary force driving continuing increases in African American enrollment in higher education as we approach the twenty-first century.

## Continuing Challenges for Desegregation

Despite the encouraging enrollment trends noted since 1985, the desegregation of higher education has obviously not occurred as thoroughly or as quickly as originally hoped. Guidelines for the desegregation of higher education specified by *Adams v. Califano* required that the proportion of African American and White high school graduates entering institutions of higher education be equal, but data in Table 4.4 indicate that the gap between White and African American enrollment in higher education has remained the same for the past decade (45.3 percent versus 39.8 percent in 1997). Similarly the gap in high school completion rate (82.7 percent versus 74.7 percent in 1997) has remained constant over the past decade, and this differential helps to fuel the disparity in enrollment numbers in higher education.

The *Adams v. Califano* guidelines for the desegregation of higher education included goals for the desegregation of faculties, and progress has also been limited in that area. For example, recent data from Louisiana indicate that state colleges are having difficulty meeting their commitment to increase racial diversity among their faculties (Shuler 1999). The current faculty at Louisiana State University (Baton Rouge) is only 3 percent African American, while the faculty at crosstown HBCU Southern University is only 18 percent White. University officials report that a major reason for the lack of

African American professors at predominantly White universities is the perennial shortage of African Americans with doctoral degrees. (See also Solmon, Solomon, and Schiff; Anderson, this volume.)

Similarly, while some progress has been made in desegregating higher education in states with dual educational systems, much work still remains. A recent research study by the Southern Education Foundation concluded that colleges were still largely segregated in twelve of the nineteen states that had segregated higher education systems (Applebome 1995; Healy 1995; Southern Education Foundation 1995). In these twelve states, HBCUs and two-year community colleges remained the destination for most African Americans while the flagship and research institutions were overwhelmingly populated by White students. Other results include the following:

- Only 9 percent of African American freshmen enrolled in their state's largest and most prestigious institutions in this study. For eight of the twelve states in the study, less than 10 percent of African American freshmen enrolled in these institutions.
- Almost 30 percent of African American freshmen enrolled in HBCUs, while 42 percent enrolled in two-year institutions in this study. For four of the twelve states in the study, more than 40 percent of the African American freshmen enrolled in HBCUs. For another four states, more than 45 percent of the African American freshmen enrolled in two-year institutions. (See also Anderson; Altbach, Lomotey, and Rivers, this volume.)
- The study concluded that higher education financial aid is now more oriented toward middle- and upper-middle-income students than toward low-income students. More federal money in the mid-1990s is being spent on loans than grants, while the opposite was true in the 1970s.

Other trends in the desegregation of U.S. higher education are becoming apparent as the twenty-first century approaches. It is apparent that the *Plessy* decision greatly impacted higher educational opportunities in the twentieth century. The most obvious impact was fifty-four years of state-sanctioned segregation that deprived African Americans of the opportunity to attend public universities. Even though the *Brown* decision reversed the separate-but-equal doctrine, it took many years of federal government intervention to force compliance. As this chapter has detailed, great strides have been made in the effort to provide equality of opportunity, but what Morris (1979) calls the "*Plessy* effect"—"the politically motivated ease of asserting the presence of equality in the absence of meaningful standards of equality"—disturbingly shadows this effort (32). Henry expands this idea by arguing that *Plessy* is still with us in the form of Justice Harlan's dissent in which he alluded to a "color-blind" society (Henry 1998).

As we examine the status of higher education desegregation today, we see a resurgence of the discussion of reverse discrimination and a call for the end of affirmative action, all in the name of a "color-blind" society. In recent years, decisions in two cases have outlawed specific affirmative action programs. In *Podberesky v. Maryland* (838 F.Supp. 1075 [D.Md. 1993], vacated 38 F.3d 147 [4th Cir. 1994], cert. denied, 115 S.Ct. 2001 [1995]), the Supreme Court upheld a lower court decision to end a "set-aside" scholarship program at the University of Maryland that was created to attract African American students in an attempt to reverse past discriminatory practices at the university. Ironically, this program was approved in 1979 by the Office of Civil Rights as part of the university's compliance under Title VI enforcement.

The following year *Hopwood v. Texas* (84 F3d 720 [5th Cir. 1996]), in which a group of White plaintiffs was denied admission to the University of Texas under the law school's affirmative action plan, ruled that all race-conscious admissions are unconstitutional. Henry's pessimistic prediction contends that *Hopwood*'s impact could end affirmative action programs, resulting in a 75 percent drop in African American enrollment at America's most prestigious universities (1998, 69).

These cases have set in motion a national debate on affirmative action, with the conservatives in Congress and the Supreme Court sensing the opportunity for extending the influence of the "*Plessy* effect." If this ploy is successful, the gains in African American enrollment in higher education over the past thirty years could be reversed, potentially increasing in the gap between African American and White higher educational attainment dramatically.

## The Development of Alternative Strategies

Ironically, the cumulative successes of the NAACP desegregation strategies, the *Brown* decision, and the 1964 Civil Rights Act in the 1954–74 period have contributed to the crisis that we now face in the desegregation of higher education. The rapid gains in African American access to and enrollment in formerly all-White institutions of higher education during this period led many to place their faith in the power of the legal system for continuing to dismantle desegregation. Events of the past decade indicate that different, nonlegal strategies will be needed in the future to advance desegregation of higher education. The limits of the courts in this arena have now been well established (Fossey 1998; Teddlie 1998).

A careful reading of this chapter suggests several strategies that may be used in conjunction with each other to further the desegregation of U.S. higher education:

- First, groups interested in the problem need to clarify their priorities on basic goals in accomplishing greater desegregation of higher education.

Just as the NAACP had to reorganize and prioritize during the Great Depression, groups seeking greater desegregation of higher education in the twenty-first century must also reorganize and prioritize. These groups must realize that some of their goals may be in conflict, as those of the NAACP and HBCU supporters have sometimes been in the past.

- Some viable goals for the next century include: increasing the completion rates of African Americans from high school, thereby increasing the pool of potential students for higher education; increasing the higher education enrollment rates for African Americans graduating from high school; increasing the number of African Americans pursuing advanced degrees (especially doctoral degrees); increasing the number of graduate programs at HBCUs; enhancing the recruitment schemes for attracting African Americans into doctoral programs at research institutions, etc.
- One strategy for increasing high school completion rates involves greater cooperation between colleges and high schools. Outreach programs from HBCUs may be particularly successful with higher risk students who have demonstrated the potential to graduate from high school.
- A strategy for increasing the enrollment of African Americans who have graduated from high school also involves cooperative arrangements between colleges/universities and high schools. For the students whom Garibaldi (1991b) described (African American students whose ACT/SAT scores and other factors makes them ineligible for admission at some schools), an outreach program from a nearby HBCU during their senior year might be particularly helpful.
- A strategy for increasing the proportion of African Americans who attend research institutions or predominantly White institutions in previously segregated states might involve some form of a "moral imperative" with administrators and faculty members. There are institutions that want to follow affirmative action guidelines, particularly if they can get some assurance that they will not be victims of "reverse discrimination" suits. With more than 3,300 institutions of higher education, some will opt to develop specific market plans to attract African American students. Developing profiles of institutions that may provide the best education for African American students (within specific curricula) would be a valuable undertaking, especially for proponents of the market system.
- Strategies for training more African Americans in doctoral programs have been tried with limited success. This goal is a linchpin for several others, since having a higher percentage of African American faculty members with doctoral degrees at any institution leads to more African American faculty members, graduate students, and undergraduate students. If there were an easy answer to the perennial question of how

to produce more African Americans with doctoral degrees, someone would have already marketed it. The hard answer is that increasing doctorates awarded to African Americans will require a significant financial commitment, especially in increasing stipends for African American graduate students and increasing salaries for new-hire African American doctorates.

Separate strategies for the desegregation of distinct types of institutions (e.g., HBCUs, flagship or research institutions, formerly all-White comprehensive institutions, etc.) may be necessary. Perhaps the most important lesson learned from the success of the NAACP in desegregating public education is the importance of developing an overall strategy and then sticking to it. If separate institutional strategies are now required for further desegregation of U. S. higher education, will a "coordinating group" emerge that develops an overall plan that cuts across separate strategies? If so, which group(s) will it be? How will they develop and implement this coordinated strategy? Answers to these questions will likely determine the success of further desegregation of higher education in the United States in the twenty-first century.

## References

Anderson, James D. 1989. Training the apostles of liberal culture: Black higher education, 1900–1935. In Goodchild and Wechsler, 455–77.

Applebome, Peter. 1995. Segregation in higher education persists, study of 12 states says. *New York Times,* May 18, 1A.

Becker, Henry J. 1978. *The measurement of segregation: The Dissimilarity Index and Coleman's Segregation Index compared.* Baltimore, MD: Johns Hopkins University Center for Social Organization of Schools.

Best, John H. 1989. The revolution of markets and management: Toward a history of American higher education since 1945. In Goodchild and Wechsler, 455–77.

Blaustein, Albert, and Clarence C. Ferguson Jr. 1962. *Desegregation and the law: The meaning and effect of the school segregation cases.* New York: Vintage Books.

Blaustein, Albert, and Robert Zangrando. 1968. *Civil rights and the American Negro.* New York: Trident Press.

Bowles, Frank, and Frank DeCosta. 1989. 1954 to the present. In Goodchild and Wechsler, 545–58.

Carter, Deborah J., and Reginald Wilson. 1995. *Thirteenth annual status report on minorities in higher education.* Washington, DC: American Council on Education.

Davis, Robert B. 1991. Social support networks and undergraduate student academic-success-related outcomes: A comparison of Black students on Black and White campuses. In *College in Black and White: African American students in predominantly White and in historically Black public universities,* edited by Walter Allen, Edgar Epps, and Nesha Haniff, 143–60. Albany: State University of New York Press.

Dentler, Robert. 1991. School desegregation since Gunnar Myrdal's American dilemma. In Willie, Garibaldi, and Reed, 27–50.

DuBois, William E. B. 1989. The talented tenth. In Goodchild and Wechsler, 842-61.

Fossey, Richard, ed. 1998. *Race, the courts, and equal education: The limits of the law.* New York: AMS Press.

Garibaldi, Antoine. 1991a. Blacks in college. In Willie, Garibaldi, and Reed, 93–99.

———. 1991b. The role of historically Black colleges in facilitating resilience among African American students. *Education and Urban Society* 24, no. 1:103–12.

Goodchild, Lester, and Harry Wechsler, eds. 1989. *ASHE reader on the history of higher education.* Needham Heights, MA: Ginn Press.

Healy, Patrick. 1995. States urged to make new efforts to end persistent segregation. *Chronicle of Higher Education* (May 26): 29A.

Henry, A'lelia Robinson. 1998. Perpetuating inequality: *Plessy v. Ferguson* and the dilemma of Black access to public and higher education. *Journal of Law and Education* 27, no. 1 (January): 47–71.

Hill, Herbert, and Jack Greenberg. 1955. *Citizen's guide to desegregation: A study of social and legal change in American life.* Boston: Beacon Press.

Morris, Lorenzo. 1979. *Elusive equality: The status of Black Americans in higher education.* Washington, DC: Howard University Press.

Myers, Samuel L., Jr. 1989. *Desegregation in higher education.* New York: National Association for Equal Opportunities in Higher Education.

Preer, Jean. 1982. *Lawyers v. educators: Black colleges and desegregation in public higher education.* Westport, CT: Greenwood Press.

Sansing, David. 1989. James Meredith. In *Encyclopedia of Southern Culture,* edited by Reagan Wilson and William Ferris, 220. Chapel Hill: University of North Carolina Press.

Shuler, Marsha. 1999. State colleges not meeting desegregation requirement. *Baton Rouge Advocate,* June 12, 1B.

Southern Education Foundation. 1995. *Redeeming the American promise.* Atlanta, GA: Southern Education Foundation.

Synnott, Marcia Graham. 1989. Desegregation. In *Encyclopedia of Southern Culture,* edited by Reagan Wilson and William Ferris, 248–49. Chapel Hill: University of North Carolina Press.

Teddlie, Charles. 1998. Four literatures associated with the study of equal education and desegregation in the United States. In Fossey, 237–58.

Teddlie, Charles, and John Freeman. 1996. "With all deliberate speed": The impact of the *Brown* decision on institutions of higher education. In *Readings on equal education, Vol. 13. Forty years after the* Brown *decision: Implications of school desegregation for U.S. education,* edited by Kofi Lomotey and Charles Teddlie, 7–51. New York: AMS Press.

Trent, William. 1991. Student affirmative action in higher education: Addressing underrepresentation. In *The racial crisis in American higher education,* edited by Philip G. Altbach and Kofi Lomotey, 107–34. Albany: State University of New York Press.

Trow, Martin. 1989. American higher education: Past, present, future. In Goodchild and Wechsler, 616–26.

U.S. Department of Education, National Center for Education Statistics. 1976. *The condition of education 1976: A statistical report.* Washington, DC: U.S. Government Printing Office.

———. 1984. *The condition of education 1984: A statistical report.* Washington, DC: U.S. Government Printing Office.

———.1987. *Higher education general information surveys, 1964–1986.* Washington, DC: U.S. Government Printing Office.

———. 1994. *Trends in enrollment in higher education, by racial/ethnic category: Fall 1982 through fall 1992.* Washington, DC: U.S. Government Printing Office.

Wilds, Deborah. 2000. *Seventeenth annual status report on minorities in higher education.* Washington, DC: American Council on Education.

Wilds, Deborah, and Reginald Wilson. 1998. *Sixteenth annual status report on minorities in higher education.* Washington, DC: American Council on Education.

Williams, John. 1991. Systemwide Title VI regulation of higher education, 1968–88: Implications for increased minority participation. In Willie, Garibaldi, and Reed, 110–22.

Willie, Charles. 1991. Summary and Recommendations. In Willie, Garibaldi, and Reed, 177–96.

Willie, Charles, Antoine Garibaldi, and Wornie Reed, eds. 1991. *The education of African Americans.* Westport, CT: Auburn House.

# Student and Campus Climate Issues

CHAPTER 5

# Racial Ideology in the Campus Community

*Emerging Cross-Ethnic Differences and Challenges*

PHILLIP J. BOWMAN AND WILLIAM A. SMITH

A more complex racial climate is emerging within historically White colleges and universities in the United States as we move into the twenty-first century. During the last half of the twentieth century, the racial climate on these campuses gradually shifted in racial ideologies, from the early days of legal segregation, through a transitional period of increasing African American student representation, to the current status of multiethnic diversification with increasing numbers of Latina/o and Asian American students (Altbach and Lomotey 1991; Allen, Epps, and Haniff 1991; Nichols and Mills 1970; Sedlacek 1987; Sue and Sue 1999). This new racial climate is tempered by three contemporary trends: (1) the growing opposition to civil rights-era policies to provide access and support services for African American college students who still remain underrepresented; (2) the increasing demands for more multiethnic institutional changes from both Latina/o and Asian American students who make up an expanding portion of the college student population; and (3) the changing racial ideologies that college students from distinct ethnic backgrounds bring to increasingly diverse campus communities (Carter and Wilson 1995; El-Khawas 1996; Tatum 1997; see also Hurtado; Chang and Kiang, this volume). Despite some clear democratic and multicultural virtues, the racial and ethnic diversification of historically White colleges has begun to produce multiple fault lines of potential cross-ethnic tensions among students that will continue to temper campus climates well into the twenty-first century. A major challenge for contemporary educational leaders and policy makers is to systematically understand both the historical context and also the contemporary forces behind such tensions. Such understanding will facilitate the development of more strategies that will effectively promote a positive racial climate and a stronger sense of campus community. (See Solmon, Solmon, and Schiff, this volume.)

Contemporary multiracial and multiethnic institutions of higher education are indeed microcosms of the broader American society. That society is
still undergoing profound sociopolitical and demographic restructuring from
predominantly White to unprecedented levels of racial and ethnic diversity.
The system of legal segregation in America, which was institutionalized in
the 1896 *Plessy v. Ferguson* case, ensured that most colleges and universities
remained essentially all-White until the 1960s (e.g., Anderson 1988; Altbach
and Lomotey 1991; Peterson et al., 1978). During the latter half of the 1960s,
unprecedented numbers of African American students gained admittance to
historically White campuses, under the impetus of both nonviolent protests in
the South and also more violent urban unrest in the North. (See Anderson;
Teddlie and Freeman, this volume.)

The representation of African American college students peaked in the
late 1970s but began to decline throughout the 1980s as a reactionary backlash surged during the Reagan years (Allen, Epps, and Haniff 1991; Deskins
1991; Feagin, Vera, and Imani 1996; Magner 1989). The 1990s brought unprecedented opposition to race-targeted, affirmative action policies, not only
in higher education but also in other policy arenas such as employment and
voting rights (Carter and Wilson 1995; Curry 1996; Fish 1993; Hacker 1992).
In higher education, both public and legal opposition to race-targeted policies
in college admissions, financial aid, academic support programs, and other
areas of campus life continues to escalate (Smith 1996, 1998). For example,
conservative organizations such as the Center for Individual Rights continue
to build on negative public sentiments, the *Hopwood* case in Texas, and
Proposition 209 in California to mobilize a growing opposition movement in
Michigan, Florida, Georgia, and beyond. (See also Tierney and Chung, this
volume.)

The opposition to policies targeted for African American students has
grown as the proportion of White students has declined and the proportion of
both Latina/o and Asian American students has continued to rise. Donald
Deskins (1991) found that, between 1976 and 1984, Black student enrollment
declined 5.2 percent while that of Latina/o students increased 23.4 percent
and that of Asian students jumped a striking 83.9 percent. The dramatic
increases in both Latina/o and Asian American college students, to some
degree, reflect immigration and related demographic changes in the broader
population (Carter and Wilson 1995; Darden, Torres, and Gutiérrez 1997;
Muñoz 1986; Olivas 1986; Shiraishi 2000; Sue and Sue 1999). For example,
the Asian American population, consisting of over twenty-five subethnic groups,
grew 800 percent during the three decades from 1960 to 1990. Moreover, the
number of Latina/os (consisting of Mexican, Puerto Rican, Cuban, and a
range of Central/South American ethnic groups) is increasing rapidly and is
projected to exceed the number of African Americans by the year 2005 (Sue
and Sue 1999). However, despite their growing numbers, Latina/os, along

with African Americans and American Indians (or First Nation Peoples), remain clearly underrepresented on college campuses.

Spurred by ongoing sociopolitical and demographic changes, most historically white colleges campuses are now composed of a more complex mixture of White, African American, Latina/o, and Asian American students than ever before. (See Solmon, Solmon, and Schiff, this volume.) The multiethnic diversification of historically White colleges has made race and ethnicity fundamental factors in ongoing efforts to monitor, understand, and promote the virtues of diversity in higher education. In this context, Latina/o and Asian students, like Black students in the 1960s and 1970s, have become political activists, organizing to demand institutional responses to their increasing representation and ethnic presence in the campus community.

## Ethnicity and Racial Ideology: A Challenge to Campus Community

On the college campuses of today, we must better understand the complex racial ideologies that students from diverse ethnic groups bring with them and how the cross-ethnic conflicts associated with such ideologies can erode campus climate and a sense of community. A growing literature on the changing racial ideology in mainstream America strongly supports two major trends: (1) increasing numbers of Americans of all races, especially young Whites, now publicly reject traditional prejudices that Blacks are genetically or inherently inferior to Whites, but (2) many Whites and significant numbers from other racial groups endorse more subtle race-related beliefs that reinforce discriminatory institutional practices and individual behaviors, especially as applied against low-income African Americans (Bobo 1996; Kinder and Sanders 1996; Sears, Sidanius, and Bobo 2000; Schuman, Steeh, Bobo, and Krysan 1997; see also Scheurich and Young, this volume).

This literature further suggests that cross-ethnic differences among college students about such concepts as modern racism, individual-system attributions, cultural pathology stereotypes, and conservative policy values may increasingly operate to undermine the racial climate and sense of community on campus.

### Contemporary Racism

The largest body of recent research on racial ideology in the contemporary American racial system has focused on a set of race-related beliefs referred to as "modern," "symbolic," "aversive," "laissez-faire," or "color-blind" racism (Bobo, Kluegel, and Smith 1997; Bonilla-Silva and Forman 2000; Dovidio, Mann, and Gaertner 1989; Kinder and Sears 1981; McConahay 1986; Sears 1988; Sears and Jessor 1996). In contrast to traditional prejudice, this literature strongly suggests that contemporary anti-Black ideology is much subtler. (See Villalpando and Bernal, this volume.)

Contemporary racism is characterized by a rather complex combination of resentment at Black demands that are perceived as unfair, feelings that Whites are unfairly losing ground to Blacks, denial that racial discrimination remains a thorny problem for Blacks, and a conservative assumption that Blacks generally do not share American values of hard work, self-reliance, and individualism. This complex belief system is considered to be a product of socialization into the contemporary American racial system and has been shown to reinforce opposition to race-targeted policies designed to reduce the persistent inequalities that African Americans face (Bobo 2000; Krysan 2000; Jones 1997; Sears, van Larr, Carrillo, and Kosterman 1997). Do contemporary college students bring such race-related beliefs to the college campus? Are there systemic differences in such beliefs among students from various race and ethnic backgrounds which may have consequences for the racial climate and sense of community on campus?

Unfortunately, nearly all past research on various aspects of modern racism or other race-related beliefs has focused on either Whites or White-Black comparisons with very little attention to other race and ethnic groups (e.g., Bobo 2000; Hughes and Tuch 2000; Hochschild 2000; Hunt 1996; Smith 1996). A major challenge for those seeking to better understand cross-ethnic differences in contemporary race-related beliefs among college students or any other segment of the population is to further deconstruct the complexity of the multiple dimensions of modern racism highlighted above. Among Whites, more focused measures of resentment of Black progress have emerged as especially powerful predictors of opposition to race-targeted policies (Kinder and Sanders 1996; Hughes 1997). However, future cross-ethnic research must better distinguish between reactionary beliefs that may be expressed as resentment or ambivalence toward Black demands for progress and a related set of concepts—individual-system attributions for persistent White-Black inequalities, cultural pathology stereotypes that Blacks in general do not share mainstream virtues, and conservative opposition to race-targeted policies to address the persistent inequalities endured by Black Americans.

*Race-Related Attributions*

Early research on causal attributions for racial inequality among Black college students and other populations often viewed individual vs. system blame in either/or terms within a bipolar framework (e.g., Gurin and Epps 1975; Kluegel and Smith 1986). That is, people tend to believe that *either* individual deficits *or* discriminatory obstacles and barriers in the larger social system should be blamed for persistent Black poverty and other social and economic inequalities. An early White-Black pattern emerged in which Whites most strongly blamed individual deficits and Blacks most strongly blamed social system barriers. More recent research shows that individual-deficit and system-barrier attributions are not always bipolar opposites or contradictory but can, and often do, coexist, especially among non-Whites (Bobo and Kluegel 1993; Kluegel and Smith 1983; Sears, Henry, and Kosterman 2000). That is, rather than always being high on one and low on the other, people can also be high on both or low on both.

In cross-ethnic terms, mainstream socialization may produce greater similarities in beliefs about individual responsibility while racial/ethnic socialization may produce greater diversity in system attributions. Like Blacks, Latina/os and Asians more often than Whites experience a "dual consciousness" with a higher correlation between individual-deficit and system-barrier attributions (e.g., Hughes and Tuch 2000; Hunt 1996). Hence, in a bicultural sense, non-Whites more often combine individual-blame beliefs (reflecting to some degree their internalization of mainstream cultural values) with high system-blame beliefs (based on their racial/ethnic socialization). This double consciousness may also reflect a greater recognition among non-Whites of the complexity and multiplicity of causes for perpetuating poverty and other racial inequalities among African Americans.

Other complex patterns have also begun to emerge in cross-ethnic comparisons, although Blacks remain highest in system blame and lowest in individual blame for inequalities they experience. For example, Michael Hughes and Steven Tuch (2000) found that Asians and Latina/os were even more likely than Whites to blame persistent Black inequalities on their individual deficiencies.

*Cultural Pathology Stereotypes*

A conservative assumption that Blacks generally do not share mainstream American values of hard work, self-reliance, and individualism continues to be a central theme in the literature on aspects of modern racism. Cultural pathology stereotypes that Blacks in general not only lack mainstream virtues but also hold self-defeating, ghetto-specific preferences may likewise play a significant role in the opposition to race-targeted policies. There is increasing evidence that a significant portion of the American population believes stereotypically that African Americans are not so much restricted by individual deficits per se, but rather by an inferior culture characterized by a tendency toward violence, a preference for welfare, and a self-perpetuating life-style of poverty (Bobo 2000; Sears, Hetts, Sidanius, and Bobo 2000; Smith 1998). Conservative leaders have popularized the notions that African Americans tend to self-segregate rather than take advantage of opportunities to move into better neighborhoods, to engage in violent crime rather than to respect the law, to be irresponsible in family roles, sexuality, and drug use, resulting in a breakdown of stable nuclear families, and to ignore expanding opportunities (D'Souza 1995; Sowell 1984, 1994; Roth 1990, 1994).

Such cultural pathology stereotypes may have combined with both a reactionary resentment of Black progress and also with individual-deficit attributions, thus diverting attention away from system barriers and resulting in a subtler form of modern prejudice that has replaced Jim Crow-era discrimination. Existing research has not adequately clarified the nature, context, and consequences of such cultural stereotypes, despite their potential importance, within ethnically diverse campus communities. Do such cultural pathology beliefs differ from other dimensions of contemporary racism (like racial resentment and individual-system attributions) among contemporary college students? How might such cultural pathology stereotypes differ among students from various ethnic backgrounds? What are the implications of cross-ethnic conflicts over such stereotypes for racial climate and a sense of community on campus?

## Conservative Values and Attitudes

An intense debate has emerged in the theoretical and empirical literature on the role of conservative political values and ideology in the growing opposition to race-targeted policies in higher education and other arenas (e.g., Sears, Hetts, Sidanias, and Bobo 2000). As highlighted above, proponents of a race-centered model have emphasized the pivotal role of modern racism, racial resentment, race-related attributions, and anti-Black stereotypes in the growing opposition to civil rights-era policies. In contrast, proponents of a politics-centered model undermine the role of race and emphasize the rational choices of the politically informed to reaffirm cherished American values and oppose unfair race-based entitlements (e.g., Sniderman and Carmines 1997; Sniderman and Hagen 1985).

This hypothesis argues that the democratic process and intensified political support for a conservative agenda reaffirming core American ideals of individualism, self-reliance, and fair play have increased the opposition to race-targeted policies. As with other race-related beliefs, differences among college students from diverse ethnic groups on conservative policy values, preferences, and attitudes may have important implications for campus discourse, climate, and community (Smith 1998). Do college students from various ethnic backgrounds differ on the classic conservative agendas such as strong opposition to traditional social welfare policies? Are there cross-ethnic differences among college students in their attitudes about the special admissions policies and other race-targeted programs that have become increasingly controversial in the multiethnic campus community? How do college students from different ethnic backgrounds vary in their level of support for opposition to African American studies, women's studies, and other multicultural-curriculum diversity initiatives?

## A Multiethnic Study

Guided by the foregoing literature, this multiethnic study addressed three major questions about race-related sentiments, attributions, stereotypes, values, and attitudes that students from diverse racial and ethnic backgrounds bring to college.

*1. Are measures of reactionary racism—individual-deficit attributions, cultural pathology stereotypes, conservative policy values, and attitudes toward race-targeted policies on campus—conceptually distinct in a multiethnic sample of college students?*

*2. What patterns emerge in intercorrelations among these critical dimensions of contemporary racial ideology in an ethnically diverse campus community?*

*3. How do White, Asian, Latina/o and African American college students differ on these critical race-related beliefs and campus diversity policy attitudes?*

## Methodology

### Subjects

We drew 178 female and 112 male students for this multiethnic study from a stratified sample of juniors enrolled at a major Midwestern, public university. Of these participants, 68 were Black (49 women and 19 men), 86 were White (51 women and 35 men), 90 were Asian Americans (54 women and 36 men), and 46 were Latina/os (24 women and 22 men). Their average age was about 20.

### Data Collection

The university at which we collected our data is well known for the high quality of its academic programs, facilities, and resources. It strongly emphasizes undergraduate education. Admissions standards are very competitive. Typically, more than half of entering students rank in the top 10 percent of their high school class, and more than 25 percent rank in the top 3 percent. Approximately 35,000 students from the United States and from some hundred foreign countries are enrolled each year in programs offered by twenty-one schools and colleges.

In addition to undergraduate education, this university is also known for its achievements in research and graduate studies. Each year the campus attracts more than $150 million in state and federal grants and contracts and in private gifts and grants. The university consistently ranks nationally among the top 10 institutions in many fields of study. Several of its colleges and departments rank among the top five universities in the nation.

Our data was collected from a sample of multiracial undergraduate students seeking majors in the College of Liberal Arts and Sciences (LAS), which has the largest enrollment of majors at the university and is the most racially diverse college. We collected data from individual participants during their first and third years. We used specific procedures[1] to reduce variation in the sample size and composition while performing different analyses. We calculated the response rate by dividing the 423 eligible[2] students by the 307 student respondents. As a result, the overall response rate was 73 percent.

## Measures and Findings

*Are measures of reactionary racism—individual-deficit attributions, cultural pathology stereotypes, conservative policy values, and attitudes toward race-targeted policies—conceptually distinct in a multiethnic sample of college students?*

To address this question, we conducted a factor analysis on a set of items selected to measure each of these key aspects of racial ideology. As shown in Table 5.1, the rotated-component factor matrix reveals loadings for the twenty items that support conceptual distinctions between the six critical dimensions of racial ideology in a multiethnic sample of college students. We selected five of these items to measure a critical dimension of contemporary racial ideology that we have defined as *reactionary racism*. We selected these five items from widely used modern or symbolic racism measures of the

---

1. We included only those students who completed two of the three questionnaires during their freshman year, who were also enrolled during their junior year, and who completed data on all measures during the junior year.

2. We included in the response rate only students with an available local address and/ or phone number listed withe the university. Of 146 available White students, 22 were unreachable, resulting in 124 eligible students. From this number, 87 students responded, for a White response rate of 70 percent. The Asian Americans had 147 available students minus 21 who were unreachable, for a total of 126 eligible students, of whom 96 responded, yielding a response rate of 76 percent. There were 78 available Latina/o students minus an unreachable 10, resulting in 68 eligible students of whom 50 responded, yielding a response rate of 74 percent. Of 124 available African American students, 19 were unreachable; of these 105 eligible students, 74 responded, a rate of 71 percent.

**Table 5.1**
**Factor Analysis of Selected Racial Ideology Items**
**in a Multiethnic Sample of College Students**

| Racial Ideology Indicators | Rotated Component Matrix |
|---|---|
| *1. Race-related Beliefs* | |
| **Reactionary Racism** (.82 alpha) | |
| Minority media | .74 |
| Minority pushy | .74 |
| Minority economics | .73 |
| Minority rights | .51 |
| School desegregation | .42 |
| **Individual-Deficit Attributions** (.71 alpha) | |
| Unintelligent | .80 |
| Lazy | .65 |
| **Cultural Pathology Stereotypes** (.61 alpha) | |
| Violence prone | .80 |
| Poverty prone | .71 |
| Prefer welfare | .69 |
| **Conservative Policy Values** (.70 alpha) | |
| Welfare reduction | .79 |
| Mandatory work for welfare | .74 |
| *2. Campus Diversity Policy Attitudes* | |
| **Race-Targeted Program Opposition** (.89 alpha) | |
| Special scholarships | .84 |
| Special admissions | .82 |
| Special support services | .80 |
| Special facilities | .44 |
| **Curriculum Diversity Opposition** (.83 alpha) | |
| Expand women's studies | .83 |
| Expand women's programs | .77 |
| Expand African American studies | .73 |
| Require multicultural courses | .59 |

negative, reactionary sentiment that social changes in response to demands from Blacks and other nondominant groups have "gone too far" (e.g., Kinder and Sears 1981; Kinder and Sanders 1996; McConahay 1986; Sears 1988).

These items, measured on a seven-point Likert-type scale ranging from "very strongly agree" to "very strongly disagree," are: *Over the past few years, (1) the government and news media have shown more respect to minorities than they deserve; (2) minorities should not push themselves where they are not wanted; (3) minorities have gotten more economically than they deserve; (4) minorities are getting too demanding in their push for equal*

*rights; and (5) Blacks and Hispanics have more influence upon school deseg-*
*regation than they ought to have.* Factor scores for these five reactionary
racism items revealed consistently high factor loadings (.74–.42) with a high
level of internal consistency for the overall scale (alpha = .82).

Table 5.1 also reveals high factor loadings (.80 and .65) and a high level
of internal consistency (alpha = .71) for the two items that tap *individual-
deficit attributions.* We selected these items from the General Social Survey.
They focus on the belief that race and class inequalities result from intellectual and motivational deficits in individuals rather than from barriers within
society: *America is an increasingly diverse population, where groups differ
widely in economic class, race, and ethnicity. Below are a few reasons some
people give to explain why there are poor people in the country. How important do you feel each of the following reasons is in explaining why there are
poor people in the country? Less intelligence than the middle class? Lack of
individual effort or hard work?* The three-point scale asked respondents to
select "not important," "somewhat important," or "very important."

The three items measuring *cultural pathology stereotypes* also came from
the General Social Survey and produced factor loadings that varied from .80
to .69 with an alpha coefficient of .67. The items to operationalize this concept focused on stereotypical overgeneralizations or beliefs about Black
Americans: *Blacks in general tend to be violence-prone rather than peace-
loving; come from poor families; and tend to prefer to live off welfare rather
than to be self-supporting.* Here we asked respondents to respond by choosing a seven-point proportion rating—from under 10 percent to over 90 percent of the entire Black population.

We measured the concept of *conservative policy values* by two items
designed for this study that produced factor loadings of .79 and .74 with a .74
alpha coefficient, again indicating a high level of internal consistency. These
items reflected political support for core conservative values regarding public
welfare: *Do you personally favor or oppose the following policy trends: (1)
reducing welfare benefits to make working for a living more attractive and (2)
requiring that people must work to receive welfare?*

In addition to broad race-related beliefs, we also designed a set of policy
attitude items to measure the level of support or opposition for campus diversity. As shown in Table 5.1, opposition to *Race-Targeted Program Opposition*
and *Curriculum Diversity Opposition* emerged as independent factors. The
four items to measure race-targeted program attitudes had a high level of
internal consistency (alpha = .89) with factor loadings ranging from .84 to
.44. We asked: *Do you personally favor or oppose: (1) special scholarships
or financial aid designated for Black or other minority students, (2) special
admission programs for Black and other minority college students,
(3) special academic support programs for Black and other minority students,*

*(4) special "cultural" facilities and services for various minority student groups on college campuses?*

The four items to tap *curriculum diversity attitudes* also had a very high level of internal consistency (alpha = .83) with factor loadings from .83 to .59: *Do you personally favor or oppose— expanding women's studies courses, minors and majors in the college curriculum; expanding programs that increase awareness of rape, sexual harassment, and other women's issues on college campuses; expanding Afro-American studies courses, minors, and majors in the college curriculum; required courses for college graduation on race, ethnicity or cultural diversity issues?*

The second prong of our inquiry was the patterns of intercorrelations that might emerge among these sets of four critical race-related beliefs in an ethnically diverse campus community. As findings reported in Table 5.2 show, the four race-related belief factors are not only internally consistent but are also modestly related to each other. In this multiethnic sample, reactionary racism is most clearly associated with both conservative policy values (r = .36, $p < .01$) and individual-deficit attributions (r = .30, $p < .01$). Moreover, the factor of individual attributes is also significantly related to both cultural pathology stereotypes (r = .34, $p < .01$) and conservative policy values (r = .26, $p < .01$). However, the factor of cultural pathology stereotypes does not have a significant relationship to conservative policy values (r = .11, $p$ = NS). These modest correlations suggest that each of these four composite measures of racial ideology may function as a distinct aspect of a broader race-related belief system in this ethnically diverse sample of college students.

**Table 5.2**

**Intercorrelations among Four Race-Related Belief Scales
in a Multiethnic Sample of College Students**
($N$ = 293)

|  | Reactionary Racism | Individual Deficit Attributions | Cultural Pathology Stereotypes | Conservative Policy Values |
|---|---|---|---|---|
| Reactionary Racism | — | .30** | .14* | .36** |
| Individual-Deficit Attributions |  | — | .34** | .26** |
| Cultural Pathology Stereotypes |  |  | — | .11 |
| Conservative Policy Values |  |  |  | — |

*Correlation is significant at the .05 level (2-tailed)
**Correlation is significant at the .01 level (2-tailed)

Our third inquiry was: *How do White, Asian, Latina/o and African American college students differ on these critical dimensions of contemporary racial ideology and policy attitudes?* As shown in Table 5.3, cross-ethnic comparisons indicate that college students from different racial and ethnic backgrounds do indeed tend to bring distinct race-related ideologies and policy attitudes to the campus community. Hence, a statistically significant difference emerges from the four ethnic groups on each of the four race-related belief scales and both campus diversity policy attitude scales. However, the cross-ethnic pattern appears to be rather complex and often distinct for particular dimensions of racial ideology.

The pattern is similar for reactionary racism and individual-deficit attributions; Whites and Asians are most likely to subscribe to such beliefs, while Latina/os and Blacks are least likely to internalize such invidious race-related beliefs. White college students tend to score a little higher than their Asian counterparts in reactionary racism but slightly lower on individual-deficit attributions. Moreover, Whites and Asians are almost identical in endorsing conservative policy values while Latina/os and Blacks tend to be less conservative about welfare. In contrast, Asian and Latina/o students are highest in stereotypes about Black cultural pathology while White students are surpris-

**Table 5.3**
**Cross-Ethnic Comparisons[a] of College Students**
**on Race-Related Beliefs and Campus Diversity Policy Attitudes**
$(N = 293)$

| | Racial and Ethnic Background | | | | |
|---|---|---|---|---|---|
| | White (N = 87) | Asian (N = 90) | Latina/o (N = 47) | Black (N = 68) | Sig. |
| **Race-Related Belief Scales** | | | | | |
| Reactionary racism | **14.6** | **13.6** | 11.0 | 8.2 | $p < .000$ |
| Individual-deficit attributions | **7.5** | **8.1** | 7.4 | 6.2 | $p < .000$ |
| Cultural pathology stereotypes | **9.5** | *11.1* | *10.9* | **9.8** | $p < .002$ |
| Conservative policy values | **7.4** | **7.5** | *6.6* | *6.3* | $p < .001$ |
| **Campus Diversity Policy Attitude Scales** | | | | | |
| Race-targeted program attitudes | 8.2 | 9.8 | **12.7** | **13.5** | $p < .000$ |
| Curriculum diversity attitudes | **14.5** | **14.7** | 15.5 | 17.9 | $p < .000$ |

[a]One-way analysis of variance

ingly similar to African Americans in not endorsing stereotypes of Blacks as violent, poor, and welfare-preferring. Black and Latina/o college students most strongly support race-targeted policies on campus, while Asian students are even stronger than White students in opposing special programs for Blacks and other students of color. Blacks are consistently the strongest supporters of curriculum diversity followed by Latina/os while both White and Asian students express lower levels of support.

## Summary and Implications

This chapter supports the importance of understanding the historical context and complexity of contemporary racial ideology. Within diverse campus communities, such an ideology may increasingly divide students from different race and ethnic backgrounds. In contrast to blatant Jim Crow racism, contemporary racial ideology is far subtler and includes both race-related beliefs and campus diversity policy attitudes. Despite modest interrelationships, each of the four race-related factors—reactionary racism, individual-deficit attributions, cultural pathology stereotypes, and conservative policy values—apparently has a distinct meaning for contemporary college students who study on ethnically diverse campuses.

The psychometric findings suggest that multidimensional constructs such as *modern, symbolic, aversive, laissez-faire,* or *color-blind* racism can be further deconstructed for more meaningful analyses of contemporary racial ideology in multiethnic contexts (Bobo, Kluegel, and Smith 1997; Bonilla-Silva and Forman 2000; Dovidio, Mann, and Gaertner 1989; Kinder and Sears 1981; McConahay 1986; Sears 1988). Moreover, psychometric findings also suggest that campus diversity policy attitudes are not unidimensional but include opposition to both race-targeted programs (admissions, financial aid, support services, and cultural facilities) and also to curriculum diversity (African American studies, women's studies, and multiethnic course requirements).

Both White and Asian American college students were consistently the most negative on all six of the indicators of racial ideology, followed by Latina/os. Blacks were least negative. African Americans consistently revealed the overall lowest internalization of the four race-related beliefs combined with the strongest level of support for the two campus diversity policy agendas. To be sure, the clear differences in both race-related beliefs and diversity policy attitudes that students from diverse ethnic backgrounds bring with them to college represent a critical challenge for those committed to building a strong sense of campus community as we move into the twenty-first century. Rather than yielding to "color-blind" denial, educational leaders and policy makers must seek to better understand the nature, context, and consequences of these cross-ethnic disparities in racial ideology so that they can more effectively address contemporary racial climate challenges on campus.

From a historical perspective, cross-ethnic disparities in racial ideology may reflect an evolving American racial system that has important implications for interracial group interests, discourse, and climate both within and outside of diverse campus communities (e.g., Blumer 1958; Bobo 1996; Hacker 1992). The pattern showing the increasing refusal to endorse contemporary racial ideology as the group of focus shifts from White and Asian, to Latina/o and then to African Americans, may reflect an emerging multiethnic hierarchy, which could transform the historical White-Black racial system in postindustrial America.

Several researchers have noted the important role of the American racial "contract," "hierarchy," "order," or racialized "social system" in racial and ethnic group relations, conflicts, and related public policy debates (Bonilla-Silva 1997; Bobo, 2000; Dawson 2000; Hochschild 2000; Mills 1997). In general, these scholars suggest that the evolving American racial system includes three key features: (1) deeply rooted cultural values about the proper role of Whites over African Americans, (2) systematic institutional practices that reinforce and fulfill these indigenous cultural values, and (3) individual beliefs and attitudes that reflect such core American cultural values, related informal arrangements, and formal practices.

The racial system in the United States has evolved over time from chattel slavery, to legal segregation, to its current status of de facto, informal, and subtle modes of anti-Black backlash or subordination. (See also Altbach, Lamotey, and Rivers, this volume.) In response to significant civil rights-era changes, a reactionary national movement during the last quarter of the twentieth century began to restructure a more contemporary racial system (e.g., Hacker 1992; Klinkner and Smith 1999; Morris 1984). The first quarter of the twenty-first century promises a continued evolution of this institutionalized racial system where White-Black "contracts" and unresolved racial "debts" will be challenged in multiethnic contexts in major cities, workplaces, and especially universities. Therefore, despite the popularity of rhetoric about a "color-blind" society, a tenacious and evolving racial system will continue to have profound effects on the ideologies of students from various ethnic groups. It will also continue to impact the racial climate in universities and at other multiethnic settings (Altbach and Lomotey 1991; Bowser, Auletta, and Jones 1993; Smith 1998; Tatum 1997; Terkel 1992). The ongoing evolution of a traditionally White-Black racial system, combined with rapid demographic changes and the diversification of the college student population, may well influence new multiethnic campus climate patterns well into the future.

## References

Allen, Walter R., Edgar G. Epps, and Nesha Z. Haniff. 1991. *College in Black and White: African American students in predominantly White and historically Black public universities.* Albany: State University of New York Press.

Altbach, Philip G., and Kofi Lomotey, eds. 1991. *The racial crisis in American higher education.* Albany: State University of New York Press.

Anderson, James D. 1988. *The education of Blacks in the South, 1860–1935.* Chapel Hill: University of North Carolina Press.

Blumer, Herbert. 1958. Race prejudice as a sense of group position. *Pacific Sociological Review* 1, no. 1: 3–7.

Bobo, Lawrence. 1996. Perceptions of racial group competition: Extending Blumer's theory of group position to a multiracial context. *American Sociological Review* 61: 951–72.

———. 2000. Race and beliefs about affirmative action. In Sears, Sidanius, and Bobo, 137–65.

Bobo, Lawrence, and James Kluegel. 1993. Opposition to race-targeting: Self-interest, stratification ideology, or prejudice? *American Sociological Review* 58: 443–64.

Bobo, Lawrence, James Kluegel, and Ryan Smith. 1997. Laissez-faire racism: The crystallization of a kinder, gentler, anti-Black ideology. In *Racial attitudes in the 1990s: Continuity and change,* edited by Steven A. Tuch and Jack K. Martin, 15–41. Westport, CT: Praeger.

Bonilla-Silva, Eduardo. 1997. Rethinkng racism: Toward a structural interpretation. *American Sociological Review* 62, no. 3: 465–80.

Bonilla-Silva, Eduardo, and Tyrone Forman. 2000. "I'm not a racist, but . . .": Mapping White college students' racial ideology in the USA. *Discourse and Society* 11, no. 1: 51–86.

Bowser, Benjamin P., Gale S. Auletta, and Terry Jones. 1993. *Toward the Multicultural University.* Madison, WI: Magna Publications, Inc.

Carter, Deborah J., and Reginald Wilson. 1995. *Thirteenth annual status report on minorities in higher education.* Washington, DC: American Council on Education.

Curry, George E. 1996. *The affirmative action debate.* Reading, MA: Addison-Wesley.

Darden, Antonia, Rodolfo D. Torres, and Henry Gutiérrez, eds. 1997. *Latinos and education.* New York: Routledge.

Dawson, Michael C. 2000. Slowly coming to grips with the effects of the American racial order on American policy preferences. In Sears, Sidanius, and Bobo, 344–58.

Deskins, Donald. 1991. Winners and losers: A regional assessment of minority enroll-
    ment and earned degrees in U.S. colleges and universities, 1974–84. In *College
    in Black and White: African American students in predominantly White and his-
    torically Black public universities,* edited by Walter R. Allen, Edgar G. Epps, and
    Nesha Z. Haniff, 17–41. Albany, NY: State University of New York Press.

Dovidio, John F., Jeffery A. Mann, and Samuel L. Gaertner. 1989. Resistance to
    affirmative action: The implication of aversive racism. In *Affirmative action in
    perspective,* edited by Fletcher A. Blanchard and Faye J. Crosby, 83–102. New
    York: Springer-Verlag.

D'Souza, Dinesh. 1995. *The end of racism: Principles for a multicultural society.* New
    York: Free Press.

El-Khawas, Elaine. 1996. Student diversity on today's campuses. In *Student services:
    A handbook for the profession,* edited by Susan Komives and Dudley Woodard,
    64–82. San Francisco: Jossey-Bass.

Feagin, Joe R., Hernan Vera, and Nikitah Imani. 1996. *The agony of education.* New
    York: Routledge.

Fish, Stanley. 1993. Reverse racism, or how the pot got to call the kettle black.
    *Atlantic Monthly,* 272, no. 5: 128–34.

Gurin, Patricia, and Edgar Epps. 1975. *Black consciousness, identity, and achieve-
    ment: A study of students in historically Black colleges.* New York: John Wiley.

Hacker, Andrew. 1992. *Two nations: Black and White, separate, hostile, unequal.* New
    York: Ballantine Books.

Hochschild, Jennifer L. 2000. Lumpers and splitters, individuals and structures. In
    Sears, Sidanius, and Bobo, 324–43.

Hughes, Michael. 1997. Symbolic racism, old fashioned racism, and Whites' opposi-
    tion to affirmative action. In *Racial attitudes in the 1990's: Continuity and change,*
    edited by Steven A. Tuch and Jack K. Martin, 45–75. Westport, CT: Greenwood
    Publishing Group, Inc.

Hughes, Michael, and Steven A. Tuch. 2000. How beliefs about poverty influence
    racial policy attitudes. In Sears, Sidanius, and Bobo, 165–90.

Hunt, Mathew O. 1996. The individual, society, or both? A comparison of Black,
    Latino, and White beliefs about the causes of poverty, *Social Forces* 75: 293–322.

Jones, James M. 1997. *Prejudice and racism.* New York: McGraw-Hill.

Kinder, Donald R., and Lynn M. Sanders. 1996. *Divided by color.* Chicago: University
    of Chicago Press.

Kinder, Donald R., and David O. Sears. 1981. Prejudice and politics: Symbolic racism
    versus racial threats to the good life. *Journal of Personality and Social Psychol-
    ogy* 40: 414–31.

Klinkner, Philip A., and Rogers M. Smith. 1999. *The unsteady march: The rise and decline of racial equality in America.* Chicago: University of Chicago Press.

Kluegel, James R., and Eliot R. Smith. 1983. Affirmative action attitudes: Effects of self-interest, racial affect, and stratification beliefs on Whites' view. *Social Forces* 61, no. 3: 797–824.

———. 1986. Beliefs about Black inequality: Americans' views of what is and what ought to be. Hawthorne, NY: Aldine de Gruyter.

Krysan, Maria. 2000. Prejudice, politics, and public opinion: Understanding the sources of racial policy attitudes. *Annual Review of Sociology* 26, no. 1: 135–68.

Magner, D. K. 1989. Blacks and Whites on campuses: Behind ugly racist incidents, student isolation and insensitivity. *Chronicle of Higher Education* (April): 1.

McConahay, John. 1986. Modern racism, ambivalence, and the modern racism scale. In *Prejudice, discrimination, and racism,* edited by John F. Dovidio and Samuel L. Gaertner, 91–125. Orlando, FL: Academic Press.

Mills, Charles W. 1997. *The racial contract.* Ithaca, NY: Cornell University Press.

Morris, Aldon. 1984. *The origins of the civil rights movement: Black communities organizing for social change.* New York: Free Press.

Muñoz, D. G. 1986. Identifying areas of stress for Chicano undergraduates. In *Latino college students,* edited by Michael A. Olivas, 131–56. New York: Teachers College Press.

Nichols, David, and Olive Mills. 1970. *The campus and the racial crisis.* Washington, DC: American Council on Education.

Olivas, Michael A. 1986. *Latino college students.* New York: Teachers College Press.

Peterson, Marvin, Robert Blackburn, Zelda Gamson, Carlos Arce, Roselle Davenport, and James Mingle. 1978. *Black students on White campuses: Impact of increased Black enrollments.* Ann Arbor: Institute for Social Research, University of Michigan.

Roth, Byron M. 1990. Social psychology's racism. *Public Interest* 98: 26–36.

———. 1994. *Prescription for failure: Race relations in the age of social science.* New Brunswick, NJ: Transaction Publishers.

Schuman, Howard, Charlotte Steeh, Lawrence Bobo, and Maria Krysan. 1997. *Racial attitudes in America: Trends and interpretations.* Cambridge: Harvard University Press.

Sears, David O. 1988. Symbolic racism. In *Eliminating racism: Means and controversies,* edited by Phyllis A. Katz and Dalmas A. Taylor, 53–84. New York: Plenum Press.

Sears, David O., P. J. Henry, and Rick Kosterman. 2000. Egalitarian values and contemporary racial politics. In Sears, Sidanius, and Bobo, 75–117.

Sears, David, John J. Hetts, Jim Sidanius, and Lawrence Bobo. 2000. Race in American politics. In Sears, Sidanius, and Bobo, 1–43.

Sears, David O., Jim Sidanius, and Lawrence Bobo, eds. 2000. *Racialized politics: The debate about racism in America.* Chicago: University of Chicago Press.

Sears, David O., and Tom Jessor. 1996. Whites' racial policy attitudes: The role of white racism. *Social Science Quarterly* 77, no. 4: 751–59.

Sears, David, Colette van Laar, Mary Carrillo, and Rick Kosterman. 1997. Is it really racism? The origins of White Americans' opposition to race-targeted policies. *Public Opinion Quarterly* 61: 16–53.

Sedlacek, William E. 1987. Black students on White campuses: 20 years of research. *Journal of College Student Personnel* 28: 484–95.

Shiraishi, Yukiko. 2000. *Attributional patterns and adjustment in the college transition: A cross-cultural study.* Unpublished dissertation, Northwestern University.

Smith, William A. 1996. Affirmative action attitudes in higher education: A multiethnic extension of a three-factor model. *Dissertation Abstracts International* 57, no. 4: 1557A. University Microfilms No. AAD96-25196.

———. 1998. Gender and racial/ethnic differences in the affirmative action attitudes of U.S. college students. *Journal of Negro Education* 6, no. 2: 127–41.

Sniderman, Paul M., and Edward G. Carmines. 1997. *Reaching beyond race.* Cambridge: Harvard University Press.

Sniderman, Paul M., and Michael G. Hagen. 1985. *Race and inequality: A study of American values.* Chatham, NJ: Chatham House.

Sowell, Thomas. 1984. *Civil rights: Rhetoric or reality?* New York: William Morrow.

———. 1994. *Race and culture: A world view.* New York: Basic Books.

Sue, Derald, and David Sue. 1999. *Counseling the culturally different: Theory and practice.* New York: John Wiley.

Tatum, Beverly Daniel. 1997. *Why are all the Black kids sitting together in the cafeteria?* New York: Basic Books.

Terkel, Studs. 1992. *Race: How Blacks and Whites think and feel about the American obsession.* New York: Anchor Books/Doubleday.

# CHAPTER 6

# Creating a Climate of Inclusion

*Understanding Latina/o College Students*

## SYLVIA HURTADO

An institution's success in attracting Latina/o students and fostering their development during college has much to do with how those students perceive the institutional climate for racial/ethnic diversity and their awareness of institutional efforts to create responsive learning environments. Colleges with relatively open access policies in states with a growing Latina/o population must respond to Latina/o-specific issues because of their sheer numbers. Over the years we have witnessed what demographers have called the "ethnic restructuring" (Estrada 1988) of previously predominantly White institutions that are becoming Hispanic-serving institutions, meaning that at least one-quarter of the student body is Latina/o in origin (i.e., Mexican American, Puerto Rican, Cuban, or Central and South American). There are now over two hundred Hispanic-serving institutions that enroll approximately two-thirds of all Latina/os in higher education.

At the same time during the 1990s, an increasing number of talented Latina/o students have elected to attend some of the nation's most elite and selective colleges. This growth may slow, however, under pressure from revised access policies that have resulted from the contemporary debate on affirmative action and other changes, particularly in the key states of California, Texas, and New York that serve a large proportion of the U.S. Latina/o population. Contrary to popular myths about how affirmative action has perpetuated stereotypes, we are now finding that stereotypes are perpetuated even under "race neutral" institutional policies. This finding suggests that institutions have not dealt successfully with the dynamics of intergroup relations that develop when majority students interact with Latina/os and other racial/ethnic groups. All selective institutions continue to face urgent questions about how to improve the climate for racial/ethnic diversity. Finding answers to these questions are key to their development as campus communities

121

inclusive of a Latina/o student presence. This chapter, drawing from national data and numerous studies on Latina/os, will highlight some of the most important issues.

## Use of "Hispanic" or "Latina/o"

Latina/o researchers have recently begun to prefer the term *Latina/o* when referring to a heterogeneous population of Mexican Americans, Puerto Ricans, Cuban Americans, Central Americans, and South Americans who inhabit regional communities (Hayes-Bautista, Schink, and Chapa 1988). However, in some regions, it is probably more appropriate to refer to the specific ethnic group if that is the unit of focus, because most Latina/os continue to refer to their specific ethnic group as a source of identity and distinct historical and political experience in this country. Latina/os of Mexican origin live primarily in the Southwest and Midwest; Puerto Ricans are more likely to be concentrated in the Northeast; and Cuban Americans are concentrated in the Southeast (Chapa and Valencia 1993). Other Latina/o groups that include Central and South Americans are typically found where there are large concentrations of these first three groups.

The term *Hispanic* is used primarily in the context of population. Most government data are reported under this umbrella term. Some areas of the country also use it as the more popular term. It also should be noted that Latina/os in some regions, New Mexico, for example, prefer *Hispanic* to emphasize the link with Spanish colonial families dating back to the 1500s. I use both terms interchangeably throughout this chapter to reflect the heterogeneity of identity and terms in use today.

## Demographic Change and Latina/o College Participation

Demographers have predicted since the mid-1970s that Latina/os are expected to become the largest group of people of color in the United States by 2005. The first evidence of this demographic shift was reported in 1998: Hispanic youth, under the age of eighteen, outnumbered African American youth by 35,000 (Vobejda 1998). A separate study conducted by educational researchers projected that, by 2020, one out of every four of the nation's children and youth under seventeen will be of Hispanic origin (Pallas, Natriello, and McDill 1989). These demographic statistics reveal that a rising fraction of the nation's elementary, middle, and high schools contains an increasingly visible Latina/o presence based on the simple fact that Latina/os comprise larger proportions of school-age and college-age student populations.

However, national data provide a sobering portrait of Latina/o educational progress relative to other groups. In 1990, only one in two Latina/o adults over age twenty-five had completed high school compared with 80 percent for non-Latina/os; and only 9 percent had completed four years of college (Chapa and Valencia 1993). By the year 2000, only 11% had completed four years of college, indicating that a very large proportion of Latina/os attending college today are first-generation college students.

It is important to recognize that educational attainment varies substantially among Latina/o ethnic groups: Cuban Americans are four times more likely than Mexican American adults (5 percent) to have attended college, a rate (20 percent) roughly comparable to non-Hispanic White adults (Chapa and Valencia 1993). Mexican Americans or Chicanos constitute 60 percent of the overall Hispanic population; therefore, college access issues are much more salient for the majority of Latina/os located in the Southwest and Midwest. Within these regions, the educational attainment gaps are greater among recent immigrants or first-generation Latina/os than among those who have lived in the United States for longer periods of time (Aponte 1997; A. Hurtado, Hayes-Bautista, Valdez, and Hernandez 1992).

Although overall growth in the Hispanic population has translated into larger enrollments in higher education (Carter and Wilson 1994), the pattern of access and choice of college has remained relatively unchanged since the 1970s when researchers reported that Chicanos, Puerto Ricans, and Native Americans were the least likely to attend college compared with all other racial/ethnic groups (Astin 1982). The Hispanic enrollment increases in higher education have not kept pace with the relatively rapid growth of the Latina/o college-age population, and some contend that the gap between college participation rates of White and Hispanics is actually greater today than it was twenty years ago (Heller 1997; Heller in press). Another recent study found that Latina/o students who had been identified as high-achieving in junior high school fared much better on several measures of college choice behaviors; however, they are still the least likely to have applied to college by the end of their senior year of all racial/ethnic groups (S. Hurtado, Inkelas, Briggs, and Rhee 1997). This pattern suggests either poor preparation in high school, a lack of social capital among families who strategically position their children to enter college, or attendance at a high school where college-going is not normative behavior or expected of Latina/o students. More than three-quarters of all Latina/os in the country attend schools where the student population is over 50 percent people of color (Orfield, Bachmeier, James, and Eitle 1997), indicating that colleges and universities must develop links with predominantly Hispanic schools to increase Latina/o access to higher education.

Using the National Educational Longitudinal Study (NELS:88) to understand the college-going behavior of a national cohort of students, I found that

44 percent of Hispanic high school seniors elect to attend four-year colleges as their first postsecondary institution, compared with 61 percent of White and 55 percent of Black high school seniors. (See Figure 6.1.) Approximately 47 percent of Latina/o seniors are likely to attend junior or community colleges as their first college, a rate much higher than White (33 percent) or Black (30 percent) students. In addition, 57 percent of *all* Hispanic enrollments are in two-year institutions, compared with 37 percent of all college student enrollments (Hauptman and Smith 1994). Again, this pattern suggests that recent Latina/o high school graduates, like students who enroll in college beyond the traditional age, are likely to be disproportionately represented in institutions with relatively open access.

An examination of Latina/os as an ethnic group (Figure 6.2) shows significant differences in where a high school senior elects to begin higher education. Mexican Americans or Chicanos are the Latina/o group least likely to attend a four-year college (40 percent), while Cuban Americans (55 percent) are about as likely as African Americans to begin their studies at a four-year college. Mexican Americans (52 percent) are more likely than any other Latina/o ethnic group to begin their postsecondary studies at a two-year or community college. Puerto Ricans (13 percent) were more likely than any other Latina/o ethnic group to begin their studies at a vocational or trade school.

**Figure 6.1. Type of First Postsecondary Institution Attended by Race/ Ethnicity**

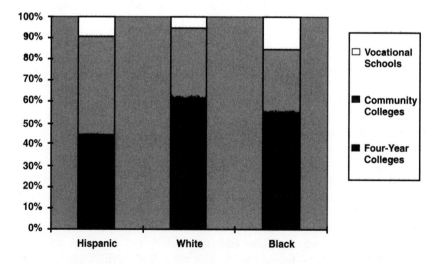

*Source:* Calculated from U.S. Dept. of Education, National Educational Longitudinal Study (1988), weighted data.

**Figure 6.2. Type of First Postsecondary Education Attended by Hispanic Ethnic Groups**

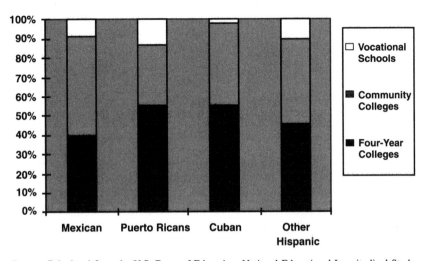

*Source:* Calculated from the U.S. Dept. of Education, National Educational Longitudinal Study (1988), weighted data.

These patterns suggest that any further constraints on admissions policies will almost certainly increase the number of Latina/os at junior and community colleges, a choice that statistically reduces their chances of achieving baccalaureate degrees, particularly if they matriculate at institutions without policies that facilitate transfer and articulation of curricula from two- to four-year colleges. Bridge programs and counseling initiatives also need to focus on Latina/o students, since studies have shown that Latina/os who participate in such programs are more likely to transfer (University 1993), primarily because the program gives them higher expectations, appropriate information about college requirements, and assistance in the transfer process. Otherwise, Latina/o community college students typically take too many courses before transferring, select courses that do not transfer to a four-year institution, and/ or have limited contact with faculty and counselors who can advise them (Rendon, Jalomo, and Garcia 1994).

**Reversing Latina/o Educational Progress**

Nearly two-thirds of the national Latina/o population is located in three states—California, Texas, and New York—and tend to live in urban areas (Chapa and Valencia 1993). Significant changes in admissions and student support policies impacting Latina/o education have occurred in these three states. California's 1996 voter initiative, Proposition 209, prohibits sensitivity to race/ethnicity in admissions and programs—a decided reversal of state initiatives to target the improvement of educational progress for various underrepresented populations. The passage of this initiative signals a significant lack of Latina/o voter influence; in contrast, a 1992 study showed that 88 percent of Latina/os in California supported special measures to ensure that the same percentage of Latina/os as other groups are admitted to college (Hurtado, Hayes-Bautista, Valdez, and Hernandez 1992). A legal challenge in Texas in 1996, *Hopwood v. State of Texas,* received a broad interpretation by the Fifth Circuit Court. It resulted in the removal of all consideration of race/ ethnicity in admissions policies, programs, and scholarships (Chapa 1999) on the grounds that such consideration violated the rights of White students. Both of these initiatives changed policies to make them "race neutral," but their most conspicuous initial effect was a significant decline in the number of Latina/o and African American students who enrolled in flagship institutions. Essentially *Hopwood* reversed enrollment gains made up until 1995.

In efforts to remain responsive to an increasingly Hispanic and racially/ ethnically diverse constituency and to stem the enrollment decline of underrepresented groups at flagship institutions, Texas legislators developed a plan which won bipartisan political support in 1997. This plan encouraged institutions to use broad admissions criteria in their decisions (e.g., first-generation status, considerations for overcoming adverse conditions, and test performance relative to similar socioeconomic groups) in addition to guaranteeing admission to students who graduate among the top 10 percent of Texas high schools. Because of the great variation in the quality of education in Texas schools, the law also requires higher education institutions to determine whether admitted students need additional college preparation and, if so, to provide remedial assistance to improve their retention.

In direct contrast, a policy instituted in January 2000 at City University of New York does not allow students to take remedial services or courses at four-year institutions and are allows them only limited entry into remedial instruction at the community-college level. This policy, which has generated widespread controversy, essentially eliminates an important way of correcting for the variability in schools attended by most Latina/os. Furthermore, it flies in the face of findings documenting the success of many CUNY graduates under an open-admissions policy. Projections indicated that Latina/o enrollments at CUNY four-year colleges would drop by half when the policy is fully implemented, and predicted significant overall enrollment declines (Lavin and Weininger 1999).

These policies affecting access and student support will almost certainly have a dramatic effect on how many of a state's Latina/o students can enter four-year institutions and thrive there. Even though the population of White youth is expected to decline by six million students by 2020 (Pallas, Natriello, and McDill 1989), in some cases, these policies have also increased White student enrollments at selective institutions of higher education—an impact that can hardly be called "race neutral," given the consistent differences in student access to quality education. Texas has managed to stem a precipitous decline in the enrollment of both African American and Latina/o students by its implementation of multiple criteria and "top 10 percent" policy (Chapa 1999), but not all institutions have regained their enrollment progress at pre-1995 levels (Hurtado and Wathington Cade, 2001). The difficulty that some institutions have in attracting a talented and diverse student body may have much to do with Latino and African American students perceptions that they will not find needed support for learning and an institutional climate that welcomes racial/ethnic diversity.

## Understanding the Climate for Racial/Ethnic Diversity

Figure 6.3 shows how these policy and sociohistorical contexts affect institutional contexts for Latina/os. Changing access policies affect Latina/o perceptions of the "right college" for them. Simultaneously, the demographic growth constitutes a new sociohistorical force that shapes institutional contexts. Student perceptions of the institutional environment are also influenced by an institution's historical legacy of exclusion, the numerical representation of Latina/os within the institution, and behaviors observed inside and outside of the classroom (S. Hurtado, Milem, et al. 1999). These factors constituting the climate for diversity are interconnected and influence each other. Even campuses with "race neutral" policies cannot avoid these racial/ethnic dynamics because all of these factors are embedded in a larger context of social relations among groups. Given that Latina/os and non-Latina/os are educated in distinct racial/ethnic contexts before coming to college (Orfield et al. 1997), they typically have had relatively few interactions and few opportunities to discuss, exchange views, and reconcile differences with diverse peers as equals before entering college.

For example, an institution's image emerges over time. Its history may contain a legacy of exclusion or resistance to the presence of students of color. In many cases, benefits to predominantly White groups are embedded in policies, rituals, and campus traditions that were created before Latina/os arrived in significant numbers on campus. Approximately nineteen states created separate systems of postsecondary education for White and non-White students during the late nineteenth century, and many campuses showed extreme resistance to desegregating institutions of higher education (Williams 1997). These segregated systems excluded both Blacks and Latina/os from access to a quality education; and even when legal doors opened, campuses

**Figure 6.3. Elements Influencing the Climate of Diversity for Latina/os**

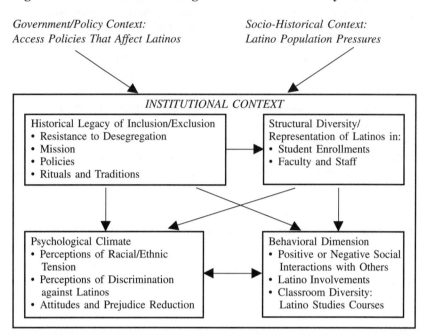

*Government/Policy Context:*                          *Socio-Historical Context:*
*Access Policies That Affect Latinos*                *Latino Population Pressures*

INSTITUTIONAL CONTEXT

Historical Legacy of Inclusion/Exclusion
• Resistance to Desegregation
• Mission
• Policies
• Rituals and Traditions

Structural Diversity/
Representation of Latinos in:
• Student Enrollments
• Faculty and Staff

Psychological Climate
• Perceptions of Racial/Ethnic
  Tension
• Perceptions of Discrimination
  against Latinos
• Attitudes and Prejudice Reduction

Behavioral Dimension
• Positive or Negative Social
  Interactions with Others
• Latino Involvements
• Classroom Diversity:
  Latino Studies Courses

*Source:* Adapted from model in Hurtado, Milem, Clayton-Pederson, and Allen, *Enacting Diverse Learning Environments,* ASHE-ERIC Report Series, Washington, DC: George Washington University Press, 1999.

still maintained exclusionary policies. For example, during the 1960s, Black and Mexican American students were prohibited from living in or visiting the dormitories of White students at the University of Texas (Lawrence and Matsuda 1997).

While many institutions have made substantial progress since the 1960s, old images die slowly—all the more slowly if students of color are few. Although many selective institutions have increased their numbers of Latina/o students, many still have administrations, faculties, and a student body that is predominantly White. Having relatively few Latina/os in an institution perpetuates stereotypes about the various Latina/o ethnic groups, in turn creating behaviors that reinforce these attitudes and perceptions. Most troubling are overt harassment or discriminatory incidents; they have high impact on the institution's image and overall climate for diversity. Discrimination in the classroom perhaps occurs more frequently but goes unreported unless institutions or researchers make an effort to document it. For example, a racial climate study on one Texas campus found that, while only 1 percent of Hispanic students reported an incident of discrimination or harassment to a proper university authority, approximately 69 percent stated that they had heard other students express negative stereotypes about different racial/ethnic groups in class (S. Hurtado, Maestas, et al. 1998). Moreover, very few courses on this campus included readings on Latina/o experiences; and less than 15 percent of White students reported taking a course that focused on different racial/ethnic groups, despite the success of such a curricular emphasis in reducing stereotypes and culturally insensitive behaviors.

Several studies reveal that many institutional factors are related to the perceptions that Latina/o students have of their college. Such views further explain the racial/ethnic dynamics within institutional contexts. Latina/os attending four-year colleges with relatively higher Hispanic student enrollments were less likely than Latinos attending institutions with low Hispanic enrollments to experience discrimination or perceive racial tension on campus (S. Hurtado 1994). Increasing Hispanic enrollments thus creates the perception that an institution welcomes Latina/os and is willing to provide a good education for them. Campuses with relatively large Hispanic enrollments provide more opportunities for White and other non-Hispanic students to interact with Latina/os and engage in a variety of classroom and out-class activities. Such interactions diminish Latina/o stereotypes and promote greater cross-cultural awareness among the student body.

Two additional perceptions are important. Latina/o students perceived smaller colleges as more welcoming than large campuses but perceived colleges in small towns as more likely to have racial tension, presumably because they were located away from Latina/o population centers and were less likely to have Latina/o cultural activities.

While most colleges can do very little about their size or location, studies revealed other factors that have a significant impact in creating an inclusive learning environment for Latina/os. A 1992 national study demonstrated that institutions were least likely to have a climate characterized by racial/ethnic tension if their students perceived the campus as student-centered and committed to diversity (S. Hurtado 1992). Interestingly, these findings held true for perceptions reported by Chicano, Black, and White students.

Another study, focused specifically on the perceptions of high-achieving Latina/o students[1] who were attending a variety of four-year colleges across the country, confirmed these findings. Latina/os were the least likely to have experienced overt discrimination or subtle racial/ethnic tension in environ-

---

1. In 1991, I conducted the National Survey of Hispanic Students (NSHS) in which high-achieving Latina/o students were selected from a national sample of the top 3,000 Latina/o PSAT scores after the junior year in high school. Many were designated semifinalists for the National Hispanic Scholars Award Program, which was analogous to other merit recognition programs, including the National Merit Scholarship Program and the National Achievement Program for Black students.

ments where they perceived that faculty demonstrated a strong interest in students and the administration was open and inclusive (Hurtado 1994). Although 68 percent of these talented Latina/os report that they attended colleges where most students know very little about Hispanic culture, their perceptions of subtle racial/ethnic tension were significantly lower on campuses where they reported discussing racial issues (inside and outside of the classroom), participating in Hispanic clubs or organizations, and socializing informally with White students.

This finding suggests that Latina/os need opportunities to interact with others when diversity is an issue and that such interactions enable students to work through differing perspectives and discover common values. At the same time, Latina/os need to interact among themselves to reinforce the development of identity, to revitalize important cultural values, and to maintain a comfort zone that buffers them when they encounter culturally insensitive students. For example, the demographic shifts described above have also increased the amount of stereotyping on predominantly White campuses. One Chicana, on the staff of the student newspaper, related:

> There was [a] memo that came in from public relations that the Hispanic population will be like 34 percent in however many years, and one of the [White] reporters turned to me and said, "Haven't you people ever heard of birth control?" And I said, "I can't take it any more!" It's one thing to be toughened up by a situation, and it's another where I don't need their money, I don't need their experience, I don't have to take it. So I quit. It was just one of those incidents— I mean it's been going on for so long in [that organization]. . . . They're backwards. They don't understand. They didn't even see a need to cover multicultural issues because "there isn't a big enough audience" at this college.[2]

She now edits a multicultural newsletter on campus but remains somewhat bitter about her experiences with the mainstream student newspaper.

Another Latino in a focus group expressed the need for involvement in Hispanic organizations to provide a "sense of home":

> [Latina/os] need that sense of home. I think we're always searching for it—a place that we belong—that's all anybody wants. And once you get that initial comfort zone in one place, you go to another club and you get ridiculed or [face discrimination], you have that place to go back to where you're comfortable, where you're safe. So I think it is essential to get involved in a Hispanic club like that—whether it be SHPE (Society for Hispanic Professional Engineers), MAES (Mexican American Engineering Society), or whatever it is.

2. Unpublished focus group transcripts that I collected in September 1999, as part of the study cited in S. Hurtado, Maestas, Hill, Inkelas, Wathington Cade, and Meader 1998. I also quote other statements from focus group participation in this chapter.

Both of these accounts illustrate the plight of Latina/o students who remain engaged and involved on predominantly White campuses despite their numerical underrepresentation. They face micro-inequities in their daily life but feel empowered enough to cope with adversity and create their own cultural spaces. One student who recruits Hispanic high school students tells them "It's gonna be [a] struggle, but that's part of who we are. We're strugglers. It's in our nature. . . . As long as you are not White, it's a struggle, in my opinion."[3] These accounts suggest that institutions need to give serious attention to the behavioral dimension of the climate, including interactions among groups, Latina/o student involvement in campus activities, and the need to engage all students in overall cultural awareness and education to prepare them for working and participating in a diverse democracy.

## The Impact of the Climate on Latina/o Students

Several studies have confirmed that the climate for diversity is not intangible and subjective but has real impact and consequences for a variety of racial/ethnic groups in college. (See S. Hurtado, Milem, et al. 1999 for a review.) Latina/os and other students of color are particularly sensitive to this climate because of its impact on their learning environment and quality of life on campus. For example, Latina/o students' perception of racial/ethnic tension negatively affects their transition from high school to four-year colleges according to several measures of academic, social, and personal-emotional adjustment, and also their attachment to the institution (S. Hurtado, Carter, and Spuler 1996). Chicano students tended to have significantly more difficulty in social adjustment at four-year colleges than other Latina/o ethnic groups but did not significantly differ on any other dimension of college adjustment.

The same study revealed that Latina/os who experienced overt discrimination were least likely to feel attached to the institution, although other measures of transition and adjustment were not significantly affected. This finding suggests that overt forms of old-fashioned racism directed at Latina/os may be rare or that students have developed support groups and ways to deal with overt discrimination. It is much more difficult, however, to deal with subtler forms of tension in the racial climate. One Latina/o in a focus group reported feeling invisible among other students and wanting recognition or some form of interaction, stating: "If our [interaction] was malicious, I would appreciate it more than if I was ignored. Because at least if it was malicious, you acknowledge that I'm here."

---

3. Although a large percentage of Latinos are racially white, the students interviewed did not consider themselves white. They talked about feeling more "brown-faced" every day and being the "only brunette" in class.

Another study confirmed that both overt and subtle hostility in the campus environment negatively affected Latina/os' overall sense of belonging to the campus community (Hurtado and Carter 1997). Students' transition to college and their sense of belonging are both directly associated with having a satisfying college experience and persistence to graduation.

## Implications for Institutional Practice:
## Developing an Inclusive Community

What practices can make a difference for Latina/o students on campus? Campuses with relatively open admissions, as the research indicates, are dealing with a higher volume of Hispanic students—many of whom are first-generation college students. Institutions that were able to increase Latina/o participation and graduation rates apparently helped Latina/o students qualify for financial aid and placed an emphasis on serving adults who were simultaneously employed and attending school despite work schedules (Richardson 1991). In essence, they reduced barriers and improved the learning environment. The same study showed that institutions with improved Latina/o participation and graduate rates also collaborated with high schools, provided special orientation programs, emphasized early warnings about academic difficulty, provided advising and mentors, used residence halls for summer bridge programs, and attended to the campus climate. Facilitating transfer from two-year to four-year colleges through special programs and improved policies will certainly continue to be critical to improving Latina/o educational progress in the foreseeable future.

To improve the climate, research suggests that institutions can create environments with relatively low racial/ethnic tension or conflict if they are attentive to a variety of issues related to diversity and if faculty and administrators demonstrate a general concern for student development (S. Hurtado 1992). Markers of institutional commitment to diversity include increasing the representation of racial/ethnic people of color among the faculty and administration, actively recruiting more students of color, taking steps to create a multicultural environment, and developing an appreciation for a multicultural society among faculty and students. In sum, attention to the interconnected dimensions of history, representation, perceptions, and behaviors may help an individual institution identify specific areas for improvement. Latina/o representation is key at all levels of the institution, not only among the various constituents that make up a campus but also in the curriculum, campus programming, and strategic planning initiatives. Further, campus planning and discussions about diversity must involve Latina/os on campus, otherwise Latina/o students, staff, and faculty will continue to feel "invisible" in predominantly White environments.

Institutions need to begin to foster a student-centered philosophy among faculty and staff that will result in transforming practices. A student-centered environment is one in which (1) faculty demonstrate an interest in students' academic and personal problems, (2) there are ample opportunities for interaction among faculty and students, (3) administrators consider student concerns when making policy, and (4) both administrators and faculty demonstrate sensitivity to the issues of students of color. As one Latina/o student said in a focus group, campus administrators "need to make an effort to come out and support us." At the same time Latina/o students struggle for recognition on predominantly White campuses, they remain committed to helping their schools create diverse learning environments and become inclusive communities.

## References

Aponte, Robert. 1997. Winds of change sweep nation as Latino population grows. *NEXO: The Newsletter of the Julian Samora Research Institute* 7 (winter): 1–17.

Astin, Alexander W. 1982. *Minorities in American higher education.* San Francisco: Jossey-Bass.

Carter, Deborah J., and Reginald Wilson. 1994. *Thirteenth annual status report on minorities in higher education.* Washington, DC: American Council on Education.

Chapa, Jorge. 1999. *Hopwood* effects and responses: The search for race-blind means of improving minority access to higher education. Paper presented at an invitational research conference sponsored by the American Council on Education, January, Washington, DC.

Chapa, Jorge, and Richard R. Valencia. 1993. Latino population growth, demographic characteristics, and educational stagnation: An examination of recent trends. *Hispanic Journal of Behavioral Sciences* 15:165–87.

Estrada, Leo. Anticipating the demographic future. 1988. *Change* 20, no. 3:14–19.

Hauptman, Arthur, and Patricia Smith. 1994. Financial aid strategies for improving minority student participation in higher education. In *Minorities in higher education,* edited by Manuel J. Justiz, Reginald Wilson, and L. G. Bjork, 78–106. Phoenix, AZ: Oryx Press and the American Council on Higher Education.

Hayes-Bautista, David B., Werner Schink, and Jorge Chapa. 1988. *The burden of support: Young Latinos in an aging society.* Stanford, CA: Stanford University Press.

Heller, Donald. 1997. Access to public higher education, 1976 to 1994: New evidence from an analysis of the states. Ph.D diss., Harvard University.

———. In press. A panel analysis of tuition prices and public college enrollments. *Review of Higher Education.*

Hurtado, Aida, David E. Hayes-Bautista, R. Burciaga Valdez, and Anthony C. R. Hernandez. 1992. *Redefining California: Latino social engagement in a multicultural society.* Los Angeles: UCLA Chicano Studies Research Center.

Hurtado, Sylvia. 1992. The campus racial climate: Contexts of conflict. *Journal of Higher Education* 63 (September/October): 539–69.

———. 1994. The institutional climate for talented Latino students. *Research in Higher Education* 35, no. 1: 21–41.

Hurtado, Sylvia, and Deborah Faye Carter. 1997. Effects of college transition and perceptions of the campus racial climate on Latino college students' sense of belonging. *Sociology of Education* 70 (October): 324–45.

Hurtado, Sylvia, Deborah Faye Carter, and Albert Spuler. 1996. Latino student transition to college: Assessing difficulties and factors in successful college adjustment. *Research in Higher Education* 37, no. 2: 135–57.

Hurtado, Sylvia, Karen Kurotsuchi Inkelas, Charlotte Briggs, and Byung-Shik Rhee. 1997. Differences in college access and choice among racial/ethnic groups: Identifying continuing barriers. *Research in Higher Education* 38, no. 1: 43–75.

Hurtado, Sylvia, Ricardo Maestas, Leon Hill, Karen Inkelas, Heather Wathington Cade, and Ellen Meader. 1998. *Perspectives on the climate for diversity: Findings and suggested recommendations for the campus community.* Ann Arbor, MI: Center for the Study of Higher and Postsecondary Education.

Hurtado, Sylvia, Jeffrey F. Milem, Alma Clayton-Pederson, and Walter A. Allen. 1999. *Enacting diverse learning environments: Improving the climate for racial/ethnic diversity in higher education.* ASHE-ERIC Report Series. Washington, DC: George Washington University Press.

Hurtado, Sylvia, and Heather Wathington Cade. 2001. Time for retreat or renewal? The impact of *Hopwood* on campus. In *The states and public higher education: Affordability, access, and accountability,* edited by Donald Heller. Baltimore, MD: Johns Hopkins University Press.

Lavin, David E., and Elliot Weininger. 1999, May. *New admissions policy and changing access to CUNY's senior and community colleges: What are the stakes?* New York: Higher Education Committee, New York City Council.

Lawrence, Charles R., III, and Mari J. Matsuda. 1997. *We won't go back: Making the case for affirmative action.* Boston: Houghton-Mifflin Company.

Orfield, Gary, Mark D. Bachmeier, David R. James, and Tamela Eitle. 1997. Deepening segregation in American public schools: A special report from the Harvard Project on School Desegregation. *Equity & Excellence in Education* 30, no. 2: 5–28.

Pallas, Aaron M., Gary Natriello, and B. L. McDill. 1989. The changing nature of the disadvantaged population: Current dimensions and future trends. *Educational Researcher* 18:16–22.

Rendon, Laura I., Romero Jalomo Jr., and Kathleen Garcia. 1994. The university and community college paradox: Why Latinos do not transfer. In *The educational achievement of Latinos: Barriers and successes,* edited by Aida Hurtado and Eugene E. Garcia, 227–58. Santa Cruz: University of California Latino Eligibility Study.

Richardson, Richard C., Jr. 1991. *Promoting fair college outcomes: Learning from the experiences of the past decade.* Denver, CO: Education Commission of the States.

University of California Latino Eligibility Task Force. 1993, November. *Latino student eligibility and participation in the University of California.* Report No. 2 of the Latino Eligibility Task Force. Santa Cruz, CA: Author.

Vobejda, Barbara. 1998. Hispanic youths outnumber Blacks. *Washington Post,* July 15, A02.

Williams, John B., III. 1997. *Race discrimination in public higher education.* Albany: State University of New York Press.

# CHAPTER 7

# New Challenges of Representing Asian American Students in U.S. Higher Education

## MITCHELL J. CHANG AND PETER N. KIANG

> I think my view of Asians changed . . . the whole model
> minority thinking that Asians are always more successful. I
> held that kind of resentment. . . . Generally, I am much
> more comfortable around Asians than I used to be. I don't
> view them as the "others" anymore.
>
> —U.S.-born White woman,
> 1999 graduate of UMass Boston

> Even when I was here two years, I still did not know what
> I really want or what I'm good in. But when I took the
> Asian American Studies courses, then it's like a light come
> in to define what really I am and what I want. I did not
> know that I would fight for justice. But when I learn those
> things, I say that's it! I want to help society to change.
> Those courses educate me for life, to see how society is
> structured and operates . . . It makes me think differently . . .
> If I do not take those courses, I will never understand who
> I really am or what I want to do in the future.
>
> —Cambodian American woman refugee,
> 1990 graduate of UMass Boston

These reflections on college learning by a U.S.-born White woman and
a female Cambodian American refugee exemplify how higher education serves
as an extraordinary setting for envisioning and (re)constructing the lives,
experiences, and circumstances of Asian Americans[1] and others in U.S. society. Post-secondary education during the past two decades has also played a

---

1. "Asian Americans" is used here to refer broadly to individuals of Asian descent
living in the United States.

remarkable social role, ideologically and structurally, in reflecting and repro-
ducing popular views and images of Asian Americans. Unlike the 1980s,
however, when the representation and critique of the model minority image
of Asian Americans in higher education were pervasive focal points—including the chapter by Sucheng Chan and Ling-chi Wang (1991) in Philip G.
Altbach and Kofi Lomotey's *The Racial Crisis in American Higher Education*—the multiple images of Asian American college and university students
moving into the twenty-first century resist reduction to simple stereotypes.

Without a doubt, images still persist of highly talented students like Yat-
pang Au who, despite his stellar academic record and array of extracurricular
activities, was rejected for undergraduate admission at the University of
California, Berkeley in 1987. A decade before California's Proposition 209,
the media simplistically depicted him as a "victim" of affirmative action, with
the implication that Asian Americans as a group, therefore, opposed these
policies (Takagi 1992, 68). Less widely portrayed but equally important,
however, are students like York Chang, the student government president at
the University of California, Los Angeles, who fought to retain race-sensitive
admissions policies in the wake of Proposition 209.

Given this spectrum of competing racial images, we argue that popular
and oversimplified characterizations of Asian Americans—coupled with the
pervasive absence of substantive learning opportunities about Asian Americans at all levels of education—have resulted in widespread misunderstand-
ings and mis/disinformation about this very diverse group. This condition has
further led to continuing policies and practices in higher education that are,
at worst, detrimental toward and, at best, silent about the complex and pressing realities of Asian Americans. This chapter challenges how higher education institutions construct and assume monolithic, racialized images about
Asian Americans. We are not the first to make this argument and, regrettably,
do not expect to be the last—at least not until more appropriate educational
policies and more authentic documentation of Asian American lives emerge
in U.S. colleges and universities.

We recognize the important contributions, not only of Chan and Wang's
chapter (1991), but also of many other significant studies about Asian Americans in higher education produced during the 1990s. These works fall, broadly,
into five categories:

1. National demographic portraits and profiles commissioned by foundations or leading professional associations such as the American Council on
Education (ACE) and Association of American Colleges and Universities
(AAC&U) to address the dearth of available information about Asian Americans in higher education (e.g., Hune 1997; Hune and Chan 1997; Suzuki
1990).

2. Integrative works on Asian American contemporary issues, particularly dynamics of race and affirmative action, for example, across the domains of both K-12 and higher education (Ancheta 1998; Fong 1998; Nakanishi and Nishida 1995; Takagi 1992; U.S. Commission 1992; Weinberg 1997).

3. Case studies from particular campuses that analyze individual or comparative groups of Asian American students using quantitative and/or qualitative methods. Though localized, these studies are particularly important in presenting voices and analyses that reflect the college experiences of South and Southeast Asian American students (Gupta 1998; Kiang 1993, 1996b).

4. Discussions of curricular and pedagogical theory and practice in the academic field of Asian American Studies, often presented in relation to Asian American student development (Hirabayashi 1997; Kiang 1998).

5. Personal narratives capturing the experiences of Asian American students and, increasingly, of Asian American faculty, often in relation to themes of survival and persistence in the academy (e.g., Kiang 2000; Matsuda 1996; Nguyen and Halpern 1989; for outstanding Latina/o narratives, see also Padilla 1997; Trueba et al. 2000).

Where appropriate, we draw on these works as illustrative examples. We also draw on our original research to suggest ways for colleges and universities to intervene productively in overcoming monolithic characterizations of Asian Americans in higher education.

## Lessons from a Racialized History

In pathbreaking recent works of history and cultural politics, Jack Tchen (1999) and Robert Lee (1999) clearly document how monolithic and ubiquitous historic representations of Asian Americans have tended to be but also how socially constructed and unstable. Race-based characterizations and the process of racialization (Omi and Winant 1986) are shaped by multiple motives which are profoundly contextual and often not readily apparent. Consider, for example, the bombing of Pearl Harbor on December 7, 1941, when, as Takaki (1989) notes, World War II "came crashing down on Asian-American communities from Hawaii to New York . . . pulling Filipinos, Koreans, Asian Indians, Chinese, and Japanese into a whirlpool of chaos and change" (357). In this context, the monolithic image of Asian Americans as economic parasites and perpetual foreigners quickly diversified, thereby enabling selected Asian ethnic groups to find temporary relief from labor discrimination and systematic exclusion. According to Takaki, for example, Chinese Americans, previously maligned as the "heathen Chinee," were suddenly regarded as friends and allies in a heroic common effort against the "Japs" (370). In stark contrast, Japanese Americans were venomously vilified as disloyal, treacherous, and untrustworthy. These characterizations, the Commission on Wartime Relocation and Internment of Civilians reported, were fueled by "race prejudice, war hysteria, and a failure of political leadership" (qtd. in Maki, Kitano, and Berthold 1999, 111) and were subsequently used to justify the detention and incarceration of over 110,000 Japanese Americans in U.S. concentration camps between 1942 and 1945 although no confirmatory evidence was ever presented (*Report* 1999).

This obvious historic example suggests that racialized images of Asian Americans can change literally overnight from one extreme to another, attesting to the power of racism and the fragility of race relations in the United States. In this case, Asian Americans were simultaneously characterized as both good and evil, as both friend and enemy. Previously negative monolithic images of Asian Americans were modified for greater precision in targeting specific Asian ethnic groups to achieve collective, albeit unconstitutional, consensus for racist hysteria and economic greed.

Furthermore, what may seem to be positive characterizations do not necessarily serve the best interests of those groups being characterized. For example, the redefined status of Filipino, Korean, Asian Indian, and Chinese American groups as allies eligible for U.S. citizenship in the post–World War II era resulted from neither a sudden national interest in their civil rights nor a desire to remedy the historical injustices perpetrated against them. If those had been the motivating factors rather than powerful, well-documented geopolitical forces and economic interests (Takaki 1989), the civil rights movement of the 1960s would not have produced such ground-breaking gains for Asian American communities.

We cite this World War II example, although it is more than half a century old, because it directly informs our understanding of racialized characterizations of Asian Americans in the late 1990s when "enemy" images of Japanese Americans during World War II (and Cold War images of "red Chinese") are inverted and reimposed on Chinese Americans as a result of national political and ideological contradictions related both to partisan campaign financing and U.S.-China relations (G. Chang 2000). In this context, a Taiwan-born U.S. citizen and nuclear physicist, Wen Ho Lee, was fired from his position at Los Alamos National Laboratory in March 1999 for allegedly leaking secrets about U.S. nuclear weapons to China, although no confirmatory evidence was ever presented and criminal charges were never initiated (*Report* 1999). A high-ranking participant in the investigation of the security leak admitted that "Mr. Lee's ethnicity was a major factor" in his being singled out for investigation and subsequent dismissal (Loeb 1999, 5).

This case is relevant to our discussion of Asian Americans in higher education because, for many Asian Americans in the sciences, research laboratories like Los Alamos are simply an extension of the government/military-funded research environments operating within universities. Furthermore, the harsh reality of Lee's case directly challenges a dominant, continuing tendency in higher education race-oriented policy research to report aggregate data for Asian American educational achievement, while ignoring the qualitative impact of racialization on their lives. For example, with no commentary and virtually no other mention of Asian Americans in their widely cited recent study, Bowen and Bok (1998) present Asian Americans as having the highest graduation rates of all racial groups after six years, both for students who graduated from the same institution they entered during their first year and for students who transferred from their initial school and graduated elsewhere (56). Similarly, in his recent review of national academic achievement data for a volume on racial diversity and higher education, Miller (1999) concludes:

> Asians are significantly better positioned than non-Asian minorities to enter and perform very well at selective colleges and universities. As a result, they are also better positioned on graduation to secure desirable entry-level professional jobs—jobs that offer career avenues to a wide variety of executive and other leadership positions in our society. (47)

Miller's facile analysis fails to recognize or represent the context in which Asian Americans like Wen Ho Lee—despite their academic achievement and status—are counter-positioned in racialized ways that specifically restrict their leadership and aggravate their insecurity, both in research environments like Los Alamos and in the larger society. Lee's personal and professional vulnerability to racialization directly contradicts Miller's image and assumptions about Asian American "security." Furthermore, though difficult to document, we hypothesize that other Asian Americans working or studying in comparable research settings, either in higher education or in other sectors, identify strongly with Lee's vulnerability because of their own racialization.

Building on these preliminary examples, we suggest that the construction of popular images of Asian Americans has a long history in the United States. It is intentional, embedded with specific motives, and linked to policy formation. Such images are also unstable, often contradictory, and subject to rapid change. It is clear that simplistic characterizations of Asian American college students and their experiences hinder rather than advance public understanding of this group. We seek to examine more closely images of Asian Americans in higher education, beginning with the most heavily critiqued yet doggedly persistent of those characterizations—the "model minority." This examination, we hope, will result in a more complex and accurate portrayal of Asian American student experiences and circumstances.

## Dismantling the Monolithic Image

During the 1980s, popular opinion-shaping media like the *New York Times Magazine* and *Time* consistently characterized Asian American students as "whiz kids" who are "going to the head of the class" and winning all "those prizes" (Brand 1987; Butterfield 1986; Graubard 1988). Despite two decades of research and publication by scholars who have critiqued these images as oversimplifications (Chun 1980; Hsia 1988; Hune 1997; Suzuki 1990), the dominance of the "model minority" image for Asian Americans in higher education has been remarkable. Here are some characteristics of the Asian American population that challenge this characterization.

Although Asian Americans still represent a small proportion of the total U.S. population, their growth has been steady and significant, nearly doubling in each of the last two decades. The U.S. Bureau of the Census reported that the Asian American population increased from 1,356,638 in 1970 to 3,726,440 in 1980 (a 174.7 percent change) and to 7,273,662 by 1990 (a 95.2 percent change from 1980–90). For 1990–96, the Census Bureau predicted an increase of 32.5 percent, with comparable growth rates expected to continue beyond the millennium.

The growth from 1980 to 1999 also dramatically diversified the ethnic composition of the Asian American population. Immigration, refugee resettlement, and higher than average birth rates for Asian Indians, Koreans, Vietnamese, Laotians, Cambodians, and Hmongs have injected much greater complexity within the population. One example of this diversification is in sharply disparate poverty levels. While the overall poverty rate for all Asian Americans in 1990, as reported by the U.S. Bureau of the Census, was 14.1 percent, compared to 9.2 percent for Whites and 13.1 percent for the total U.S. population, the rates for some Asian American ethnic groups were much higher. For example, the poverty rates were 17.1 percent for Pacific Islanders, 25.7 percent for Vietnamese, 34.7 percent for Laotians, 42.6 percent for Cambodians, and 63.6 percent for Hmongs. Southeast Asian Americans have had higher poverty rates than other immigrant groups, in large part because they nearly always arrived as refugees. Because of the monolithic racialization of Asian Americans, however, the disparity in Asian American poverty rates is often wrongly overlooked when colleges and universities design financial aid, outreach, and admissions programs for low-income students. Disaggregating Asian American data is important to provide a more accurate account of their lives and circumstances in higher education and the larger society. Disaggregated profiles from the 2000 census by factors such as ethnicity, generation, and migration status, for example, will be essential. (See also Villalpando and Delgado Bernal, this volume.)

Basic population growth has contributed to the nationwide increase in Asian American student enrollment in higher education; however, Asian

Americans still comprise only a small fraction of the nation's college enroll-ment. The U.S. Department of Education's National Center for Education Sta-tistics reported that Asian Americans in U.S. undergraduate education nearly doubled from 3.2 percent of the total 1984 undergraduate population to about 5.6 percent in 1995. However, this figure masks a diverse and complex reality.

Shirley Hune and Kenyon Chan (1997) recently documented Asian American demographic and educational trends in a comprehensive report for the American Council on Education. By drawing from national data and by carefully attending to important variabilities within and between groups, they effectively illustrated the complexity, fluidity, and expansiveness of the popu-lation at all levels of the educational pipeline. Among their many important findings is that 55.1 percent of all Asian Americans between ages eighteen and twenty-four were enrolled in college during 1990, compared to 34.4 percent for the total population, 36.8 percent for Whites, 22.9 percent for Latina/os, 27.1 percent for African Americans, and 21.6 percent for American Indians—in short, almost double the rate for other people of color. These excellent enrollment rates, however, were distributed unevenly within ethnic groups. Chinese, Japanese, Asian Indian, and Korean Americans were twice as likely as Hmong, Guamanian, Samoan, Hawaiian, and Laotian Americans to be enrolled in college. The 1990 college enrollment rates ranged from a high of 66.5 percent for Chinese Americans to a low of 26.3 percent for Laotian Americans (Hune and Chan 1997). Thus, the data suggest that as a whole, Asian Americans are enrolling in higher education at a brisk rate but that only some ethnic groups are enrolling at above-national average rates. (See also Solmon, Solmon and Schiff, this volume.)

The monolithic image of Asian Americans also breaks up when we con-sider selected fields of study. Asian American students are often criticized as too academically "narrow," interested only in mathematics and applied sci-ences. However, Hune and Chan (1997) found that Asian Americans who earned baccalaureate degrees in 1994 did so in a broad range of fields, be-ginning with business, the most popular major for all undergraduates. While 32 percent of Asian Americans majored in engineering and the sciences, 22.4 percent majored in business, and 25.9 percent chose the social sciences and the humanities. Although only 5.5 percent chose the health fields and 4.1 percent the arts, these percentages mirror those of all degree earners in those two fields of study. Because American-born and middle-class Asian Ameri-cans are less likely to choose mathematics and applied science careers (Hsia 1988), Chan and Hune projected that each new generation of American-born Asian Americans will broaden the range of their majors even further.

Another popular image of Asian American students from the 1980s is that they typically enroll in selective and elite colleges and universities. This char-acterization was largely fueled by steady increases in the number of Asian American applicants and students enrolled in a few universities concentrated in

California and New England. Although this growth has not abated, it should be placed into perspective. In their annual rank ordering of degree-producing institutions for students of color, *Black Issues in Higher Education* (1998) identified the institutions that granted the most baccalaureate degrees to Asian Americans in 1996. Asian Americans received 25 percent of the total baccalaureate degrees (433) granted that year by Stanford, 18.3 percent of Harvard's (330), 30.7 percent of MIT's (376), and 20.2 percent of Columbia's (280). These private Research I universities, commonly regarded as "elite" institutions, were among the top forty-nine schools awarding baccalaureates to Asian Americans; but none of them placed in the top thirty.

The top producer in 1996, the University of Hawaii at Manoa, granted 2,104 degrees—or 75.6 percent of its total baccalaureate degrees—to Asian Americans, a significantly greater number than the sum awarded to Asian Americans by all four elite private institutions. The fifth highest that year, San Francisco State University, and the seventh, San Jose State University, granted 1,168 (29.8 percent) and 986 (25.8 percent) degrees respectively. With the high concentration of Asian Americans in California, the selective University of California (UC) campuses were, as expected, well represented on the *Black Issues in Higher Education* list. UC Berkeley, Los Angeles, and Irvine ranked second, third, and fourth respectively. Other UC campuses in the top ten included Davis (eighth) and San Diego (ninth). California State University, Long Beach, was tenth; the University of Washington, sixth.

These rankings, compiled yearly by *Black Issues,* suggest that Asian American students enrolled in a variety of institutional types, particularly public institutions, in the Northeast and on the West Coast where Asian Americans are concentrated. The list also suggests that, while an impressive number of Asian American students earn degrees from elite institutions, a much larger number graduate from less selective schools. In fact, 40 percent of Asian Americans in higher education in 1995 were enrolled in two-year institutions compared to 37 percent for White students (Hune and Chan, 1997, Table 4, "Total Enrollment in Higher Education by Type of Institution and Race/Ethnicity: Selected Years, Fall 1984 to Fall 1995"). Moreover, the large numbers of Asian American students who are unprepared for college and need remedial work challenge notions that they tend to be highly competitive and successful college applicants. In the California State University (CSU) system, for example, of the entering Asian American first-year students in 1999, 62 percent needed remedial work in English and 41 percent needed remedial work in mathematics (Weiss 2000). Although these rates have dropped from the previous year, the big urban campuses tend to have even higher percentages of first-year students who must enroll in remedial classes because they failed entry-level math or English placement tests.

These aspects of undergraduate Asian American diversity and complexity are only a fraction of the work that needs to be done to dismantle the monolithic image. Such work includes the full educational pipeline from preschool through graduate and professional education. But it is enough to reinforce that message of scholarly colleagues who have insisted for two decades that Asian Americans and their experiences in higher education are extremely varied and cannot be reduced to simplistic, one-dimensional categories.

Despite this growing body of scholarly research, however, simple monolithic characterizations have endured in part because they are useful for advancing political agendas. The influx of Asian American students into the nation's educational system—particularly at elite schools and in states like California and New York which have major cultural, political, and economic influence on the nation as a whole—has elevated their political significance. As such, Asian Americans now play an important role in high-stake, hot-button social issues. Advocates on either extreme of a particular educational issue or cause have effectively used one-sided characterizations of Asian Americans to make a case for their political position. The next section examines one such case and the costs that Asian American students and their communities pay for politically contrived and conflicting characterizations.

## Conflicting Characterizations and Costs

The recognition of diversity is the recognition of contradictory images. While many Asian American high school students receive 4.0 grade point averages, graduate as valedictorians, and enroll at Harvard or Stanford, even more barely pass high school, enroll at local community colleges, or never participate in postsecondary institutions. Both images are true—facets of the reality of the stratified U.S. educational system intersecting with the fundamental diversity of Asian American experiences and circumstances. For example, in Boston, a city renowned for its universities, 32 percent of the adult Asian American population in 1990 had earned a bachelor's degree or higher, compared to 37 percent of the White population and 14 percent of the Black population. But an even higher percentage of Asian American adults (38 percent) had less than a twelfth-grade education, compared with 19 percent Whites and 33 percent Blacks (Watanabe 1996).

Still, in educational debates, policymakers and politicians can and do use Asian American students' experiences and circumstances as compelling examples on both sides of a debate, a strategy that conveniently allows advocates to make a case for their individual political or ideological positions. One notable example concerns the debate over affirmative action. (See also Anderson, this volume.) Asian Americans have been simultaneously portrayed as either opponents or supporters of racial remedies. In *The Retreat from Race,* Dana Takagi (1992) documented how opponents of affirmative action regularly characterized Asian American students and communities as victims of those policies and practices. According to Takagi, opponents used the Asian American admissions controversy, whereby some of the nation's most selective institutions were accused of placing a quota to limit the enrollment of Asian American students in the late eighties, as "an important launching pad for renewed scrutiny of affirmative action" (52). Neoconservatives, Takagi argues, cast the admissions controversy as another example of how affirmative action discriminated against those Asian American and White students who can compete on the basis of merit. In contrast, most Asian American activists did not view the controversy as a problem with affirmative action or diversity but framed it as a straightforward case of discrimination.

Nevertheless, the neoconservative message resonated with many Asian Americans, and indeed there are Asian American groups who actively seek to dismantle affirmative action. In a case decided in 1999, for example, Chinese American families successfully sued Lowell High School, a selective magnet school in San Francisco and the top feeder school into the University of California system, over its affirmative action practices (J. Chang 1999).

Similarly, supporters of affirmative action can likewise conveniently portray Asian American students and communities as supporters and beneficiaries of race-sensitive interventions. They can, for example, cite an incident that coincidentally occurred at a different Lowell High School (Lowell, Massachusetts) in 1998. In this example, Southeast Asian and Latina/o students and parents accused guidance counselors and administrators of discriminatory college advising, scholarship recommendations, and disciplinary punishment, which allegedly reduced the numbers of these ethnic students who had access to higher education opportunities (Massachusetts 1998).

Supporters can also evoke a more recent example whereby Asian American students along with Black, Latino/a students filed a civil rights lawsuit in March 1999 against the University of California at Berkeley, concerning the admissions policies and procedures that that university adopted after the ban on affirmative action (*Rios et al. vs. The Regents of the University of California;* case #C 99-0525 SI). Assisting the students in this class-action lawsuit is a coalition of civil rights groups, including the Asian Pacific American Legal Center, Mexican American Legal Defense and Educational Fund, and NAACP Legal Defense and Educational Fund, among others. The plaintiffs had charged that UC Berkeley's admissions process following the ban, which no longer considered the race of applicants, disproportionately denies to qualified minority applicants, without adequate educational justification, an equal opportunity to compete for admission to undergraduate studies. Following tremendous protest and national pressure, the University of California Board of Regents unanimously announced on May 16, 2001 that they adopted a resolution which rescinded their previous ban of affirmative action efforts.

Surely, as more diverse images of Asian Americans emerge due in large part to the growing body of scholarship, competing images will naturally surface. What is interesting, as the above case suggests and as documented elsewhere in this chapter, is that the dismantling of the monolithic image coupled with Asian Americans' ascending political clout have provided both sides of a controversial educational issue with politically expedient examples to advance their competing positions. Whether Asian American students are showcased as overrepresented in elite private education or in need of remedial public education, or whether they are portrayed as student activists or politically apathetic, racialized characterizations of Asian Americans are both purposeful and pointed. Like the stereotypes that sprang up in the wake of Pearl Harbor, today's Asian American students can be simultaneously upheld as heroes and vilified as villains according to political interests.

Perhaps more importantly, as sociologist Mia Tuan (1998) clearly demonstrates, racialization results in a real and substantial cost to Asian Americans and other communities of color, even if a monolithic characterization seems favorable at any particular moment. For example, when educators view Asian American students as academic superstars, their institutions may be more reluctant to provide educational services to those students, particularly immigrants, who may need additional assistance to improve their language skills. Conversely, when educators view Asian American students as a population needing remedial attention to learn English, they are less likely to encourage those students to pursue academic majors or professions that demand strong verbal, writing, or social skills. Without these skills, Asian American students may be barred from future leadership roles.

Similarly, the conflicting characterizations of Asian American students as either opponents or supporters of racial remedies also have serious policy implications. Those who seek to end affirmative action have aligned Asian American students with their White counterparts as victims of race-based policies and practices (D'Souza 1991). This characterization often wrongly ignores, perhaps intentionally, the continual importance of race-based policies in protecting Asian Americans against hate crimes, job discrimination, labor exploitation, anti-immigrant sentiment, segregation, and other civil rights-related interests. Moreover, such a characterization fails to acknowledge that Asian Americans have indeed benefited from affirmative action.

Interestingly, in 1997, John Ready, who is White, filed a lawsuit against the University of Wisconsin's Board of Regents, charging that the university had violated Title VII of the Civil Rights Act of 1964 when he was passed over in favor of an Asian American man for a tenure-track job teaching sculpture on the La Crosse campus (Schneider 1999). The university contended that its affirmative action plan justified the use of race as a determining factor in this faculty-hiring decision. Although the U.S. district court ruled in Ready's favor in the fall of 1999, the judge did not address the lawfulness of the plan itself. This example shows that, in some cases, Asian

Americans are the direct beneficiaries of affirmative action practices and subsequently, have a vested interest in retaining such policies.

By contrast, characterizing Asian Americans as ardent supporters of 1960s-style civil rights fails to recognize both the changing racial landscape of American society (particularly dramatic growth in Asian and Latina/o communities) and the fundamental limitations of a civil rights paradigm framed in Black/White terms. For example, Takagi (1996) argues that the educational profile of Asian Americans as reviewed earlier, is now pivotal in shaping the popular and legal understanding of civil rights, particularly the concept that "parity" is the best measure of equality. Although Asian Americans may be said to have achieved parity to Whites in undergraduate enrollment, they still experience systemic discrimination and racial barriers within and beyond campus walls. The nation's traditional civil rights leadership has been slow or unclear in articulating an inclusive, persuasive vision for Asian American partnership in civil rights struggles. Instead, there is a tendency to marginalize or render invisible Asian American concerns and to rely on Black/White frameworks that focus on parity as a primary goal (Cho 1996). Failure to recognize the need to rearticulate and reenvision a civil rights agenda that accounts for rapidly changing racial landscapes and circumstances inevitably hastens the demise of traditionally defined civil rights policies and programs in the United States.

Including Asian Americans in educational debates is an important first step toward understanding new multicultural realities and moving beyond the outdated Black/White paradigm that still drives the civil rights agenda. Takagi (1994) argues that including group experiences that have been overlooked or even intentionally omitted from historical narratives, like those of Asian Americans, forces us to confront the multiethnic realities of post-civil rights politics. The act of "including" Asian Americans in racial politics and educational debates is, however, a very delicate matter as illustrated above. Because Asian American experiences can be cast to advance certain positions, it is equally important, according to Takagi, to regularly challenge and analyze the social and political interests and historical conditions under which Asian American experiences are evoked in social and political controversies. Accordingly, the intent and purpose of each image are as important as its accuracy in portraying Asian American lives, experiences, and circumstances.

## The Role and Responsibility of Higher Education

Institutions of higher education have an important civic role and responsibility as knowledge producers and interpreters to intervene in the cycle of distortion. But where can the cycle be disrupted? How can more accurate portrayals and authentic perspectives about Asian Americans be identified or produced? Who is doing this essential work in universities? In most institutions, we find that Asian American students are still the primary agents of these changes, even though more than three decades have passed since students first demanded ethnic studies and Asian American studies at San Francisco State College (Umemoto 1989). At this writing in fall 1999, for example, ten Asian American students from the University of Texas-Austin are on trial for misdemeanor charges of criminal trespassing after they refused to leave a campus building when they demanded to speak with the interim dean of the College of Liberal Arts about her failure to appoint a director for their university's new Asian American studies program. In an open letter about the case, political scientist Pei-te Lien, a close observer of trends in Asian American political mobilization nationally, explained:

> The students took it upon themselves to change the status quo of the wholesale denial of their own identity and place in America. Like their counterparts at the University of California at Berkeley and at Columbia University [who also conducted sit-ins for ethnic studies in 1998–99], they were arrested after a peaceful sit-in demanding an equal right to learn about themselves as Americans of Asian ancestry. Unlike the arrested students on these two campuses, the ten students at UT-Austin will soon make history when they go on trial because their President refused to drop the misdemeanor charges against them. (e-mail communication, 3 October 1999)

The struggles at campuses like UT-Austin in the South or comparable demands for Asian American studies programs at Northwestern University and the University of Illinois-Urbana Champaign in the Midwest are important indicators, not only of the increased presence of Asian American students in regions other than the West and East coasts—a significant change in the past thirty years—but also of students' unfulfilled demands for a relevant curriculum—a continuing theme over the same period.

Reflecting on teaching introductory Asian American studies courses for the past twenty years at several East Coast colleges and universities, Jean Wu recently observed how similar the student writings are across time, both in expressing excitement about the educational power of Asian American studies and in questioning why they had so little previous exposure to such courses in the rest of their college or high school curricula (personal communication, 21 May 1999). Despite frequent marginalization by institutional racism in universities, ethnic studies programs including, but not limited to, Asian American studies have persevered and their educational significance is becoming increasingly apparent. The historical role and fundamental contributions of ethnic studies have been to transform academic culture—how the curriculum is defined and represented, the nature of scholarship, the practice and methods of research, expectations for pedagogy, the empowerment of diverse students, and the engagement with communities. The role and contributions of ethnic studies are closely aligned with current calls for improving the civic and social relevance of undergraduate education. (See also Altbach, Lomotey, and Rivers, this volume.)

The recent blue-ribbon report by the Kellogg Commission on the Future of State and Land-Grant Universities (1999), for example, sounds an urgent, millennial call for public higher education institutions to become "engaged" by responding to the diverse demographic profiles of students, by connecting students' learning with real-world research and practice, and by allocating resources to address the critical issues of communities. Indeed, these are exactly the same powerful commitments that ethnic studies programs have sustained and institutionalized within universities over the past thirty years.

Though leaders and funders involved with higher education innovation rarely embrace or recognize Asian American studies and other ethnic studies, these programs exemplify how various strands of current best practice in higher education reform—from service-learning and faculty professional outreach to institutional engagement and diversity research—can be integrated holistically and sustained meaningfully, together with core commitments to inspirational teaching, critical scholarship, and curricular transformation (Arches et al. 1997). We believe that colleges and universities are not only critical sites for engaging and struggling with important issues like racial politics, but are also locales where lives and relationships can be transformed positively and proactively. In recognizing that Asian American studies holds extraordinary transformative possibilities and that demands for it continue to represent a primary focus of Asian American students at U.S. colleges and universities, we devote the remainder of this chapter to a discussion of trends and lessons from the field of Asian American studies. This discussion also updates the work of Chan and Wang (1991), who addressed the transformative intentions and benefits of ethnic studies and Asian American studies in *The Racial Crisis in American Higher Education* (Altbach and Lomotey 1991).

## The Field of Asian American Studies

Asian American studies is an interdisciplinary academic field which documents and interprets the histories, identities, social formations, contributions, and contemporary concerns of Asian and Pacific Americans and their communities in the United States. The field has institutional roots nationally in the campus ethnic studies movements of the late 1960s (including Black studies, Chicano and Puerto Rican studies, etc.) when the country's first departments and programs in Asian American studies were established at West Coast universities (San Francisco State University, UC Berkeley, UCLA, the University of Washington, etc.). As such, Asian American studies is grounded in intellectual traditions and sociocultural interests distinct from either Asian studies or American studies area programs, although linkages to both have been important to forge campus-by-campus and through national professional associations.

More recently, the sweeping demographic changes of the 1980s and 1990s have driven the dramatic expansion of new Asian American studies programs at institutions of all ranks across the country, from the Ivy League (Cornell, University of Pennsylvania, Columbia, etc.) to the Big Ten (University of Michigan, University of Wisconsin, etc.) to small liberal arts institutions (Loyola Marymount, Oberlin, Wesleyan, etc.) to urban public and private colleges and universities (Queens College, Seattle Central Community College, New York University, etc.) and even some public and private high schools, including Berkeley High (CA), Brookline High (MA), and Milton Academy (MA).

Students organize to establish and expand Asian American studies in part because they recognize its contributions in developing theories, methods, and empirical studies that engage critical questions in the social sciences, humanities, and various professional fields. These include:

- The social, cultural, economic, political, religious, and environmental consequences of massive demographic shifts within the U.S. population during the past thirty years due to immigration and refugee resettlement—40 percent of which has come from Asia.
- The racialization of individuals and groups as well as the interrelationships among and between various racial groups historically and currently, who do not fit the bipolar, White-Black paradigm of race relations.
- The economic, political, social, and cultural changes resulting from the globalization of capital, labor, information, and popular media as well as the ways in which transnational, diasporic populations such as Indian, Chinese, and Vietnamese communities in the United States are products of and agents in that globalization process.
- The social and psychological impacts of traumatic experiences and healing practices, and their relationships to dynamics of identity and culture, as exemplified by the situations of Cambodian and Vietnamese refugee survivors and their families.
- The critical and commercial success of writers, designers, and musicians whose cultural works have incorporated Asian and Asian American forms, traditions, aesthetics, and themes in original and powerful ways.

In these and numerous other academic areas, Asian American studies scholars are making significant intellectual contributions within and across a wide range of disciplines and professions. Furthermore, because of its democratizing educational commitments, the field of Asian American studies has also made important contributions to the development of exemplary principles and practices for general education within the academy. These include:

- Demonstrating the richness of interdisciplinary approaches to teaching and learning as well as for research.
- Developing pedagogical theories and practices that respond effectively to the needs of diverse student populations.
- Enabling students of all backgrounds to develop the critical thinking skills and sensibilities essential for community-building, community service, and social responsibility.
- Preparing students to function fully and comfortably in a multiracial, multicultural society.
- Integrating instruction in the classroom with practices of mentoring and role modeling outside of the classroom to address the holistic, social, and academic needs of students.

Despite its contributions and rapid growth, however, the field of Asian American studies is still far from transforming higher education. For example, in a review of undergraduate course catalogues for nineteen public higher education institutions in Massachusetts in 1996 (eleven community colleges, four state colleges, and four state universities), Kiang and Wong (1996) counted a total of 15,318 courses offered. Of that total, they identified 180 as Asian studies—mainly language and literature classes—and 116 as multicultural studies courses which might include Asian American content. Only eight courses (0.05 percent) were actual Asian American studies courses, six of which were offered at UMass Boston. The Massachusetts data described a reality in which Asian American studies courses were completely or nearly absent from the formal curriculum of all public colleges and universities across the state.

The often-contentious development and instability of Asian American studies programs observed on many college campuses across the country have been linked to what scholars have called a systematic "institutional undermining" of ethnic studies (M. Chang 1999; Hirabayashi 1998; Hu-Dehart 1995). However, substantive commitments to Asian American studies produce learning that is enormous and lasting. Although there are no data available nationally about the long-term impact of Asian American studies, a recent quantitative and qualitative study by Kiang (1999) at one campus found that alumni who had taken at least one Asian American studies course before graduating between 1987 and 1999 reported that their Asian American studies courses had "much" or "very much" increased their understanding of the immigrant experience (91 percent), raised their awareness of racial stereotypes (86 percent), enabled them to make friends with people different from their own backgrounds (70 percent), and helped them interact more comfortably with Asian Americans (83 percent). For nonresidential university settings in which student attitudes and competencies related to diversity are largely developed in the classroom, these are powerful effects.

While these positive impacts cut across all groups, regardless of race, gender, number of courses taken, or year of graduation, Asian American alumni specifically targeted increased identity awareness (becoming more aware of who they are in U.S. society) as being nearly as powerful as their gains in social awareness through learning about the immigrant experience and racial stereotyping. Furthermore, when the responses of Asian American alumni are differentiated by gender, results suggest that Asian American studies may also have specific effects that enable Asian American women and men to redefine traditional gender roles and relationships outside of school. Men reported that the courses had a strong impact on their attitudes toward family while women reported significant effects from Asian American studies courses on their jobs and careers. Other domains of impact showed little variation by gender. These striking results suggest that Asian American studies may be important aids by which Asian American students and alumni develop social awareness and clear identities and also redefine traditional gender roles and relationships.

Qualitative data from interviews consistently supported the survey results in illustrating the long-term impact of Asian American studies across both race and many dimensions of learning for Asian American and non-Asian alumni. Alumni interviewed for the study reported that they regularly referred to and applied what they had learned in these courses. For example, many drew on their knowledge about Southeast Asian refugee resettlement to interpret and understand the refugee crisis facing ethnic Albanians in Kosovo and Yugoslavia. These conscious connections reflect their continuing capacities to apply lessons and perspectives from their Asian American studies coursework to changing contexts, populations, and issues in complex and nonracialized ways. Interviewees also consistently provided concrete examples about how this educational opportunity enabled them to become better educators, policy makers, community leaders, care providers, friends, family members, and neighbors. Such lessons and skills could not be more appropriate, valuable, or urgently needed in a society that is currently experiencing tremendous demographic, cultural, and technological shifts. Thus, when colleges and universities make a substantial and sustained commitment to Asian American studies, they elevate their capacity to transform lives and relationships in positive, meaningful, and proactive ways.

## Conclusions

In referring to his bicultural awareness or "double consciousness" within both African American and White majority societies, W. E. B. Du Bois asserted: "I view them [White Americans] from unusual points of vantage. Not as a foreigner do I come, for I am native, not foreign, but bone of their thought and flesh of their language. Mine is not the knowledge of the traveler or the colonial composite of dear memories, words and wonder" (qtd. in Fine et al. 1977, vii).

In contrast, non-Asians cannot usually claim vantage points in relation to Asian American voices, contexts, and histories that are comparable in consciousness, intimacy, and experience to Du Bois's experience. Bowen and Bok (1998) hint at this social distance—noting with surprise that the percentage of White college matriculants who knew well two or more Black peers (56 percent) was almost the same as those who knew well two or more Asian peers (58 percent)—even though Asians far outnumbered Blacks on these campuses (233). This distance from Asian Americans in universities functions for all racial groups, including many Asian Americans themselves (Liu 1998). This social distance intensifies when a lack of Asian American studies in the curriculum prevents students from learning in more substantial, complex ways about Asian American experiences and circumstances.

In this light, Kiang's (1999) findings and the educational benefits of Asian American studies take on even greater significance. If 70 percent who take an Asian American studies course can make friends with people different from their own backgrounds and 83 percent can interact more comfortably with Asian Americans, then it seems clear that curricular and pedagogical commitments effectively reduce students' academic and social distance from Asian Americans.

Our nation and its institutions of higher education continue to suffer "double unconsciousness" in understanding and representing Asian Americans. Charles Aaron (1999) uses this term to depict, somewhat ironically, the inversion of Du Bois's double consciousness in which individuals and groups live under a illusion of "oneness," based on denying the power and influence of racism in society and in their own lives. Historically and currently, the acceptance and internalization of racialized characterizations of Asian Americans contribute to the pervasive illusion that Asian American experiences and circumstances fit nicely under one label. This delusion is sustained by the habitual denial of racism. In this chapter, we not only challenge the invalid assumptions that frame data and images of Asian Americans in monolithic, albeit competing, ways which have contributed to this double unconsciousness, but also, and more importantly, we criticize the cynical self-interests that underlie such image manipulation and exact real costs from the Asian American community, especially in higher education institutions where these complex dynamics play out for better or worse. Finally, we show that institutional commitment to Asian American studies overcomes double unconsciousness by disrupting the manipulation and distortion of Asian American images, replacing them with more accurate portrayals and perspectives, and transforming institutions, individuals, and relationships.

Yet just as students and scholars in Asian American studies critique public stereotypes in portraying Asian Americans, they must also examine the limitations of their own visions and take greater collective responsibility for transforming the nation's higher educational system, including its systemic engagement with K-12 education and with Asian American communities. The racial crisis in U.S. higher education does not begin or end inside university walls. Neither should the commitments of Asian Americans, in all their complexity and with all their contradictions.

## References

Aaron, Charles. 1999. Black like them. *Utne Reader* (March–April): 68–73.

Ancheta, Angelo N. 1998. *Race, rights, and the Asian American experience.* New Brunswick, NJ: Rutgers University Press.

Arches, Joan, Marion Darlington-Hope, Jeffrey Gerson, Joyce Gibson, Sally Habana-Hafner, and Peter Kiang. 1997. New voices in university-community transformation. *Change* 29, no. 1: 36–41.

*Black issues in higher education.* 1998. Special Report. 15, no. 10 (July 9): 38–65.

Bowen, William G., and Derek Bok. 1998. *The shape of the river: Long-term consequences of considering race in college and university admissions.* Princeton, NJ: Princeton University Press.

Brand, David. 1987. The new whiz kids [cover story]. *Time,* August 31, 42–51.

Butterfield, Fox. 1986. Why Asians are going to the head of the class. *New York Times Magazine*, August 3, 19–24.

Chan, Sucheng, and Ling-chi Wang. 1991. Racism and the model minority: Asian-Americans in higher education. In *The racial crisis in American higher education,* edited by Philip G. Altbach and Kofi Lomotey, 43–67. Albany: State University of New York Press.

Chang, Gordon, ed. 2000. *Asian American politics.* Stanford, CA: Stanford University Press.

Chang, Jeff. 1999. On the wrong side. *Color Lines* 2, no. 2 (summer): 12–14.

Chang, Mitchell J. 1999. Expansion and its discontents: The formation of Asian American studies programs in the 1990s. *Journal of Asian American Studies* 2, no. 2: 181–206.

Cho, Sumi. 1996. Confronting the myths: Asian Pacific American faculty in higher education. Paper presented at the Asian and Pacific Americans in Higher Education, San Francisco.

Chun, Ki-Taek. 1980. The myth of Asian American success and its educational ramifications. *IRCD Bulletin/Teachers College* 15, nos. 1–2: 1–12.

D'Souza, Dinesh. 1991. *Illiberal education: The politics of race and sex on campus.* New York: Free Press.

Fine, Michelle, Lois Weis, L. C. Powell, and L. M. Wong. 1977. *Off White: Readings on race, power, and society.* New York: Routledge.

Fong, Timothy P. 1998. *The contemporary Asian American Experience.* Upper Saddle River, NJ: Prentice Hall.

Graubard, S. G. 1988. Why do Asian pupils win those prizes? *New York Times,* January 29, A35.

Gupta, A. 1998. At the crossroads: College activism and its impact on Asian American identity formation. In *A part, yet apart: South Asians in Asian America,* edited by L. D. Shankar and R. Srikanth, 127–45. Philadelphia: Temple University Press.

Hirabayashi, Lane R. 1997. Asian American studies and institutional politics. In *Asian Pacific Americans and the U.S. Southwest,* edited by T. K. Nakayama and C. F. Yoshioka, 23–38. Tempe: Arizona State University.

———. 1998. *Teaching Asian America.* Westport, CT: Rowman and Littlefield.

Hsia, Jayjia. 1988. *Asian Americans in higher education and at work.* Hillsdale, NJ: Lawrence Erlbaum Associates.

Hu-Dehart, Evelyn. 1995. The undermining of ethnic studies. *Chronicle of Higher Education* (October 20): B1.

Hune, Shirley. 1995. Rethinking race: Paradigms and policy formation. *Amerasia* 21, no. 1: 29–40.

———. 1997. *Asian Pacific American women in higher education.* Washington, DC: Association of American Colleges and Universities.

Hune, Shirley, and Kenyon S. Chan. 1997. Special focus: Asian Pacific American demographic and educational trends. In *Fifteenth report on the status of minorities in higher education,* edited by Deborah Carter and Reginald Wilson, 39–107. Washington, DC: American Council on Education.

Kellogg Commission on the Future of State and Land-Grant Universities. 1999, February. *Returning to our roots: The engaged institution, third report.*

Kiang, Peter N. 1993. Stratification of public higher education. In *Bearing dreams, shaping visions,* edited by L. A. Revilla, G. M. Nomura, S. Wong, and Shirley Hune. Pullman: Washington State University Press.

———. 1996a. Southeast Asian and Latino parent empowerment: Lessons from Lowell, Massachusetts. In *Education reform and social change: Multicultural voices, struggles, and visions,* edited by C. E. Walsh, 59–69. Mahwah, NJ: Lawrence Erlbaum Associates.

———. 1996b. Persistence stories and survival strategies of Cambodian Americans in college. *Journal of Narrative and Life History* 6, no. 1: 39–64.

———. 1998. Writing from the past, writing for the future: Healing effects of Asian American studies in the curriculum. *Transformations: A Resource for Curriculum Transformation and Scholarship* 9, no. 2: 132–49.

———. 1999. *Long-term effects of diversity in the curriculum: Analyzing the impact of Asian American studies in the lives of alumni from an urban commuter university.* Final report. Washington, DC: National Association of Student Personnel Administrators.

———. 2000. Wanting to go on: Healing and transformation at an urban public university. In *Immigrant voices: In search of Pedagogical Reform,* edited by Enrique T. Trueba and Lilia Bartolomé. Lanham, MD: Rowman and Littlefield.

Kiang, Peter N., and Kenneth Wong. 1996. *The status of Asian Americans in public higher education in Massachusetts: Asian American studies in the curriculum.* Conference Report of the Institute for Asian American Studies, University of Massachusetts Boston.

Lee, Robert. 1999. *Orientals: Asians in American popular culture.* Philadelphia: Temple University Press.

Liu, Eric 1998. *The accidental Asian.* New York: Vintage.

Loeb, V. 1999. Ethnicity is linked to spying accusation. *Boston Globe,* August 17, 5.

Maki, Mitchell T., Harry H. L. Kitano, and Megan Berthold. 1999. *Achieving the impossible dream: How Japanese Americans obtained redress.* Urban-Champaign: University of Illinois Press.

Massachusetts Advisory Committee to the U.S. Commission on Civil Rights. 1998. *Civil rights briefing* (November 6): 13–21.

Matsuda, Mari. 1996. *Where is your body?* Boston: Beacon Press.

Miller, L. Stuart. 1999. Promoting high academic achievement among non-Asian minorities. In *Promise and dilemma: Perspectives on racial diversity and higher education,* edited by E. Y. Lowe, 47–91. Princeton, NJ: Princeton University Press.

Nakanishi, Don, and Tina Y. Nishida, eds. 1995. *The Asian American educational experience.* New York: Routledge.

Nguyen, Lucy H., and Joel M. Halpern, eds. 1989. *The Far East comes near: Autobiographical accounts of Southeast Asian students in America.* Amherst: University of Massachusetts Press.

Omi, Michael, and Howard Winant. 1986. *Racial formation in the United States.* New York: Routledge.

Padilla, Felix M. 1997. *The struggle of Latino/a university students: In search of a liberating education.* New York: Routledge.

*Report of the Select Committee on U.S. National Security and Military/Commercial Concerns with the People's Republic of China,* Report 105–851. 1999. Published in its declassified version as *The Cox Report.* Washington, DC: Regnery Publishing.

Schneider, A. 1999. Wisconsin loses case over race-based hiring. *Chronicle of Higher Education* (September 17): A18.

Suzuki, Bob H. 1990. Asians. In *Shaping higher education's future: Demographic realities and opportunities, 1990–2000,* edited by A. Levine and Associates, 87–114. San Francisco: Jossey-Bass.

Takagi, D. Y. 1992. *The retreat from race: Asian American admissions and racial politics.* New Brunswick, NJ: Rutgers University Press.

————. 1994. Post civil rights politics and Asian American identity: Admissions and higher education. In *Race,* edited by S. Gregory and R. Sanjek, 229–42. New Brunswick, NJ: Rutgers University Press.

————. 1996. Into the 21st century: Asian Americans and civil rights. Paper presented at the Asian and Pacific Americans in Higher Education Conference, San Francisco.

Takaki, R. 1989. *Strangers from a different shore.* Boston: Little, Brown and Company.

Tchen, Jack. 1999. *New York before Chinatown: Orientalism and the shaping of American culture, 1776–1882.* Baltimore, MD: Johns Hopkins University Press.

Trueba, Henry T., Lila Jacobs, Jose Cintrón, and Cecil Canton, eds. 2000. *The politics of survival in academia: Narratives of inequity, resilience, and success.* Albany: State University of New York Press.

Tuan, Mia. 1998. *Forever foreigners or honorary Whites?* New Brunswick, NJ: Rutgers University Press.

Umemoto, Karen. 1989. "On strike!" San Francisco State College strike, 1968–69: The role of Asian American students. *Amerasia Journal* 15, no. 1: 3–41.

U.S. Commission on Civil Rights. 1992, February. *Civil rights issues facing Asian Americans in the 1990s.* Washington, DC: U.S. Commission on Civil Rights.

U.S. Department of Education, National Center for Education Statistics. 1998. *The condition of education, 1998.* Washington, DC: National Center for Education Statistics.

Watanabe, Paul. 1996. *A dream deferred: Changing demographics, challenges, and new opportunities for Boston.* Boston: Institute for Asian American Studies and the Boston Foundation.

Weinberg, Meyer. 1997. *Asian-American education: Historical background and current realities.* Mahwah, NJ: Lawrence Erlbaum.

Weiss, Kenneth R. 2000. Cal State sees dip in need for remedial help. *Los Angeles Times,* March 15, A3, A18.

# CHAPTER 8

# Educational Choices and a University's Reputation

*The Importance of Collective Memory*

JOE R. FEAGIN, HERNÁN VERA,
AND NIKITAH IMANI

Like space and territory, the individual and collective sense of time and memory can be socially and racially colonized. What passes for a society's history is usually the dominant group's version of that history. White Americans, particularly White officials, historians, media commentators, and movie makers, have long tried to control and sanitize the collective memories and understandings of the interracial history of the United States. A "whitewashed" version of this racial past has often been popularized in the mass media, especially in major movies such as *The Birth of a Nation* (1911), *The Littlest Rebel* (1935), *The Little Colonel* (1935), and *Gone with the Wind* (1939). These and other movies, together with most White-authored novels and nonfiction books until the 1960s, portrayed a gallant American South run by genteel White aristocrats who had earned the loyalty of faithful Black slaves. The Black struggle for freedom was of no interest. Not until 1989 was the heroism of even one of the many Black units in the Union army chronicled, in the movie *Glory* (1989) (Vera and Cordon 1995). To this day, Hollywood's White moviemakers have shown very little interest in most other aspects of the lives of African Americans during slavery or legal segregation. Significantly, the White prohibition during slavery on teaching African Americans to read relegated the understanding of the slave past from the Black slave perspective mostly to oral traditions.

---

This chapter is reprinted from *The Agony of Education,* by Joe R. Feagin, Hernán Vera, and Nikitah Imani, 21–48. Minimal editing has been done for stylistic conformity in punctuation and capitalization. (© 1995) by permission of Routledge.

During slavery and ever since, not only White filmmakers but also White historians and publishing companies have largely controlled the record of the racial history of the United States. For example, in a recent review of a dozen leading high school textbooks, sociologist James Loewen (1995) found that most tiptoed around the harsh realities of America's racist past. He found no discussion of White racism as a persisting causal factor lying behind the racial barriers faced by African Americans. Most strikingly, not one of the major high school textbooks makes significant use of African American sources; not one "lets African Americans speak for themselves about the conditions they faced" (161).

One consequence of the White control of the understanding of U.S. racial history is that the African American oral tradition has had to place a heavy emphasis on familial and community memories of African American history. The Black students and parents that we interviewed repeatedly emphasized the time dimension of their experience by drawing on a strong and often perceptive sense of the racial past and present, recalling memories and understandings that are not only individual but also familial and communal.

African Americans place a heavy emphasis on education because of its role in family and community. Education is about a liberated future that must be better than the oppressive past. Pressing hard for higher education for children today is linked to the strong educational aspirations of African Americans in the distant and recent past. The prospect of a successful future for one's children and grandchildren helps to justify and give distinctive meaning to the collective suffering and struggles of the past and the present. In many ways, Black parents do not differ from other parents who work hard to put their children through college. However, for Black parents the education of their children gives meaning to their struggle against racism as well as to other aspects of their individual and familial histories.

The biography of each student who comes to college is rooted in individual and familial histories. Chances for success and for intellectual growth depend in part on skills, predispositions, and discipline developed in the home and community. The parents in the focus groups provided illustrations of how they regarded their children's coming to college as part of a collective history. One father noted the pressure he felt during his school years:

> If I don't perform I [lose] my scholarship; if I don't perform, I'm not going to be able to get a job; if I don't perform, I'm not going to be able to perpetuate the family's goals. In other words, I have to do better than my father. My father had to do better than his father, so forth down the line.[1]

---

1. Comments from the focus groups have been edited to protect the respondents' anonymity.

This familial pressure is common to many American families, but it takes on an added dimension for those who are members of an oppressed group that has faced major racial barriers to education. The ways in which such cross-generational pressures shape Black parents' conceptions of their own and their children's futures will become apparent as we examine accounts of the racial reputation and climate at a predominantly White university. As we will observe, a university's reputation is generally a condensation of individual and group memories of experience with that university.

Significantly, the concept of a collective past and future allows one to understand many African American responses to encounters with anti-Black discrimination. In addition to the immediate pain and stress that come from hostile encounters with Whites, such experiences have over time a significant *cumulative* impact on individuals, their families, and surrounding communities. The lives of most African American are regularly disrupted by racial mistreatment, suffered personally or endured by friends and family members. The cumulative impact of these instances of discrimination is often very distressful and damaging. Typically, a Black victim of discrimination communicates the incident to family and friends, and the pain of the incidents is passed along to a larger social group. Moreover, the negative effects of present discriminatory incidents are enhanced because they are laden with individual and group memories of centuries of racial oppression, which included accounts of lynchings and other anti-Black brutality and violence (Feagin and Sikes 1994, 16–23; Delany and Delany 1993, chap. 6 and passim).

The Black parents and students in our focus groups did not view most acts of discrimination as unusual disruptions in their everyday lives, but rather as recurring and integral parts of the experience of being Black in a White-dominated society. In this sense, the past is a constant part of the present; African Americans speak about events and evaluate them based on both their own and their historical group experience. Some analysts have argued that a traditional African perspective, elements of which are present in African American thought, includes two concepts of time—sacred cyclical time and ordinary linear time. Sacred time has no "past" because it is not part of a linear conception; ancestors and their experiences live in the present. This sacred cyclical time joins the past, present, and future at any point in time and space, making the present especially significant (Mbiti 1970; Eliade 1959, 21; Richards 1985, 218).

Other cultures and groups share aspects of this perspective on time, but it can be particularly important for those groups that have suffered oppression. One critical dimension of time is the sense people have of the character and pace of social change. This understanding of change is important because an appraisal of the future—Are things changing for the better or worse? What type of world will our children face?—affects to a substantial extent how we view the past, experience the present, and see the future. This sense of the possibility for social transformation is particularly momentous for groups, such as African Americans, that have a long history of oppression.

Certain heralded analysts of higher education have argued that predominantly White colleges and universities are undergoing a dramatic revolution that is radically decentering White interests in favor of the concerns and interests of racial minorities (Bloom 1987, 91; D'Souza 1991, 113–15, 229–44; Bernstein 1994; Schlesinger 1991). According to this interpretation, the racial reputations of most predominantly White colleges and universities are now quite liberal and signal correctly that minorities dominate much of campus life, much of the curriculum, and much of the discussion in college classrooms.

However, the images of the majority-White colleges and universities held by the Black parents and students whom we interviewed are often dramatically different from the views of these critics of higher education. These Black parents and students view majority-White campuses as generally inhospitable for Black students. In this regard they are much like other parents and leaders in communities of color across the nation. For example, the University of Texas (Austin) has long had a reputation for academic excellence and liberalism both nationally and in its own region. Yet a recent survey of Black and Latina/o leaders at the university and in local communities found that the university had a reputation for being racist and unwelcoming to students of color. According to one report, the Black and Latina/o leaders objected to the university's failure "to remove statues of Confederate leaders" and its failure "to recruit and retain Black and Hispanic students" (Ackerman 1994, A31). Here we see a clear example of the importance of collective memory in shaping the reputation of a university campus. The symbolism of campus statues of Confederate officials is very negative in communities of color in Texas and many other states, although most Whites do not seem to understand the strong linkage of this type of symbolism to a predominantly White university's negative reputation for people of color or to its problems in retaining students of color on campus.

In this chapter, we investigate the question of a university's racial reputation and explore the educational dilemmas that the continuing racial barriers at a predominantly White university force on parents and students of color. The temporal dimensions of a university's reputation and its campus climate—including collective memories and their present and future effects—are a central concern in this chapter.

## Parental Hopes and Aspirations: "You're Going to Get an Education, Period"

African American parents and students told us about their daily lives and basic choices—what their past was like, what was happening to them in the present, and how they saw their futures. For these parents, the children's college education was the natural continuation of their individual and familial hopes and ambitions, and their children's success in college is understood as justifying many sacrifices. The parents in one focus group began with a discussion of educational plans for their children. One successful entrepreneur described the pressure to fulfill the family goals he had felt in his youth. He contrasted this pressure with his desire for his son to get an education for its intrinsic value:

> I want him to go get an education for one reason only—to broaden his mind, period. See, he's not going to go to school or college like I did with the pressure of—if I don't perform I [lose] my scholarship. . . . If I don't perform, I'm not going to be able to perpetuate the family's goals. . . . In other words, "You're going to go to school. You're going to get an education, period." And then, we'll see how things work out after that.

This father's education was a multigenerational family project that transcended the individual. He wants to spare his son the heavy familial pressures that he experienced. Still, his parental concerns and demands on his son suggest a continuing familial dimension to the educational decisions.

A little later in the discussion, the mother of a teenager who was considering a community college took up the last speaker's topic. She noted a contrasting family history and how her experience has affected what she wants for her children:

> I want them to do things better because I didn't, and you know I really didn't have nobody to talk to me, like, "What you want to do?" Push me, you know. So I kind of talk to them: "If that's what you want to do, go for it," as long as they want something that's right, not messing with drugs or nothing.

In this focus group, the participants build on each other's ideas. Like the father above, this mother wants a better life for her children, a life without the pitfalls she has had to live through. While her experience is different from the previous parent, like him she shapes her behavior to help her children. The hopes and plans for a child's education are rooted in the parent's and student's familial past and extend into the family's future.

### Selecting a College: "It's Important for All Children . . . to Be Nurtured, as Far as Education Is Concerned"

All the parents we interviewed, whether they had graduate degrees or had never been to college, considered the selection of a college for their children to be a serious matter. In addition to taking account of their children's particular needs, they make college decisions in light of issues of racial identity and African American culture. The problem of racism in predominantly White institutions often came up naturally as the parents talked about general college matters.

In response to a general question about what colleges the parents were considering for their children, one father noted his displeasure with his son's going to a business college. He indicated that his son needed to learn to spell and write better, skills apparently not provided by the college. He suggested, thus, that his wife would be to blame for his son's getting a low-end job since she "pushed him" into that business college. There was parental conflict over the son's needs and the college he should have attended. Although this man's response did not address the question directly, his emotional statement had an impact on the group that set the tone for the following statements. As the conversation moved around the table, other parents took up the theme that colleges should be chosen according to the children's needs and abilities.

The next person to speak, the mother of two children nearing college age, cast her comment in the temporal terms we have described. For her there is a personal and collective past and a future that, in this case, looks hopeful:

> I think I would like my children to go to [a local university], a Black institution. And that's because of the topic that we're discussing—racism in higher educational [settings]. There is or has been a lot of racism within this state's institutions. . . . I didn't attend that school [State University], but I know lots of people who did, and the Black people who attended . . . all experienced racist attitudes among the students and among the teaching staff there. I think things may change. . . . They now have a Black administrator.

The past experience of racism at predominantly White universities is an important element in Black parents' decisions concerning their children's college choices. The future—in this case, the hope that things may change because of the presence of a Black administrator—may also guide some parental decisions.

Next, an educator and mother of two children presented a past experience at a predominantly White university, which she contrasted with that of a previous speaker:

> I didn't experience the racism that you're talking about. And I guess because when I was in school, I was very naive. I mean, I had gone to a predominantly Black state university in a nearby state prior to going to a local White university like State University. And I went there for two years. . . . But when my father died, I decided to come home to go to school, and I think going to the local university really helped me as far as a broad perspective, as far as getting . . . my career, or my job, or my profession as a teacher, but as far as my children are

concerned, . . . a lot of it depends on your child. . . . Well, this child needs to be close to home; [but] this one can, you know, go off on his or her own. So I really haven't considered it, but I know they will go to college. I do know that.

This parent, while not denying the problem of campus racism that the previous parents brought up, notes a different personal experience. Looking to the future, she refocuses the discussion by making children's abilities and inclinations a key to a decision about a predominantly White or a Black college. In each of the parent groups, one or more parents introduced contradictory experiences or disclaimers about not facing discrimination, and each group examined the matter of racial barriers openly and critically.

As the group continued, the collective effort to examine the difficult issues thoroughly became apparent. To illustrate the idea that children's abilities and interests are the key element in a college decision, another mother addressed the issue of identity:

Well, I have two sons who are . . . very different. One is extremely bright and could go anywhere, and the other one struggles, so we really worked hard to find a college for them. Now, . . . I didn't consider a college in this state; my husband did. My son received a scholarship to an Ivy League college, but he refused to take it. [He] had gone to predominantly White schools in the lower grades and high school, and he decided for himself that he wanted to go to a school that was predominantly Black—that he . . . would be more comfortable [there], even though he was quite competent academically; but he wanted to immerse himself in this culture. And so for that reason, he decided that he wanted to go to a predominantly Black university.

The interest in this question was intense and several parents raised their hands seeking to participate in the discussion. The previous speaker continued:

The second one . . . who's not as bright, . . . didn't want to go [to the Black college], so he chose State University . . . and he struggled with it academically . . . and they're now both in grad school.

In the beginning of this line of discussion, we should recall, the issue of choosing a college was posed in the conflict between a husband and a wife who, according to the husband, had pushed their son into a business school. In subsequent comments that initial issue was framed broadly to encompass the matter of children's talents and interests, including an interest in African American culture that can usually be nurtured best at a predominantly Black college.

In her comments, the last speaker indicated that the choice between a predominantly Black or a predominantly White college involves more than academic matters. Predominantly Black colleges have much to offer, including a more hospitable social and cultural environment. Some research shows that, on average, African American students at predominantly Black colleges make greater relative academic gains than those on White campuses because there is a more supportive academic environment and because there is a better match between the academic and social needs of the students and existing campus programs. On mainly Black campuses, students make better psychosocial adjustments and have a stronger awareness of African American history and culture (Allen and Haniff 1991, 96; Fleming 1984, 47–63). The group discussions make it clear that African American parents do not make the often agonizing choice about colleges for their children abstractly. The abilities, needs, and inclinations of the children are factored into the decision, as are the academic, social, and cultural environments of the college campuses that are considered.

Then another educator in this group introduced another time-related factor relevant to college choices—that of late-blooming children:

> Sometimes people tend to say that a child is a certain way when they see them growing up as children. However, when they become older, they blossom. Sometimes, experiences make them not do as well in school as maybe parents would like for them to do; but if they have the ability and if they have guidance that parents have already given them and nurturing, more than likely they'll do well. They just need average ability in order to go to college, so I feel that a child should never be discouraged from going to college. Just like she said, her son, who she felt was not as strong academically as the other child, made it; and that's the key—making it, making it into a college. But now, my children . . . will go to college. My husband graduated from a Black institution. . . . My children are living in an environment where they are truly a minority. . . . It's important for all children . . . to be nurtured, as far as education is concerned. And I find sometimes that there is not a sensitivity to African American children . . . by teachers that are non-African American. . . . I just believe that African American schools nurture our children more.

A father of two children doing well in school then asked the last speaker a question to settle the issue of White and Black colleges:

> Based on . . . you being a graduate of [a predominantly White university] and your husband being a graduate of a Black college, . . . have you thought about a comparison as to the level of educational environment made available by both schools? How would you compare that—one-on-one equal? or one more than the other?

Thinking deeply about the matter, she replied to him and thus completed her previous thought about the critical role of classroom teachers:

> To me, the key is the person that's standing in front of that classroom presenting the information. That is the key. It's not private, public, this reputation, that

reputation. Sometimes reputation is an important factor, but the person that is giving out that information—that is teaching—is the key to the learning.

At this point, the line of discussion reached closure. More than which college or university has a superior academic reputation, the critical issues for these mothers and fathers included the interests of children and the sensitivity of teachers. These parents confronted the issues of academic quality, racist reputations and attitudes, campus culture, a child's skills and desires, and the sensitivity of teachers as elements in the decision to choose a college. Very important here are what we have called the temporal aspects of these college choices. The personal, familial, and community events these parents note are not inert quantities that can be ignored. Past events and experiences are powerfully active factors that must be considered to act in the future. The discriminatory or unsupportive climates of predominantly White institutions vs. the supportive climates at Black institutions are among the important college realities that are faced by Black parents and their children.

## State University's Reputation: "You Go to School for a Lot of Experiences, Not Just the Academics"

We have just followed an important discussion in which difficult decisions about colleges involve, among other factors, consideration of a college's racial reputation. Parental and student judgments regarding the degree to which a predominantly White university will facilitate personal and cultural development are based in large part on reported experiences of other African Americans who have attended or attempted to attend that university, as well as on events involving the university that are reported in the media.

The parent focus groups generally opened with a dialogue about questions regarding higher education which were not initially focused on racial matters. Soon, the parents or moderator turned the discussion to State University. One of the questions explored in the focus groups was the reputation this predominantly White university had in local Black communities. Both in their focus group comments and in responses to an exit questionnaire, the Black parents were often explicit about SU's reputation. On the exit questionnaire, we asked each participant, "What would you say is State University's reputation today as an institution of higher education for Blacks within the Black communities you know in this state?" The overwhelming majority (83 percent) replied that SU's reputation was somewhat or mostly negative. Only 10 percent said that the school's reputation was somewhat positive, and not one parent chose the option of "mostly positive." The rest were uncertain.

In reply to the question, "In regard to serving the Black community and Black students in this state, has the reputation of State University changed in a positive or negative direction over the last five years?" 30 percent felt that its reputation had become somewhat or a lot more negative, and 24 percent said, "No change." Only 17 percent thought SU's reputation had become somewhat more positive, and no one thought it had become much more positive. The rest were uncertain. (One person did not answer this question.)

In the focus groups, the parents engaged the question of SU's reputation. Some attempted to achieve a balance in their opinions. Their views of negative aspects of State University were frequently mixed with their views of the good they saw there, as in the following statement:

> Very often, Blacks will feel that [at] State University . . . they can get a good academic background. However, for Blacks, they feel that there's a lot more negative kinds of feelings, emotions, considerations going on there. In fact, even with their Black programs here that they have—the student programs—there's not enough knowledge of the cultural differences, not enough allowances for expressing the cultural differences. So the students—while they may be academically sound, you're talking about a total person, and especially on the undergrad level—are not able to develop into a full-fledged whole person who feels good about himself or herself.

African Americans quickly pick up on certain White aspects of the campus. The lack of knowledge of cultural differences and the lack of "allowances for expressing the cultural differences" are traits of State University as a distinctive place. Thinking in terms of a positive-to-negative scale, another parent added this comment on SU's reputation:

> I would say that definitely not on the positive, but in between neutral and negative . . . because when you hear Blacks talk of State University, "Oh certainly it does have a good academic program," but just like [a previous speaker] said, you need [to be] a whole person. . . . You go to school for a lot of experiences, not just the academics, and I hear that Black students have negative experiences there. They're called various names. They're treated a certain way, and that cannot be positive as far as I'm concerned.

These parental evaluations of a major U.S. university's image illustrate the problems for African Americans who are considering predominantly White universities in the United States. Like other Black parents across the nation, these parents weigh the value of such a university's academic programs for students' careers against the racial costs of schools that fail to provide support for the development of the "whole Black person."

Both the moderator and the parents made a serious effort to include positive points about predominantly White universities in their discussions, although their attempts to do this were sometimes punctuated with laughter, thereby indicating that this was a difficult task. Asked by the group moderator if anyone there had heard anything positive in support of State University, one parent responded:

In support of? [Group laughter] Yeah, you do hear things. A few years ago the media came out with this . . . Do you know Mr. Jones [a Black professional]? . . . I believe he's employed out at State University because of the perception that had gone up.

This is a modest example, one that notes the efforts of SU to add racial diversity to the campus; it suggests that Black communities pay attention to small gains. Previous research has found a tendency on the part of many African Americans to try hard to find something positive to say about Whites even in situations of serious racial barriers and hostility (Feagin and Sikes 1994, 307–11). The desire to acknowledge a situation's positive aspects seems to involve more than a concern with avoiding the appearance of being one-sided. Some social analysts have suggested that among many people of African descent there is a view that the "good" often emerges out of the substance of the "bad." Such a perspective accents change and sees human interactions and situations as in the process of being transformed from one state to the other (Ani 1994). For the university to represent a legitimate educational option for many African Americans, it must have some positive dimensions, as well as at least the possibility for future change in the positive direction.

In the focus groups, the Black parents sometimes viewed SU's sports programs as a positive aspect of the school's reputation. Commenting on the university's image in the Black community, one father noted:

They have a positive image in [so] far as people that I'm in touch with . . . in my neighborhood. . . . I gather the kids around and try to show them something positive as I take them along with me. And . . . their older members of their family—cousins and brothers— . . . some of them are in different schools. Some aspire to go to State University. . . . Lots of guys [say], "Hey, I can get there and get some exposure playing football and possibly prepare myself [for] professional sports.

However, other parents' assessments of the sports programs at SU had a less positive tone, as in the case of this mother who knew SU only by its reputation:

We were just discussing the issue of the sports thing there. It's just not happening. They won't accept you there, and they just won't accept you if you're not involved with athletics there.

Another mother also noted that SU's reputation was one of seeking Black students for their sports abilities:

It's just really like for sports, if you're good in sports.

A father noted that he saw the university keeping itself separate from local Black communities:

Now, where all the Black people live, that's something else. That is totally
separate from State University. The only reason why [the university] ventures
out, in my opinion, back in the seventies . . . to make any contact with the Black
people, they needed athletes. That was the only reason.

Another parent added: "They needed federal monies, you see."

Although many African Americans, especially young people, see sports as
an avenue of upward mobility, these Black parents were aware of the racial
contradictions in college athletic programs. College athletics provide a means
for some talented Black students to finance their college educations; but from
the perspective of White university officials and alumni, these athletes are often
little more than grist for the athletic mill. There is evidence that Black athletes
are important in the generation of revenue for White colleges and universities,
as well as in the building of a regional or national reputation. Recent figures
indicate that about 37 percent of NCAA Division I football players and 56
percent of Division I men's basketball players are African American. However,
well over half of these Black football and basketball players score in the lowest
quartile on the SAT, and 61 percent have high school GPAs in the lowest
quartile (*Studies* 1989). Once admitted to predominantly White colleges, these
students are worked very hard by the coaches in their primary occupation,
which is college athletics. During the season for their sport, they typically
spend more time practicing and playing than on academic matters. In one
survey, three-quarters of Black athletes at predominantly White institutions
reported that it was hard for them to make the grades they were capable of
achieving. More than four in ten had been on academic probation. Seven in ten
gave their coaches a "fair" or worse rating in regard to encouraging good
coursework and listening to their academic problems. It appears that many
Black athletes are not recruited to enhance their educations and career prospects outside the area of athletics (*Studies* 1989).

Black parents know that the role of Black athletes at mainly White colleges is primarily to enhance the reputation and revenues of the school. Still,
some parents and students gamble on the athletic route in the remote hope of
recruitment by a professional athletic team.

## Racism and the University's Reputation:
## "A Bad Reputation"

As discussed above, parents attempt to balance their positive and negative comments, noting the importance of the university's academic programs
and athletics in shaping its reputation. On the whole, however, the positive
comments about State University were drowned out in a chorus of negative
sentiment about racial barriers on the campus. When asked if State University

had a reputation in Black communities, one group's spontaneous comments went this way:

> Group: Yes.
> One father: I say yes.
> Moderator: And what is that reputation?
> Group: Racist.
> First father again: I hear that.
> Moderator: Now you have to talk up. You're the lowest speaker.
> One mother: Racist.
> Another mother: Racist.
> First father again: Because my daughter just the other day was asking about that. And a friend of ours, their son is going to come out of there, and they're the ones that said, "No, you don't want to go there because it is racist." My wife went there for one semester going at night, and I can see how it is there.

The comments in another focus group about the university's reputation in local Black communities were similar:

> One mother: A bad reputation.
> One father: Yes! A bad one. . . .
> Another mother: Negative. Negative. . . .
> Another father: I'm neutral only because my knowledge of it is limited.
> Another mother: My sister went to State University, and she said it's very prejudiced; there's a lot of racists there. And I'm going by word of mouth.

Parents in the other groups replied in the same vein to a question about whether the reputation was positive or negative:

> One mother: For me it would go towards neutral to negative.
> Moderator: Neutral to negative? Okay, what makes you say that?
> Mother: Well, it's a majority White school. I think that the Black kids there, . . . —this is just my perception—they get kind of lost there if they're not an athlete, and the focus there is on the athletic team.
> One father: I've heard from other students, some White, some Black, and from what I get, they are still prejudiced at State University.
> Another father: Getting back to the school—nobody ever said anything good about it. I never heard anybody say anything good about the school at all.

Unquestionably, SU has a reputation in the state's Black communities of being socially inhospitable to Blacks. The Black parents' willingness to use the strong word *racist* in assessing SU's reputation, together with the resolution and emotion shown in many of their comments, suggests that such an appraisal is common in Black communities and not considered excessive. In each focus group, the negative views expressed by individual parents were generally validated by the group as a whole. Contrary to much White commentary on Black "paranoia" about racism, most African Americans usually do not choose such strong words until the experiential evidence is substantial.

The parents' sources of information about SU's racial reputations are diverse, as one speaker made clear:

> I've only heard that, you know, basically what I'm hearing now, that there were some problems, racial problems, out there.
> Moderator: Who did you hear it from?
> First speaker: . . . I've talked to several people . . . because I was thinking about going to State University. . . . After I started to talk to some people about myself and going to State University, then it started coming up that they were racial. . . . And then just looking at the news, you know incidents that have happened out at State University, the racial incidents that are going on out there.

Personal contacts and the mass media both play a role in the Black construction of a predominantly White university's reputation and image. Drawing on what he had heard and on his own experience, one father described the SU campus and its reputation in chilling terms:

> The first time I rode through, it looked like Ku Klux Klan country. . . . State University . . . just looked cold when I rode there, and I didn't like it, and I had already heard negative things before I went there.
> Moderator: What did you hear?
> Father: They were racist. And just driving through, I was only through a half hour, and I felt like I was in the heart of Alabama.

The image of this White campus as "Klan country" is a strong historical association for a Black man to make. The Klan was created after the Civil War as a White organization designed to create a condition of semi-slavery for ostensibly free Black Americans. Certain unnamed aspects of the campus triggered in his mind personal or familial memories of racial oppression. The Klan, still a White supremacy organization in many states, is part of a seamless web of White racism that reaches from past to present.

Indicating yet another source of information on SU's reputation, one mother presented some evidence suggesting that SU was not viewed positively in the local Black communities:

> I interview students—graduating high school seniors— who are going to college in the fall. I interview about fifty a year; and out of each group

of fifty students, I don't think I have five students who are interested in State University.

Moderator: Now, is that all of your students or African American students?

Mother: All minority students, and very few are interested in [State University].

Sources of information about SU's reputation include peer networks, as another parent explained in his assessment of how a racial reputation spreads:

Among the [Black] undergraduate college group and so forth, it [SU] has a very negative reputation. And I think the reason for that is students from schools in the area effectively party together and so forth, and they hear the sad stories and so many nonsuccess stories from so many students at State University. . . . Now when my son was going to college, he was very lucky. He was offered a four-year, expense-paid scholarship to State University, and I really begged him to take it, but he turned it down flat. I think it was specifically for this reason— what the peers were saying.

Peer groups among young African Americans are important receptacles of collective memory; they accumulate positive and negative accounts of students' experiences with a variety of colleges and universities. The poor reputation of White universities acts as a powerful deterrent on some Black high school students' consideration of SU as a desirable locale to obtain an education.

Reflecting on how a Black state university welcomed Black students, one mother noted the different attitude that the Black community perceived at State University:

This is to tell you how they [SU] reached out to their population. [The Black] people who lived right in that [SU's] community, the students that I met that summer—well, you know how you spend the summer on campus—from SU's area, they didn't go to SU; they went to a Black state university. So, if they [SU] were interested in bringing these Black people in and if they were being good servers to the community, I would think that . . . [Black people] would say, "You know what? That school right there will really service us well. We should go there." But no! They go all the way over to the Black university.

The decision of Black students living nearby to attend other educational institutions signals that SU has a reputation of little interest in serving nearby Black communities. Some students report that Black students, in their experience, are not actively recruited by State University. This absence of aggressive recruitment evidently contributes to Black parents' and students' lack of interest in State University.

### Parents' Views of SU's Service to Black Communities: "It Can Burn Down"

The collective memory of African American families and communities accumulates accounts of negative experiences with SU that can affect present-day views and decisions. On the exit questionnaire, we asked the parents if they agreed or disagreed with this statement: "In the past, historically, State University has done a poor job of serving the Black community and Black students." Three-quarters said they agreed with this negative assessment of SU's past performance, while only 14 percent disagreed. The rest were uncertain or gave no answer.

In the group discussions, some parents noted that SU's historical background of referring or discouraging Black applicants played a role in their current thinking, as was the case in this dialogue:

> One father: Looking back—I was raised here, and I've been in this county most of my life—and I can remember people applying to go to State University, and they would be referred to, because of their race, you know, "Wouldn't you be more comfortable at the predominantly Black universities?" They would invariably try to refer you to a Black school.
> One mother: That's true. . . . They would do that. If you go to them, they would refer or they would recommend or suggest that you could go to another college.
> Moderator: I wonder—is that [referrals to Black colleges] to keep down racial tension, maybe?
> Another father: No, that's to keep Blacks out of universities! [Group laughter]

Later in this focus group's discussion, the last speaker added this strongly worded comment:

> If you picked up State University and dropped it off the face of the earth, I would not miss it.
> Moderator: Anything driving that feeling?
> Father: Well, I thought about it, and I thought, "What drove me to think about it like that?" And I've got to go back to—I'm from this state. And from kindergarten to sixth grade I was a segregated Black student. From seventh grade, boom, integration. They dropped you into a predominantly White school. . . . Well I did go to college—to a White college. I was in an English class, and I turned in a paper in the English class, and it came back in three days marked "E—this does not sound like your work." So these are the types of things that made up my mind quick that I'm going to scamper right to a Black college where I don't

have to worry about that aspect. That qualifies that statement. None of the peers that I grew up with went to State University. They went to the predominantly Black universities. Like I said, "It can burn down."

This father's anger is palpable. Significantly, no other parent took issue with his harsh comment. The history of racial separation in the United States lays the foundation for and now blends into current parental decisions, which may sometimes be oriented away from unwelcoming, predominantly White colleges and universities and toward more hospitable, predominantly Black colleges and universities.

## Students' Views of State University's Reputation: "Whites Really Rule the Campus"

As we have seen in the parents' comments, the parent and student decisions about college settings are affected by a college's reputation. Before most Black students in the focus groups came to SU, they had heard about the university's reputation. As with the parents, on the exit questionnaire, we asked all of the students about SU's reputation: "What would you say is State University's reputation today, as an institution of higher education for Blacks, within the Black communities you know in this state?" The pattern of student responses was generally similar to that of the parents. A large majority (70 percent) felt that SU's reputation in local communities was mostly or somewhat negative. Twenty-two percent said that SU's reputation was somewhat positive, and only 3 percent (one student) replied, "Mostly positive." The rest were uncertain. Taken together with the strong parental views, these results are unmistakable—they show that SU's racial reputation is substantially negative in the state's Black communities.

In the focus groups, the Black students discussed what they had heard about SU's reputation before they came and about their reasons for choosing SU. Their comments were similar to those of the parents. They included some positive assessments of its location, sports programs, academic reputation, and reasonable cost. In their college choices, the students indicated a desire for an academically first-rate university that would prepare them well for good careers in business or the professions. Not surprisingly, most of these young scholars relied on family and friends in sorting out SU's and other colleges' reputations, as this student indicated:

Well, my mother liked the idea. My two choices for college were both predominantly White anyway, and this was the better of the two. Because it was between this and another predominantly White university, which was having a lot of racial problems right before I came to college. So she was okay with it.

Also noting the importance of the academic reputation, one male student described his college choice:

> I have a cousin who recently graduated from here. She had nothing but good things to say about this university. She graduated with honors, and she's in law school right now. She kind of swayed me in this university's direction.

Another student also noted that he had heard good things about the academic program:

> I didn't hear anything about any racism or nothing like that. All I heard—all I knew was that they had a good business school, and that's basically why I decided to come.

Interestingly, another positive factor about SU's reputation cited by several students in the group interviews was the fact that this predominantly White campus does have some African American students. As one male student noted, "I didn't know the percentage when I decided to go here. I just knew they had Blacks."

This issue of the visibility or invisibility of Black students on campus is important in shaping SU's image as a hospitable place for parents and students. The relatively small number of Black students there has caused the residents of the state's Black communities to see SU as a *White* university. Several of the Black students reported that they were discouraged from selecting this university by friends or relatives who felt they would be relegated to the margins in a mostly White setting. Replying to the moderator's question about whether people said things to discourage students from coming to SU, one young woman replied:

> Yeah. Because it's a predominantly White school—and that I should go to a predominantly Black school, which I did not want to do. Because I knew the whole world was not Black, and with me coming from an all Black town. . . .

Bringing up the large size of the university, one student in another focus group reported that she faced tough questioning from some of her Black friends:

> "Why are you going to that White school? All those White people up there." And then . . . a lot of my friends were talking about the fact of how this university was so big, "Oh, you are just going to be a number. You're just going to be a number. You should go to a smaller school."

Here the common student complaint of "just being a number" takes on racial connotations. Being lost in a crowd is a common experience for all college students at large universities, but being lost in a sea of White faces elevates the common problem to another level of difficulty for Black students.

As we have noted previously, such experiences are not unique to Black students considering State University. Advice from relatives and other Black adults that warns students away from mostly White universities is common-place in many Black communities across the nation. For example, a junior at the University of North Carolina (Chapel Hill) was recently quoted in *Essence* magazine: "Before I decided to go to North Carolina, a lot of people encouraged me to consider universities that were a little less racially intense. UNC had a history and a reputation for being a racist campus" (Tarpley 1993, 65). Collective memories shape Black students' decisions about education in many communities.

Reflecting a realistic tone about postgraduation opportunities, another student at State University noted the university's image among his friends:

> I heard something like that too, . . . not from my parents but from friends. They say that since it was an all-White school I might have some problems. But to me, I just looked at it [as a] situation where if we're talking about going to an all-Black college—but the world is not all Black. So if you have to deal with these people eventually, you might as well deal with them now.

In reply to the focus group moderator's question about what he had heard about SU's reputation before he came, one student discussed the views of his parents about the White-oriented staff at State University:

> I heard that since it's predominantly White that the Whites really rule the campus. And my parents tried to tell me not to come. . . . Like programs that would go on—most of the stuff was geared toward the White[s]. . . . The staff would tend to you more, care about you more, if you went to a Black college.

Racial barriers can take a variety of forms, blatant or subtle, overt or hidden. One student explained that she had heard about the character of certain barriers on campus:

> The racial atmosphere was okay, but a lot of the racism was, like, underlying. It wasn't very blatant . . . but that you always have to be on your guard.

Unquestionably, agonizing educational choices are created for Black parents and students by the racial reputation of predominantly White universities like SU. The choice of such a college may sometimes be made against the advice of relatives and friends, who may warn the students of subtle and blatant discrimination on a campus where Whiteness is omnipresent in student body composition, staff services, and a variety of campus facilities and affairs. Still, these students have decided to come to State University anyway. Some explain, often with an air of resignation, that they might as well get used to dealing with mostly White, socially inhospitable environments while they are young.

We have previously noted the importance of space and place in the way that racial relations are arranged or managed. As we have just seen, a number of the student commentaries indicate the importance of that spatial environment. The interaction in one focus group made the significance of place even clearer. After the moderator asked what factors students considered in choosing a university, one senior commented sharply on the issues pressed on her by family and friends:

> I had so many, like, people my parents' age and people older than that, going, "Oh girl, don't go there," you know, and people just telling me that it was the worst place for me to go. "Go to another state university." . . . [Names another] was the one they kept telling me to go [to] since it's predominantly Black. But they just said under no circumstances was I to go to State University. I mean I had friends who are a bunch of years older than me going here, and they still said, "Don't go there."

This comment is similar to those previously examined, but this student accents both the spatial and temporal aspects of her important decision. The vocabulary of spatial relations is striking: "Don't go *there*," and "it was the worst *place* for me to go." Replying to the moderator's follow-up question about why she had received such advice, the same student alluded to SU's past history in regard to African American students. She suggested that the university had had few Black students until the late 1960s, then added:

> And the environment just wasn't conducive, I guess, to Black students, so it's just the kind of thing that we knew we weren't wanted here. I guess that was what they meant.

Again, the collective memory of Black families and communities in regard to racial discrimination is underscored.

In what at first appears to be a move in a different direction, the next student in the group interview focused on her own parents' fears about substance abuse on campus:

> The thing that my family did . . . and I was coming from out-of-state. So that was, like, "That school has drugs. You don't need go there." So I mean, that was just a major thing because that was so much in the news and everything. And every place else was drug-free, according to them, except State University.

The family's sense of danger is focused on the "place" that is State University. Then the next student speaker in this particular group drew on her past experiences to discuss the reputation of State University:

I didn't know anything about this school. . . . I used to pass through this campus all the time. I used to always see these White girls. I'd tell myself, "I wouldn't go to that school. . . . "There's no Black people here." I live right in the neighborhood. It's like I didn't know one Black person that came here.

## Racial Climate and Racial Reputation:
## "You Were . . . Just an Unseen Person"

Not surprisingly, the parents' perceptions of SU's racial climate are ingredients in their views of SU's reputation. On the exit questionnaire, we asked the parents how they felt about this statement: "Today State University is a college campus where Black students are generally welcomed and nurtured." Most (71 percent) disagreed with this statement, while only 14 percent agreed. The rest were uncertain. The parents were also asked, "How often have you heard about racial discrimination or racial problems at State University in the last ten years?" Fifty-four percent replied "fairly often" or "very often," while 32 percent replied "not very often." One person said "not at all," and the rest were not sure. In spite of SU's efforts over the last decade to improve its image among African Americans in the state, most of the Black parents still have a negative view of the situation of Black students on campus.

In the group discussions of SU's racial climate, some of the parents drew on their own or their children's experiences there; others based their views of the campus on discussions with friends and relatives or accounts in the local media. The favorable assessments of SU indicated that acquaintances or relatives had made it through with no serious problems. A few of the parents spoke in this fashion:

> One mother: I know of three people . . . who attended [SU]. . . . The three people had no complaints.
> One father: A real close friend of mine, . . . attended State University. He had no problems at State University. [As] a matter of fact, he raved about [the] school. [That's] my only experience.

Even positive accounts sometimes have an undercurrent that suggests something is amiss. There is no clear suggestion in any of the parental accounts that the experience of Black SU students was highly rewarding beyond the attainment of a good education and a college degree. For many White students, in contrast, the university experience doubtless marks a special time in their lives which creates fond memories and which enhances their self-esteem and personal and collective identities.

Drawing on the experiences of his wife and his wife's friend, one father suggested that there were positive and negative aspects to SU's racial climate:

> I have negative and positive points about State University. My wife's girlfriend went to State University and . . . we went over there constantly to visit her; she stayed on campus. We never got any negative response from her about the school. . . . My wife [is] . . . a high school teacher, and they approached her about taking a job, or [doing] her internship at State University's computer program. But being the so-called aggressive Black woman she is, she said, "I'm not taking the position where I would be a clerk typist or whatever." I mean, she has her master's degree.

Several participants noted that some relatives and acquaintances had positive experiences at SU or at least had not made negative statements. A few referred to specific events. One Black student was offered a university job; another was welcomed back by a mixed group of friends. Two parents specifically mentioned that Black athletes had a more positive environment. Again there is the hint in such comments that Black students who are athletes may be seen by many Whites as in their appropriate "place" at a predominantly White university.

Significantly, some participants had relatives who did not talk much or at all about their personal experiences as students at SU. Providing some family details, one parent mentioned the eloquent silence of a sister-in-law about her student days at SU:

> My sister-in-law graduated from State University, and I had a lot of respect for her because I thought highly of that institution as far as academically being able to graduate. Now, she never ever had anything to say about the college. You know, I graduated from a Black public university. And, yeah, we had this, and I had great friends, and we were doing this, and the campus was doing this. And we were political signers. We were signing people up to vote this, that, and the other. [Yet] she never had anything good [to say about State University], I mean, there was nothing. She worked. She went to school. She came home. . . . College is one of the best times of your life! You never, ever should cheat yourself out of that. She never had—as far as I'm concerned—she never had that. . . . Because I know somebody who graduated, who was an excellent teacher, who benefitted from that education, who was strong enough, academically and socially, and must [have] had a wonderful self-esteem . . . to get through a situation where you were sort of like, you know, just an unseen [person]. You weren't seen.

This speaker reveals another potential consequence of an African American's choice of a predominantly White educational institution. She interprets her sister-in-law's lack of any commentary, either positive or negative, about her experiences at SU as a sign of social isolation. She concludes that it took great personal strength for her sister-in-law to succeed as an "unseen" person on the campus. Comments touching on the lack of recognition were numerous in the parent and student focus groups. Such experiences bring to mind yet again Ralph Ellison's (1989) comment in his *Invisible Man* about the White inability to truly "see" African Americans as individuals: "I am invisible, understand, simply because people refuse to see me" (3).

Significantly, *not one* participant in the parent groups indicated they had *often* heard from friends, relatives, or other Black residents of the state that SU's campus was strongly supportive of its Black students. The best many could say was that their acquaintances or relatives had gotten though the university with "no serious problems."

## Advice to Potential College Students:
## "I Wouldn't Recommend Anybody to Go to That School"

The ultimate test of one's views of a university campus is the type of recommendation one would make to a young person selecting a university. In this way, individual, family, and collective knowledge of a university's reputation moves from the present to future generations. The reputation of a university is linked in central ways to its position in local communities, Black or non-Black. On the exit questionnaire we asked parents, "If you were asked by a Black high school student to recommend a college in this state, would you recommend State University very favorably, somewhat favorably, somewhat unfavorably, or very unfavorably with respect to the racial climate there?" Two-thirds said that they would give a somewhat or very unfavorable recommendation to a high school student, while a quarter said that they would give a somewhat favorable recommendation. Only one person would give a very favorable recommendation, and a few others were uncertain.

Several parents gave a very negative reply to an open-ended question about recommending SU. For example, one parent answered this way: "I wouldn't recommend anybody to go to that school, with low self-esteem." And another parent underscored his point this way:

> To most of them I would say, just because of experience and because it's tough enough, there are enough challenges, and you don't want to add that one on unless there's some overriding reason.
> Moderator: I get a sense you're discouraging them.
> Father: For most Black students, yes, I would discourage them from going to State University. Whereas two years ago I would have offered some encouragement. Basically the only competitive edge it has is cost.

Drawing on their *experience,* a common process in the interview groups, some Black parents judged the personal and psychological stress generated by racial hurdles at SU to be so great as to outweigh the benefits for potential students.

However, the majority view seemed to be that their advice on colleges would be tailored to the needs and strengths of a particular student, a point this expressive parent underscored:

> I think that an individual brings an experience to their own education. Everyone's isn't always the same.
> Another parent: Even if it makes them uncomfortable?
> First parent: No. Different people react differently to a situation. And there are many people who are successful— African Americans who have had successful experiences. So I wouldn't limit anyone by saying, "Don't go because of the racial attitude." I might say, "You'll run into racism at the university just as you'll run into racism—"
> Another parent: Any place else.
> First parent: —It's how you handle it and how you feel about yourself. My only problem is how I feel about young people in the seventeen-to-nineteen age group. It's such an evolutionary period that so much harm can be done. It would depend on the person.

A number of the parents amplified this point by arguing that only those students who are "tough" should take on the racial climate at universities like State University. In these probing commentaries, the parents bring up issues that we saw them discuss in regard to their own children; we see the accent on individual and collective experience with racism as the inevitable backdrop of much Black decision making about higher education.

One mother answered the question about encouraging a high school student in this manner:

> I think if I was going to encourage someone to go there because, for instance, they want to go to the school of [names a SU program] because it's one of the best in the country . . . it would have to be someone who is very highly motivated. And . . . there has to be some kind of support system there for them. And I think it would be incumbent upon the parents and the other students to, [in the] freshman year, try to get together and at least form some kind of unit to help these kids get through there because, like he said, otherwise they're just lost.

Suggesting that SU is for the highly motivated, this speaker recommended the defensive strategy of banding together. In contrast to certain critics of higher education like D'Souza and Bloom, many Black parents see Black students' sticking together in traditionally White places as necessary for their personal and academic survival, not as some type of organized anti-White activity. These peer-group settings give many first-year college students a place to be themselves and to find supportive friends without the intrusion of racial barriers.

Accenting the requirement of mental toughness, one focus group participant added this penetrating social commentary:

> The people that I've spoken with over the past couple of years . . . who attended [State University] . . . have had negative things to say. But they all graduated, and they are all successful in their respective careers. So, I guess . . . it strikes a balance. I think there are some things they went through that were challenging, and I guess, if you're mentally strong enough, you can rise above and get what you want out of the program. But a lot of the stories I remember and the one that I related—just little things that I felt were kind of demeaning to us as Black people just should not have [happened]. It's sad that . . . a person has to learn in that type of atmosphere—that you have to go through that kind of thing.

The approach of the majority of the parents to advising students about how to deal with predominantly White universities like SU was not usually one of avoidance and retreat. For many of the parents, the choice of a predominantly White college must be made with eyes open and a certain realism about the omnipresence of racist attitudes, as this parent emphasized:

> I think they have a lot to offer. I think there's a good academic program there. I think once you get a degree, . . . you can go far. It's something that is respected nationwide, and I would not steer a young person away from the university simply because it's racism everywhere. . . . You can tell the child to go down [to] the basement, and I'll open up a college down there, and that's going to be perfect. But I just wouldn't—I would not—steer this child away from State University solely on [the] racial climate there, because . . . it may be moving worse than somewhere else, but it's still tension; it's everywhere.

A certain resignation about racial impediments and animosity in everyday life in the United States creeps into many of the answers of both the parents and the students. The predominantly White university is not an island of tolerance in an ocean of intolerance, as it has often been pictured. From the Black perspective, it is another major arena of everyday intolerance and racism.

Phrasing his answer eloquently, one father noted that advice giving and decision making about majority-White colleges and universities was like being part of a military campaign:

> I don't think that I could ever be so shallow as to say to a student or a guy or a girl who wants to go to college [at] State University, "Don't go there because [of the] prejudice or there's a history of racism." . . . So, if a student, . . . —let's say that this is an intelligent child—is looking at the academics that they could achieve at this university, and they're looking at

184 FEAGIN, VERA, AND IMANI

what I could get at this university [that] will help me do what I want in life, okay, then, I would say, "Well, this university's a good school for this thing, that, and the other. However, I think you should be well advised to know that you will probably—I'm not saying you will, but you may probably—experience this sort of problem, so I'm just telling you so."

Moderator: What sort of problem?

Father: Racial prejudice. . . . A White student is treated like a number; a Black student is treated . . . less than a number. See, because the White student goes to school, he says, "Well, I'm going to get an education first, and the college has this atmosphere." A Black student going to a White town is war.

The parental remarks on the recommendation they might or might not make to a high school student considering State University illustrate the complex situations and difficult choices that confront Black parents and children in dealing with higher education in the United States. Many felt that SU's academic programs warranted a young Black person's consideration, yet they suggested that the Black student who chooses SU will likely require much familial, peer, and other social support to survive personally and academically. These African American parents generally seem to believe that only strong and highly motivated Black students should choose a predominantly White college or university.

## Conclusion

Across the nation, African American parents and students face distinctive, difficult, and often agonizing dilemmas in making choices about higher education. Central to these dilemmas are the racial reputations of traditionally White college and university campuses. The military language—such as "struggle" and "war"—sometimes used in the focus groups indicates the painful labor and effort that a racist environment imposes on African American students seeking greater academic opportunities. African American students in majority-White university settings must be able to put up with racial slurs, to avoid becoming "lost," to protect themselves from personal "harm," and to endure or confront the often negative racial climate. Such conditions do not describe a truly positive educational experience for any person.

Within the geographical area that it serves, a predominantly White university's reputation is a condensation of individual and collective memories. From the data we have seen on predominantly White universities, this reputation can be very different for Black and White families. Judging from academic quality reports and alumni publications, most major public universities have reputations accenting excellent academic programs and supportive social environments in the White communities which send students to these universities. However, while Black communities typically regarded these universities' academic programs as very good, their racial climates are often another matter. Many African American parents feel that a typical Black student will pay a heavy personal price for participation in the desirable academic environments at these traditionally White colleges and universities.

In general, African American parents and students want the same things from a college education as White parents and students. They seek solid college credentials and a broadening of the mind within a personally and socially supportive campus atmosphere. Yet the choice of a college for African Americans involves serious dilemmas and major struggles not generally faced by White Americans. The racial barriers of the past and the hope that the racial situation will change in the future color the temporal aspects of these educational choices and dilemmas. African American parents' expectations for their children are grounded in their own experiences as well as those of other family members and the larger African American community. References to past racial segregation and violence-prone supremacist groups like the Ku Klux Klan are notable because they point to how violent White hostility has been in the past and the present. African American parents cannot afford to ignore this nation's racialized past, whether it be the racism of yesterday or of decades past, if they are going to make intelligent decisions about their children's futures.

# References

Ackerman, Todd. 1994. UT [University of Texas] minority survey critical. *Houston Chronicle,* January 29, A31.

Allen, Walter R., and Nesha Z. Haniff. 1991. Race, gender, and academic performance. In *College in Black and White: African American students in predominantly White and historically Black public universities,* edited by Walter R. Allen, Edgar G. Epps, and Nesha Z. Haniff, 95–109. Albany: State University of New York Press.

Ani, Marimba. 1994. *Yurugu: An African-centered critique of European cultural thought and behavior.* Trenton, NJ: Africa World Press.

Bernstein, Richard. 1994. *Dictatorship of virtue: Multiculturalism and the battle for America's future.* New York: Alfred A. Knopf.

Bloom, Allan. 1987. *The closing of the American mind: How higher education has failed democracy and impoverished the souls of today's students.* New York: Simon and Schuster.

Delany, Sarah, and A. Elizabeth Delany. 1993. *Having our say: The Delany sisters' first 100 years.* New York: Kodansha International.

D'Souza, Dinesh. 1991. *Illiberal education: The politics of race and sex on campus.* New York: Vintage.

Eliade, Mircea. 1959. *The sacred and the profane.* New York: Harcourt Brace.

Ellison, Ralph. 1952. 1989. *Invisible Man.* New York: Vintage Books.

Feagin, Joe R., and Melvin P. Sikes. 1994. *Living with racism: The Black middle class experience.* Boston: Beacon Press.

Fleming, Jacqueline. 1984. *Blacks in college: A comparative study of students' success in Black and in White institutions.* San Francisco: Jossey-Bass.

Loewen, James W. 1995. *Lies my teacher told me: Everything your American history textbook got wrong.* New York: New Press.

Mbiti, John S. 1970. *African religions and philosophies.* New York: Anchor Press.

Richards, Dona Marimba. 1980. European mythology: The ideology of progress. In *Contemporary Black thought,* edited by Molefi Asante and Abdulai Vandi, 59–79. Beverly Hills, CA: Sage.

Schlesinger, Arthur M., Jr. 1991. *The disuniting of America: Reflections on a multicultural society.* New York: W. W. Norton.

*Studies of intercollegiate athletics: The experiences of Black intercollegiate athletes at NCAA Division I institutions.* 1989. Palo Alto, CA: American Institutes for Research, Center for the Study of Athletics.

Tarpley, Natasha. 1993. Voices from the college front. *Essence,* October, 65–71.

Vera, Hernan, and Andrew Cordon. 1995. The beautiful American: Fictions of the White Messiah in the American cinema. Unpublished research paper, University of Florida.

PART III

# Faculty and Administrative Issues

# CHAPTER 9

# Outsiders Within

*Race, Gender, and Faculty Status in U.S. Higher Education*

WALTER R. ALLEN, EDGAR G. EPPS,
ELIZABETH A. GUILLORY, SUSAN A. SUH,
MARGUERITE BONOUS-HAMMARTH,
AND MARTHA L. A. STASSEN

The underrepresentation and low academic status of women and faculty of color is a persistent problem in U.S. higher education. Research on African American and female faculty reveals continued underrepresentation at most colleges and universities. The limited numbers of women and people of color within the professoriat are also concentrated at the lower levels of the academic prestige system. The hierarchy, which favors men over women and Whites over non-Whites, typically penalizes faculty who are Black and female.[1] Women professors and African American faculty are less likely to be tenured, spend more time on teaching and administrative tasks v. research, are located at less prestigious institutions, and have lower academic ranks compared to their White male peers. Additionally, a multiplicative effect of race and gender exists such that Black women occupy lower academic status compared to Whites, males, White men, White women, and Black men (Gregory 1995; H. Astin et al. 1997). Race and gender inequities are implicated in the persistent problem of underrepresentation and low academic status among African American and women college faculty generally—and among African American women faculty specifically.

Higher education institutions are greatly influenced by, and cannot be analyzed apart from, the larger social, historical, and cultural context. Attempts to improve the status of people of color and women must therefore consider how higher education is organized and how it functions. Higher education is characterized by an academic hierarchy, which assigns schools

---

1. This chapter uses "African American" and "Black" interchangeably.

to various prestige levels based on numerous criteria, for example, average test scores, faculty/student ratio, and selectivity of admissions. The opportunities available to different race/gender groups in American society are linked to their degree of access to higher prestige colleges and universities (Epps 1998). For reasons of historical and ongoing discrimination, the operation of the academic prestige hierarchy contributes to the maintenance of substantial educational inequality, not only among institutions, but also among different student constituencies.

The positions of different racial, ethnic, socioeconomic and gender groups within the academic hierarchy are consistent with their differential status, wealth, and power in American society (Blackwell 1981; Bowen and Bok 1998). Racial and ethnic people of color (i.e., African Americans, Latina/os, and Asian Americans), as well as women, face barriers due to the historical, cultural, and social factors that have frequently shaped their relations with Whites and/or males in American society. Pervasive attitudes of racism and sexism, and differential access and power, continue to limit educational opportunities for people of color and for women in America. Such inequities produce the achievement discrepancies in contemporary American education that explain the relative scarcity of people of color and women faculty in academia (Nation 1998).

This study examines the status of people of color and women faculty in higher education and its relationship to access and success in the American professoriate. In particular, we compare people of color and female faculty characteristics, experiences, and achievement to those of White and male faculty. Our focus is on the opportunity structure, resources, and academic/ nonacademic demands, as these factors are related to the entrance and advancement of people of color and women in the professoriate.

## The Academic Prestige Hierarchy

In the prestige hierarchy of the American professoriate, the rank of "professor" is a highly valued, powerful status in which people of color and women continue to be vastly underrepresented. Previous literature suggests that academics are among the "upper" classes of American society (Epps 1998). In addition to such benefits as tenure and choice of working hours, much of the status value of the professoriate is based on its relative exclusivity. The status of faculty members is determined not only by the quality/ quantity/visibility of their research but also by the prestige of the institutions where they are employed.

The academic hierarchy in American higher education has been described as follows: Major research universities (especially Ivy League schools and similar institutions) are at the top of the academic hierarchy, followed by highly selective liberal arts colleges, public and private colleges that grant graduate degrees, nonselective four-year colleges, and community colleges (Clark 1987). Research also points out that faculty culture differs significantly at the various types of institutions (Clark 1987). However, the most prestigious or leading universities set the standards that other institutions emulate if they aspire to improve their relative positions in the academic hierarchy. With each passing decade, the reward system of promoting academics on the grounds of research and published scholarship has become more deeply rooted in universities (H. Astin and Snyder 1984).

The prestige of both the graduate program and the employing institution influences a young faculty member's opportunities for becoming a productive, respected scholar. In each case, the stronger the research tradition, the greater the likelihood that young scholars will acquire the knowledge, values, resources, and opportunities that lead to research productivity. Academics of color are more likely to graduate from institutions with weak research traditions and more limited resources. They are also more likely to find their first jobs in similar institutions. As a result, scholars of color are at a cumulative disadvantage compared to graduates of higher-ranked, better-resourced universities for positions in prestigious institutions. Effectively recruiting and retaining racial/ethnic faculty members have been major concerns in higher education for the past three decades. Nonetheless, the increase in the small percentages of minorities across faculty ranks has been negligible (H. Astin et al. 1997). The related goal of recruiting/retaining female faculty has achieved considerably greater success over this same period (H. Astin et al. 1997).

The prestige rankings of the institutions where individuals earn doctoral degrees often determine the prestige of the institutions where they obtain employment. The relative paucity of scholars of color in high-prestige doctoral programs partially accounts for the difficulties they encounter when they apply for faculty positions at elite institutions (Smelser and Content 1980). Further, the low representation of students of color at prestigious undergraduate institutions leads to their low representation at highly prestigious graduate schools. This situation in turn leads to low representation of scholars of color among the faculties of major research universities.

The absence of faculty of color lessens the probability that students of color will complete graduate and professional programs at the same rate as White students. Research shows that the most persistent, statistically significant predictor of enrollment and graduation of African American graduate and professional students is the presence of faculty of color (Blackwell 1981). Institutions that are successful in recruiting and retaining Black faculty do a far better job of recruiting, enrolling, and graduating Black students than those with few or no Black faculty members (Blackwell 1981). There is growing evidence that faculty—and students—of color experience severe marginalization on campuses (Aguirre, Hernandez, and Martinez 1994; Boice

1993; Bourguignon et al. 1987; Nakanishi 1993; Olivas 1988). (See also Chang and Kiang; Hurtado, this volume.) This marginalization significantly reduces their access to networks, resources, and experiences necessary for academic success. Simply put, it is a pipeline (A. Astin 1982) or flow of the river (Bowen and Bok 1998; Olivas 1988) problem: Too few people of color successfully traverse the qualifying stages which lead to scarce, treasured positions at the top of the academic hierarchy.

## Obstacles Encountered by Faculty of Color

Women faculty and faculty of color often encounter obstacles that constrain their ability to move up the academic hierarchy. Two obstacles of particular concern are (1) the tendency of female faculty and faculty of color to be overburdened with teaching and service responsibilities, and (2) the inflexible expectations of universities and colleges about research and publication.

Like all faculty, female faculty and faculty of color have teaching, counseling, and committee responsibilities as well as expectations that they will conduct research and produce scholarly publications (Nettles and Perna 1995; ASA Commission 1984). Female faculty and faculty of color often place a higher value on teaching and service. Consequently, they spend more time counseling students, advising/mentoring students, and serving on committees. In the academic prestige hierarchy, these activities are less likely to be recognized or rewarded than research, grantsmanship, and publication (Banks 1984; Blackwell 1996; Menges and Exurn 1983; Nakanishi 1993). Teaching responsibilities also tend to be heavier at less research-oriented institutions, while publication opportunities are fewer. Because many scholars of color begin their careers in institutions that emphasize teaching over research, they frequently have heavy teaching loads and relatively few opportunities for research and publication. As a result, they often do not compile a significant list of publications and remain outside the academic mainstream throughout their careers.

Female professors and faculty of color regularly complain about overwhelming counseling responsibilities. Officially, counseling assignments are the same for all faculty, regardless of race or gender. However, many women faculty and faculty of color find themselves in situations where students' expectations add complications. Students typically expect women faculty and faculty of color to be available when they need to discuss academic or personal problems. They are not very receptive to explanations about the faculty member's need to conduct research and to publish. In addition, female faculty and faculty of color often feel intense personal obligations to serve as advisors to female student groups and student groups of color. Many female faculty and faculty of color also undertake disproportionate burdens for supervising junior and senior papers, master's theses, and doctoral dissertations in areas where they are among the few faculty with expertise. These advisory activities can be very consuming, draining time and energy away from research and writing.

Mentoring is an important role that most professors assume in some form. However, many women faculty and faculty of color, through a sense of obligation to their students, elect to become mentors to many more students than is typical for their White and male peers. This is not entirely a voluntary process. Most predominantly White institutions employ only a few faculty of color, and many departments employ few women. Therefore, students seeking experts on race/ethnicity or gender-related topics, or those simply looking for supportive role models who share their background and experiences, are drawn to the small group of professors of color and women for direction, advice, and moral support. This is a role that most women professors and professors of color feel obligated to accept, given the history of race/gender inequities in this society. Again, time demands can be considerable, e.g., providing students with social support and guidance, writing letters of recommendation, assisting with graduate or professional school selection, and critiquing numerous drafts of job and fellowship applications.

Female faculty and faculty of color may also find themselves overburdened with departmental, university, and community obligations (Bowen and Schuster 1986). In addition to standard committees, female faculty and faculty of color are also expected (by the administration, faculty, colleagues, students, and sometimes community members) to serve on committees dealing with issues of color and gender, campus security, race relations, recruiting faculty/students of color, university relations, and community outreach. Faculty members in such situations feel keen responsibilities to their departments, the university, students, and to larger constituencies. Usually they view improving campus relations, enlarging opportunities for female students/faculty and those of color, and strengthening support systems for nontraditional students as vitally important objectives, well worth the time and energy devoted to them. However, they undertake such work almost always at the cost of reducing their efforts in other areas. More often than not, work on such fronts is viewed as avocation, not vocation; it seldom "gets counted" on measures of academic career advancement.

Frequently, female faculty and faculty of color deal with overload by postponing or downshifting research and publication efforts. Nevertheless, universities expect the same level of productivity from women faculty and those of color as from the faculty at large. The evaluation processes leading to academic security and success typically give little consideration to the detrimental effects of excessive counseling, advising, mentoring, or committee work demands (Padilla 1994).

Additionally, faculty of color whose scholarship focuses on ethnic issues express tremendous concern that their work will be devalued and dismissed as polemical, self-serving, or out-of-the-mainstream (Bourguignon et al. 1987). Because their scholarly work and community involvement are often focused on social change and issues of color, they must confront judgments that these activities are nonacademic and inappropriate (Collins 1998; H. Astin et al. 1997; Banks 1984; Bourguignon et al. 1987).

In general, the underrepresentation of faculty of color in American colleges and universities is well documented (Blackwell 1981; A. Astin, Korn, and Dey 1991; H. Astin et al. 1997; Sax et al. 1996). (See also Scheurich and Young; Villalpando and Delgado Bernal; Teddlie and Freeman; Anderson, this volume.) Thus, this study discusses the academic prestige hierarchy in higher education and its relationship to Black, female, and Black female access to the professorate. We also focus on various barriers to the recruitment, retention, and success of African American faculty. In particular, this chapter addresses various obstacles encountered by African American and female faculty. Of special interest are the academic and nonacademic demands on time and resources that interfere with their professorial advancement and contribute to the marginalization of their research. We conclude by considering the impact of affirmative action and recruitment strategies on the progress of female faculty and faculty of color, especially African Americans.

## Problem and Methods of Study

The data in this study are from campuses with successful institutional responses to African American students (i.e., increased enrollment, retention, and graduation rates). These campuses also represented different institutional contexts according to the Carnegie classification system of higher education institutions, e.g., comprehensive university, private research I, public research I, liberal arts college, and doctoral or regional university. We gathered data at three private institutions (Northwestern University, Oberlin College, and Lewis College) and at three public institutions (Southern Illinois University, Cleveland State University, and Eastern Michigan University). We collected self-completed, mail questionnaire data from 1,189 college and university faculty in 1990 during a study based at the University of Michigan, Ann Arbor, under the direction of Walter R. Allen, Gerald Gurin, and Marvin Peterson.

The measures in this study can be grouped into background factors, intervening factors, and outcome factors. More detail about these factors and the verbatim questions used to measure or represent each factor are in the appendix. Two sets of outcome factors are of interest here: faculty workload focus and faculty satisfaction. The faculty workload focus item measured the estimated mean number of hours devoted in a typical week to teaching, research, and administrative/committee work (question 8). We measured faculty satisfaction with a general question (3) and a series of specific questions (4B, 4D, 4G) about satisfaction with salary, faculty resources, and institutional leadership. This study included five background measures: race (African American, White); gender (female, male); number of years on faculty; academic rank (professor, associate, assistant, other); and academic tenure (tenured, not tenured).

It is our sense that, generally, relationships and pathways of influence flow from the background factors through the intervening factors to produce the observed outcomes. This paper describes and compares faculty across race, gender and race/gender groups. For this purpose, we use univariate statistics (frequencies, measures of central tendency, measures of dispersion) and bivariate statistics (cross-tables, analysis of variance). In addition to examining race and gender differences, we examine race/gender subgroup differences.

**Findings**

Our initial descriptive analyses are based on data from the entire sample of faculty who responded to the survey (i.e., Asian American, African American, Latina/o, and White faculty). Table 9.1 summarizes the general characteristics of all faculty who responded to our survey. Consistent with studies cited above and with general patterns in U.S. higher education, our faculty respondents are mostly White (91 percent) and male (72 percent). White males are the largest single race/gender subgroup (65 percent) followed by White women (26 percent). Asian American and African American males comprise 4 percent and 2 percent respectively. In no case does any non-White/female faculty subgroup exceed 1 percent (African American female = .9 percent, Latina = .4 percent, Asian American female = .7 percent).

The six campuses represent diverse contexts in terms of public/private control, student enrollment, state of residence, and urban/rural setting. The largest contingent of faculty respondents is from Eastern Michigan University (24 percent), the smallest from Lewis College (4 percent). Thirty-eight percent of respondents teach at private institutions (Northwestern University, Oberlin College, Lewis College). The remainder are employed at public institutions (Eastern Michigan University, Southern Illinois University, Cleveland State University). Almost a third of respondents are relative newcomers, having been at their current institution fewer than five years. Nearly half of these faculty have been at their current institutions for more than a decade (49 percent); of these, 20 percent have over twenty years' service. A sizable majority of respondents are tenured (66 percent).

**Table 9.1**
**Characteristics of All Faculty in Study**

|                                | | *Frequency* | *Percent* |
|--------------------------------|--|---------|---------|
| *Racial Group/Gender*          | | | |
| Black woman                    | | 10      | 0.9%    |
| Black man                      | | 25      | 2.2     |
| White woman                    | | 290     | 25.8    |
| White man                      | | 734     | 65.2    |
| Latina                         | | 4       | 0.4     |
| Latino                         | | 9       | 0.8     |
| Asian American woman           | | 8       | 0.7     |
| Asian American man             | | 46      | 4.1     |
|                                | Total $N =$ | 1,126 | |
| *Current Institution*          | | | |
| Eastern Michigan University    | | 280     | 23.5%   |
| Lewis                          | | 45      | 3.8     |
| Oberlin                        | | 134     | 11.3    |
| Northwestern                   | | 270     | 22.7    |
| Cleveland State University     | | 216     | 18.2    |
| Southern Illinois University   | | 244     | 20.5    |
|                                | Total $N =$ | 1,189 | |
| *Years at Institution*         | | | |
| 0–4 years                      | | 352     | 31.2%   |
| 5–10                           | | 222     | 19.6    |
| 11–20                          | | 325     | 28.8    |
| Over 20 years                  | | 231     | 20.4    |
|                                | Total $N =$ | 1,130 | |
| *Rank*                         | | | |
| Instructor                     | | 42      | 3.6%    |
| Assistant professor            | | 291     | 25.2    |
| Associate professor            | | 338     | 29.2    |
| Professor                      | | 449     | 38.8    |
| Lecturer                       | | 36      | 3.1     |
|                                | Total $N =$ | 1,156 | |
| *Seniority*                    | | | |
| Tenured                        | | 782     | 65.8%   |
| Not tenured                    | | 384     | 32.3    |
|                                | Total $N =$ | 1,166 | |

Tables 9.2 through 9.6 summarize responses for questions in five areas of work experience for all faculty across the four racial groups: satisfaction, teaching, student advising, committee work, and publications/research re-

**Table 9.2**
**Satisfaction Questions for All Faculty in Study: Univariate Statistics**

|  |  | *Percent* |
|---|---|---|
| *General Satisfaction with Institution* |  |  |
| Very good |  | 37.0% |
| Fairly good |  | 52.8 |
| Not place for me |  | 10.3 |
|  | Total $N =$ | 100.0% |
| *Satisfaction with Salary* |  |  |
| Dissatisfied/very |  | 39.5% |
| Neutral |  | 20.0 |
| Satisfied/very |  | 40.5 |
|  | Total $N =$ | 100.0% |
| *Satisfaction with Resources* |  |  |
| Dissatisfied/very |  | 47.4% |
| Neutral |  | 19.8 |
| Satisfied/very |  | 32.8 |
|  | Total $N =$ | 100.0% |
| *Satisfaction with Leadership* |  |  |
| Dissatisfied/very |  | 50.1% |
| Neutral |  | 26.0 |
| Satisfied/very |  | 23.9 |
|  | Total $N =$ | 100.0% |

spectively. At first glance, faculty in this study seem to be highly satisfied with their profession. Nearly 90 percent feel "very good" (37 percent) or "fairly good" (53 percent) about the institution where they work. (See Table 9.2.) However, 40 percent are "dissatisfied" or "very dissatisfied" with salary. Almost half (48 percent) expressed dissatisfaction with available resources. Half are likewise either "dissatisfied" or "very dissatisfied" with institutional leadership (50 percent).

It could well be that these faculty members enjoy their work but are nonetheless burdened by the weight of demands. Data presented in Table 9.7 shows heavy workloads (mean weekly hours = 52); their schedules are filled with both teaching and nonteaching (i.e., committee work, administrative work, and research) responsibilities. In approximate increments, they spend just over half of their weekly work time teaching/advising students (mean hours = 28) while one-quarter of the week's time is spent on scholarly research (mean hours = 14). Table 9.3 shows that two-thirds (64 percent) teach both undergraduate (mean = 69 students) and graduate students (mean = 8 students). Table 9.5 shows that, by their estimate, administrative/committee work requires one full day per week (mean hours = 9.84), although these

## Table 9.3
## Teaching Questions for All Faculty in Study: Univariate Statistics

|  | Percent | Mean | SD | N |
|---|---|---|---|---|
| *Problems Teaching "Academically Underprepared Students"?* |  |  |  |  |
| Disagree/strongly | 46.4% |  |  |  |
| Neutral | 27.2 |  |  |  |
| Agree/strongly | 26.4 |  |  |  |
| Total N = | 1,038 |  |  |  |
| *Teaching Responsibilities in Last Five Years* |  |  |  |  |
| Entirely undergrads | 29.2% |  |  |  |
| Both | 64.4 |  |  |  |
| Entirely grads | 4.3 |  |  |  |
| Not teaching | 2.1 |  |  |  |
| Total N = | 1,036 |  |  |  |
| *Communicate with Black Students* |  |  |  |  |
| Less well/much less | 17.3% |  |  |  |
| Neutral | 78.8 |  |  |  |
| Somewhat better/much better | 3.9 |  |  |  |
| Total N = | 1,019 |  |  |  |
| Hours teaching per week |  | 22.81 | 10.88 | 1,030 |
| Number of LD undergrads this term |  | 47.18 | 81.27 | 1,011 |
| Number of UD undergrads this term |  | 22.34 | 27.67 | 1,010 |
| Number of grads this term |  | 7.96 | 14.55 | 1,010 |
| Number of Black LD undergrads |  | 5.17 | 12.48 | 1,011 |
| Number of Black UD undergrads |  | 1.93 | 3.90 | 1,009 |
| Number of Black grads |  | 0.78 | 3.48 | 1,012 |

## Table 9.4
## Student Advising Questions for All Faculty in Study: Univariate Statistics
### (N = 1,000)

| *Hours per Week with Students Outside of Class* | Percent | Mean | SD |
|---|---|---|---|
|  |  | 5.94 | 5.17 |
| *Academic Counseling to Undergrads* |  |  |  |
| None | 11.0% |  |  |
| Few | 44.4 |  |  |
| Less than half | 22.0 |  |  |
| At least half | 22.6 |  |  |
| Total N = | 1,003 |  |  |
| *Career Counseling to Undergrads* |  |  |  |
| None | 5.5% |  |  |
| Few | 45.4 |  |  |
| Less than half | 28.1 |  |  |
| At least half | 21.1 |  |  |
| Total N = | 1,008 |  |  |

**Table 9.5**

**Committee Work Questions for All Faculty in Study: Univariate Statistics**

(*N* = 1,027)

| Hours per Week Administrative and Committee | Percent | Mean | SD |
|---|---|---|---|
| | | 8.94 | 8.76 |
| *Serve on department committee on minority issues?* | | | |
| Yes | 5.8% | | |
| No | 94.2 | | |
| Total *N* = 1,041 | | | |
| *Serve on institutional committee on minority issues?* | | | |
| Yes | 7.9% | | |
| No | 92.1 | | |
| Total *N* = 1,041 | | | |
| *Member of organization concerned with Black issues?* | | | |
| Yes | 12.5% | | |
| No | 87.5 | | |
| Total *N* = 1,034 | | | |

**Table 9.6**

**Research/Publications Questions for All Faculty in Study: Univariate Statistics**

(*N* = 1,028)

| Hours per Week Research | Percent | Mean | SD |
|---|---|---|---|
| | | 14.16 | 12.25 |
| *Number of Articles Submitted in Past Two Years* | | | |
| Never | 15.8% | | |
| 1–2 times | 31.3 | | |
| 3–4 times | 25.3 | | |
| 5–10 times | 20.2 | | |
| > 10 times | 7.5 | | |
| Total *N* = 1,040 | | | |
| *Number of Presentations in Past Two Years* | | | |
| Never | 17.8% | | |
| 1–2 times | 29.0 | | |
| 3–4 times | 26.4 | | |
| 5–10 times | 18.1 | | |
| > 10 times | 8.7 | | |
| Total *N* = 1,045 | | | |
| *Number of Publications in Past Two Years* | | | |
| Never | 31.5% | | |
| 1–2 times | 31.0 | | |
| 3–4 times | 19.5 | | |
| 5–10 times | 12.8 | | |
| > 10 times | 5.2 | | |
| Total *N* = 1,037 | | | |

**Table 9.7**
**Breakdown of Work Activities (Means Hours)**

| Activity | Hours/Week | SD |
|---|---|---|
| Teaching | 22.81 | 10.88 |
| Other time with students | 5.94 | 5.17 |
| Administration, committee | 8.94 | 8.76 |
| Research | 14.16 | 12.25 |
| Average total hours per week: | 51.85 | |

workloads vary greatly (SD = 8.76). Table 9.6 shows that over half of these faculty respondents also submitted articles for publication and/or presented papers at professional meetings three or more times in the past two years.

These data also reveal interesting patterns of faculty involvement with Black students and with campus issues of color more generally. Close to half of the faculty report that they have no problems effectively teaching students who are academically unprepared. (See Table 9.3.) However, a sizable proportion—over one-quarter—do report some difficulties in providing effective instruction for students who are not adequately prepared academically. While the great majority of these faculty do not believe that they have any difficulties understanding and communicating with their African American students (79 percent), a sizable 17 percent believe that they communicate less well with Black students than with other students. Strikingly, a miniscule percentage of faculty serve on department committees (6 percent) and university committees (8 percent) concerned with issues of color. (See Table 9.5.) These small percentages look suspiciously like the percentages of faculty of color in this sample, suggesting that the committees dealing with university affairs of color are largely drawn from their ranks. A slightly larger percentage of faculty claimed membership in organizations that were concerned with Black issues.

## Black and White Faculty

We now consider faculty work experiences by race, gender, and race/gender subgroups. When we compare where African American faculty work, academic rank, and tenure status in this midwestern sample with White peers, we find only one statistically significant difference. (See Table 9.8A.) African American faculty have significantly fewer mean years at their institutions than Whites (1.76 v. 2.44, $p < .001$). This finding suggests that Black faculty are more recent recruits to these campuses. Indeed, 41 percent of Black faculty are assistant professors v. 25 percent of White faculty. By contrast, 40

## Table 9.8A
## Faculty Characteristics by Race and Gender

| | African American | White | Women | Men |
|---|---|---|---|---|
| *Current Institution* | | | | |
| Eastern Michigan University | 22.9% | 23.8% | 32.7% | 20.3%*** |
| Lewis | 2.9[a] | 3.8 | 5.7 | 3.0 |
| Oberlin | 28.6 | 10.9 | 10.3 | 12.0 |
| Northwestern | 14.3 | 22.4 | 128.3 | 23.6 |
| Cleveland State University | 14.3 | 18.1 | 14.3 | 19.4 |
| Southern Illinois University | 17.1 | 21.0 | 18.7 | 21.7 |
| Total *N* = | 35 | 1,024 | 300 | 759 |
| *Rank* | | | | |
| Lecturer | | 3.1 | 5.2 | 2.1 |
| Instructor | | 3.7% | 7.9% | 1.9%*** |
| Assistant professor | 41.2% | 24.5 | 36.8 | 20.5 |
| Associate professor | 35.3 | 29.2 | 30.6 | 28.9 |
| Professor | 23.5 | 39.6 | 19.6 | 46.7 |
| Total *N* = | 34 | 1,005 | 291 | 748 |
| *Seniority* | | | | |
| Tenured | 62.9% | 67.7% | 51.8% | 73.7%*** |
| Not tenured | 37.1 | 32.3 | 48.2 | 26.3 |
| Total *N* = | 35 | 1,021 | 299 | 757 |
| Many years at institution | 1.76 | 2.44*** | 2.06 | 2.55*** |
| SD | 0.94 | 1.13 | 1.03 | 1.13 |
| Total *N* = | 33 | 990 | 289 | 734 |

[a]Cell count < 5.
*** *p*  .001 level

percent of White faculty are full professors v. 24 percent of Black faculty—
a near-exact reversal of pattern. Contrary to findings from previous research,
the percentage of Black and White faculty with tenure is approximately the
same in this sample (63 and 68 percent respectively). However, African
American faculty are much more likely than their White peers to be employed at private institutions (46 v. 37 percent). This fact takes on special
significance when we recall that 75 percent of currently enrolled African
American college students attend public institutions (Nettles and Perna 1995).
  We must, of course, be mindful of the vast difference in the total number
of African American faculty (*N* = 35) compared with the total number of
White faculty (*N* = 1,024) in this sample. This huge discrepancy requires that
we be cautious in drawing conclusions. The discrepancy also goes to the

heart of a key concern of this chapter—the persistent and dramatic underrepresentation of African Americans among the nation's college and university faculty. Too often this discrepancy is explained as the intractable result of a limited pool of eligible faculty, but this explanation does not pay enough attention to the patterns of institutional discrimination that block the recruitment, hiring, and retention of qualified African American candidates.

There are sizable gender differences, which show women in academe to be at a distinct disadvantage compared to their male peers. (See Table 9.8A.) In this sample, women—most of whom are White—are significantly more likely to have lower status as manifest by nontenure track academic appointments; 5 percent of women v. 2 percent of men are lecturers while 8 percent of women v. 2 percent of men are instructors. Men are also more likely to hold high-prestige appointments like professor (47 v. 20 percent) and to be tenured (74 v. 52 percent). Consistent with these patterns, women are also more recent arrivals at their institutions. They have fewer mean years at the institutions (2.06 v. 2.55), and overall their employment distribution is skewed toward the lower academic ranks.

As we expected, inequities in faculty employment status are more vividly revealed when we take account of race and gender simultaneously. (See Table 9.8B.) First, we see that African American women faculty are far and away the smallest group, outnumbered 2.5 to 1 by African American males. In turn, White women faculty outnumber Black male faculty by a factor of 10 and are themselves outnumbered 2.5 to 1 by White males. For every African American woman on the faculty in this representative sample, there are 73 White males and 29 White females! Men are advantaged within and across race in terms of academic prestige: 47 percent of White males and 28 percent of Black males are full professors, the highest academic rank. In comparison, only 20 percent of White women and 11 percent of Black women in this sample are full professors. Males of both races are also more likely to be tenured (White men—74 percent; Black men—68 percent). In contrast, 52 percent of White female faculty and 50 percent of Black female faculty are tenured. Finally Whites, especially White males, have more mean years of service at their institutions (White men—2.58 years; White women—2.07 years) than African Americans (Black men—1.79 years; Black women—1.67 years).

We see interesting, and in some cases significant, differences in levels of faculty satisfaction by race/gender. (See Table 9A.) Although no race differences achieve statistical significance, they are nonetheless revealing. For instance, while 37 percent of White faculty expressed the highest general satisfaction with their institutions, only 23 percent of Black faculty were so positive. Similarly, just under half (49 percent) of the African American faculty in this sample were "dissatisfied" or "very dissatisfied" with their salaries compared to only 40 percent of Whites. Equal percentages of Black (40

## Table 9.8B
## Faculty Characteristics by Race/Gender

| | African American | White | Women | Men |
|---|---|---|---|---|
| *Current Institution* | | | | |
| Eastern Michigan University | 20.0%[a] | 24.0% | 33.1% | 20.2%*** |
| Lewis | | 4.0[a] | 5.9 | 3.0 |
| Oberlin | 40.0[a] | 24.0 | 9.3 | 11.6 |
| Northwestern | | 20.0 | 19.0 | 23.7 |
| Cleveland State University | 20.0[a] | 12.0[a] | 14.1 | 19.6 |
| Southern Illinois University | 20.0[a] | 16.0[a] | 18.6 | 21.9 |
| Total *N* = | 10 | 25 | 290 | 734 |
| *Rank* | | | | |
| Lecturer | | | 5.3 | 2.2 |
| Instructor | | | 8.2% | 1.9%*** |
| Assistant professor | 44.4%[a] | 40.0% | 36.5 | 19.8 |
| Associate professor | 44.4[a] | 32.0 | 30.1 | 28.8 |
| Professor | 11.1[a] | 28.0 | 19.9 | 47.3 |
| Total *N* = | 9 | 25 | 282 | 723 |
| *Seniority* | | | | |
| Tenured | 50.0% | 68.0% | 51.9% | 73.9%*** |
| Not tenured | 50.0 | 32.0 | 48.1 | 26.1 |
| Total *N* = | 10 | 25 | 289 | 732 |
| Many years at institution | 1.67 | 1.79 | 2.07 | 2.58*** |
| SD | 0.87 | 0.98 | 1.03 | 1.13 |
| Total *N* = | 9 | 24 | 280 | 710 |

[a]Cell count < 5.
*** *p* .001

percent) and White (41 percent) faculty responded "satisfied" or "very satisfied" with their salaries.

Looking at gender differences, men seem to be more satisfied than women. (See Table 9.9A.) Males are significantly more likely to express highest general satisfaction (40 v. 30 percent). Moreover, female faculty are much less satisfied with institutional resources (55 v. 44 percent) and with institutional leadership (54 . 49 percent). They more often express extreme dissatisfaction (45 v. 38 percent) and less often report strong satisfaction (36 v. 42 percent) with their salaries than their male counterparts.

Comparisons across faculty race/gender subgroups reveal that African American women professors are generally the most dissatisfied. (See Table

**Table 9.9A**
**Faculty Satisfaction by Race and Gender**

|  | African American | White | Women | Men |
|---|---|---|---|---|
| *General Satisfaction with Institution* | | | | |
| Very good | 22.9% | 37.4% | 29.9% | 39.8%** |
| Fairly good | 65.7 | 52.3 | 58.1 | 50.7 |
| Not place for me | 11.4[a] | 10.2 | 12.1 | 9.6 |
| Total $N$ = | 35 | 1,015 | 298 | 752 |
| *Satisfaction with Salary* | | | | |
| Dissatisfied/very | 48.6% | 39.2% | 44.8% | 37.5% |
| Neutral | 11.4[a] | 20.3 | 19.1 | 20.3 |
| Satisfied/very | 40.0 | 40.5 | 36.1 | 42.2 |
| Total $N$ = | 35 | 1,017 | 299 | 753 |
| *Satisfaction with Resources* | | | | |
| Dissatisfied/very | 42.9% | 47.5% | 55.2% | 44.3%** |
| Neutral | 22.9 | 19.7 | 15.7 | 21.5 |
| Satisfied/very | 34.3 | 32.7 | 29.1 | 34.3 |
| Total $N$ = | 35 | 1,014 | 299 | 750 |
| *Satisfaction with Leadership* | | | | |
| Dissatisfied/very | 47.1% | 50.2% | 53.9% | 48.7% |
| Neutral | 38.2 | 25.6 | 26.6 | 25.7 |
| Satisfied/very | 14.7 | 24.2 | 19.5 | 25.6 |
| Total $N$ = | 34 | 1,017 | 297 | 754 |

[a]Cell count < 5.
*** $p$    .001
** $p$    .01

9.9B.) White male faculty are four times more likely than Black female professors to express the highest general satisfaction with their institutions (40 v. 10 percent). White female and Black male professors are three times more likely than their Black female peers to express highest general satisfaction (31 and 28 percent respectively, v. 10 percent). By the same token, three of five Black women professors (60 percent) express strong dissatisfaction with their salaries compared to 44 percent of Black men and White women and 37 percent of White men. Paradoxically, given their expressed dissatisfaction with the institution and with their salaries, Black female professors are the least critical of institutional leadership (i.e., fewer answered "dissatisfied" or "very dissatisfied" with leadership)— those very individuals most directly responsible for setting salaries and the general tenor of the institution. However, at the other extreme, Black female faculty are the least likely to answer "satisfied" or "very satisfied" with institutional leadership.

**Table 9.9B**
**Faculty Satisfaction by Race/Gender Subgroups**

|  | | African American Women | African American Men | White Women | White Men |
|---|---|---|---|---|---|
| *General Satisfaction with Institution* | | | | | |
| Very good | | 10.0%[a] | 28.0% | 30.6% | 40.2%* |
| Fairly good | | 80.0 | 60.0 | 57.3 | 50.3 |
| Not place for me | | 10.0[a] | 12.0[a] | 12.2 | 9.5 |
| | Total $N$ = | 10 | 25 | 288 | 727 |
| *Satisfaction with Salary* | | | | | |
| Dissatisfied/very | | 60.0% | 44.0% | 44.3% | 37.2% |
| Neutral | | 10.0[a] | 12.0[a] | 19.4 | 20.6 |
| Satisfied/very | | 30.0[a] | 44.0 | 36.3 | 42.2 |
| | Total $N$ = | 10 | 25 | 289 | 728 |
| *Satisfaction with Resources* | | | | | |
| Dissatisfied/very | | 50.0% | 40.0% | 55.4% | 44.4% |
| Neutral | | 10.0[a] | 28.0 | 15.9 | 21.2 |
| Satisfied/very | | 40.0[a] | 32.0 | 28.7 | 34.3 |
| | Total $N$ = | 10 | 25 | 289 | 725 |
| *Satisfaction with Leadership* | | | | | |
| Dissatisfied/very | | 40.0%[a] | 50.0% | 54.4% | 48.6% |
| Neutral | | 50.0 | 33.3 | 25.8 | 25.5 |
| Satisfied/very | | 10.0[a] | 16.7[a] | 19.9 | 25.9 |
| | Total $N$ = | 10 | 24 | 287 | 730 |

[a]Cell count < 5.
*$p$  .05

Overall teaching obligations seem to be comparable by race and gender, although there are several noteworthy differences. (See Table 9.10A.) Commenting on their teaching responsibilities over the past five years, 49 percent of Black faculty and 29 percent of White faculty taught only undergraduates. On average, African American faculty teach one and a half more hours per week than Whites (24.1 v. 22.8 hours). Black faculty also teach slightly more undergraduates on average (82 v. 69) and slightly fewer graduates (7.3 v. 8.0). In particular, African American faculty teach more Black students than their White colleagues, twice as many Black undergraduates on average (13 v. 7) and one-quarter more Black graduate students (.94 v. .78).

In a related vein, more African American faculty disagree that they have problems teaching "academically unprepared" students than do White faculty (66 v. 46 percent respectively). In contrast, slightly more White than Black faculty agree with this assessment (27 v. 20 percent respectively). Black and White faculty are starkly differentiated in their self-reported ability to understand and communicate with Black students: 47 percent of African American faculty claim to be "better" or "much better" in this regard compared with 2 percent of White faculty. At the other end of the spectrum, 18 percent of White v. no Black faculty claim to do "much less" or "less well" in understanding and communicating with Black students.

While few gender differences in faculty teaching responsibilities rise to the level of statistical significance, there are important, patterned discrepancies. (See Table 9.10A.) Women in this sample are significantly more likely to teach only undergraduate students (37 v. 26 percent), although in sheer numbers men teach more undergraduates. Women also teach significantly more hours weekly on average than men (25 v. 22 hours a week respectively). Female faculty are much more likely to disagree that they have problems teaching "academically unprepared" students (52 v. 44 percent).

Our examination of faculty race/gender subgroups reveals differences in teaching responsibilities that were masked under previous race and gender comparisons. (See Table 9.10B.) African American women in this faculty sample are disproportionately involved in undergraduate teaching; seven out of ten taught only undergraduates over the past five years, compared with 40 percent of African American men, 36 percent of White women, and 26 percent of White men. We also see significant differences in the extent to which Black men, Black women, White women, and White men deny having problems teaching "academically unprepared" students (respective percentages: 72, 50, 52 and 44). While vast race differences separate faculty in terms of the ability to understand and communicate with Black students, only minor gender differences are revealed within race. Half of Black female faculty and 46 percent of Black males—compared with 3 percent of White women and 2 percent of White men—claim to communicate better with Black students. Interestingly, African American males and White females teach more hours weekly (25 hours for both) than African American females (23 hours) and White males (22 hours). African American female and male faculty teach roughly twice as many Black undergraduate students compared to White female and White male faculty. Black and White female faculty have more Black graduate students than their male counterparts; moreover, White male faculty teach only three Black graduate students for every four taught by faculty from the other race/gender subgroups.

Beyond faculty teaching is faculty engagement with students outside class hours, most often taking the form of student advising. Broadly speaking, these faculty members devote one and a half hours daily (six to seven hours a week) to working with students outside class. (See Table 9.11A.) African American and female faculty spend more hours per week advising students on academics or future careers than Whites and males. Roughly 10

**Table 9.10A**
**Teaching Questions for All Faculty by Race and Gender**

|  | African American | White | Women | Men |
|---|---|---|---|---|
| *Problems Teaching Academically Underprepared?* | | | | |
| Disagree/strongly | 65.7% | 45.8% | 51.5% | 44.4% |
| Neutral | 14.3 | 27.6 | 23.2 | 28.7 |
| Agree/strongly | 20.0 | 26.6 | 25.3 | 26.8 |
| Total $N =$ | 35 | 1,003 | 293 | 745 |
| | | | | |
| *Teaching Responsibilities in Last Five Years* | | | | |
| Entirely undergrads | 48.6% | 28.5% | 36.9% | 26.1%*** |
| Both | 45.7 | 65.0 | 56.9 | 67.3 |
| Entirely grads | 5.7ᵃ | 4.3 | 3.4 | 4.7 |
| Not teaching |  | 2.2 | 2.8 | 1.9 |
| Total $N =$ | 35 | 1,001 | 290 | 746 |
| | | | | |
| *Communicate with Black Students* | | | | |
| Less well/much less |  | 17.9%*** | 16.8% | 17.5% |
| Neutral | 52.9% | 79.7 | 78.8 | 78.8 |
| Somewhat better/much better | 47.1 | 2.4 | 4.5 | 3.7 |
| Total $N =$ | 34 | 985 | 292 | 727 |
| Hours teaching per week (SD) | 24.09 | 22.77*** | 24.53 | 22.14*** |
|  | (12.32) | (10.83) | (10.55) | (10.93) |
| Number of LD undergrads this term | 55.32 | 46.89 | 42.30 | 49.08 |
|  | (74.87) | (81.50) | (73.71) | (83.99) |
| Number of UD undergrads this term | 26.35 | 22.20 | 22.36 | 22.33 |
|  | (29.63) | (27.60) | (27.86) | (27.61) |
| Number of grads this term | 7.29 | 7.98 | 6.93 | 8.36 |
|  | (13.49) | (14.59) | (14.04) | (14.74) |
| Number Black LD undergrads | 9.26 | 5.03 | 4.94 | 5.26 |
|  | (11.87) | (12.48) | (15.94) | (10.85) |
| Number of Black UD undergrads | 3.82 | 1.87** | 1.61 | 2.06 |
|  | (5.85) | (3.80) | (3.00) | (4.19) |
| Number of Black grads | 0.94 | 0.78 | 0.95 | 0.72 |
|  | (1.89) | (3.52) | (5.63) | (2.12) |

ᵃCell count < 5.
*** $p$  .001
** $p$  .01

Table 9.10B
**Table 9.10B**
**Teaching Questions for All Faculty by Race/Gender**

| | | African American Women | African American Men | White Women | White Men |
|---|---|---|---|---|---|
| *Problems Teaching Academically Underprepared?* | | | | | |
| Disagree/strongly | | 50.0% | 72.0% | 51.6% | 43.5%* |
| Neutral | | 20.0ᵃ | 12.0ᵃ | 23.3 | 29.3 |
| Agree/strongly | | 30.0ᵃ | 26.0ᵃ | 25.1 | 27.2 |
| | Total *N* = | 10 | 25 | 283 | 720 |
| *Teaching Responsibilities in Last Five Years* | | | | | |
| Entirely undergrads | | 70.0% | 40.0% | 35.7% | 25.7%*** |
| Both | | 20.0ᵃ | 56.0 | 58.2 | 67.7 |
| Entirely grads | | 10.0ᵃ | 4.0ᵃ | 3.2 | 4.7 |
| Not teaching | | | | 2.9 | 1.9 |
| | Total *N* = | 10 | 25 | 280 | 721 |
| *Communicate with Black Students* | | | | | |
| Less well/much less | | | | 17.4% | 18.1%*** |
| Neutral | | 50.0% | 54.2% | 79.8 | 79.7 |
| Somewhat better/much better | | 50.0 | 45.8 | 2.8 | 2.3 |
| | Total *N* = | 10 | 24 | 282 | 703 |
| Hours teaching per week (SD) | | 23.00 | 24.52 | 24.58 | 22.06** |
| | | (13.50) | (12.13) | (10.47) | (10.88) |
| Number of LD undergrads this term | | 42.70 | 60.58 | 42.28 | 48.68 |
| | | (55.20) | (82.17) | (74.38) | (84.08) |
| Number of UD undergrads this term | | 15.60 | 30.83 | 22.61 | 22.04 |
| | | (15.32) | (33.12) | (28.20) | (27.38) |
| Number of grads this term | | 4.20 | 8.58 | 7.03 | 8.36 |
| | | (9.82) | (14.75) | (14.17) | (14.75) |
| Number Black LD undergrads | | 9.70 | 9.08 | 4.77 | 5.13 |
| | | (9.63) | (12.87) | (16.11) | (10.76) |
| Number of Black UD undergrads | | 3.50 | 3.96 | 1.54 | 2.00* |
| | | (5.02) | (6.26) | (2.89) | (4.09) |
| Number of Black grads | | 1.00 | 0.92 | 0.95 | 0.71 |
| | | (2.54) | (1.61) | (5.71) | (2.14) |

ᵃCell count < 5.
*** *p*  .001
** *p*  .01
* *p*  .05

**Table 9.11A**
**Student Advising Questions for All Faculty by Race and Gender**

| | African American | White | Women | Men |
|---|---|---|---|---|
| *Hours per Week Working with* | | | | |
| *Students Outside of Class* (SD) | 6.97 | 5.91 | 6.33 | 5.79 |
| | (5.31) | (5.16) | (6.04) | (4.78) |
| *Academic Counseling to Undergrads* | | | | |
| None | 10.0% | 11.0% | 9.5% | 11.5%*** |
| Few | 43.3 | 44.4 | 33.9 | 48.5 |
| Less than half | 23.3 | 22.0 | 25.8 | 20.6 |
| At least half | 23.3 | 22.6 | 30.7 | 19.4 |
| Total *N* = | 30 | 973 | 283 | 720 |
| *Career Counseling to Undergrads* | | | | |
| None | | 5.6% | 3.5% | 6.2%** |
| Few | 43.8% | 45.5 | 38.2 | 48.3 |
| Less than half | 28.1 | 28.1 | 31.6 | 26.7 |
| At least half | 28.1 | 20.8 | 26.7 | 18.8 |
| Total *N* = | 32 | 976 | 285 | 723 |

[a]Cell count < 5.
*** *p* .001
** *p* .01

percent of all faculty, regardless of race or gender, offer no academic counseling to undergraduate students outside class. Fewer than 4 percent of all
faculty fail to provide career counseling of any type. More White than African American faculty and more men than women provide no career counseling to students. Thirty-one percent of female faculty, compared with 19 percent
of male faculty, see at least half of their students outside class during the
course of a term to provide academic counseling. When race and gender are
simultaneously taken into account (Table 9.11B), Black males and White
females spend more hours weekly outside of class working with students (7.7
and 6.4 hours respectively) than White males (5.7 hours) and Black females
(5.1 hours). There is a three-fold difference between Black and White women
and Black and White men in the proportion of faculty who provide no academic counseling to undergraduate students. Also, significantly more African
American males than females (25 v. 17 percent) and more White females than
males (31 v. 19 percent) provide academic counseling outside class to at least
half of their undergraduate students. (See also Villalpando and Delgado Bernal,
this volume.)

Although there are no statistically significant differences in the number
of hours devoted to administrative and committee work by different race or

## Table 9.11B
## Student Advising Questions for All Faculty by Race/Gender

|  | African American | White | Women | Men |
|---|---|---|---|---|
| *Hours per Week Working with* |  |  |  |  |
| *Students Outside of Class* (SD) | 5.11 | 7.7 | 6.37 | 5.73 |
|  | (4.31) | (5.56) | (6.09) | (4.75) |
| *Academic Counseling to Undergrads* |  |  |  |  |
| None | 33.3% | 4.2%[a] | 9.0% | 11.8%*** |
| Few |  | 54.2 | 34.7 | 48.3 |
| Less than half | 50.0[a] | 16.7[a] | 25.3 | 20.7 |
| At least half | 16.7[a] | 25.0 | 31.0 | 19.3 |
| Total $N$ = | 6 | 24 | 277 | 696 |
| *Career Counseling to Undergrads* |  |  |  |  |
| None |  |  | 3.6% | 6.4%** |
| Few | 25.0%[a] | 50.0% | 28.6 | 48.2 |
| Less than half | 50.0[a] | 20.8 | 31.0 | 26.9 |
| At least half | 25.0[a] | 29.1 | 26.7 | 18.5 |
| Total $N$ = | 8 | 24 | 277 | 699 |

[a]Cell count < 5.
*** $p$  .001
** $p$  .05

gender faculty, we can surmise that there are pronounced differences in the types of committee work involved. (See Tables 9.12A and 9.12B.) We see large standard errors, suggesting that there are in fact "administrative specialists" or select faculty who have much heavier administrative burdens than others. White faculty devote an average of 9 hours per week to administration/committee work v. 6.3 hours for Blacks. It is patently clear, however, that African American faculty disproportionately work on departmental and institutional committees concerned with issues of color.

The value of a specific race/gender subgroup focus is again revealed. We see that Black men and White women spend more hours per week in administrative and committee work than do their counterparts. (See Table 9.12B.) We also see that Black men and especially Black women are significantly more likely than their White peer faculty to serve on "minority issue" committees and to be members of organizations concerned with Black issues. While White males are far and away the largest race/gender faculty subgroup numerically, they are consistently the least likely to serve on committees dealing with issues of color or to be members of organizations concerned with Black issues. In contrast, Black females are consistently the most likely to serve on committees dealing with issues of color and to be members of Black-oriented organizations.

**Table 9.12A**
**Committee Work Questions for All Faculty by Race and Gender**

| | African American | White | Women | Men |
|---|---|---|---|---|
| Administrative and Committee Work (hours/week) | 6.31 (9.17) | 9.02 (8.74) | 9.36 (8.82) | 8.78 (8.73) |
| Serve on Department Committee on Minority Issues? | | | | |
| Yes | 22.9% | 5.2%*** | 6.8% | 5.4% |
| No | 77.1 | 94.8 | 93.2 | 94.6 |
| Total $N$ = | 35 | 1,006 | 296 | 745 |
| Serve on Institutional Committee on Minority Issues? | | | | |
| Yes | 27.3% | 7.2%*** | 9.4% | 7.3% |
| No | 72.7 | 92.8 | 90.6 | 92.7 |
| Total $N$ = | 33 | 1,008 | 298 | 743 |
| Member of Organization Concerned with Black Issues? | | | | |
| Yes | 51.4% | 11.1%*** | 18.4% | 10.1%*** |
| No | 48.6 | 88.9 | 81.6 | 89.9 |
| Total $N$ = | 35 | 999 | 294 | 740 |

[a]Cell count < 5.
*** $p$  .001

**Table 9.12B**
**Committee Work Questions for All Faculty by Race/Gender**

| | African American Women | African American Men | White Women | White Men |
|---|---|---|---|---|
| Administrative and Committee Work (hours/week) | 6.31 (9.17) | 9.02 (8.74) | 9.36 (8.82) | 8.78 (8.73) |
| Serve on Department Committee on Minority Issues? | | | | |
| Yes | 30.0%[a] | 20.0% | 5.9% | 4.9%*** |
| No | 70.0 | 80.0 | 94.1 | 95.1 |
| Total $N$ = | 10 | 25 | 286 | 720 |
| Serve on Institutional Committee on Minority Issues? | | | | |
| Yes | 30.0%[a] | 26.1% | 8.7% | 6.7%*** |
| No | 70.0 | 73.9 | 91.3 | 93.3 |
| Total $N$ = | 10 | 23 | 288 | 720 |
| Member of Organization Concerned with Black Issues? | | | | |
| Yes | 60.0% | 48.0% | 16.9% | 8.8%*** |
| No | 40.0[a] | 52.0 | 83.1 | 91.2 |
| Total $N$ = | 10 | 25 | 284 | 715 |

[a]Cell count < 5.
*** $p$  .001

There are statistically significant differences by gender and race in the time and energy spent on faculty research. (See Table 9.13A.) Men average nearly six hours more per week devoted to research activities than women (15.7 v. 10.3 hours). Predictably, these differences in time commitments translate into significant differences in research productivity. More women than men have not submitted an article for publication during the past two years (17 v. 15 percent). By the same token, more men submitted five or more articles for publication over the time period (30 v. 21 percent). Female faculty are also significantly more likely to have no publications (37 v. 29 percent) or to have only one or two publications (35 v. 29 percent) than male faculty. Women are slightly more likely to make presentations: 31 percent of women v. 25 percent of men made five or more presentations during the previous two years. The standard deviations suggest greatest variability from top to bottom in research commitments among men and among Whites, compared with women and Blacks respectively.

Faculty differences by race are also apparent in research time commitments and in research productivity. White faculty spend on average over two hours more per week than their African American peers in research activities. (See Table 9.13A.) Despite this sizable difference in time on task, Black and White faculty have comparable rates of article submission. Thirty-three percent of Black faculty and 28 percent of White faculty submitted five or more articles. However, while 8 percent of Whites submitted over ten articles, no African American faculty submitted articles for publication at this pace. Although larger numbers of Whites than Blacks did not publish during the two-year time period (32 v. 28 percent), more White faculty also published at least five articles (18 v. 13 percent).

Disaggregating by race and gender reveals hidden differences in faculty research commitments and research productivity. (See Table 9.13B.) White males have a striking advantage in the amount of weekly time given to faculty research. White men devote roughly half a day more per week to their research compared to the other race/gender faculty subgroups. We also see that the within-subgroup variation in faculty research hours is greatest for Whites as a group, males as a group, and White men specifically. Interestingly, the White male advantage in research productivity is not nearly as pronounced as one might have expected. Thirty-one percent of White males submitted five or more articles compared to 20 percent of White women, 28 percent of Black men, and a whopping 50 percent of Black women. The different race/gender faculty subgroups are nearly indistinguishable in number of presentations, though it should be noted that White males made the fewest presentations of any subgroup. On the other hand, one in five White male faculty published at least five articles compared to one in eight White females, one in eight Black females, and one in eight Black males.

**Table 9.13A**
**Research/Publications Questions for All Faculty by Race and Gender**

| | African American | White | Women | Men |
|---|---|---|---|---|
| *Research Hours per Week* | 11.66 | 14.24 | 10.32 | 15.67*** |
| | (9.53) | (12.32) | (10.30) | (12.62) |
| *Number of Articles Submitted in Past Two Years* | | | | |
| Never | 15.2% | 15.8% | 16.8% | 15.3%** |
| 1–2 | 33.3 | 31.2 | 39.1 | 28.1 |
| 3–4 | 18.2 | 25.5 | 23.2 | 26.1 |
| 5–10 | 33.3 | 19.8 | 15.5 | 22.1 |
| > 10 | | 7.7 | 5.4 | 8.3 |
| Total *N* = | 33 | 1,007 | 297 | 743 |
| *Number of Presentations in Past Two Years* | | | | |
| Never | 9.1%[a] | 18.1% | 17.9% | 17.8% |
| 1–2 | 36.4 | 28.8 | 25.0 | 30.6 |
| 3–4 | 27.3 | 26.4 | 26.0 | 26.6 |
| 5–10 | 18.2 | 18.1 | 22.3 | 16.4 |
| > 10 | 9.1[a] | 8.7 | 8.8 | 8.7 |
| Total *N* = | 33 | 1,012 | 296 | 749 |
| *Number of Publications in Past Two Years* | | | | |
| Never | 28.1% | 31.6% | 36.9% | 29.4%** |
| 1–2 | 37.5 | 30.7 | 34.9 | 29.4 |
| 3–4 | 21.9 | 19.4 | 14.9 | 21.3 |
| 5–10 | 6.3[a] | 13.0 | 9.8 | 14.0 |
| > 10 | 6.3[a] | 5.2 | 3.4 | 5.9 |
| Total *N* = | 32 | 1,005 | 295 | 742 |

[a]Cell count < 5.
*** p   .001
** p   .01

## Summary, Conclusions, and Implications

Research shows that at the beginning of the twenty-first century, despite three decades of antidiscrimination legislation and affirmative action, women faculty and faculty of color continue to be underrepresented on college and university faculties (A. Astin, Korn and Dey 1991; H. Astin et al. 1997; Sax et al. 1996). The underrepresentation of African American faculty at higher education institutions other than historically Black colleges and universities (HBCUs) is especially acute. Evidence suggests that, where women and people of color are able to gain entrance to the professoriate, they are more often than not penalized by reward and prestige systems that favor men over women and

**Table 9.13B**
**Research/Publications Questions for All Faculty by Race/Gender**

| | African American Women | African American Men | White Women | White Men |
|---|---|---|---|---|
| *Research Hours per Week* | 11.78 | 11.61 | 10.28 | 15.80*** |
| | (8.89) | (9.96) | (10.35) | (12.68) |
| *Number of Articles Submitted in Past Two Years* | | | | |
| Never | | | 20.0% | 17.3% | 15.2%** |
| 1–2 | | 50.0%[a] | 28.0 | 38.8 | 28.1 |
| 3–4 | | | 24.0 | 23.9 | 26.2 |
| 5–10 | | 50.0[a] | 28.0 | 14.5 | 21.9 |
| > 10 | | | | 5.4 | 8.6 |
| Total $N$ = | 8 | 25 | 289 | 718 |
| *Number of Presentations in Past Two Years* | | | | |
| Never | | 12.5%[a] | 8.0%[a] | 18.1% | 18.1% |
| 1–2 | | 37.5[a] | 36.0 | 24.7 | 30.4 |
| 3–4 | | 12.5[a] | 32.0 | 26.4 | 26.4 |
| 5–10 | | 25.0[a] | 16.0[a] | 22.2 | 16.4 |
| > 10 | | 12.5[a] | 8.0[a] | 8.7 | 8.7 |
| Total $N$ = | 8 | 25 | 288 | 724 |
| *Number of Publications in Past Two Years* | | | | |
| Never | | 25.0%[a] | 29.2% | 37.3% | 29.4% |
| 1–2 | | 37.5[a] | 37.5 | 34.8 | 29.1 |
| 3–4 | | 25.0[a] | 20.8 | 14.6 | 21.3 |
| 5–10 | | | 8.3[a] | 10.1 | 14.2 |
| > 10 | | 12.5[s] | 4.2[a] | 3.1 | 6.0 |
| Total $N$ = | 8 | 24 | 287 | 718 |

[a]Cell count < 5.
*** $p$ .001
** $p$ .01

Whites over non-Whites. As a rule, African American faculty are less often tenured, earn less money, work at less prestigious institutions, have lower academic rank, and have less academic stature compared to their White peers. There seems to be a negative, multiplicative effect: Black women hold lower status compared to Black men, and Blacks at "lesser" institutions have lower academic rank compared with those employed at more prestigious schools. In short, faculty status in U.S. higher education continues to be problematic in raced and gendered ways.

This chapter examined faculty status by race and gender on six predominantly White, midwestern campuses. The general question guiding this study was: "Are there significant differences by race and gender in faculty status, workload and satisfaction?" More specifically, we examined differences by race (Black v. White), gender (female v. male), and race/gender (Black female v. others) in faculty academic rank, years at institution, academic tenure, teaching workload, administrative workload, student relations, and overall satisfaction. As expected, we saw that Blacks and women are systematically and significantly disadvantaged on all measures relative to Whites and men. Moreover, we found that race and gender had a patterned, significant multiplicative disadvantage—that is, African American female faculty occupy the most disadvantaged position of the four faculty race/gender subgroups studied. To the extent that it is true, Blacks as a group, females as a group, and Black female faculty experience systematic, significant disadvantages, which can result in serious, persistent obstacles to their recruitment, retention, and success in U.S. higher education.

This study confirms the value of "situated analysis"; that is, we discovered multiple race-, gender- and race/gender-specific answers to our questions about faculty workload and satisfaction. How a particular faculty member answers these questions is related to race, gender, institution, career stage, professional standing, and a host of other specific characteristics. Collins (1998) reminds us of the need to see these faculty within the complex of patterned, hierarchically structured relationships where they are located. This approach values disaggregation, the search for unique subgroup patterns, over aggregation, and the search for universal or general patterns. Thus, although Black men, Black women, and (to a lesser degree) White women share a disadvantaged status among the professorate in U.S. higher education, there are important differences.

The disadvantages for White female academics assume different forms than for their African American counterparts— female and male. Thirty years of affirmative action have produced dramatic gains in the representation of White women among college faculty. From 1983 to the present, the proportion of White females in the professorate grew from 9.9 percent to 29.2 percent, representing a 300-fold increase. To be sure, White women are still outnumbered by White males in the ranks of college professors, and they occupy less prestigious positions in the academic hierarchy. Relative to White men in academe, White women continue to be disadvantaged; they have come a long way, but they still have a long way to go toward achieving parity with White men.

However, the disadvantages of White female academics pale in comparison to those of Black faculty—males and especially females. In point of fact, White women academics are advantaged relative to their Black peers. In this sample, White female professors outnumbered Black females 29 to 1, a ratio lower than the 73 to 1 for White male professors, but nonetheless powerfully significant. Given these dramatic differences in sheer numbers, it is only reasonable to exercise caution when discussing the relative disadvantages of White female, Black female, and Black male faculty. While Blacks generally and Black women in particular continue to struggle for access to college faculty positions, White women have gained more of a foothold. But make no mistake—the real and overwhelming winners in the competition for faculty positions continue to be White males.

The relatively rapid entry and rise of White women among the ranks of college faculty stand in stark contrast to the situations of African American women and men. Herein lies a lesson about how gender, race, and class discrimination function in American society to produce distinct and shared, separate and multiplicative effects. Universities have indeed become more diverse over the past three decades; there are now more faculty who can be defined as "other," due to gender, race, ethnicity, and class differences from White men (Johnsrud and Sadao 1998). It is revealing to note, however, that these institutions—rooted in Anglo-Saxon traditions and culture *and* dominated by Whites—have been slow to incorporate faculty of African, Latin/ Hispanic, Native American—and yes, even Asian, ancestry.

A recent study attributes the exclusion of Blacks and other people of color from faculty positions to the operation of "elite racism." Teun Van Dijk (1993) defines elite racism as the critical role played by political, media, corporate, and academic elites in the reproduction of contemporary racial and ethnic inequality. He concludes that through their influential text and talk, these elites "manufacture the consent needed for the legitimization of their own power in general, and for their leadership in the dominance of the white group in particular" (Van Dijk 1993, 8).

A recent study by Linda Johnsrud and Kathleen Sadao (1998) found that the elite racism practiced by White Western academics was manifest in their adherence to dominant cultural norms, values, and ideologies that made no room for different cultures and/or worldviews. More explicitly, this dominant view defined ethnic and racial faculty as " 'other.' They are different and differentness is perceived as deficient, not in keeping with the standards of the academy" (339). Further, White faculty developed mechanisms that reinforced their dominant values and their "power to define who is to be included and who is to be excluded from—or remain peripheral to—the academy" (339).

Seen through the lens of elite racism in the academy, the racial disparities that this study reveals in access to the professorate and in relative levels of success are brought into clearer focus. While the data of this particular study are not sufficient to test the hypothesis of elite racism, personal experience, coupled with the empirical findings cited above, lend credence to such a hypothesis. The scene has been replayed many times in faculty meetings discussing the qualifications of African American candidates. All too often, calls for recognizing and valuing diversity are heard as special pleadings to recruit and hire unqualified professors.

African American professors present different profiles from the mainstream in their research, in their backgrounds, and in their race. They confront an institutional context that interprets such differences as grounds for exclusion. Moreover, those holding these racial stereotypes and beliefs that underlie such systematic discrimination deny or equivocate: "Individuals do not see themselves or their judgements as racist," point out Johnsrud and Sadao (1998). "Rather they see themselves as part of something larger and grander— as part of the educated elite whose collective responsibility is to uphold standards of scholarly integrity" (338). (See also Scheurich and Young, this volume.)

In any case, the end result is the same: Black women and Black men continue to be scarce among the nation's faculty. They exist within a larger pattern of systematic discrimination and deprivation. Since they share culture, race, and experiences with White males, the dominant group, White women are—relative to Blacks—somewhat privileged; they find more niches in these walls of discrimination and exclusion (Frankenberg 1993). Put simply, the system of *White male patriarchy* makes some room for the inclusion of White women among the professoriat—albeit in decidedly subservient roles and numbers. However, its cousin, "White supremacy" (operating in the guise of individual and institutional racism) more vigorously resists yielding access to the professoriate to African Americans, even in clearly subordinated roles and numbers.

Future research needs to examine the relative status of White women and African Americans in the professoriat. How do the dynamics of exclusion and inclusion differ for the different race/gender groups? What are the key personal and institutional predictors of faculty workload and satisfaction?

**Note**

Data are from "Black Students in White Institutions: The Effectiveness of Different Institutional Approaches," a University of Michigan, Ann Arbor-based study directed by Walter R. Allen, Gerald Gurin, and Marvin Peterson. Cheryl Presley, Martha Stassen and Michelle Gilyard served as graduate research assistants on this project. The Spencer Foundation provided funding for this research project. The Andrew Mellon Foundation funded the preparation of this report. Ophella Dano provided editorial and secretarial assistance. We are indebted to the institutions and faculty that consented to participate in this research project.

**Appendix**

3. In general, how do you feel about this institution?
    It is a very good place for me.
    It is a fairly good place for me.
    It is not the place for me.

4. How satisfied are you with each of the following?
Very dissatisfied
Dissatisfied
Neither satisfied nor dissatisfied
Satisfied
Very satisfied
B.   Your salary in comparison with that of your peers at this institution
D.   Resources for faculty teaching and research
G.   Institutional leadership and priorities

8. During the term, how many *hours* do you give to each of the following activities *in a typical week?*
Teaching (include class preparation and student advising).
Research
Administrative and committee work

## References

Aguirre, Adalberto, Jr., Anthony Hernandez, and Ruben O. Martinez. 1994. Perceptions of the work place: Focus on minority women faculty. *Initiatives* 56, no. 3:41–50.

ASA Commission on the Status of Women in Sociology. 1984. Unique barriers women of color faculty encounter. In *Equity issues for women faculty in sociology departments,* 20–24. Washington, DC: American Sociological Association Commission on the Status of Women in Sociology.

Astin, Alexander W. *Minorities in American higher education.* 1982. San Francisco: Jossey-Bass.

Astin, Alexander W., William S. Korn, and Eric L. Dey. 1991. *The American college teacher: National norms for the 1989–1990 HERI faculty survey.* Los Angeles: Higher Education Research Institute, UCLA.

Astin, Helen S., Anthony L. Antonio, Christine M. Cress, and Alexander W. Astin. 1997. *Race and ethnicity in the American professorate, 1995–1996.* Los Angeles: Higher Education Research Institute, UCLA.

Astin, Helen S., and Mary Beth Snyder. 1984. Women's education and career choice: Disparities between theory and practice. In *Women and education: Equity or equality,* edited by Elizabeth Fennema and Jane Ayer, 187–87. Berkeley, CA: McCutchan.

Banks, William M. 1984. Afro-American scholars in the university: Roles and conflicts. *American Behavioral Scientist* 27 (January/February): 325–39.

Blackwell, James E. 1981. *Mainstreaming outsiders: The production of Black professionals.* Bayside, NY: General Hall.

————. 1996. Faculty issues: The impact on minorities. In *Racial and ethnic diversity in higher education,* edited by Caroline Sotello Viernes Turner, Mildred Garcia, Amaury Nora, and Laura Rendon, 315–26. Needham Heights, MA: Simon and Schuster Custom Publishing.

Boice, Robert. 1993. New faculty involvement for women and minorities. *Research in Higher Education* 34, no. 3:291–333.

Bourguignon, Erika, S. A. Blanshan, L. Chiteji, K. J. MacLean, S. J. Meckling, Mary Ann Sagaria, A. E. Shuman, and M. T. Taris. 1987. *Junior faculty life at Ohio State: Insights on gender and race.* Columbus: Ohio State University, Affirmative Action Grant Program.

Bowen, Howard R., and Jack H. Schuster. 1986. *American professors: A national resource imperiled.* New York: Oxford University Press.

Bowen, William G., and Derek Bok. 1998. *The shape of the river: Long-term consequences of considering race in college and university admissions.* Princeton, NJ: Princeton University Press.

Clark, Burton R. 1987. *The academic life: Small worlds, different worlds.* Princeton, NJ: Princeton University Press.

Collins, Patricia Hill. 1998. *Fighting words: Black women and the search for justice.* Minneapolis: University of Minnesota Press.

Epps, Edgar G. 1998. Affirmative action and minority access to faculty positions. *Ohio State Law Journal* 59, no. 3:755–74.

Frankenberg, Ruth. 1993. *White women, race matters: The social construction of Whiteness.* Minneapolis: University of Minnesota Press.

Gregory, Sheila T. 1995. *Black women in the academy: The secrets to success and achievement.* New York: University Press of America.

Johnsrud, Linda K., and Kathleen C. Sadao. 1998. The common experience of "otherness": Ethnic and racial minority faculty. *Review of Higher Education* 21, no. 4:315–42.

Menges, R. J., and W. H. Exum. 1983. Barriers to the progress of women and minority faculty. *Journal of Higher Education* 54, no. 2:123–43.

Nakanishi, Don T. 1993, Spring. Asian Pacific Americans in higher education: Faculty and administrative representation and tenure. In *Building a diverse faculty,* edited by Joanne Gainen and Robert Boice, 51–59. New Directions for Teaching and Learning, No. 53. San Francisco: Jossey-Bass.

The Nation: Faculty and Staff. 1998. *Chronicle of Higher Education.* (1998–1999 Almanac Issue) (August 28).

Nettles, Michael T., and Laura W. Perna. 1995. Sex and race differences in faculty salaries, tenure, rank, and productivity: Why, on average, do women, African Americans, and Hispanics have lower salaries, tenure, and rank? Paper presented at the Association for the Study of Higher Education annual meeting. ERIC Document Reproduction Service No. ED 391 402.

Olivas, Michael A. 1988. Latino faculty at the border: Increasing numbers key to more Hispanic access. *Change* 20, no. 3:6–9.

Padilla, Amado M. 1994. Ethnic minority scholars, research, and mentoring: Current and future issues. *Educational Researcher* (May): 24–27.

Sax, Linda J., Alexander W. Astin, Marisol Arredondo, and William S. Korn. 1996. *The American college teacher: National norms for the 1995–1996 HERI faculty survey.* Los Angeles: Higher Education Research Institute, UCLA.

Smelser, Neil J., and Robin Content. 1980. *The changing academic market: General trends and a Berkeley case study.* Berkeley: University of California Press.

Van Dijk, Teun A. 1993. *Elite discourse and racism.* Newbury Park, CA: Sage.

# CHAPTER 10

# White Racism among White Faculty

*From Critical Understanding to Antiracist Activism*

### JAMES JOSEPH SCHEURICH AND
### MICHELLE D. YOUNG

In 1986 Gaertner and Dovidio began to discuss the emergence of a new form of racism among Whites, which they called "aversive" racism. At about the same time, Sears (1988) coined the term "symbolic racism" to refer to a similar new type of White racism. Whatever the term that is used, this new racism allows Whites to sincerely believe that they as individuals are no longer supportive of racism, while the numerous effects, old and new, of racism continue unabated. This is particularly clear in the academy, which typically sees itself as a liberal force for racial equity. Rare indeed is a faculty member in education who does not see herself or himself as strongly against racism, even though college of education curricula and pedagogies continue to reflect White racial privilege and bias and even though the students trained by these faculty continue to maintain schools that positively serve middle-class White children and negatively serve children of color.

One of the main reasons that education faculty, university faculty in general, and the U.S. White public are able to see themselves as not racist, even though racism and its effects continue to eviscerate the lives of people of color, is that racism is seen as solely a function of what an individual consciously believes. Thus, if an individual faculty member consciously believes that she or he is not a racist, that is the end of the issue for that person and the end of her or his responsibility. While we argue that this individual-level effect of the civil rights movement of the 1950s and 1960s is an important gain historically, individual, conscious racism is only one level of racism. Racism also exists at three other, broader levels—the institutional, the societal, and the civilizational. Consequently, as long as White faculty stop with an individual-level understanding, racism will be left to permeate the university deeply and pervasively.

221

Our purpose here, then, is, first, to discuss each of four categories or levels of racism—individual (subdivided into overt and covert), institutional, societal, and civilizational. Second, we hope to provide recommendations on what faculty can do to be explicitly antiracist. In fact, we believe that, given the depth and breadth of racism in the academy, an explicit antiracist approach is a necessity. Without this latter approach, institutional, societal, and civilizational racism will continue to dominate the university.

The first two categories of racism we discuss—overt and covert racism—operate at the level of individual consciousness. The next two are organizational and social categories— institutional and societal racism. In effect, they create the social context for the prior two categories. The final category, civilizational, creates or constitutes the possibility for all of the prior four categories. Further, it is the civilizational racism that is most salient for discussions regarding the racism at the very heart of the university—the racial bias of research epistemologies. Figure 10.1 illustrates and positions these categories. The individual level, which includes both overt and covert racism, sits within the institutional level, which sits within the societal level. All four sit, in a hierarchy of smaller to larger and broader, inside the largest and broadest category, the civilizational level.

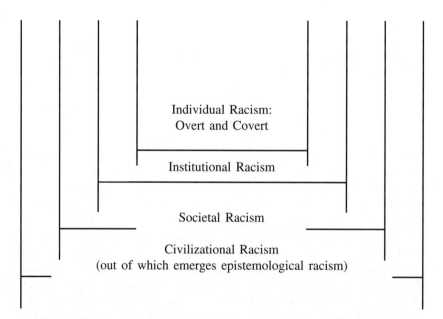

Individual Racism:
Overt and Covert

Institutional Racism

Societal Racism

Civilizational Racism
(out of which emerges epistemological racism)

**Figure 10.1. Levels of racism, each of which is "broader" and "deeper" than any above it.**

## Two Categories of Individual Racism: Overt and Covert

Racial bias or racism is typically understood in popular culture and in academia in terms of individual acts of overt prejudice that are racially based, that is, *overt racism* (see, for example, Kluegel and Smith 1986; Rizvi 1993; Scheurich 1993; Tatum 1992). For example, if a college professor makes a racial slur during a class lecture, this is seen as overt racism. Overt racism, then, is a public, conscious, and intended act, including speech acts, by a person or persons from one race with the intent of doing damage to a person or persons of another race chiefly because of the race of the second person or persons.[1] While there are still many in the United States who are overt racists, there is a general social consensus, at least at the public level, that these behaviors are socially unacceptable (though verbalizations of overt racism are constitutionally protected in most cases).

A second kind of individual racism is *covert racism*. The only real difference between overt and covert racism is that the latter is not explicitly public. For example, a professor may consciously choose not to mentor a Mexican American doctoral student because of racial biases, even though factually the Mexican American may be qualified to receive such mentoring. While this professor may be consciously acting in a racist manner, she or he will publicly provide a socially acceptable reason for her or his decision. Persons making covert, racially biased decisions do not explicitly broadcast their intentions; instead, they hide their biases and provide reasons that are acceptable within the discourses of the academy. A public (and a university) consensus, though perhaps not as strong as the one for overt racism, also

---

1. The difference between White racism and the racism of people of color is a highly contentious issue. We strongly agree with Tatum (1992), who teaches a course entitled "Group Exploration of Racism" attended primarily by White students who typically evaluate the course as one of their best college educational experiences. She says, "A distinction must be made between the negative racial attitudes held by individuals of color and White individuals, because it is only the attitudes of Whites that routinely carry with them the social power inherent in the systematic cultural reinforcement and institutionalization of those racial prejudices. To distinguish the prejudices of students of color from the racism of White students is *not* to say the former is acceptable and the latter is not; both are clearly problematic. The distinction is important, however, to identify the power differential between members of the dominant and subordinate groups" (3; emphasis hers). Similarly, Hacker (1992) says, "Individuals who do not have power may hold racist views, but they seldom cause much harm" (29; see also Feagin and Vera 1995, ix–x). Consequently, for individual racism, we have stated our definitions in race-neutral terms, though the tendency to define racism solely as individual is chiefly done by Whites; for all of the other types of racism we discuss, our definitions are constructed in terms of the racism of the dominant group.

exists with regard to covert acts of racism; and, in fact, many laws prohibit such acts, particularly in the area of employment practices.

Whether covert or overt, however, racism in the United States is over-whelmingly seen as an individual phenomenon (Kluegel and Smith 1986). And this is as much true in academia as in popular culture (Scheurich 1993). If a faculty answers "no" to the question of whether she or he is racist, the respondent typically means that she or he does not, as an individual, engage in conscious, intended racism or that she or he is not, as an individual, consciously racist. University faculty, just like other members of this society, typically judge their own lack of racism based on personal evaluations that they do not, as an individual, have a negative judgment of another person just because that person is a member of a particular race. While this individual-ized, conscious, moral, or ethical commitment to antiracism is a significant and meaningful individual and historical accomplishment, born mainly of the civil rights movement, the fact that it restricts our understanding of racism to a conscious, individualized ethical arena easily becomes a barrier to a broader, more comprehensive understanding of racism—for society and for faculty.

In addition, understanding that we need to get beyond issues of indi-vidual racism, whether overt or covert, is critical to initiating a consideration of the racism that is imbedded in our basic research assumptions, that is, our epistemologies. For example, if we, as researchers, were to read an article arguing that our research epistemologies were racially biased and if we dis-agreed with this argument because we did not consider ourselves, as individu-als, to be consciously or intentionally racist, this judgment would indicate that we did not understand the broader and deeper levels of racism. The error here is that racial critiques of research epistemologies have virtually nothing to do with whether an individual researcher is overtly or covertly racist. A researcher could be adamantly antiracist in thought and deed and simulta-neously be committed to excluding research epistemologies that are race/culture-oriented, which we would argue is a form of epistemological racism. Consequently, researchers considering the issue of epistemological racism need to get beyond the question of whether they personally are racists be-cause this latter judgment is not related to judgments about epistemological racism.

## Institutional Racism

*Institutional racism* exists when institutions or organizations, including educational ones, have standard operating procedures (intended or unintended) that hurt members of one or more races in relation to members of the domi-nant race. (For further discussions of institutional racism, see Feagin and Vera 1995; Hacker 1992.) Institutional racism also exists when institutional or

organizational cultures, rules, habits, or symbols have the same racially bias-
ing effect. For example, if an institution's procedures or culture (such as that
of a university or college), favors Whites for promotion to a full professorship
over persons of color, this is institutional racism. If a university's standard
pedagogical method is culturally congruent with the culture of White students
but not with the cultures of students of color, this is institutional racism. (For
discussion of this widespread problem, see, for example, Cummins 1986;
Ladson-Billings 1995; Hilliard 1992; J. E. King 1991; Lee, Lomotey, and
Shujaa 1990, among many others.)

One particularly important type of institutional racism that occurs in
research communities arises when racially biased beliefs or assumptions are
embedded within a research discipline or a particular community of researchers or within the variables, labels, or concepts of a discipline or community
(Paredes 1977; Stanfield 1985, 1993a, 1993b). For example, if educational
researchers commonly use, as they once typically did, a phrase like "culturally disadvantaged" or "cultural deprivation" to indicate why some students
of color did not succeed educationally, this is institutional racism (McCarthy
1993). While not using this particular phrase ("institutional racism"), Gordon,
Miller, and Rollock (1990) have argued that this kind of racism is endemic
to the social sciences: "*Much of the social science knowledge* referable to
Blacks, Latinos, and Native Americans ignores or demeans [members of these
races and] . . . often presents distorted interpretations of minority conditions
and potentials" (14; emphasis ours).

But Gordon, Miller, and Rollock (1990) are not the only ones who have
made this point about the endemic institutional racism of social science research. James Banks (1995) and Shuey (1958), among many others spread
across the different social science disciplines, have asserted that "scientific"
knowledge has commonly been based on racially biased assumptions, labels,
perspectives, etc. From Linneaus' 1735 categorization that related race to
psychological attributes and positioned the White race as having superior
psychological attributes (Webster 1992) and Caldwell's similar contentions in
1830 to *The Bell Curve* (Herrnstein and Murray 1994) and the works of
Shockley (1992) in the present era, scientists and social scientists have per-
sistently used racist ideas regarding inherited characteristics of different racial
groups (Banks 1995).

Unfortunately, educational researchers have been and continue to be key
participants in this elaboration, reproduction, and maintenance of institutional
racism. Other examples of such racism by educational researchers in the past
include the mental and intellectual measures taken from "cranium estimates,"
"theories of racial difference" taken from anthropology and biology, "theories
of race and intelligence" taken from genetics, and "curriculum theories" arguing that "Black families and Black communities . . . were 'defective' and
'dysfunctional' " (McCarthy 1993, 332). While the use of these racially oriented

"cranium estimates" or other such categories would now be considered unacceptable in education, label-based institutional racism continues to exist. For example, higher percentages of students of color are currently more likely to be labeled "at-risk," "learning disabled," or "emotionally disturbed" (Ortiz, Garcia, Wheeler, and Maldonado-Colon 1986). In addition, various kinds of "deficit" models continue to be verbalized and applied to students of color at all levels of the educational system (Valencia 1997).

But while institutional racism is much more widespread than is commonly realized (Hacker 1992; Feagin and Vera 1995) and while expanding our understanding of it is a necessity, institutional racism is still not the deepest level of racism that infects the university. For instance, one could use either racist or antiracist concepts or labels within a positivist or a constructivist epistemology, but research epistemologies themselves are not necessarily a function of the concepts or labels with which they are used. (It could be argued that this is not true for the critical tradition; many of its advocates would consider racist assumptions to be incongruent with its epistemology, a point we will address later.)

### Societal Racism

The second type of social racism is *societal racism*. Societal racism is similar to institutional racism, but it exists on a broader, societywide scale, though societal racism has received even less attention than institutional racism. In fact, it usually takes major social conflicts, like those of the mid- and late-1960s, or major social events, like the O. J. Simpson trial, for societal racism to receive broad social attention within the dominant White culture, as, for example, in the *Report of the National Advisory Commission on Civil Disorders* (1968). This report is, of course, the one that used the often-quoted statement that "our Nation is moving toward two societies, one Black, one White—separate and unequal" (p. 1). This report also argued that the "most fundamental" cause of the inequitable bifurcation was a long-term national history of "White racism" (p. 5) and that this racism deeply pervaded numerous facets of national life, from employment and housing to education and political representation.

Societal racism, then, can be said to exist when prevailing societal or cultural assumptions, norms, concepts, habits, expectations, etc., favor one race over one or more other races (Hacker 1992; Feagin and Vera 1995). For example, while it is certainly true that there is a complex range of definitions of good leadership within the mainstream of public life in the United States, that range is actually relatively limited compared to definitions of good leadership in other cultures, in or outside the United States. The widely respected anthropologist James Clifford (1988) has demonstrated how mainstream definitions of leadership disadvantaged a Native American tribe, the Mashpee Wampanoag. In a 1977 U.S. federal court trial, held to determine the validity of the Mashpee's status as a tribe, the mainstream culture's definition of leadership was used to weaken the testimony of the Mashpee chief, especially in terms of proving whether the chief was a "true" or "real" leader. The "proof" that the tribe's leadership was not "real" leadership was then used to undermine the legitimacy of the Mashpee's claim to be a tribe. Without legitimacy as a tribe, the Mashpee were unable to successfully claim land for a redress of historical grievances or even claim the town of Mashpee although, until 1964, the Mashpee had dominated this area of Martha's Vineyard, Massachusetts. Other tribes in the area had been more successful in their efforts.

Similarly, if the socially promoted idea of a good family is primarily drawn from the dominant culture's social and historical experience, that is societal racism. The privileging of one view over others results in social practices that have direct negative effects on families that deviate from the dominant norm (Billingsley 1968; Hill 1972; Littlejohn-Blake and Darling 1993). The idea that a Mashpee definition of leadership or an African American definition of a family might be considered as equal to a mainstream definition is typically not seen as reasonable or warranted in formal or informal social practices within the dominant White culture.

However, societal racism is, also, not epistemological racism. The latter is drawn from a more fundamental level than societal racism. Epistemological racism comes from or emerges out of what we have labeled the civilizational level, the deepest, most primary level of the culture of a people. The civilization level is the level that encompasses the deepest, most primary assumptions about the nature of reality (ontology), the ways of knowing that reality (epistemology), and the disputational contours of right and wrong or morality and values (axiology). But these presumptions emerge from a broader terrain than just the United States. The presumptions to which we refer are fundamental to Euro-American modernism, the historical period within which the ontologies, epistemologies, and axiologies of contemporary Western civilization have arisen (see, for example, Bernstein 1992). Our argument, then, is that the racism of research itself, i.e., epistemological racism, is drawn from the civilizational level; and, thus, it is to the civilizational level that we must turn to engage directly the question of whether our research epistemologies are racially biased.

## Civilizational Racism

The civilizational level is the level of broad civilizational assumptions—assumptions that, though they construct the nature of our world and our experience of it, are not typically visible to most members of a civilization (Foucault 1979). These assumptions are deeply embedded in how those members think and in what they name "the world" or "the Real" (Said 1979; Stanfield 1985, 1994). But these assumptions are different for different civilizations, such as the Hopi civilization (Loftin 1991) or the Zuni civilization (Roscoe 1991); and, thus, each civilization constructs the world differently for its inhabitants: "Not all people [i.e., civilizations, in this case] 'know' in the same way" (Stanfield 1985, 396).

In addition, large, complex civilizations often include a dominant culture and one or more subordinate cultures. In this context, subordinate cultures, races, and other groups often have different civilizational assumptions: "Just as the material realities of the powerful and the dominated produce separate [social, historical experiences] . . . , each [racial or social group] may also have distinctive epistemologies or theories of knowledge" (Collins 1991, 204). One consequence is that "dominant racial group members and subordinate racial group members do not think and interpret realities in the same way because of their divergent structural positions, histories, and cultures" (Stanfield 1985, 400). For instance, "What is considered theory in the dominant academic community is not necessarily what counts as theory for women-of-color" (see, for example, Anzaldúa 1990, xxv).

The name for the Euro-American culture's construction of "the world" or "the Real" is modernism. Modernism is an epistemological, ontological, and axiological network or grid that "makes" the world as the dominant Western culture knows and sees it (see, for example, Foucault 1972, 1973, 1979; Goldberg 1993). Though this grid has evolved and changed to some degree, it has, nonetheless, maintained a kind of coherence and consistency, particularly in terms of some of its primary assumptions (that is, its civilizational-level assumptions). One of these primary assumptions, the one we are addressing here, is *civilizational racism*.

The modernist period begins roughly in the 1600s, depending on who is doing the dating. Starting in that century, European colonial expansion was typically undertaken under the rationale of the supremacy of White civilization. For instance, Hacker (1992) asserts: "For at least half a dozen centuries, . . . 'white' has implied a higher civilization based on superior inheritance" (7; see also Takaki 1993). To the English of Shakespeare's time who were attending the Globe Theater to see *The Tempest*, "Caliban [the character who epitomizes the native people of the "new" world] represented what Europeans had been when they were *lower* on the scale of development" (Takaki 1993, 32; emphasis ours), while Prospero [the character who depicts the English conqueror] declares that he came to the new world "to be the lord on't" (Shakespeare, quoted in Takaki 1993, 35). Widely circulated racial hierarchies and exclusions such as these became, then, a central feature in the emergence of Western modernism; and modernist thought and, consequently, White racism or White supremacy were woven into the founding fabric of modernist Western civilization. (For an extended discussion of this point, see Goldberg 1993, but also Stanfield 1985).

These racial rationales were, of course, central, along with other rationales, to the founding of the United States. Taking land from and killing Native Americans was justified by the Whites' definition of property as well as the supposed supremacy of White civilization—like that depicted in Thomas More's *Utopia* (Takaki 1993, 35). Similar rationales were used in taking the Southwest from the Mexicans, whom Stephen F. Austin, one of the prominent political leaders of the "Texas revolution," disparagingly called "a mongrel Spanish-Indian and negro race" (qtd. in de León 1983, 12). The enslavement of African Americans and the "subsequent decades of Jim Crow laws, peonage, tenancy, lynchings and second-class citizenship" (West 1993, 256) were also justified in the same racially exclusionary terms (Feagin and Vera 1995; Hacker 1992; Harris 1993), although, of course, these justifications were not the only ones driving slavery or the appropriation of Native American and Mexican American land.

While this is an extremely brief summary of a complex argument about White racial supremacy and the fact that it was interlaced with the founding assumptions of Western civilization, our point can be made in a simpler way. The White race—what Stanfield (1985) has called "a privileged subset of the population" (389)—has unquestionably dominated Western civilization during all of the modernist period (i.e., hundreds of years). When any group significantly dominates other groups for hundreds of years, the ways of the dominant group (its epistemologies, ontologies, and axiologies) not only become the dominant ways of that civilization, but these ways also become so deeply embedded that they typically are seen as "natural" or appropriate norms rather than as historically evolved social constructions (Stanfield 1985). To a large degree, the dominant group makes its own "community the center of the universe and the conceptual frame that constrains all thought" (Gordon, Miller, and Rollock 1990, 15). Thus, the dominant group creates or constructs "the world" or "the Real" and does so in its own image, in terms of its ways, its social historical experiences (Banks 1993; Minh-ha 1989; Morrison 1992; Stanfield 1985, 1994; see, esp., Said 1979, for an entire volume that discusses how the West gave "reality" to its construct of "the Orient").

In this view, ontologies, epistemologies, and axiologies are not outside history or sociology; they are deeply interwoven with the social histories of particular civilizations and with particular groups within those civilizations. As Gordon, Miller, and Rollock (1990) assert, "Knowledge, technology, and the production of knowledge are cultural products. . . . Knowledge production operates within communicentric [ontological and epistemological] frames of reference, which dominate and enable it" (14). Similarly, Stanfield (1994) has said:

> The experiences that construct paradigms in sciences and humanities are derivatives of cultural baggage imported into intellectual enterprises by privileged residents of historically specific societies and world systems. This is important to point out, because it is common for scholars to lapse into internal analyses while discussing paradigms and thus to ignore the rather commonsense fact that sciences and humanities are products of specific cultural and historical contexts that shape the character of intellectual work. (181–82)

Or as James Banks (1993) more simply states, "All knowledge reflects the values and interests of its creators" (4).

Consider who the major, influential philosophers, writers, politicians, corporate leaders, social scientists, and educational scholars have been over the course of Western modernism. They have virtually all been White. And it is they who have constructed the world we live in—named it, discussed it, explained it. It is they who have developed the ontological and axiological categories or concepts, like individuality, truth, education, free enterprise, good conduct, social welfare, etc., that we use to think (that think us?) and that we use to socialize and educate children. This racially exclusive group has also developed the epistemologies—the legitimated ways of knowing—that we use. And it is these epistemologies and their allied ontologies and axiologies, taken together as a lived web or fabric of social constructions, that make or construct the world or the Real and that relegate other socially constructed "worlds," like those of African Americans or the Cherokee, to the "margins" of our social life and to the margins of legitimated research epistemologies.

These influential Whites and their "world-making" or "reality-making" activities or practices, however, are not separate from the social history within which they live: "All knowledge is relative to the context in which it is generated" (Gordon, Miller, and Rollock 1990, 15). And, thus, "when academics . . . construct knowledge[,] . . . they are influenced by the ideas, assumptions, and norms of the cultures and subsocieties in which they are socialized" (Banks 1995, 16). Just as Julius Caesar was "constructed" by the social history of his particular group, seeing and understanding the world in terms of the social constructions of his time and place, the influential White authors of modernism have been constructed by their position, place, and time. Just as Caesar did not see the world from the point of view of the other cultures that Rome dominated, these influential Western modernists did not see the world from within the epistemologies and ontologies of other races and cultures in or outside of Western modernity. "How we create, define, and validate social knowledge [and, thus, reality] is determined largely through our cultural context" (Stanfield 1985, 388).

Our argument, however, is not that these influential White individuals were involved in a racial conspiracy or moral bad faith (which they may or may not have been), but that these individuals overwhelmingly named and knew only from within the social history in which they lived. While we seem to have little trouble understanding that those far away in time existed in terms of their social contexts (e.g., Julius Caesar), we seem to resist understanding this concept about ourselves. We, as our predecessors did, live, understand, work, think, and act within a particular social history, within a particular social construction. We do not live, in some universal sense, above culture or history. We live inside a culture, inside a civilizational social construction. We live in the terms and ways of a particular social history.

This, then, is our argument about epistemological racism. Epistemologies, along with their related ontologies and axiologies, arise from the social history of a particular social group. Different social groups, races, cultures, societies, or civilizations evolve different epistemologies, each of which reflects the social history of that group, race, culture, society, or civilization. In short, no epistemology is context free. Yet all of the epistemologies currently legitimated in education arise almost exclusively from the social history of the dominant White race. They do not arise from the social history of African Americans, Latina/o Americans, Native Americans, Asian Americans, or other racial/cultural groups—social histories that are much different than that of the dominant race. This difference is due, at least partially, to the historical experience of racism itself (see, for example, Collins 1991). Cornell West (1993) validates this judgment when he says "social practices . . . [and research is a social practice] are best understood and explained . . . by situating them within . . . cultural traditions" (267).

By epistemological racism, then, we do not mean that the researchers using, say, positivism or postmodernism are overtly or covertly racist as individuals, though they may be. Nor do we mean that epistemological racism is a conscious institutional or societal conspiracy in favor of Whites (Gordon 1993, 267), although this certainly happens in some situations. Epistemological racism means that our current range of research epistemologies—positivism to postmodernism—arises from the social history and culture of the dominant race, that these epistemologies logically reflect and reinforce that social history and that racial group (while excluding the epistemologies of other races/cultures), and that this dynamic has negative results for people of color in general and scholars of color in particular. In other words, our "logics of inquiry" (Stanfield 1993a) are the social products and practices of the social, historical experiences of Whites; therefore, these products and practices carry forward the social history of that group and exclude the epistemologies of other social groups. The critical problem, then—for all of us, both Whites and people of color—is that the resulting epistemological racism, besides unnecessarily restricting or excluding the range of possible epistemologies, creates profoundly negative consequences for those of other racial cultures with different epistemologies, ontologies, and axiologies.

## The Negative Consequences of Epistemological Racism

First, epistemologies and research that arise from other social histories, such as African American social history or Cherokee social history, are not typically considered legitimate within the mainstream research community (see, for example, Anzaldúa 1990; Gordon 1990 1993; Minh-ha 1985; Sarris 1993; Stanfield 1993a; 1993b; 1994; among many others). As Reyes and Halcón (1988) suggest, "The traditional Euro-centric perspective used to evaluate their [scholars of color] scholarship disadvantages nontraditional [race-based] research because predominantly White male academics lack the appropriate cultural perspectives from which to judge its real merit" (307). Similarly, Collins (1991) contends that "while Black women can produce knowledge claims that contest those advanced by the White male community, this community does not grant that Black women scholars have competing knowledge claims based in another [equally warranted] knowledge validation process" (204; see also Stanfield 1994, 176). Or, as Sarris (1993) asks, "Can Apache stories, songs, and so forth be read (or heard) and thus understood in terms of Euroamerican-specific expectations of language and narrative [i.e., Euro-American epistemologies]?"

Second, there has been a large chorus of scholars of color (including Anzaldúa 1990; Collins 1991; Paredes 1977; Sarris 1993; Stanfield 1994 among others) who have contended that dominant group epistemologies and methodologies—the epistemologies and methods themselves and not just "bad" applications of these epistemologies and methodologies—tend to distort the lives of other racial groups. For example, Gordon, Miller, and Rollock (1990) have asserted:

> Examination of the social and educational research knowledge bases relative to Afro-Americans indicated that these sciences have traditionally attempted to understand the life experiences of Afro-Americans from a narrow cultrocentric perspective and against equally narrow cultrocentric standards [i.e., epistemological racism]. (15)

Consequently, as Stanfield (1985) has said, mainstream "social science knowledge production about racial minorities still dwells on the pathological and on the sensational" (411). A result of this is that these negative distortions pass into the dominant culture as "truth," thus becoming the basis of individual, group, and institutional attitudes, decisions, practices, and policies, that is, institutional and societal racism. Another result is that these distortions are often enculturated into those who are the victims of the distortions (hooks 1990; Rebolledo 1990), especially children of color who have less ability to resist (McCarthy 1993), necessitating "painful struggle[s] of accepting and rejecting internalized negative and disenabling self-conceptions" (West

1993, 270). A further result is that, frequently, the "minority scholar's time is consumed in efforts to refute or neutralize fallacious findings, questionable theories, and inappropriate interpretations" (Gordon, Miller, and Rollock 1990, 16) of mainstream research and scholarly commentary.

Third, the dominant research epistemologies—from positivism to postmodernisms—implicitly favor White people because they accord most easily with their social history (Banks 1993; Gordon 1993; Stanfield 1985). Thus, even though it may be unintended, the "clothes" that an epistemology could be said to be, fit better and are more comfortable on White researchers because White researchers themselves are a product of the social history of Whites, just as the dominant epistemologies are a product of White social history. That is, the range of epistemologies that have arisen from the social history of Whites "fits" Whites because they themselves, the nature of the university and of legitimated scholarship and knowledge, and the specifications of different re- search methodologies are all cultural products of White social history. While scholars of color have had to wear these "White" clothes (be bicultural) so that they could succeed in research communities, however sociologically, histori- cally, or culturally ill-fitting those clothes might be, White scholars have virtu- ally never had to think about wearing the epistemological clothes of people of color or even to consider the idea of such "strange" apparel.

The negative consequence for scholars of color, however, is that they must learn and become accomplished in epistemologies that arise from a social history that has been profoundly hostile to their race and that ignore or exclude alternative race-based epistemologies because mainstream research communities have assumed that their epistemologies are not derived from any particular group's social history—that is, are free of any specific history or culture. That scholars of color have successfully become epistemologically bicultural to survive as scholars is a testament to them—their strength, their courage, their perseverance, and their love of scholarship—rather than a tes- tament to the race/culture-free nature of mainstream research epistemologies.

However, one White-dominated research epistemology, the critical tradi- tion, might argue that it has not participated in the production of these nega- tive consequences, that it has consistently opposed racism in all of its many aspects or forms (for examples of critical tradition-based, antiracist work, see among many others Scheurich and Imber 1991; Scheurich and Laible 1995). And to a significant extent this is true. Many White scholars have literally devoted their careers to antiracism. In addition, the critical tradition has for many scholars of color been the only epistemologically friendly set of "clothes" (West 1993, 78–79; Stanfield 1994). Some scholars of color even contend that, to some extent, the "new" epistemologies (to be discussed shortly) based on the sociocultural histories of people of color are significantly derived from the critical tradition (e.g., Gordon, Miller, and Rollock 1990, 18–19). Consequently, it is important that the critical tradition be honored for its antiracist work, for its insights into racism, and for its willingness to question and oppose racism in academic environments that are often hostile to such efforts.

Nonetheless, the critical tradition, even if more favored by intellectuals of color, is itself almost exclusively drawn from White social history, from what Stanfield (1985) has called "European-derived paradigms" (399). The critical tradition's ontology, epistemology, and axiology are predominantly the creation of White scholars and their social context (e.g., Gordon 1993, or Stanfield 1994). Cornell West (1993), an African American and one of the eminent scholars of the critical tradition, argues, therefore, that the dependency of intellectuals of color on the critical tradition may be "debilitating for black intellectuals because the cathartic needs it [critical theory] satisfies tend to stifle the further development of black critical consciousness and attitudes" (79). In addition, virtually all of the different critical approaches, including critical theory, feminism, lesbian/gay orientations, and critical postmodernism, have been repeatedly cited for their racial biases (see, for example, Alarcón 1990; Bell 1992; Frankenberg 1993; hooks 1990; Huggins 1991; Minh-ha 1989; Stanfield 1994, 179–81; West 1993). Consequently, as Ellsworth (1989) has argued in a different context, while critical theory has been important to antiracist efforts and perhaps important to the development of new race-based epistemologies, it is not necessarily the appropriate epistemological frame for all race-oriented emancipatory work. Advocates for the critical tradition, therefore, need to support the emergence and acceptance of other epistemologies that are derived from different racial or cultural social histories[2] if this tradition is going to maintain its strong commitment to antiracism.

## Antiracist Alternatives

It is important for White faculty to broaden our understanding of racism and how it operates in our research and practice and for us to broaden our understanding of epistemologies that are derived from different racial or cultural histories. But unless we White faculty are actively engaged in working against racism through our own research and practice, we have not taken our efforts far enough:

---

2. Race-based discussions of research epistemologies and methodologies by scholars of color in the United States, like the many cited here, can provocatively be seen as a significant contribution to global postcolonial studies. In fact, this U.S. discussion can be seen as an "internal" or "domestic" version of postcolonial literature. A theme-oriented comparison between the literature cited here and that contained in collections like *The Postcolonial Studies Reader* (1995) will readily make our point.

Universities are considered responsible for helping to shape the racial attitudes of students and are widely criticized for racial incidents that take place. Universities cannot solve society's problems nor can they compensate for government policies which have contributed to racial tensions. Yet they are expected to provide a model. (Altbach 1991, 15)

Universities cannot, however, provide an effective model without modeling. Indeed, working against racism will require commitment to antiracism among a wide community of scholars.

Unfortunately, the tendency of Whites, White scholars, and White society to define racism in individual terms limits the ability to develop a concerted effort to fight racism in all its manifestations. As described previously, seeing racism so narrowly allows Whites to believe that they are not supporting, participating in, or reinforcing racism, leaving them free of any obligation to confront, interrupt, rethink, or work against it. However—and we cannot say this strongly enough—they are—we all are—participating in the system of racism regardless of our individual beliefs or intentions. Indeed, through our usually well-meaning actions and inactions, we are supporting and perpetuating racism at the institutional and societal levels. More importantly, however, we White faculty are unconsciously promulgating racism on an epistemological level. As we teach and promote epistemologies like positivism to postmodernism, we are, at least implicitly, teaching and promoting the social history of the dominant race to the exclusion of people of color, scholars of color, students of color, and the possibility for research based on other race/culture epistemologies.

The single most important effort, then, is for White researchers to develop a critical understanding of the different levels of racism, particularly epistemological racism, and of the ways these different levels of racism work on and through us. That is, faculty must develop a more sophisticated understanding of racism that moves well beyond the individual level and be able to apply that understanding to their own personal and professional practice. Then White faculty must begin to put these understandings and their opposition to racism to work—to do antiracist work, that is, efforts that work in opposition to racism.

One area in which White faculty can put their understandings and opposition to work is in their course work, particularly in research methods courses. Faculty must begin to study, teach, and thus, legitimate the research epistemologies that arise from the social histories of people of color. Research that has been conducted from race-based epistemologies should be included in our required course readings. Often "students get the message either directly or indirectly that ethnic-related research is not something that they should engage in as part of their training or for their dissertation research" (Padilla 1994, 24). As professors, we need to support informed understandings and the skillful use of these race-based epistemologies by interested students of color. But we ought not to try to force them in this direction, as most students of color typically know that race-oriented scholarship is riskier than mainstream-oriented scholarship.

Furthermore, such courses should highlight and explore the argument made by scholars of color that dominant group epistemologies and methods tend to distort the lives of people of color and the arguments made by scholars on the ethics of cross-race research, for example, a White researcher studying Latina students. None of this literature is likely to have an important impact, however, if we do not also explore with our students the levels of racism, especially the epistemological level of racism. Such course content would provide students with a good start and some resource materials. However, if we are serious about our antiracist work, we must do more than help our students think about racism in research; we must also teach them to identify and work against it in both their research and practice.

We know that such efforts are possible. We have taught research methods courses in which we cover other race/culture-based epistemologies (African American, Latino/a American, Native American, and Asian American, among other racial designations), along with positivism to poststructuralism. We have facilitated and participated in class discussions of racism, cross-race research, and the effects of dominant research paradigms on people of color. We have also incorporated antiracist teaching strategies into our courses. Furthermore, we know of professors at other universities who have been doing the same.

White faculty can also take antiracist action outside of the classroom. As research mentors and dissertation chairs, we must support studies drawn from these new race-based epistemologies. As scholars, we need to increase our awareness of work that has drawn from race-based epistemologies, and we need to work with our colleagues to increase our valuation of race-oriented journals during tenure and promotion proceedings. As journal editors, editorial board members, and journal reviewers, we must study and support the publication both of discussions of these epistemologies and of studies based on them, like that of Ladson-Billings (1995). Even better, we need to solicit this kind of work, including doing special editions of our journals. As editors and reviewers for publishing companies, we must insist on the inclusion of race-based perspectives in research methods textbooks.

Another very important effort that is needed is an ongoing and vigorous debate/dialogue at the local and national level among scholars of all races, particularly including those who write the commonly used methods textbooks and who edit widely read and respected research journals. Of all the myriad issues crucial to educational research, surely this ought to be a hotly debated one. For instance, we know there are many scholars who would oppose our contention that epistemologies arise from the social history of specific groups. Many traditional researchers or social scientists, for instance, argue that their epistemology reaches above history toward a context-free kind of truth. These scholars, among others, should be part of the discussion. If the possibility that our typical epistemologies are racially biased is not genuinely worth the price of a spirited intellectual debate, what is?

Obviously these suggestions are insufficient, but they are intended only as initial steps toward a crucially needed antiracist effort that to date, unfortunately, has largely been overlooked or avoided by White scholars. Our hope is that we have provided a helpful discussion of epistemological racism as well as a convincing argument for faculty in institutions of higher education to rethink their understanding of racism and the ways in which their research and practice are affected by racism. It is also our hope that such a rethinking will enable White researchers to see and to begin to take action against racism in their work and work settings. It is time for higher education faculty, particularly those who prepare students to work in the field of education or to carry out educational research, to join these efforts.

## Conclusion

Racism has a long and horrible legacy; and it continues, though its forms and tools have transformed over time, to have terrible consequences for its victims as well as for its perpetrators. Perhaps one of the most frustrating forms of racism for any generation or group is the one we do not see, the one that is invisible to our lens, the one we participate in without consciously knowing or intending it. Are we not seeing the biases of our time just as those a hundred years ago did not see the biases of their time? Will those who look back at us in time wonder why we resisted seeing our racism? The unfortunate truth is that we can be strongly antiracist in our own minds but be promulgating racism in profound ways we do not understand (Pine and Hilliard 1990, 595). As Cose (1993) says in *The Rage of a Privileged Class,* "People do not have to be racist—or have any malicious intent—in order to make decisions that unfairly harm members of another race" (4). It is our contention here, based on the germinal, groundbreaking work of scholars of color, that we educational researchers are unintentionally involved at the epistemological heart of our research and practice in a racism— epistemological racism—that we generally do not see or understand.

However, simply because we have not seen it in the past does not mean that we cannot see it once it is pointed out. We can study it, discuss it, and reflect on it. Once we see and understand it, however, we cannot continue in our old ways. In the words of Ruth Farmer (1993), "In the academic community, much is written about racism, race dynamics, and racial attitudes, yet little is done about these same issues personally, departmentally, or institutionally. Race is viewed abstractly" (201). As university faculty, we have an obligation to move beyond abstractions to action. It is time to take seriously the call to rethink and work against racism.

## References

Alarcón, Norma. 1990. The theoreti-cal subject(s) of *This bridge called my back* and *Anglo-American feminism*. In *Making face, making soul haciendo caras: Creative and critical perspectives by feminists of color,* edited by Gloria Anzaldúa, 356–69. San Francisco: Aunt Lute Books.

Altbach, Philip G. 1991. The racial dilemma in American higher education. In *The racial crisis in American higher education,* edited by Philip G. Altbach and Kofi Lomotey, 3–17. Albany: State University of New York Press.

Anzaldúa, Gloria. 1990. Haciendo caras, una entrada. In *Making face, making soul haciendo caras: Creative and critical perspectives by feminists of color,* edited by Gloria Anzaldúa, xv–xxviii. San Francisco: Aunt Lute Books.

Banks, James A. 1993. The canon debate, knowledge construction, and multicultural education. *Educational Researcher* 22, no. 5:4–14.

———. 1995. The historical reconstruction of knowledge about race: Implications for transformative learning. *Educational Researcher* 24, no. 2:15–25.

Bell, Derrick. 1992. *Faces at the bottom of the well: The permanence of racism.* New York: Basic Books.

Bernstein, Richard J. 1992. *The new constellation: The ethical-political horizons of modernity/postmodernity.* Cambridge: MIT Press.

Billingsley, Andrew. 1968. *Black families in White America.* Englewood Cliffs, NJ: Prentice-Hall.

Clifford, James. 1988. Identity in Mashpee. In *The predicament of culture: Twentieth-century ethnography, literature and art,* edited by James Clifford, 277–345. Cambridge: Harvard University Press.

Collins, Patricia Hill. 1991. *Black feminist thought: Knowledge, consciousness, and the politics of empowerment.* New York: Routledge.

Cose, Ellis. 1993. *The rage of a privileged class.* New York: HarperCollins.

Cummins, Jim. 1986. Empowering minority students: A framework for intervention. *Harvard Educational Review* 56, no. 1:18–36.

de León, Arnoldo. 1983. *They called them greasers: Anglo attitudes toward Mexicans in Texas, 1821–1900.* Austin: University of Texas Press.

Ellsworth, Elizabeth. 1989. Why doesn't this feel empowering? Working through the repressive myths of critical pedagogy. *Harvard Educational Review* 59, no. 3:297–325.

Farmer, Ruth. 1993. Place but not importance: The race for inclusion in academe. In *Spirit, space and survival: African American Women in (White) Academe,* edited by Joy James and Ruth Farmer, 192–217. New York: Routledge.

Feagin, Joe R., and Hernán Vera. 1995. *White racism.* New York: Routledge.

Foucault, Michel. 1972. *The archaeology of knowledge.* New York: Pantheon.

———. 1973. *The order of things: An archaeology of the human sciences.* New York: Vintage.

———. 1979. *Discipline and punish: The birth of the prison.* New York: Vintage.

Frankenberg, Ruth. 1993. *The social construction of Whiteness: White women, race matters.* Minneapolis: University of Minnesota Press.

Gaertner, Samuel L., and John F. Dovidio. 1986. The aversive form of racism. In *Prejudice, discrimination, and racism,* edited by John F. Dovidio and Samuel L. Gaertner, 61–89. Orlando, FL: Academic Press.

Goldberg, David Theo. 1993. *Racist culture: Philosophy and the politics of meaning.* Oxford, UK: Blackwell.

Gordon, Beverly M. 1990. The necessity of African-American epistemology for educational theory and practice. *Journal of Education* 172, no. 3:88–106.

———. 1993. Toward emancipation in citizenship education: The case of African-American cultural knowledge. In *Understanding curriculum as racial text: Representations of identity and difference in education,* edited by Louis A. Castenell Jr. and William F. Pinar, 263–84. Albany: State University of New York Press.

Gordon, Edmund W., Fayheese Miller, and David Rollock. 1990. Coping with communicentric bias in knowledge production in the social sciences. *Educational Researcher* 19, no. 3:14–19.

Hacker, Andrew. 1992. *Two nations: Black and White, separate, hostile, unequal.* New York: Charles Scribner's Sons.

Harris, Cheryl. 1993. Whiteness as property. *Harvard Law Review* 106, no. 8:1707–91.

Herrnstein, Richard J., and Charles Murray. 1994. *The bell curve: Intelligence and class structure in American life.* New York: Free Press.

Hill, Robert Bernard. 1972. *The strengths of Black families.* New York: Emerson Hall.

Hilliard, Asa G., III. 1992. Behavioral style, culture, and teaching and learning. *Journal of Negro Education* 61, no. 3:370–77.

hooks, bell. 1990. *Yearning: Race, gender, and cultural politics.* Boston: South End Press.

Huggins, Joyce. 1991. Black women and women's liberation. In *A reader in feminist knowledge,* edited by Sneja Gunew, 6–12. London: Routledge.

King, Joyce F. 1991. Dysconscious racism: Ideology, identity, and the miseducation of teachers. *Journal of Negro Education* 60, no. 2:133–46.

Kluegel, James R., and Eliot R. Smith. 1986. *Beliefs about inequality: Americans' views of what is and what ought to be.* New York: Aldine de Gruyter.

Ladson-Billings, Gloria. 1995. Toward a theory of culturally relevant pedagogy. *American Educational Research Journal* 32, no. 3:465–91.

Laible, Julie, and Sandra Harrington. 1998. The power and the possibility of leading with alternative values. *International Journal of Leadership in Education* 1, no. 2:111–35.

Lee, Carol D., Kofi Lomotey, and Mwalimu Shujaa. 1990. How shall we sing our sacred song in a strange land? The dilemma of double consciousness and the complexities of an African-centered pedagogy. *Journal of Education* 172, no. 2:45–61.

Littlejohn-Blake, Sheila M., and Carol Anderson Darling. 1993. Understanding the strengths of African American families. *Journal of Black Studies* 23, no. 4:460–71.

Loftin, John D. 1991. *Religion and Hopi life in the twentieth century.* Bloomington: Indiana University Press.

McCarthy, Cameron. 1993. Beyond the poverty of theory in race relations: Nonsynchrony and social difference in education. In *Beyond silenced voices: Class, race, and gender in United States schools,* edited by Lois Weis and Michelle Fine, 325–46. Albany: State University of New York Press.

Minh-ha, Trinh T. 1989. *Woman native other.* Bloomington: Indiana University Press.

Morrison, Toni. 1992. *Playing in the dark: Whiteness and the literary imagination.* Cambridge: Harvard University Press.

National Advisory Commission on Civil Disorders. 1968, March 1. *Report of the National Advisory Commission on Civil Disorders.* Publication No. 1968 O-291-729. Washington, DC: U.S. Government Printing Office.

Ortiz, Alba A., Shernaz B. Garcia, David S. Wheeler, and Elba Maldonado-Colon. 1986. *Characteristics of limited English proficient students served in programs for the speech and language handicapped: Implications for policy, practice, and research.* Austin: University of Texas, Department of Special Education, Handicapped Minority Research Institute on Language Proficiency. ERIC No. 292 280.

Padilla, Amado M. 1994. Ethnic minority scholars, research, and mentoring: Current and future issues. *Educational Researcher* 23, no. 4:24–27.

Paredes, Americo. 1977. On ethnographic work among minority groups: A folklorist's perspective. *New Scholar* 6:1–32.

Pine, Gerald J., and Asa G. Hilliard III. 1990. Rx for racism: Imperatives for America's schools. *Phi Delta Kappan* 71:593–600.

Rebolledo, Tey Piana. 1990. The politics of poetics: Or, what am I, a critic, doing in this text anyhow? In *Making face, making soul haciendo caras: Creative and critical perspectives by feminists of color,* edited by Gloria Anzaldúa, 346–55. San Francisco: Aunt Lute Books.

Reyes, María de la Luz, and John J. Halcón. 1988. Racism in academia: The old wolf revisited. *Harvard Educational Review* 58, no. 3:299–314.

Rizvi, Fazal. 1993. Children and the grammar of popular racism. In *Race identity and representation in education,* edited by Cameron McCarthy and Warren Crichlow, 126–39. New York: Routledge.

Roscoe, Will. 1991. *The Zuni man-woman.* Albuquerque: University of New Mexico Press.

Said, Edward W. 1979. *Orientalism.* New York: Vintage.

Sarris, Greg. 1993. Hearing the old ones talk: Reading narrated American Indian lives in Elizabeth Colson's *Autobiographies of three Pomo women.* In *New voices in Native American literary criticism,* edited by Arnold Krupat, 419–52. Washington, DC: Smithsonian Institution Press.

Scheurich, James Joseph. 1993. Toward a White discourse on White racism. *Educational Researcher* 22, no. 8:5–10.

Scheurich, James Joseph, and Julie Laible. 1995. The buck stops here—in our preparation programs: Educative leadership for all children (No exceptions allowed). *Educational Administration Quarterly* 31, no. 2:313.

Scheurich, James Joseph, and Michael Imber. 1991. Educational reforms can reproduce societal inequities: A case study. *Educational Administration Quarterly* 27, no. 3:297–320.

Sears, David O. 1988. Symbolic racism. In *Eliminating racism: Profiles in controversy,* edited by Phyllis A. Katz and Dalmas A. Taylor, 53–84. New York: Plenum.

Shockley, W. 1992. Society has a moral obligation to diagnose tragic racial IQ deficits. In *Shockley on eugenics and race: The application of science to the solution of human problems,* edited by R. Pearson, 212–18. Washington, DC: Scott-Townsend.

Shuey, Audrey M. 1958. *The testing of Negro intelligence.* Lynchburg, VA: Bell.

Stanfield, John H., II. 1985. The ethnocentric basis of social science knowledge production. *Review of Research in Education* 12:387–415.

———. 1993a. Epistemological considerations. In *Race and ethnicity in research methods,* edited by John H. Stanfield II and Rutledge M. Dennis, 16–36. Newbury Park, CA: Sage.

———. 1993b. Methodological reflections. In *Race and ethnicity in research methods,* edited by John H. Stanfield II and Rutledge M. Dennis, 3–15. Newbury Park, CA: Sage.

————. 1994. Ethnic modeling in qualitative research. In *Handbook of qualitative inquiry,* edited by Norman K. Denzin and Yvonna S. Lincoln, 175–88. Newbury Park, CA: Sage.

Takaki, Ronald T. 1993. *A different mirror: A history of multicultural America.* Boston: Little, Brown.

Tatum, Beverly D. 1992. Talking about race, learning about racism: The application of racial identity development theory in the classroom. *Harvard Educational Review* 62, no. 1:1–24.

Valencia, Richard R., ed. 1997. *The evolution of deficit thinking: Educational thought and practice.* London: Falmer.

Webster, Yehudi O. 1992. *The racialization of America.* New York: St. Martin's Press.

West, Cornell. 1993. *Keeping faith: Philosophy and race in America.* New York: Routledge.

# CHAPTER 11

# A Critical Race Theory Analysis of Barriers that Impede the Success of Faculty of Color

OCTAVIO VILLALPANDO AND
DOLORES DELGADO BERNAL

> I encountered a rude awakening to the horrors of being a junior faculty member in a department where at the time, sexism and racism operated rampantly. As the only African American female, with an overabundance of doctoral students to advise, two graduate courses a semester, one-quarter time in an interdisciplinary research center, I questioned the efficacy of academic pursuits. . . . I had been awarded grants from [the] National Science Foundation, Rockefeller Foundation . . . and had established the reputation of being a competent scholar, researcher, and teacher. . . . However, it became increasingly clear that my contribution was not valued by my colleagues, and at my three-year review, I received a negative evaluation of my work. Although individuals in central administration were very supportive, I decided that the institutionalized racism and sexism within the department [were] larger than I.
>
> —Professor Linda F. Winfield (1997, 203)

Recent and emerging literature on the American professorate suggests that Winfield's account represents experiences endured by many faculty of color. In this chapter, "faculty of color" refers to persons of African American, Chicana/o/Puerto Rican/Other Latina/o, American Indian, and Asian American ancestry. (See, e.g., Altbach and Lomotey 1991; Gainen and Boice

We want to recognize that the writing of this chapter was a collaborative effort in which both authors contributed equally. For their valuable feedback on earlier drafts, we thank William A. Smith, Philip G. Altbach, Kofi Lomotey, Lavina Fielding Anderson, and our colleagues at the University of Utah: Bryan Brayboy, Ed Buendia, Donna Deyhle, Andrew Gitlin, Frank Margonis, and Audrey Thompson.

243

1993; Padilla and Chavez 1995; Turner, Garcia, Nora, and Rendon 1996; Turner and Myers 2000; Turner, Myers, and Creswell 1999. Faculty of color appear to encounter institutional barriers at most stages of their academic careers. These barriers are frequently racially biased double standards that penalize faculty of color for not performing better than their White male colleagues (Turner, Myers, and Creswell 1999). They often include an expectation for a higher quantity and quality of publications, heavier teaching and advising loads, required visibility when it is in the department's best interest to have a "minority" scholar, and "token" membership on "diversity" committees (Padilla and Chavez 1995; H. Astin, Antonio, Cress, and Astin 1997; Niemann 1999; Turner and Myers 2000). Yet despite the unmistakable racial bias inherent in these double standards, higher education refuses to acknowledge them, insisting that its academic reward structure is a neutral, objective, and meritocratic process. (See also Allen et al.; Scheurich and Young, this volume.)

In this chapter, we use critical race theory to provide a structural analysis of the racialized barriers that impede the success of faculty of color. We first outline critical race theory as an interpretive framework and explain its appropriateness to our examination of higher education's failure to hire, retain, promote, and tenure faculty of color. We then use thirty-year national trend data to examine the stratification of faculty of color by institutional type, academic department, and academic rank. From these data, we argue that an apartheid of knowledge for faculty of color separates and devalues the type of research, teaching, and scholarship they produce. We examine how faculty of color compare with White faculty on productivity and work roles and how the academic reward structure operates differently for them. We explore the plausibility of the reasons often cited by higher education institutions and the mainstream literature to explain the lack of success in hiring, retaining, promoting, and tenuring faculty of color. Analyzing the data using critical race theory allows us to contest these reasons and identify some of the racialized barriers for faculty of color. Finally, we suggest how institutions and White faculty can genuinely begin to eliminate these racialized barriers and offer insights for faculty of color on navigating these obstacles.

## Critical Race Theory As an Interpretive Framework

Critical race theory is a theoretical framework generated by legal scholars of color who are concerned about racial oppression in society (Crenshaw, Gotanda, Peller, and Thomas 1995; R. Delgado 1995; Matsuda, Lawrence, Delgado, and Crenshaw 1993). It explores how so-called race-neutral laws and institutional policies perpetuate racial/ethnic subordination. This framework emphasizes the importance of viewing policies and policy making in the proper historical and cultural context to deconstruct their racialized content (Bell 1995; Crenshaw, Gotanda, Peller, and Thomas 1995). It challenges dominant liberal ideas such as color blindness and meritocracy and shows how these concepts disadvantage people of color and further advantage Whites (R. Delgado and Stefancic 1994). Critical race theory commonly uses counterstories in the form of dialogues, chronicles, and personal testimonies because it acknowledges that some members of marginalized groups, by virtue of their marginal status, tell stories different from those White scholars usually hear (R. Delgado 1990). Counterstories are both a method to tell stories of often-untold experiences and also a tool for analyzing and challenging the dominant discourse and the stories of those in power (R. Delgado 1989). They provide data that offer individuals a way to see the world through others' eyes and enrich their own reality. In this chapter, we offer counterstories to corroborate our quantitative data and analysis. The following defining elements form the basic assumptions, perspectives, research methods, and pedagogies of critical race theory (Matsuda, Lawrence, R. Delgado, and Crenshaw 1993). Each is important to our examination of the racialized barriers that impede success for faculty of color. Critical race theory:

- recognizes that racism is endemic to American life.
- expresses skepticism toward dominant claims of neutrality, objectivity, color blindness, and meritocracy.
- challenges ahistoricism and insists on a contextual/historical analysis of institutional policies.
- insists on recognizing the experiential knowledge of people of color and our communities of origin in analyzing society.
- is interdisciplinary and crosses epistemological and methodological boundaries.
- works toward the end of eliminating racial oppression as part of the broader goal of ending all forms of oppression.

These defining elements form a framework that applies to real-life social problems, especially in education. In fact, a number of education scholars have begun to use critical race theory as a way to further define and examine problems endemic to education, schools, and the schooling processes (Delgado Bernal 2002; Ladson-Billings and Tate 1995; Lynn 1999; Parker 1998; Solorzano 1998; Solorzano and Villalpando 1998; Tate 1997; Villalpando forthcoming A). Solorzano applies critical race theory in his research to challenge "the dominant discourse on race and racism as it relates to education by examining how educational theory, policy, and practice are used to subordinate certain racial/ethnic groups" (Solorzano 1998, 122). The six defining elements of critical race theory, along with Solorzano's application of critical race theory in education, provide our framework in identifying and analyzing the racialized barriers that impede the success of faculty of color in academia.

## The Heterogeneity of Faculty of Color

Aside from H. Astin, Antonio, Cress, and Astin's (1997) recent analysis of race and ethnicity in the American professorate and the biannual faculty reports issued by the UCLA Higher Education Research Institute, most analyses of national data for faculty of color are seldom disaggregated by race, ethnicity, and gender. Data for faculty of color are often aggregated and reported in a homogenous analysis of "minority faculty" that, unfortunately, tends to confound their distinct experiences in the academy, often leading to the erroneous conclusion that all faculty of color share the same sociohistorical experiences, demographic characteristics, professional values, aspirations, and levels of success.

To avoid this limitation, our analysis in this chapter has, wherever possible, disaggregated data for African American, Asian American, American Indian, Chicana/o/Mexican American, and Puerto Rican faculty. We have drawn from the UCLA Higher Education Research Institute's national faculty data sets and other sources that collect and report data by racial/ethnic groups. What also makes our analysis unique is that we weave the counterstories of faculty of color with the disaggregated quantitative data to present both distinct and shared experiences of faculty of color.

Asian American faculty are central to any discussion of the heterogeneity of faculty of color, since most available data on the professorate note their marked success over the last thirty years (A. Astin, Korn, and Dey 1990; H. Astin, Antonio, Cress, and Astin 1997; Sax, Astin, Korn, and Gilmartin 1999; Turner and Myers 2000). The data on Asian Americans suggest that, as a group, they have performed better in several important dimensions, in contrast to other ethnic/racial groups, including White faculty in some cases. For example, in comparison to other faculty of color, Asian Americans are the best represented ethnic/racial group, are more likely to hold a Ph.D., publish more, and earn higher salaries (H. Astin, Antonio, Cress, and Astin 1997). Their representation in the professoriat is often also considered to be near parity with their representation in the U.S. population.

However, there are several problems associated with data on Asian Americans (Suzuki 1989). First, even though they constitute a highly heterogeneous population, data and analysis on Asian American faculty are seldom disaggregated (Escueta and O'Brien 1991). (See also Chang and Kiang, this volume.) Most analyses do not distinguish among ethnic groups, generation status, or national origin, to name only a few of the characteristics that shape distinct identities and experiences among Asian American groups. The experiences of a first- or second-generation Vietnamese American faculty member are likely to differ sharply from those of a sixth-generation Japanese American. Thus, grouping all Asian Americans together confounds and camouflages the distinct and diverse experiences of each group.

Second, the suggestion that their representation in the professoriat has brought them to parity with their representation in the U.S. population is very misleading. As Cho (1996) explains, parity (or overparity) at the entry level does not always translate into parity at the higher academic levels. Parity in certain academic disciplines masks underparity in other disciplines. In fact, she argues that the assumptions drawn from Asian Americans' aggregated parity status hides the varied needs of a heterogeneous population. In support of Cho's argument, Turner and Myers (2000) assert: "The concept of parity speaks to a statistical picture of numerical 'inclusion' but does not say anything about the quality of that inclusion" (40). For these two reasons, our analysis does not dwell on explaining differential levels of success over the last thirty years between Asian American faculty and other faculty of color. Asian American faculty are exposed to racist policies and practices as much as other faculty of color (Nakanishi 1993). In fact, some would argue that, if it were not for these exclusionary practices, Asian American faculty would have achieved even greater successes in the professorate.

**Shortcomings of the "Pipeline" Explanation**

The underrepresentation of faculty of color is often attributed to the doctoral production "pipeline problem"—not enough qualified doctoral graduates of color to fill vacant faculty positions (A. Astin 1982; Turner, Meyers, and Creswell, 1999). The conventional explanation for the underrepresentation of faculty of color asserts that institutions are interested in hiring faculty of color but that there are few people of color in the doctorate pool and even fewer who are actually qualified. bell hooks (1996) captures this standard explanation succinctly:

> Whenever I called attention to the relative absence of Black women scholars at this institution, naming the impact of sexism and racism, I was told again and again by White male colleagues, "If Black women are not here, it is not because Yale is racist, it is that Black women are simply not good enough." (367)

We acknowledge the importance of the doctoral pool as a pipeline into the professorate. We also recognize that the underrepresentation of faculty of color is partly due to documented leaks that begin very early in their educational pipeline. However, we concur with Allen et al. (this volume) that "too often, this discrepancy [in underrepresentation of faculty of color] is treated as the intractable result of a limited pool of eligible faculty." By overemphasizing the "pipeline problem" as a principal explanation for the underrepresentation of faculty of color, we risk disregarding some of the equally insidious racialized structures and practices that contribute to a cycle of exclusion for faculty of color. While the pipeline certainly contributes to the available pool of faculty of color, it is really the *members* of the academic profession who hire individuals from the pool for available faculty positions. Whether intended or not, individual faculty members can promote racist procedures and engage in behavior that sustains an institutional racist framework. This is true even though, as Scheurich and Young (this volume) point out, faculty are usually not aware of how they perpetuate a racist institutional structure by using rigid hiring and promotion practices that devalue the qualifications and scholarship of faculty of color.

For these reasons we reject the "pipeline problem" as a conventional explanation for faculty of color's underrepresentation. If we do not analyze how higher education's racialized structures and practices undergird institutional racism, then we unintentionally relieve higher education and White faculty of the responsibility for removing barriers to success for faculty of color. Our framework—critical race theory—recognizes that racism is endemic to higher education and exists in many forms, though one of the most prevalent appears to be institutional racism (Padilla and Chavez 1995; Reyes and Halcon 1996). Institutional racism most often exists in higher education as "standard operating procedures . . . that hurt members of one or more races in relation to members of the dominant race" (Scheurich and Young, this volume). Thus, we do not adopt the "pipeline argument" to explain why there are so few faculty of color. Instead, we analyze the racialized practices and procedures that exclude and stratify faculty of color by institution, department, and rank.

## De Facto Segregation: Faculty of Color in Different Institutions

In the last quarter century, faculty of color have increased their representation in American higher education by less than 6 percent (H. Astin and Villalpando 1996; Sax, Astin, Korn, and Gilmartin 1999). In 1972, 95 percent of all faculty self-identified as White, and only about 4 percent as faculty of color. In 1998, nearly 92 percent self-identified as White and approximately 9 percent as faculty of color (Sax, Astin, Korn, and Gilmartin 1999). As appalling as this lack of improvement is, perhaps equally astonishing is how little the individual composition has changed for each of the faculty ethnic/racial groups. No one ethnic/racial group has grown by more than 2 percent over the last twenty-five years. In fact, as Table 11.1 demonstrates, the largest ethnic/racial group is currently represented by Asian Americans at only about 3 percent (Sax, Astin, Korn, and Gilmartin 1999).

Similarly, women, regardless of race, have increased their representation as a percentage of all faculty only by approximately 7 percent since 1989 (Sax, Astin, Korn, and Gilmartin 1999). Thirty-six percent of all faculty in

1998 were women. Women of color represented only about 10 percent of all women in the professorate, though they represented a higher proportion among all faculty of color, ranging from 30 percent to 48 percent within most racial/ethnic groups (H. Astin, Antonio, Cress, and Astin 1997). (See also Allen et al., this volume.)

The representation of faculty of color varies slightly across different types of higher education institutions. The largest representation of faculty of color is at public two-year institutions, where in 1998, approximately 12 percent of the faculty self-identified as persons of color, an increase of 7 percent since 1972. The lowest representation is among private four-year colleges and universities, where less than 8 percent of the faculty self-identified as members of an underrepresented ethnic/racial group in 1998, an increase of only 5 percent since 1972 (Milem and Astin 1993; Sax, Astin, Korn, and Gilmartin 1999). Faculty of color comprised less than 9 percent of the professoriat at public four-year colleges and universities in 1998, an increase of only 3 percent since 1972 (Milem and Astin 1993; Sax, Astin, Korn, and Gilmartin 1999). These patterns also hold true for women of color, who had the largest proportional representation in public two-year institutions, and the smallest representation in private universities (H. Astin, Antonio, Cress, and Astin 1997).

The data in Table 11.1 illustrate the stratification of faculty of color by institutional type, size, and prestige. The smallest and more prestigious institutions, like private four-year colleges and universities, have had the smallest percentage of faculty of color since the early 1970s. In contrast, the largest and less prominent two-year institutions have had among the highest percentage and growth of faculty of color during the same period. For example, American Indian faculty have improved their overall representation in the professoriat by about 1 percent since 1972 but grew primarily at two-year institutions.

These data suggest that despite an official end to de jure racial segregation, higher education continues to reflect a state of de facto racial segregation and gender stratification (Delgado Bernal 1999; see also Allen et al.; Scheurich and Young, this volume.) Faculty of color are not only concentrated in institutions of lesser prestige and fewer resources but can expect lower levels of lifetime earnings and restricted social mobility as a result of working in these types of institutions (A. Astin 1982, 1993; Carnevale 1999; Karabel 1977). The popular claims that higher education is objective, meritocratic, color blind, and race neutral and that it provides equal opportunities for all (Bennett 1984; Bloom 1987; D'Souza 1991; Schlesinger 1993) clearly do not hold up when analyzing the racial segregation and gender stratification of faculty. Higher education's claims, interpreted through a critical race lens, are a camouflage for the self-interest, power, and privilege of dominant groups in U.S. society who exert significant influence over higher education (Calmore 1992; R. Delgado 1984).

## Table 11.1
### Trends in Distribution of Faculty of Color, by Type of Institution (in percentages)

|  | Total | | African American | Asian American | American Indian | Chicano/ Mex American | Puerto Rican |
|---|---|---|---|---|---|---|---|
|  | White | Fac Col |  |  |  |  |  |
| **All Institutions** |  |  |  |  |  |  |  |
| 1972 | 95.0 | 3.7 | 1.3 | 1.3 | .7 | .2 | .2 |
| 1989 | 90.9 | 7.0 | 2.1 | 2.9 | .8 | .8 | .4 |
| 1998 | 91.7 | 9.3 | 2.6 | 3.3 | 2.0 | 1.0 | .4 |
| % change | -3.3 | 5.6 | 1.3 | 2.0 | 1.3 | .8 | .2 |
| **Public Universities** |  |  |  |  |  |  |  |
| 1972 | 95.9 | 3.0 | .7 | 1.4 | .7 | .2 | 0.0 |
| 1989 | 90.1 | 7.3 | 1.3 | 4.1 | .7 | .8 | .4 |
| 1998 | 91.3 | 8.9 | 2.3 | 4.2 | 1.2 | .9 | .3 |
| % change | -4.6 | 5.9 | 1.6 | 2.8 | .5 | .7 | .3 |
| **Private Universities** |  |  |  |  |  |  |  |
| 1972 | 95.7 | 3.5 | 1.2 | 1.7 | .4 | .0 | .2 |
| 1989 | 92.1 | 5.5 | 2.0 | 2.8 | .4 | .2 | .1 |
| 1998 | 91.3 | 8.2 | 2.5 | 3.9 | .7 | .8 | .3 |
| % change | -4.4 | 4.7 | 1.3 | 2.2 | .3 | .8 | .1 |

**Table 11.1**
*Continued*

| | Total | | African American | Asian American | American Indian | Chicano/ Mex American | Puerto Rican |
|---|---|---|---|---|---|---|---|
| | White | Fac Col | | | | | |
| **Public Four-Year** | | | | | | | |
| 1972 | 92.2 | 5.5 | 1.9 | 1.6 | .8 | .2 | 1.0 |
| 1989 | 90.6 | 7.4 | 2.4 | 3.2 | 1.0 | .6 | .2 |
| 1998 | 91.1 | 9.2 | 2.6 | 3.6 | 1.7 | .9 | .4 |
| % change | -1.1 | 3.7 | .7 | 2.0 | .9 | .7 | -.6 |
| **Private Four-Year** | | | | | | | |
| 1972 | 96.3 | 2.6 | 1.1 | .7 | .6 | .1 | .1 |
| 1989 | 93.3 | 5.0 | 1.4 | 1.7 | .5 | .3 | 1.1 |
| 1998 | 92.5 | 7.6 | 2.9 | 2.5 | 1.5 | .7 | .4 |
| % change | -3.8 | 5.0 | 1.8 | 1.8 | .9 | .6 | .3 |
| **Public Two-Year** | | | | | | | |
| 1972 | 94.0 | 4.6 | 2.0 | 1.2 | .8 | .6 | 0.0 |
| 1989 | 89.4 | 8.8 | 3.3 | 2.3 | 1.2 | 1.8 | .2 |
| 1998 | 92.1 | 11.5 | 2.7 | 2.3 | 4.3 | 1.5 | .7 |
| % change | -1.9 | 6.9 | .7 | 1.1 | 3.5 | .9 | .7 |

*Sources*: Milem and Astin 1993; A. Astin, Korn, and Dey 1990; Sax, Astin, Korn, and Gilmartin 1999.

## An Apartheid of Knowledge:
## Faculty of Color in Academic Departments

In addition to their disproportionate stratification among types of higher education institutions, faculty of color are also unevenly represented in different types of academic departments. Faculty of color are concentrated in departments that are often held in low regard and considered less prominent and prestigious within higher education, such as humanities, ethnic studies, women's studies, education, and the social sciences (Allen et al., this volume; Garza 1993). Garza (1993) called this phenomenon the "ghettoization" and "barrioization" of faculty of color and their scholarship. The data appear to support these assertions. For example, in 1995, 32 percent of African American faculty had appointments in the humanities or in education, while less than 2 percent were in the physical sciences (H. Astin, Antonio, Cress, and Astin 1997). Similarly, almost 37 percent of all Chicana/o faculty held appointments in the humanities or in education while only 2 percent taught in the physical sciences. Women of color follow an equally disproportionate representation in these fields, with 34 percent teaching in the humanities or in education, and 3 percent in the physical sciences (H. Astin, Antonio, Cress, and Astin 1997).

We argue that faculty of color are concentrated in the humanities, social sciences, and education because of both personal choice and opportunity structure. First, as Oakes's (1985) research demonstrates, students of color are often tracked into "low ability" groups or "low-achieving" classrooms from elementary school through high school. As a result, students of color are often placed in vocational tracks or academic tracks that do not prepare them for science-based fields. Students of color often tend to be concentrated in racially segregated K-12 urban schools with very scarce resources, inexperienced faculty, and neglected physical facilities (González 1990; Kozol 1991; Valencia 1991). Academic tracking and poor schooling conditions contribute to public education's inability to support and develop talent among students of color who are interested in the natural or physical sciences or in other science-based fields. Few students of color can benefit from adequate resources and support to pursue their interests in these fields and are consequently excluded from graduate programs in the sciences and, hence, from academic science as a profession. Moreover, according to Shirley Brown, strict exclusionary practices

> sanctioned by custom and law in both private and public higher education, continued well into the mid-twentieth century for all minority groups including Black-Americans, American Indians, Hispanics, and Asian Americans. Thus, the lack of representation of minorities throughout the range of disciplines continues to exist. (Qtd. in Turner and Myers 2000, 13).

The second reason for the concentration of faculty of color in these fields is related to their sense of responsibility to their community (Villalpando 1996). They often enter fields where they can teach and research social justice issues that address the status of their politically and socioeconomically disenfranchised communities. They produce scholarship that addresses different forms of social inequality, often through the fields of humanities, education, social sciences, and ethnic studies.

Scholarship produced by faculty of color in these fields, however, is often undervalued by the academic profession, even though, as Garza (1993) notes:

> Most of the national and international politics and principal movements for change of at least the last quarter century centered on racial and ethnic group matters. Therefore, this kind of scholarship and the scholars who do it should be accorded the necessary respect and legitimacy it and they deserve. (40)

Rather than receiving respect, this kind of scholarship is often regarded as illegitimate, biased, or too subjective (Turner and Myers 2000; Turner, Myers, and Creswell 1999).

For faculty of color, an apartheid of knowledge separates the research, teaching, and scholarship they often produce from mainstream scholarship. This apartheid of knowledge goes beyond the high value society places on the positivist tradition of the "hard sciences" and its low regard for the social sciences. It ignores and discredits the epistemologies—systems of knowing and understanding—of faculty of color. This apartheid of knowledge is sustained by an epistemological racism that defines what the mainstream research community considers legitimate epistemologies. (See also Scheurich and Young, this volume.) Too frequently, research epistemologies based on the social history and culture of the dominant race have produced scholarship which portrays people of color as culturally, socially, and/or biologically deficient and inferior. Within their respective disciplines, faculty of color have responded by conducting research based on epistemologies and theories that arise from their social histories (Delgado Bernal 1998; Collins 1991; Dillard 1997; Flores-Ortiz 1998; Ladson-Billings 1995; Perez 1999). For example, based on the findings of the 1992 American Indian Survey, Stein (1996) documents the story of a American Indian who serves on the faculty of a large four-year institution in the Southwest. As Stein explains, this faculty member's scholarship on American Indians is often devalued and seen as biased by his White colleagues:

> [He] understands that his personal area of research is not highly valued by his colleagues because it is outside the mainstream and is on American Indian issues. Further, many journals in his field suspect his work because it is about Indians and he is an American Indian. [He] has been told that it would be impossible for him to do objective scientific research on his own people. (392)

Similarly, Professors María de la Luz Reyes and John Halcón (1996), describe why it is important to conduct research that is grounded in the social history of Chicana/os, despite the taboo of "brown-on-brown" research:

> We want to provide our own perspectives regarding prevailing negative assumptions about our values, culture, and language. This explains our interest in such topics as dropouts, bilingual education, second language literacy, Chicano literature, and the education of minority students. . . . Tired of reading about ourselves in the social science literature written by non-minorities, we want to speak for ourselves, to define, label, describe, and interpret our own condition from the "inside out." (342)

Our critical race analysis of the disproportionate stratification of faculty of color across academic departments suggests that there is an epistemological racism endemic to higher education that results in the creation of an apartheid of knowledge. Rather than recognizing the contributions of the epistemologies that faculty of color bring to academia and the importance of scholarship that crosses epistemological and disciplinary boundaries, the academic reward structure in higher education excludes their access to a broader field of academic disciplines and departments.

## Double Standards: Academic Ranks and Tenure Rates

In addition to their disproportionate stratification along types of higher education institutions, faculty of color are also stratified by academic rank— and the disparities appear to have remained relatively unchanged in nearly twenty-five years. Between 1972 and 1989, faculty of color improved their representation at the rank of professor by less than 4 percent. In 1989, approximately 92 percent of professors were White and less than 7 percent were faculty of color (Milem and Astin 1993). (The remaining 1 percent identified as "other" or declined to state their race/ethnicity.) Overall, men, regardless of race, are two to three times more likely than all women to achieve this rank, and it continues to be most elusive for women of color as a group. For example, only 9 percent of all Latina faculty and only 12 percent of all American Indian women faculty hold the rank of professor (H. Astin, Antonio, Cress, and Astin 1997).

The largest representation of faculty of color has consistently been in the lower and less prestigious academic ranks. (See Table 11.2.) Between 1972 and 1989, African Americans, Chicana/os, Puerto Ricans, American Indians, and Asian Americans comprised between 7 percent to about 12 percent of the lowest academic ranks—lecturers and instructors. This clustering constituted the largest and most stable presence of faculty of color among all academic

**Table 11.2**

**Trends in Distribution of Faculty of Color, by Academic Rank (in percentages)**

| | Total | | African American | Asian American | American Indian | Chicano/o Mex American | Puerto Rican |
|---|---|---|---|---|---|---|---|
| | White | Fac Col | | | | | |
| Professor | | | | | | | |
| 1972 | 95.7 | 3.4 | 1.8 | 1.0 | .4 | .2 | 0.0 |
| 1989 | 92.2 | 6.5 | 2.1 | 3.0 | .8 | .5 | .1 |
| % change | -3.5 | 3.1 | .3 | 2.0 | .4 | .3 | .1 |
| Assoc. Professor | | | | | | | |
| 1972 | 93.8 | 4.9 | 2.2 | 1.7 | .6 | .2 | .2 |
| 1989 | 89.5 | 8.3 | 3.4 | 3.3 | .7 | .6 | .3 |
| % change | -4.3 | 3.4 | 1.2 | 1.6 | .1 | .4 | .1 |
| Asst. Professor | | | | | | | |
| 1972 | 91.8 | 6.2 | 3.3 | 1.3 | .8 | .2 | .3 |
| 1989 | 85.2 | 11.3 | 5.6 | 3.6 | .7 | .8 | .6 |
| % change | -6.6 | 5.1 | 2.3 | 2.3 | -.1 | .6 | .3 |
| Lecturer | | | | | | | |
| 1972 | 85.5 | 11.4 | 6.1 | 3.4 | 1.4 | .1 | .5 |
| 1989 | 86.4 | 9.6 | 5.4 | 1.8 | .9 | .7 | .8 |
| % change | .9 | -1.8 | -.7 | -1.6 | -.5 | .6 | .3 |
| Instructor | | | | | | | |
| 1972 | 91.2 | 7.3 | 4.3 | 1.5 | 1.0 | .4 | .1 |
| 1989 | 86.1 | 11.5 | 6.0 | 2.4 | .6 | 1.6 | .9 |
| % change | -5.1 | 4.2 | 1.7 | .9 | -.4 | 1.2 | .8 |

*Sources:* Milem and Astin 1993; Higher Education Research Institute 1989.

ranks (Milem and Astin 1993), suggesting that even the minuscule growth of faculty of color that did occur was largely limited to the lower ranks of the professorate. Again, women, regardless of race, are appointed lecturers and instructors in larger proportions than men. Among faculty of color, this pattern is repeated, with women of color representing a larger proportion than men in these ranks. For example, 37 percent of all Latina faculty, and 41 percent of all American Indian women faculty are lecturers or instructors (H. Astin, Antonio, Cress, and Astin 1997).

A frequently cited reason for the few faculty of color at higher ranks of the academic profession is their alleged lack of academic certification, as measured by advanced degrees. The assumption is that their promotion and tenure rates are significantly impeded by their lack of graduate degrees in high-demand fields. However, data on the highest degrees completed by faculty in 1989 and 1995 document little difference between the types of degrees that White faculty and faculty of color earn (H. Astin, Antonio, Cress, and Astin 1997). Given this relatively equal distribution of highest degrees earned, why then are tenure rates so disproportionate between White faculty and faculty of color? Table 11.3 reviews the disproportionate tenure rates between full-time tenure-track faculty, both White and of color, during three periods. It excludes faculty who are in nontenure-earning positions (Carter and Wilson 1992). The table clearly indicates that White faculty have consistently received tenure at a higher rate than all faculty of color, regardless of academic discipline.

One explanation for these unequal tenure rates is the double standard for faculty of color, who often report being held to different expectations than their White colleagues (Brown 1998; Nakanishi 1993). One faculty member of color, Herman Garcia, was denied early tenure based on this double standard. His counterstory gives meaning and reason to these data and is essential in providing a critical race theory analysis, as it allows us to recognize the importance of experiential knowledge and helps us examine the alleged neutral, objective, and meritocratic tenure process.

### Table 11.3
### Full-Time Faculty Tenure Rates for Selected Years in All Fields
(in percentages)

|      | Whites | Total Faculty of Color |
|------|--------|------------------------|
| 1983 | 71.3   | 62.8                   |
| 1985 | 72.1   | 62.5                   |
| 1989 | 71.9   | 60.7                   |

*Source:* Carter and Wilson 1992.

The academy has treated Chicano faculty poorly and unfairly. In my case, for example, I have always had to fill the "minority slot" in an array of college committees while my Euro-American colleagues have been left to their scholarship. My committee service met affirmative action guidelines but kept me from my own scholarly pursuits. In the final analysis, I was not given the credit warranted for my service to the university, but in fact I was penalized during my tenure and promotion efforts. . . . I went up for promotion and tenure a year early with the unanimous support of my department head, dean, associate deans, and the college faculty. But at the level of the graduate college, my promotion and tenure were delayed one year. . . . Yet there had been White faculty members who went up early, and who had fewer publications and [less] service than I, who were tenured and promoted. (Garcia 1995, 156, 159)

Although tenure and promotion are usually determined through a formula based on faculty members' productivity in research, teaching, and service, this counterstory illustrates how subjective the formula can be for faculty of color. The double standard that often exists for them during the tenure and promotion process also helps explain their lack of progress across academic ranks.

These effects are intensified for women of color. While both male and female faculty of color are underrepresented across all institutions, departments, and academic ranks and have been since the early 1970s, women of color are more underrepresented than men in the most prestigious institutions, academic departments, and in the higher academic ranks. (See also Allen et al., this volume.) The subjectivity of the tenure process certainly contributes to some of these patterns of exclusion and merits additional analysis. The following section further examines the subjectivity of the tenure process based on faculty productivity and work roles.

## Faculty Productivity and Work Roles

Much of the literature on faculty careers and productivity agrees that certain roles and activities are more beneficial in the tenure and promotion process (Boyer 1990; Finkelstein 1984; Glassick, Huber, and Maeroff 1997), especially research and publishing (Bowen and Schuster 1986; Menges and Exum 1983). Even though a majority of all faculty are more interested in and spend more time engaged in teaching than in research, the academic reward structure (Boyer 1990) more readily acknowledges and compensates their research and publication productivity (Higher Education Research Institute 1989).

White faculty and faculty of color share the same degree of interest in research, yet they appear to be rewarded differentially for their interests. Results from the 1989 HERI Faculty Survey suggest that, as a group, faculty of color may be just as productive in research and publications as their White colleagues (Higher Education Research Institute 1989). Even after controlling for institution type, slightly more faculty of color (66 percent) than White faculty (64 percent) reported spending at least sixteen hours per week on research and scholarly writing. Likewise, as a group, nearly 8 percent of all faculty of color reported publishing between twenty-one and fifty articles in academic or professional journals, a figure which compares very favorably to approximately 9 percent of all White faculty (Higher Education Research Institute 1989). Thus, across all institutions, faculty of color as a group appear to be as productive in research as White faculty, yet they do not seem to be rewarded equally with their White colleagues.

Critical race scholars offer a specific example of how faculty of color are unequally recognized and rewarded through the "politics of citation" (R. Delgado 1984; Espinoza 1990; Matsuda 1988). In some institutions and academic fields, citation counts are often a standard measure of academic prestige and contribution. Retention, tenure, and promotion committees often ask whether a candidate's work is cited in a given field of study. Matsuda (1988) points to the politics of citation as one means by which the apartheid of knowledge keeps the scholarship of faculty of color invisible and unrewarded:

> Scholars proceed in research and information-gathering by following a trail of footnotes. In addition to following footnotes, people cite what they have read and discussed with their academic friends. When their reading and their circle of friends are limited, their citations become limited. The citations then breed further self-reference. This process ignores a basic fact of human psychology: human beings learn and grow through interaction with difference, not by reproducing what they already know. A system of . . . education that ignores outsiders' perspectives artificially restricts and stultifies the scholarly imagination. (3)

At best, the politics of citation restrict innovative scholarship for faculty of color at institutions that rely on this measure of productivity. At worst, this process ignores the epistemologies of those faculty of color and rejects their scholarship on the basis that it is biased, illegitimate, and/or inferior.

In the area of teaching, White faculty and faculty of color again share the same degree of interests, yet faculty of color spend more time engaged in teaching (H. Astin, Antonio, Cress, and Astin 1997; A. Astin, Korn, and Dey 1990; Boyer 1990). More faculty of color than White faculty report spending over seventeen hours per week preparing to teach and actually teaching; and nearly 10 percent more faculty of color than White faculty report spending at least five hours per week advising/counseling students (Higher Education Research Institute 1989). As a group, more faculty of color than White faculty believe it is very important or essential to: (1) prepare undergraduates for employment, (2) develop their moral character, (3) prepare them for family living, and (4) help them develop personal values—all functions that the general public defines as important roles for higher education (Higher Education Research Institute 1989). Despite the public interest in promoting greater faculty involvement in teaching and despite the closer alignment of faculty of color's teaching activities with the public's expectation that faculty should spend more time working to enhance the undergraduate educational experience (Bok 1986; Boyer 1987), faculty of color achieve tenure less frequently than White faculty.

To illustrate the teaching and advising roles of faculty of color, we share the personal narrative of Yolanda Flores Niemann (1999), a woman of color who struggled for tenure in a large, predominantly White, urban university. Her counterstory is consistent with the experiences of most faculty of color and supports the documented disparities between the teaching load of faculty of color and White faculty, as well as the disparities between male and female faculty (Johnsrud 1993). As she points out, these disparities are often exacerbated for women of color and can reveal a department's unstated but obvious perceptions of faculty of color:

My teaching and advising load was unprecedented for recently hired junior members of the department. In the four years I was a member of that department, I taught four different graduate seminars and three different undergraduate courses. From my discussions with colleagues, I learned that most new professors in the department taught only one or two graduate seminars in their area of specialty, which they continued teaching for the first few years before they added others. . . . I was also the principal advisor for eight graduate students as well as chair of their thesis and/or dissertation committees. . . . Two of the other program faculty, both full professors, had only two graduate students each, and one of those students later transferred to me. . . . This workload may be contrasted with that of the faculty member I replaced. She was White, a graduate of an elite university . . . , and the department had high expectations of her. Although she taught two critical graduate courses, she had been sheltered from extensive advising responsibilities. After three years in the department, she was formally advising only one student, an advising load consistent with department standards for junior professors. The difference in the department's perception of us was evident by the disparities in our workloads.

I was assigned complex and time-consuming administrative tasks necessary for the program. What this workload meant was that there was little time for research. . . . The assigned teaching and administrative load was made significantly heavier by unassigned responsibilities and obligations. As a woman of color, I felt duty-bound to respond to students who felt marginalized in the institution, especially ethnic/racial minorities. These students often sought me out to advise their student organizations and to listen to their experiences of racism, sexism, or homophobia in the university. . . . Of course, at one level, I did have the choice of turning these students away. Emotionally, however, I felt pulled to respond to them. . . . Furthermore, I would not have been able to face myself if I had turned away these students, especially knowing about the difficulties for students of color in predominantly White institutions. (121–22)

This counterstory helps to demonstrate how faculty of color participate in many of the activities that the public considers important faculty tasks. It also reveals how faculty of color feel an emotional and moral sense of responsibility to students who are also marginalized and treated like second-class citizens within academia. (See also Allen et al., this volume.) Our analysis suggests that faculty of color across all institution types are actively engaged in research, teaching, and service— all of the traditional roles of the professorate. Yet as valuable as these activities are, faculty of color, unlike their White colleagues, are apparently not rewarded for these roles.

**Discussion**

In this section, we synthesize our major findings on the racialized barriers to success for faculty of color and suggest how they may improve their status in the hiring, promotion, and tenure processes, the three major components of the faculty reward structure.

Through our critical race analysis, we have contested the conventional justifications offered to explain the lack of progress for faculty of color and have reexamined the data to reveal how higher education has inhibited their success in the academy. The data suggest that, while many complex factors have influenced the lack of progress for faculty of color, most of the responsibility lies on the racialized structures, policies, and practices that guide hiring, retention, and promotion. The suggestions we make in this section are grounded in a critical race theory framework that calls for higher education to correct the policies and practices that exclude or devalue faculty of color.

*Hiring Faculty of Color*

As Stein (1996) contends, one of the most damaging perceptions held by higher education and White faculty is that faculty of color are hired only because they are members of a "minority group" and not because they possess the qualifications for the job. Stein describes how, for example, American Indian faculty "often feel that they must work twice as hard as their non-Indian counterparts to prove themselves" (Stein 1996, 392). Padilla and Chavez (1995) also offer personal accounts by Latina/o faculty, underscoring the extent to which this misperception affects their success as faculty members. To begin eliminating racialized barriers for faculty of color, higher education needs to alter these damaging perceptions and develop an understanding of the potential benefits of hiring faculty of color. Not only are faculty of color equally qualified, but they actually bring epistemologies and cultural resources that contribute to the goals of higher education. As we have shown, faculty of color perform roles that the public endorses as important functions of higher education. It is in the best interest of higher education to acknowledge the potential contributions of faculty of color and undertake concrete strategies to increase their entry into the academy.

Hiring committees can help alter these misperceptions about faculty of color by developing recruitment protocols and job descriptions that consider as assets the cultural resources and experiential knowledge that faculty of color can contribute to the learning environment. Similarly, institutions should consider actively recruiting faculty of color by offering specific types and levels of support to help ensure their success in the department. Some universities have developed innovative approaches to their recruitment and hiring processes that appear to be yielding some early successes. For example, one large, primarily White, Research I university in the West, recently took very proactive steps to recruit and hire new faculty of color by offering them such innovative forms of support during their early years as academic employment for their spouses, reduced teaching responsibilities, research funding, technological support, and limited time off to engage in research and writing.[1] These recruitment strategies convey the institution's commitment to hiring faculty of color and enhancing their chances of success, thereby increasing the likelihood that other faculty of color will also be attracted to the campus (Olivas 1988). These recruitment strategies also counter an ideology of objectivity in the hiring process by acknowledging that faculty of color face racialized barriers. While these strategies alone certainly do not ensure any new faculty's success, they enhance their possibility of succeeding in the academy when combined with a sincere effort to correct racist policies and practices within the retention, promotion, and tenure process.

## Promotion and Tenure for Faculty of Color

Higher education has embraced the meritocratic illusion that it has been, is, and should remain objective and color-blind (Berube and Nelson 1995; Bowen and Bok 1998; Jencks and Phillips 1998; Orfield and Miller 1998). It believes that it provides equal opportunities to all, yet our analysis reveals a

---

1. It is important to note that these strategies often require support from centralized "faculty diversity" offices or initiatives. In this case, within approximately three years, about seven new faculty of color were hired in tenure-track positions in the university's graduate school of education with strong support from the office of the associate vice president for diversity and faculty development, the ethnic studies program, key faculty, administrators, and students within the school.

continuing, deep racial and gender stratification in academe. Higher education's assertions of neutrality maintain existing race, class, and gender privileges within its academic reward structure.

Our data are particularly distressing in showing that faculty of color representation has changed so little during the last three decades. Faculty of color, especially women, continue to be severely underrepresented. Faculty of color comprise less than 9 percent of the total academic profession, while women of color represent only 39 percent of this 9 percent. All faculty of color continue to be concentrated in less prestigious types of institutions, like public two-year colleges, and in academic departments that are often held in low regard.[2] All faculty of color continue to occupy the lowest academic ranks and are tenured at lower rates than White faculty, regardless of academic discipline.

Why do these disparities continue and how do we eliminate them? Critical race theory proposes some insights and suggestions through a contextual analysis of educational policies and practices. Our contextual analysis of the promotion and tenure process for faculty of color found that the process does not acknowledge how institutional racism influences formal and informal operating procedures in higher education. The process operates under meritocratic claims of objectivity, yet applies a double standard to faculty of color by devaluing their experiential knowledge and scholarship. An important step in valuing experiential knowledge is to recognize the cultural resources that both male and female faculty of color bring to the university and how these different resources contribute to the goals of higher education and to the overall knowledge base in academia. By embracing the perspectives of faculty of color, higher education will stimulate and encourage further scholarly creativity. It is also important to recognize that publications in gender- or race-related journals, or research on systems of oppression, constitute important contributions to academia. Promotion and tenure reviews should place a higher value on this type of scholarship so that the extensive talent of scholars of color can be fully recognized by higher education.

Moreover, one of the most important reasons for supporting the success of faculty of color is the content of their teaching and research (Villalpando forthcoming B), which often focus on correcting different forms of social inequality. This point alone deserves special consideration in the academy,

2. While we make this point throughout the chapter, we realize that it is the hierarchical structure inherent in higher education that ranks institutions, disciplines, and departments, placing more prestige on that which is valued more in society. We personally place a high value on teaching institutions and on disciplines and fields that are often held in low regard (ethnic studies, women's studies, education, the arts, etc.), yet we realize that many faculty of color have been systematically excluded from certain institutions and disciplines, giving them little choice in where they can go.

yet the research of faculty of color is often dismissed as biased or too subjective. (See also Scheurich and Young, this volume.) Similarly, their teaching often focuses on issues of race, class, gender, and "diversity/multiculturalism." Again, these issues focus on improving social relationships that promote greater equality. Critical race theory suggests that this type of scholarship ought to be more highly valued, as it works toward eliminating all forms of subordination and creating a more just society.

## Conclusion

Our analysis reveals that across all institutions, faculty of color as a group, compared to White faculty, appear to be about as productive in research and publications, to teach more courses, and to engage in roles more closely aligned with the public's expectations for faculty. Yet faculty of color and women of color achieve success in the academy at lower rates than their White colleagues and are disproportionately overrepresented in less prestigious academic departments, ranks, and institutions.

We examine these issues using critical race theory for two reasons. First, we encourage the academic profession to reverse the dismal representation of people of color, especially women of color, in the professoriat by reexamining the effects of a racialized academic reward structure. Second, and equally important, through our quantitative and qualitative data, we validate the experiences of faculty of color. We are the people who represent the numbers and the voices heard through the counterstories in this chapter. We want to remind other faculty of color that they are not alone in experiencing alienation, marginalization, and racism in the academy. As Solorzano (1998) notes:

> In that space or moment when one connects with these experiences, these stories can be the catalyst for one's own coming to voice, of not feeling alone, and knowing that someone has gone before them, had similar experiences, and succeeded. . . . In an area for further research, we must examine the ways in which scholars of color navigate around and through these macro- and micro-barriers. (131)

Indeed, part of our intent in this chapter is also to call for additional research, especially by scholars of color, on ways of eliminating racialized barriers to their success. We encourage research with methods and theoretical frameworks that contribute new perspectives to old and persisting problems. By applying critical race theory in our reexamination of data on faculty of color, we challenge the conventional deficit-based explanations of their lack of progress and reveal how higher education has inhibited their success in the academy.

# References

Altbach, Philip, and Kofi Lomotey, eds. 1991. *The racial crisis in American higher education.* Albany: State University of New York Press.

Astin, Alexander W. 1982. *Minorities in American higher education: Recent trends, current prospects, and recommendations.* San Francisco: Jossey-Bass.

———. 1993. *What matters in college? Four critical years revisited.* San Francisco: Jossey-Bass.

Astin, Alexander W., William Korn, and Eric Dey. 1990. *The American college teacher: National norms for the 1989–90 HERI faculty survey.* Los Angeles: Higher Education Research Institute, UCLA.

Astin, Helen S., Anthony Antonio, Christine Cress, and Alexander W. Astin. 1997. *Race and ethnicity in the American professoriate, 1995–96.* Los Angeles: Higher Education Research Institute, UCLA.

Astin, Helen S., and Octavio Villalpando. 1996. A demographic profile of today's faculty. In *Integrating research on faculty: Seeking new ways to communicate about the academic life of faculty.* Results from the 1994 Forum Sponsored by the National Center for Education Statistics (NCES), the Association for Institutional Research (AIR), and the American Association of State Colleges and Universities (AASCU), 96–849. Washington, DC: U.S. Department of Education, Office of Educational Research and Improvement.

Bell, Derrick. 1995. Who's afraid of critical race theory? *University of Illinois Law Review,* 1995, no. 41:893–910.

Bennett, William. 1984. *To reclaim a legacy.* Washington, DC: National Endowment for the Humanities.

Berube, Michael, and C. Nelson. 1995. *Higher education under fire: Politics, economics, and the crisis of the humanities.* New York: Routledge.

Bloom, Allan. 1987. *The closing of the American mind: How higher education has failed democracy and impoverished the souls of today's students.* New York: Simon and Schuster.

Bok, Derek. 1986. *Higher learning.* Cambridge: Harvard University Press.

Bowen, Howard R., and Jack H. Schuster. 1986. *American professors: A national resource imperiled.* Oxford, UK: Oxford University Press.

Bowen, William G., and Derek Bok. 1998. *The shape of the river: Long-term consequences of considering race in college and university admissions.* Princeton, NJ: Princeton University Press.

Boyer, Ernest. 1987. *College: The undergraduate experience in America.* Carnegie Foundation for the Advancement of Teaching. New York: Harper & Row.

————. 1990. *Scholarship reconsidered: Priorities of the professorate.* Princeton, NJ: Carnegie Foundation for the Advancement of Teaching.

Brown, Shirley V. 1998. *Increasing minority faculty: An elusive goal.* Princeton, NJ: Educational Testing Service.

Calmore, John. 1992. Critical race theory, Archie Shepp, and fire music: Securing an authentic intellectual life in a multicultural world. *Southern California Law Review* 65:2129–31.

Carnevale, Anthony P. 1999. *Education = success: Empowering Hispanic youth and adults.* A product of the ETS/Hispanic Association of Colleges and Universities Collaboration. Princeton, NJ: Educational Testing Service.

Carter, Deborah, and Reginald Wilson. 1992. *Tenth annual status report on minorities in higher education.* Washington, DC: American Council on Education.

Cho, Sumi K. 1996, March. Confronting myths: Asian Pacific American faculty in higher education. In *Ninth Annual APAHE [Asian Pacific American Higher Education] Conference Proceedings,* 31–56. San Francisco.

Collins, Patricia Hill. 1991. *Black feminist thought: Knowledge, consciousness, and the politics of empowerment.* New York: Routledge.

Crenshaw, Kimberle, Neil Gotanda, Gary Peller, and Kendall Thomas, eds. 1995. *Critical race theory: The key writings that formed the movement.* New York: New Press.

D'Souza, Dinesh. 1991. *Illiberal education: The politics of race and sex on campus.* New York: Free Press.

Delgado Bernal, Dolores. 1998. Using a Chicana feminist epistemology in educational research. *Harvard Educational Review* 68, no. 4:555–52.

————. 1999. Chicana/o education from the civil rights era to the present. In *The elusive quest for equality: 150 years of Chicano/Chicana education,* edited by J. F. Moreno, 77–108. Cambridge: Harvard Educational Publishing Group.

————. 2002. Toward a critical race-gender epistemology: Recognizing students of color as holders of knowledge. *Qualitative Inquiry* 8, no. 1.

Delgado, Richard. 1984. The imperial scholar: Reflections on a review of civil rights literature. *University of Pennsylvania Law Review* 132:561–78.

————. 1989. Storytelling for oppositionists and others: A plea for narrative. *Michigan Law Review* 87:2411–41.

————. 1990. When a story is just a story: Does voice really matter? *Virginia Law Review* 76, no. 1:95–111.

————, ed. 1995. *Critical race theory: The cutting edge.* Philadelphia: Temple University Press.

266   VILLALPANDO AND DELGADO BERNAL

Delgado, Richard, and Jean Stefancic. 1994. Critical race theory: An annotated bibliography [in] 1993, a year of transition. *University of Colorado Law Review* 66:159–93.

Dillard, Cynthia. 1997. The substance of things hoped for, the evidence of things not seen: Toward an endarkened feminist ideology in research. Paper presented at the American Educational Research Association Annual Meeting, April, Chicago.

Escueta, E., and E. O'Brien. 1991. *Asian Americans in higher education: Trends and issues.* American Council on Education Research Briefs, 2, no. 4. Washington DC: American Council on Education Research, Division of Policy Analysis and Research.

Espinoza, Leslie. 1990. Masks and other disguises: Exposing legal academia. *Harvard Law Review* 103:1878–86.

Finkelstein, Martin. 1984. *The American academic profession: A synthesis of social scientific inquiry since World War II.* Columbus: Ohio State University Press.

Flores-Ortiz, Yvette. 1998. Voices from the couch: The co-creation of a Chicana psychology. In *Living Chicana Theory,* edited by Carla Trujillo, 102–22. Berkeley, CA: Third Woman Press.

Gainen, Joanne, and Robert Boice, eds. 1993. *Building a diverse faculty.* New Directions for Teaching and Learning, No. 53. San Francisco: Jossey-Bass.

Garcia, Herman. 1995. Toward a postview of the Chicano community in higher education. In *The leaning ivory tower: Latino professors in American universities,* edited by Raymond Padilla and Rudolfo Chavez Chavez, 156–59. Albany: State University of New York Press.

Garza, Hisauro. 1993. Second-class academics: Chicano/Latino faculty in U.S. universities. In Gainen and Boice, 33–41.

Glassick, C., M. Huber, and G. Maeroff. 1997. *Scholarship assessed: Evaluation of the professorate.* An Ernest L. Boyer Project of the Carnegie Foundation for the Advancement of Teaching. San Francisco: Jossey-Bass.

González, G. G. 1990. *Chicano education in the era of segregation.* Cranbury, NJ: Associated University Presses.

Higher Education Research Institute. 1989. *1989 weighted faculty norms, special tabulations.* Los Angeles: University of California, Los Angeles.

hooks, bell. 1996. Black women intellectuals. In Turner, Garcia, Nora, and Rendon, 360–69.

Jencks, Christopher, and M. Phillips. 1998. *The Black-White test score gap.* Washington, DC: Brookings Institution Press.

Johnsrud, Linda. 1993. *Women and minority faculty experiences: Defining and responding to diverse realities.* New Directions for Teaching and Learning, No. 53:3–16. San Francisco: Jossey-Bass.

Karabel, Jerome. 1977. Community colleges and social stratification: Submerged class conflict in American higher education. In *Power and ideology in education,* edited by Jerome Karabel and A. H. Halsey, 232–54. New York: Oxford University Press.

Kozol, J. 1991. *Savage inequalities: Children in America's schools.* New York: Harpers Collins.

Ladson-Billings, Gloria. 1995. Toward a theory of culturally relevant pedagogy. *American Educational Research Journal* 32, no. 3:465–91.

Ladson-Billings, Gloria, and William Tate. 1995. Toward a critical race theory of education. *Teachers College Record* 97:47–68.

Lynn, Marvin. 1999. Toward a critical race pedagogy: A research note. *Urban Education* 33, no. 5:606–26.

Matsuda, Mari. 1988. Affirmative action and legal knowledge: Planting seeds in plowed-up ground. *Harvard Women's Law Journal* 11:1–17.

Matsuda, Mari, Charles Lawrence, Richard Delgado, and Kimberle Crenshaw, eds. 1993. *Words that wound: Critical race theory, assaultive speech, and the First Amendment.* Boulder, CO: Westview Press.

Menges, R. J., and W. H. Exum. 1983. Barriers to the progress of women and minority faculty. *Journal of Higher Education* 54, no. 2:123–43.

Milem, Jeff, and Helen Astin. 1993. The changing composition of the faculty. *Change* 25, no. 2:21–28.

Nakanishi, Don. 1993. Asian Pacific Americans in higher education: Faculty and administrative representation and tenure. In Gainen and Boice, 51–59.

Niemann, Yolanda Flores. 1999. The making of a token: A case study of stereotype threat, stigma, racism, and tokenism in academe. *Frontiers: A Journal of Women Studies* 20, no. 1:111–34.

Oakes, Jeanne. 1985. *Keeping track: How schools structure inequality.* New Haven, CT: Yale University Press.

Olivas, Michael. 1988. Latino faculty at the border: Increasing numbers key to more Hispanic access. *Change,* 20, no. 3:6–9.

Orfield Gary, and E. Miller. 1998. *Chilling admissions: The affirmative action crisis and the search for alternatives.* Cambridge: The Civil Rights Project, Harvard University/Harvard Education Publishing Group.

Padilla, Raymond, and Rudolfo Chavez Chavez, eds. 1995. *The leaning ivory tower: Latino professors in American universities.* Albany: State University of New York Press.

Parker, Larry. 1998. "Race is . . . Race ain't": An exploration of the utility of critical race theory in qualitative research in education. *International Journal of Qualitative Studies in Education* 11, no. 1:43–55.

Perez, Emma. 1999. *The decolonial imaginary: Writing Chicanas into history.* Bloomington: Indiana University Press.

Reyes, María de la Luz, and John Halcón. 1996. Racism in academia: The old wolf revisited. In Turner, Garcia, Nora, and Rendon, 337–48.

Sax, Linda, Alexander Astin, William Korn, and Shannon Gilmartin. 1999. *The American college teacher: National norms for the 1998–99 HERI faculty survey.* Los Angeles: Higher Education Research Institute, UCLA.

Schlesinger, Arthur M., Jr. 1993. *The disuniting of America: Reflections on a multicultural society.* New York: W. W. Norton.

Solorzano, Daniel G. 1998. Critical race theory, racial and gender microaggressions, and the experiences of Chicana and Chicano scholars. *International Journal of Qualitative Studies in Education* 11:121–36.

Solorzano, Daniel G., and Octavio Villalpando. 1998. Critical race theory: Marginality and the experiences of students of color in higher education. In *Sociology of education: Emerging perspectives,* edited by Carlos Torres and Theodore Mitchell, 211–24. Albany: State University of New York Press.

Stein, Wayne J. 1996. The survival of American Indian faculty. In Turner, Garcia, Nora, and Rendon, 390–97.

Suzuki, Bob. 1989. Asians. In *Shaping higher education's future: Demographic realities and opportunities, 1990–2000,* edited by Arthur Levine and Associates, 87–115. San Francisco: Jossey-Bass.

Tate, William. 1997. Critical race theory and education: History, theory, and implications. *Review of Research in Education* 22:195–247.

Turner, Caroline Sotello Viernes, Mildred Garcia, Amaury Nora, and Laura Rendon, eds. 1996. *Racial and ethnic diversity in higher education.* Needham Heights, MA: Simon and Schuster Custom Publishing.

Turner, Caroline Sotello Viernes, and Samuel L. Myers Jr. 2000. *Faculty of color in academe: Bittersweet success.* Boston: Allyn and Bacon.

Turner, Caroline Sotello Viernes, Samuel L. Myers Jr., and John W. Creswell. 1999. Exploring underrepresentation: The case of faculty of color in the Midwest. *Journal of Higher Education* 70, no. 1:27–59.

Valencia, R. R. 1991. The plight of Chicano students: An overview of schooling conditions and outcomes. In *Chicano school failure and success: Research and policy agendas for the 1990s,* edited by R. R. Valencia, 3–26. London: Falmer Press.

Villalpando, Octavio. 1996. The long-term effects of college on Chicana and Chicano students: Other-oriented values, service careers, and community involvement. Ph.D. diss., University of California, Los Angeles.

Villalpando, Octavio. Forthcoming a. Self-segregation or self-preservation? A critical race theory and Latina/o critical theory analysis of findings from a longitudinal study of Chicana/o college students. *International Journal of Qualitative Studies in Education.*

Villalpando, Octavio. Forthcoming b. The impact of diversity and multiculturalism on *all* students: Findings from a national study. *National Association of Student Personnel Administrators Journal.*

Winfield, Linda F. 1997. Multiple dimensions of reality: Recollections of an African American woman scholar. In *Learning from our lives: Women, research, and autobiography in education,* edited by Anna Neumann and Penelope L. Peterson, 194–208. New York: Teachers College Press.

# CHAPTER 12

# Affirmative Action in a Post-*Hopwood* Era

## WILLIAM G. TIERNEY AND JACK K. CHUNG

In April 1998, the University of California (UC) campuses released their admissions data for the 1998 first-year class. The first-year class accepted immediately *after* Proposition 209 took effect in California looked very different from previous classes at the UC campuses. Admissions of underrepresented students of color—those from African American, Chicana/o/Latina/o, and American Indian backgrounds, dropped more than 8.6 percent for fall 1998. The drop was even more alarming given that overall acceptances to the UC system *increased* 3.5 percent (UCOP 1999). Scholars studying the effects of Proposition 209, which eliminated affirmative action programs in the California public higher education system, had predicted such a drop in enrollments of students of color (Schrag 1997; Kane and Dickens 1997).

The argument for race-targeted admissions stems from the original intent of Lyndon Johnson's 1965 executive order to use affirmative action to reach out to applicants without regard to race or ethnicity. Wherever appropriate, affirmative action seeks "to [extend] a hand to eminently qualified people previously held back by bias" (Cose 1997). Yet critics of affirmative action, such as Stephan Thernstrom (1998) and Dinesh D'Souza (1995), and policy groups such as the Center for Individual Rights (1999a), have spoken against the use of race as a criterion for college admissions and of the ameliorating consequences of eliminating affirmative action in higher education. The critics contend that, if affirmative action calls for the use of different admissions standards for Whites and students of color and favors students of color with lower test scores and GPAs, then it is inherently flawed.

Citizens in California and Washington state, and the Fifth Circuit Court in Texas, apparently agree. With the passage of Proposition 209 in November

The authors wish to thank Michael Olivas, Ben Baez, and Jon Alger for their thoughtful comments on an earlier version of this paper.

1996, of Initiative 200 in November 1998, and the March 1996 *Hopwood v. State of Texas* court decision, considerations of race are now illegal in public institutions of higher education in California,[1] Washington, and Texas. Impending lawsuits against affirmative action programs at the University of Michigan, the University of Maryland Medical School, and the University of Washington Law School, combined with political scrutiny, further endanger affirmative action programs on college campuses.

In September 1998, William G. Bowen and Derek C. Bok published a comprehensive statistical analysis of the effects of affirmative action policies entitled *The Shape of the River: Long-Term Consequences of Considering Race in College and University Admissions.* Their book provides a quantitative look at the encouraging results of affirmative action between 1976 and 1989. A second text, *Chilling Admissions: The Affirmative Action Crisis and the Search for Alternatives* (Orfield and Miller 1998) reaches a conclusion similar to that of Bowen and Bok. A handful of critics have suggested that such research is flawed by the same race-based assumptions as previous arguments for affirmative action (A. Thernstrom 1998; Greve 1999). However, most reviewers have concluded that these texts have succeeded in refocusing public interest on affirmative action and have demonstrated the importance of diversity in higher education through careful statistical analyses (Tierney and Chung, in press).

In this chapter, we review recent developments pertaining to college admissions and affirmative action, specifically (1) legislative developments, (2) legal cases and civil rights initiatives, and (3) institutional responses to the end of racial considerations in admissions policies. In doing so, we will consider only institutions of postsecondary education. We focus in particular on college admissions for students of color, rather than on issues such as faculty hiring. Our goal is to point out the lessons that have been learned and to consider the implications of what happens when affirmative action is eliminated.

One caveat is in order. Policies pertaining to affirmative action are protean. When we began writing this chapter and when we completed it, particular policies had changed or new ones had been implemented. We fully expect that by the time this chapter is published, additional issues will have been decided and new ones proposed. Our purpose here, however, is to offer an overview of a dynamic policy that is being reformulated, rather than attempt a historical exegesis of a policy that is no longer debated.

---

1. On May 16, 2001, the University of California Board of Regents unanimously agreed to approve a resolution which rescinded SP-1 and SP-2 which prohibited the use of preferences in admissions, hiring, and contracting practices.

## Legislation

On November 3, 1998, Washington State voters passed Initiative 200, a measure that bars the use of race as a criterion to admit students, hire employees, or award contracts to public universities in the state. Patterned after California's Proposition 209 (November 1996), this legislation sought to end affirmative action programs at the state university system in Washington. To say the least, this legislation generated a lot of controversy. Seeking to continue his anti-affirmative action efforts, Ward Connerly, a leader on the UC Board of Regents who initially dismantled affirmative action in California, was also at work on a similar initiative in Florida. Connerly had hoped to coalesce state opinions into a national policy against the use of race in higher education admissions, but he was met with initial resistance from state leaders.

In the meantime, Florida Governor Jeb Bush has announced that the state's four-year public colleges would voluntarily stop using race as a factor in undergraduate and graduate admissions, and would instead admit the top 20 percent of graduates of every high school in the state. His plan has met with much resistance.

## Litigation and Civil Rights

Alongside spreading legislation banning race as a criterion to consider in college admissions, lawsuits against individual colleges and universities supporting affirmative action programs have become increasingly common. Such legal challenges to affirmative action not only denounce race in colleges but also attack scholarship opportunities and outreach programs for students of color. (See also Teddlie and Freeman, this volume.) Here are four significant cases in higher education that are currently pending:

1. On March 5, 1997, the Center for Individual Rights (CIR) filed a class-action lawsuit against the University of Washington School of Law on behalf of Katuria Smith, now a law student at Seattle University. CIR is a legal organization most famous for its victory over the University of Texas School of Law in the *Hopwood* case. Smith, along with other UW School of Law applicants from 1994 who felt they were not given equal consideration because they were White, claimed reverse racial discrimination. As in the *Hopwood* case, CIR challenged the school's alleged practice of admitting students of color with lower combinations of test scores and GPAs, while rejecting White students with higher combinations of scores and GPAs.

2. On October 14, 1997, CIR sued the University of Michigan on behalf of two White students denied undergraduate admissions the previous year.

3. CIR followed with another suit against the University of Michigan Law School on December 3, 1997. Again, it charged that the university's

affirmative action policies discriminated against qualified White applicants in favor of unqualified students of color. The University of Washington and the University of Michigan have acknowledged that race is one of the many considerations used in admitting students, but they defend such policies on the grounds of underrepresentation of students of color, historical discrimination, and the importance of diversity (Center 1999b). Both of these cases are pending.

4. Rob Farmer filed a complaint in May 1998 against the University of Maryland School of Medicine for "maintaining drastically lower standards for the admission of members of certain favored minority groups" (Alger 1999, 6). Farmer, a student at a medical school in the Netherlands Antilles, alleged that his application for admission was rejected even though his "grades, test scores, and other criteria used by the University were far above the average of Black students who were accepted for the class entering in Fall 1996" (Alger 1999, 6). The case is under consideration in Maryland.

These four cases underscore the point that lawsuits claiming reverse discrimination and preferential affirmative action are no longer sporadic or isolated incidents in higher education. At least two reasons exist for the rise in such legal challenges. First, courts are becoming increasingly critical of programs in higher education that use race as a criterion for admissions without "just" cause. Second, conservative think tanks such as the Center for Individual Rights (CIR) have the funds necessary to challenge university policies. This conservative trend will continue unless the philosophical beliefs of the courts change, more pro-affirmative action judges are appointed, or policy groups that support affirmative action have funding equivalent to CIR's.

Race-targeted scholarships also have come under attack. A male student sued the Oklahoma State Regents for Higher Education in October 1998 over the legality of a scholarship program with different test-score requirements for members of different racial groups. Similar lawsuits by CIR against the National Science Foundation in June 1998 and against a federal summer science program at Texas A&M University in December 1997 were settled in favor of White plaintiffs (Alger 1999). In the case of the NSF, where a White graduate student protested the exclusion of White applicants to the Minority Graduate Research Fellowship Program, the court compelled NSF to marshal its programs into one single new program of graduate fellowships that awards funds to institutions rather than to individual students. In the case of Texas A&M, a federally sponsored summer science program designed to attract students of color into biomedical and health professions agreed to abandon its race and ethnicity criteria to accommodate a White female plaintiff.

As with the lawsuits against universities cited earlier, the same legal rationale has been used to dismantle race-targeted scholarships. Affirmative action is often defended in higher education as a means to redress past discriminatory practices and to uphold the benefits of diversity. In some court jurisdictions, the evidence to meet those standards has been raised. Institutions must show specific instances of past de jure or "legal" discrimination on their campuses to prove the need for affirmative action. Further, race as a criterion for admissions when it is based on the benefits of diversity must pass the strict scrutiny of the court and be "necessary to further a compelling [state] interest" (Olivas 1999, 227). Thus, many courts see race-targeted scholarships used simply to increase the numbers of students of color on campus as unjustified.

In contrast, in 1997 a White female faculty member sued the University of Nevada at Reno for discrimination when she was hired at a salary considerably lower than that paid a recently hired African American faculty member because of a "minority bonus program." The state supreme court upheld the university's "compelling interest in fostering a culturally and ethnically diverse faculty. . . . A failure to attract minority faculty perpetuates the university's White enclave and further limits student exposure to multicultural diversity" (*University and Community College System of Nevada v. Farmer*, 930 P. 2d 730 [Nev. S. Ct. 1997], cert. denied [1998]).

Although the rulings cited earlier attacked fundamental aspects of affirmative action, their conflicts with previous Supreme Court decisions remain unresolved. The U.S. Supreme Court's 1978 decision in *Regents of the University of California v. Bakke* continues to set the precedent for future verdicts on race-targeted policies and is still the law of the land (Aldave 1996). The attorney general of Texas has, in fact, petitioned *Hopwood* back into the Fifth Circuit Court of Appeals for further consideration of the federal *Bakke* precedent. Racial considerations in admissions policies are still valid, provided that such policies are subject to constitutional "strict scrutiny" (Olivas 1997). The focus of legal criticism now is on the justification for admissions plans that include affirmative action.

To highlight the legal limitations, CIR released two handbooks (1998, 1999a) on what it defines as "racial preferences" in higher education—one for college leaders and trustees, and one for students. The handbooks read like exploratory legal arguments against affirmative action programs. They point universities to recent legislation and lawsuits that ended affirmative action programs and describe possible actions on behalf of students against universities that continue to insist on continuing racial considerations. "Race, like religion," argues CIR, "must be placed beyond the reach of the state" (Center 1999a, 1).

Groups of color and pro-affirmative action groups have responded with counter arguments. Reverend Jesse Jackson led marches against the effects of Proposition 209 in California. Professors Ron Takaki and Bill Banks rallied Oakland teachers' unions and Berkeley students to call for the admission of hundreds of underrepresented students of color with 4.0+ GPAs who were denied entrance to UC Berkeley. The American Association of University

Professors (1997) released a strong statement in support of diversity goals in university admissions:

> The Eighty-third Annual Meeting of the American Association of University Professors expresses its continuing concern over the reduction or elimination of affirmative action programs that have important educational benefits for all students. Actions during the past year by courts, voters on ballot measures, and university trustees, among others, have served to weaken affirmative action programs, notwithstanding the contribution of these programs to remedying past discrimination, promoting diversity among student bodies, faculty, and administrations, and improving opportunities for women and people of color. Underrepresentation of these groups in the academy remains a serious problem. . . . We remind colleges and universities that federal law, through Executive Order 11246, requires entities receiving federal contracts to maintain affirmative action plans. The plans must include affirmative action goals. Colleges and universities are legally obligated to adhere to these requirements in order to remain eligible for receipt of federal funds. (1)

The American Civil Liberties Union continues to denounce lawsuits filed against affirmative action. The U.S. Department of Education, in response to a complaint under Title VI, has also warned the University of California that it plans to investigate whether the dismantling of affirmative action may have led to violations of federal civil rights laws (Affirmative 1998). In February 1999, eight students of color and three organizations of color filed a class-action lawsuit against the University of California at Berkeley. They charge that the university violates federal antibias laws by placing too much emphasis on standardized test scores and completion of advanced placement courses and, in consequence, causing disparate impact on certain groups of color.

## Institutional Responses

Although *Bakke* remains the law of the land, what happens if affirmative action is eliminated? Texas and California might be seen as rogue states insofar as their state policies contradict *Bakke*. However, what might we learn about affirmative action if we investigate the effects of anti-affirmative action legislation, rulings, and initiatives in Texas and California? Simply stated, without affirmative action programs, public institutions in California and Texas have seen their admissions of students of color plummet. In California, acceptances of students of color recovered somewhat in the second first-year class selected for UC campuses after Proposition 209. Overall numbers of admissions of students of color (excluding Asian Americans) in 1999 were comparable to 1997 figures, although admissions for African Americans were still down 7.9 percent from 1997. (See Table 12.1.)

**Table 12.1**

**Undergraduate Admissions, University of California, 1997–99**

| Group of Color | 1997 | 1998 | % Change '97–'98 | 1999 | % Change '98–'99 | Overall % Change '97–'99 |
|---|---|---|---|---|---|---|
| African American | 1,510 | 1,248 | −17.4% | 1,390 | +11.0% | − 7.9% |
| Chicano/Latino | 5,622 | 5,258 | − 6.9% | 5,753 | + 9.0% | + 2.3% |
| American Indian | 334 | 316 | − 5.4% | 296 | − 6.0% | −11.4% |
| Asian American | 13,649 | 13,697 | 0.0% | 15,414 | +13.0% | +12.9% |
| White | 17,654 | 16,016 | − 9.3% | 19,634 | +22.6% | +11.2% |
| Other | 1,025 | 640 | −37.6% | 854 | +33.4% | +16.7% |
| Declined to state | 2,141 | 6,216 | +214% | 3,579 | −42.0% | +67.2% |
| Total | 41,935 | 43,391 | + 3.5% | 46,921 | + 8.1% | +11.9% |

*Source:* University of California (1999)

**Table 12.2**
**Percentage of Students of Color in First-Year Admissions,**
**University of California, 1997–99**

| Group of Color | 1997 | 1998 | 1999 |
|---|---|---|---|
| African American | 3.6% | 2.9% | 3.0% |
| Chicano/Latino | 13.4% | 12.1% | 12.3% |
| American Indian | 0.8% | 0.7% | 0.6% |
| Asian American | 32.5% | 31.6% | 32.9% |
| White | 42.1% | 36.9% | 41.8% |
| Other | 2.4% | 1.5% | 1.8% |
| Declined to state | 5.1% | 14.3% | 7.6% |
| Total | 100% | 100% | 100% |

*Source:* University of California (1999)

However, this "recovery" in admissions of students of color is somewhat misleading, given that overall admissions to the UC system jumped 11.9 percent. Factoring in the overall increase in admissions and holding the percentage of admissions of students of color steady from 1997, the enrollment data reveal a 12.3 percent drop in the enrollment of students of color. Corrected analysis of the percentage of student of color admissions to the UC system over the last three years shows a continuing decline since 1997. (See Table 12.2.) The University of Texas has seen a similar decrease in its enrollments[2] of students of color in the aftermath of *Hopwood*. (See Table 12.3.) (See also Hurtado; Teddlie and Freeman; Altbach, Lomotey, and Rivers; Anderson, this volume.)

At the most selective campuses of the University of California—Berkeley and UCLA—and at the University of Texas, Austin, applicants of color have fared even worse. Two years after the passage of Proposition 209, admissions of African American students to UC Berkeley had decreased 51 percent and those of Latina/os by 41 percent (Weiss 1999). At the least selective UC campuses, acceptances of students of color actually *increased.* For example, admissions of African American first-year students at UC Riverside increased 9 percent from 1996 to 1998 while the admission of Latina/o students went up 27 percent (UCOP 1999). Such a bifurcation generates concern that the University of California may develop into a two-tiered system where students of color are segregated in the least prestigious campuses (University of California 1998).

---

2. The University of Texas system releases data on student enrollments on campuses, rather than admissions.

**Table 12.3**
**Enrollments of Students of Color, University of Texas, 1996–98**

| Group of Color | 1996 | 1997 | 1998 | Overall % change '96–'98 |
|---|---|---|---|---|
| African American | 6,555 | 6,127 | 6,211 | – 5.2% |
| Hispanic | 45,455 | 45,421 | 45,688 | + 0.5% |
| American Indian | 656 | 674 | 667 | + 1.7% |
| Asian American | 10,584 | 11,126 | 11,489 | + 8.6% |
| White | 76,001 | 74,166 | 72,462 | – 4.7% |
| Other | 8,060 | 8,331 | 8,984 | +11.5% |
| Declined to state | 0 | 0 | 103 | — |
| Total | 147,311 | 145,845 | 145,604 | – 1.2% |

*Source:* University of Texas System (1999)

The University of Texas, Austin, shows a similar drop in African American and Hispanic enrollment. (See Table 12.4.)

Institutions like UC Berkeley and UCLA are caught between changes in state laws and legal regulations on the one hand and their growing concern for the decreasing admissions of students of color on the other. Predictably, institutional leaders have responded with (1) revisions of their admissions policies and (2) different ways of reaching out to potential applicants of color without affirmative action. The University of Massachusetts at Amherst, for example, announced on March 1, 1999, that it would rely less on race and more on socioeconomic factors and extracurricular activities. The University of California at Irvine spent a good deal of effort reworking its admissions policies to

**Table 12.4**
**Enrollments of Students of Color, University of Texas, Austin, 1996–98**

| Group of Color | 1996 | 1997 | 1998 | Overall % change '96–'98 |
|---|---|---|---|---|
| African American | 1,911 | 1,720 | 1,616 | –15.4% |
| Hispanic | 6,207 | 6,148 | 5,964 | – 3.9% |
| American Indian | 209 | 230 | 239 | 14.3% |
| Asian American | 4,989 | 5,300 | 5,619 | 12.6% |
| White | 31,346 | 32,069 | 31,572 | 0.7% |
| Other | 3,346 | 3,390 | 3,793 | 13.4% |
| Declined to state | 0 | 0 | 103 | — |
| Total | 48,008 | 48,857 | 48,906 | 1.9% |

*Source:* University of Texas System (1999)

create a broader, more holistic way to think about the strength of applicants (Wilbur and Bonous-Hammarth 1998). Michael Olivas has also written extensively about what undergraduate and graduate admissions committees might do to ascertain the quality of an applicant so that an institution gains a more complete view of a candidate, rather than basing a decision simply on test scores that have low predictive validity (Olivas 1997 and in press).

Texas is in its second year of a program that accepts the top 10 percent of graduates from each high school into its public colleges. Similarly, when Gray Davis became governor of California in 1999, he worked with the Board of Regents at the University of California to pass a proposal to guarantee admission to one of the UC campuses to the top 4 percent of graduates from each high school in the state, based on UC-required courses. This approach thus acknowledges different educational opportunities that exist at well-financed high schools vs. those less endowed in the inner city or rural areas. Whether such an approach will be successful in increasing enrollments of color on UC campuses has yet to be determined.

Thomas Kane (1998) argues against policies based on socioeconomic status in college admissions. He points out that students of color may once again be disadvantaged in "class-based" admissions since White students make up the *majority* of graduating seniors from low-income backgrounds. Therefore, policies that give preference to those from low socioeconomic circumstances will not necessarily compensate for the drop in admissions of color following the end of race-targeted affirmative action programs.

The bifurcation of admissions to the most and least selective institutions in the UC system, given the recent trends, is another important concern. Admissions of color to the UC system may increase somewhat, but these students will end up at the least selective institutions.

Additional initiatives taken by colleges and universities also include increased outreach efforts to school systems graduating historically underrepresented students. In instances where there previously existed little, if any, relationship between the university system and these schools, there is now an increasingly closer working relationship between college administrators, K-12 counselors, and teachers. Efforts range from structured college preparation programs to SAT training to informational seminars about the possibilities of attending a specific institution. Working relationships are also being forged between specific universities and specific schools.

## Conclusion

Some believe that racial preferences in higher education admissions are illegal and inherently racist—that they violate the very nature of civil liberties (Greve 1996). They argue that if affirmative action programs preferentially favor some groups of color over other groups, then these programs ought to be found unconstitutional and eliminated. Those who believe that affirmative action is needed in higher education counter that underrepresented groups of color still do not compete on a level playing field (Cose 1997). A thirty-year demographic study of median incomes released in May 1997 (Hernandez 1997), for example, shows that incomes of people of color have dropped against those of Whites. To the degree that some societal standards favor Whites over groups of color, argue proponents of affirmative action, then affirmative action is still needed to level the playing field. Further, an increasing body of research points out how diverse campuses and classrooms benefit the learning environment for all students (Schrag 1999).

Obviously, affirmative action is still hotly contested—and defended—in higher education, even with legislation banning it in California and Washington and lawsuits filed against it in institutions across the nation. Without affirmative action, admissions numbers for students of color have plummeted, forcing campuses to devise creative—but not necessarily more effective— ways to reach out to underrepresented students. Critics continue to argue affirmative action's issues of legality. One way of analyzing this problem is to ask, What is the purpose of public higher education today? Whether affirmative action continues as a viable program into the future may depend on the answer to this fundamental question.

## References

The affirmative action and diversity project: A web page for research. 1998. *News and announcements: 1997.* Retrieved March 25, 1998 from http://humanitas.ucsb.edu/projects/aa/pages/news.html.

Aldave, Barbara B. 1996. *Hopwood v. Texas:* A victory for "equality" that denies reality—an afterword. *St. Mary's Law Journal* 28 (fall): 147–48.

Alger, Jonathan. 1999. *Affirmative action in higher education: A current legal overview.* Washington, DC: American Association of University Professors.

American Association of University Professors. 1997. *Resolution on affirmative action.* Passed at 83rd AAUP Annual Meeting, June, 1997. Washington, DC: Author.

Bowen, William G., and Derek Bok. 1998. *The shape of the river: Long-term consequences of considering race in college and university admissions.* Princeton, NJ: Princeton University Press.

Center for Individual Rights. 1998. *Racial preferences in higher education: A handbook for college and university trustees.* A Project of the Center for Individual Rights and the Pope Institute for the Future of Higher Education. Washington, DC: CIR/Pope Institute.

------. 1999a. *Civil rights principles and objectives.* Washington, DC: Author. Retrieved April 29, 1999, from http://www.wdn.com/cir/cr-aa.htm.

------. 1999b. *Memorandum of law in support of motion to intervene.* Washington, DC: Author. Retrieved April 29, 1999, from http://www.wdn.com/cir/uintmem.htm.

Cose, Ellis. 1997. *Color-blind: Seeing beyond race in a race-obsessed world.* New York: HarperCollins.

D'Souza, Dinesh. 1995. *The end of racism: Principles for a multiracial society.* New York: Free Press.

Greve, Michael S. 1996. Ruling out race: A bold step to making colleges color-blind. *Chronicle of Higher Education* (March 29): B2.

------. 1999. A river runs dry. *Policy Review* 94 (April/May): 77–82.

Hernandez, E., Jr. 1997. Growing gap seen between minority and White income. *Los Angeles Times,* May 11, A3, A25.

Kane, Thomas J. 1998. Misconceptions in the debate over affirmative action in college admissions. In Orfield and Miller, 17–31.

Kane, Thomas J., and William T. Dickens. 1997. *Racial and ethnic preference in college admissions.* Brookings Policy Brief, No. 9. Washington, DC: Brookings Institute.

Orfield, Gary, and Edward Miller. 1998. *Chilling admissions: The affirmative action crisis and the search for alternatives.* Cambridge: The Civil Rights Project, Harvard University/ Harvard Education Publishing Group.

Olivas, Michael A. 1997. Affirmative action: Diversity of opinions. *University of Colorado Law Review* 68, no. 4:1065–1122.

------. 1999. The legal environment: The implementation of legal change on campus. In *American higher education in the twenty-first century: Social, political, and economic challenges,* edited by Philip G. Altbach, Robert O. Berdahl, and Patricia J. Gumport, 216–40. Baltimore, MD: Johns Hopkins University Press.

------. In press. Higher education admissions and the search for one important thing. *University of Arkansas Law Review.*

Schrag, Peter. 1997. When preferences disappear. *American Prospect* 30 (January/February): 38–41.

------. The diversity defense. 1999. *American Prospect* 46 (September/October): 57–60.

Tierney, William G., and Jack Chung. In press. Review essay. [Review of William G. Bowen and Derek Bok, *The shape of the river: Long-term consequences of considering race in college and university admissions* and Gary Orfield and Edward Miller, *Chilling admissions: The affirmative action crisis and the search for alternatives*]. *Journal of Higher Education.*

Thernstrom, Abigail. 1998. A flawed defense of preferences. *Wall Street Journal,* October 2, A14.

Thernstrom, Stephan. 1998. Farewell to preferences? *Public Interest* 130 (winter): 34–49.

UCOP. University of California Office of the President. 1999. *Office of the president news.* Retrieved April 29, 1999: http://www.ucop.edu/

University of California: Black students moving down into the less selective campuses. 1998. *Journal of Blacks in Higher Education,* no. 19 (spring): 28.

University of Texas System. 1999, February. Reporting Package for the Board of Regents.

Weiss, Kenneth R. 1999. Minority admissions at UC almost at 1997 level. *Los Angeles Times,* April 3, A1, A17.

Wilbur, Susan, and Marguerite Bonous-Hammarth. 1998. Testing a new approach to admissions: The Irvine experience. In Orfield and Miller, 111–22.

# About the Contributors

## Editors

**William A. Smith** is Co-Director of the Center for the Study of Race and Diversity in Higher Education and an Assistant Professor at the University of Utah in the Department of Education, Culture, and Society and the Ethnic Studies Program. Dr. Smith's teaching and research interests are in the areas of social foundations and social justice of higher education, focusing on issues of diversity, gender, race, and student persistence. His current research focuses on inter-ethnic relations, racial attitudes, racial identity, academic colonialism, affirmative action, and the impact of student diversity on university and college campuses. He was awarded a postdoctoral research fellowship at the University of Illinois-Chicago's Center for Urban Educational Research and Development (CUERD) from 1997 to 1999. Dr. Smith's research efforts at CUERD have cumulated in articles, book chapters, and the initial development of this volume. Dr. Smith has taught in the African American Studies and Sociology departments at Western Illinois University. He can be reached at the Department of Education, Culture, and Society, University of Utah, 1705 E. Campus Center Drive, Rm. 307, Salt Lake City, UT 84112-9256; telephone: (801) 587-7814; e-mail: WASmith@ed.utah.edu.

**Philip G. Altbach** is J. Donald Monan SJ Professor of Higher Education and Director of the Center for International Higher Education at Boston College. Dr. Altbach is editor of the *Review of Higher Education* and has written widely on higher education issues. He is the author of *Comparative Higher Education, Student Politics in America, The Knowledge Context,* and other books.

**Kofi Lomotey** is currently the President of Fort Valley State University in Fort Valley, Georgia. He has also been the Senior Vice President and Provost at Medgar Evers College of the City University of New York. He previously taught at Louisiana State University, SUNY at Buffalo, and the University of California at Santa Cruz. Dr. Lomotey's research interests include African American principals, independent African-centered schools, and issues of race in higher education. He is the editor, coeditor, or author of seven books and has published numerous articles and book chapters. He edits *Urban Education* and is the Secretary/Treasurer of the Council of Independent Black Institutions (CIBI), an umbrella organization for independent African-centered schools.

## Authors

**Walter R. Allen,** Ph.D., is Professor of Sociology at the University of California, Los Angeles. He is codirector of CHOICES, a longitudinal study of college attendance among African Americans and Latinos in California. Dr. Allen's research and teaching focus on family patterns, socialization and personality development, race and ethnic relations, social inequality and higher education. Dr. Allen's more than eighty publications include *The Color Line and the Quality of Life in America* (1987), *Enacting Diverse Learning Environments: Improving the Climate for Racial/Ethnic Diversity in Higher Education Institutions* (1999), *College in Black and White* (1991), and *Black American Families, 1965–84* (1986). Dr. Allen has also been a consultant to industry, government, and the courts on issues related to race, education, and equity. His degrees in the field of sociology are from Beloit College (B.A., 1971) and the University of Chicago (M.A., 1973; Ph.D., 1975). Dr. Allen has held teaching appointments at the University of Michigan (1979–89) and the University of North Carolina (1974–79). Address queries to him at Department of Sociology, 2201 Hershey Hall, 610 Charles E. Young Drive, Los Angeles, CA 90095-1551.

**James D. Anderson,** Ph.D., is a Professor of the History of Education at the University of Illinois. He specializes in history of American education, history of African American education, and race in American life and culture. His current research interests include African American higher education. Selected publications include "Race, Meritocracy, and the American Academy during the Immediate Post–World War II Era," *History of Education Quarterly* 33, no. 2 (summer 1993): 151–75; "How We Learn about Race through History," in *Learning History in America,* edited by Lloyd Kramer, Donald Reid, and William Barney (Minneapolis: University of Minnesota Press, 1994), 87–106; and "Literacy and Education in the African American Experience," in *Literacy among African-American Youth,* edited by Vivian Gadsen (Cresskill, NJ: Hampton Press, 1995), 19–37. Professor Anderson received his doctorate from the University of Illinois in 1973.

**Marguerite Bonous-Hammarth,** Ph.D., is a Research Associate in the UCLA Department of Education, and Research Project Director for "CHOICES: Access, Equity and Diversity in Higher Education." Her research and teaching interests focus on the influence of individual and organizational value congruence or Person-Environment Fit, and on productivity and learning outcomes. She is a member of the W. K. Kellogg Forum on Higher Education Transformation, a multi-institutional, multi-researcher team examining organizational change and transformation. Dr. Bonous-Hammarth's recent publications include "Value Congruence and Organizational Climates for Undergraduate Persistence," in *Higher Education: Handbook of Theory and Research,* Vol. 15 (New York: Agathon, 2000); and "Testing a New Approach to Admissions: The Irvine Experience" with Susan Wilbur, in *Chilling Admissions: The Affirmative Action Crisis and the Search for Alternatives* (Boston, MA: The Civil Rights Project, Harvard University). She received her Ph.D. in Education from the Program in Higher Education and Organizational Change at UCLA. Address queries to her at 3101B Moore Hall, UCLA Graduate School of Education and Information Studies, Los Angeles, CA 90095; telephone: (310) 206-5114; e-mail: mbonoush@ucla.edu.

**Phillip J. Bowman,** Ph.D., is Professor of Urban Planning and Policy and African American Studies, and Director of the Institute for Research on Race and Public Policy at the University of Illinois at Chicago. Dr. Bowman received his Ph.D. in social psychology from the University of Michigan where he later directed a postdoctoral training program in survey research methodology and helped to develop a series of landmark national studies on African American life at the Institute for Social Research. He has held prior faculty appointments at the University of Michigan, University of Illinois at Urbana-Champaign, and Northwestern University in psychology, African American studies, and education and social policy. He has served as both a Rockefeller Foundation Fellow and Senior Ford Postdoctoral Fellow and continues to conduct studies that bridge social psychological theory and culturally sensitive research methods to address pressing race and public policy issues. Recent publications include: *Culturally Competent Research Methods* (1999); *Unmarried African American Fathers: A Comparative Life Span Analysis* (1998); *Instrumental and Expressive Family Roles among African American Fathers* (1997); and *Education and Responsible Fatherhood among African Americans: Socialization, Mobilization and Allocation Challenges* (1996). Professor Bowman is also an active national lecturer and consultant on cultural diversity issues in psychology, research methods, and urban public policy arenas such affirmative action, joblessness, and family poverty. Address queries to him at the Institute for Research on Race and Public Policy, College of Urban Planning and Public Affairs, University of Illinois at Chicago, Chicago, IL 60607; e-mail: pjbowman@uic.edu.

**Mitchell J. Chang,** Ph.D., is an Assistant Professor in the Graduate School of Education and Information Studies at the University of California, Los

Angeles. He has previously worked as a college administrator at Loyola Marymount University where he was Associate Dean in the College of Liberal Arts and Director of Asian American Studies, and as a school administrator for the Alum Rock Union Elementary School District in San Jose where he was a program evaluator. Professor Chang has researched, taught and written about the educational effects of diversity in higher education, racial representation and identity, and Asian American Studies. He was recently recognized for outstanding research by the American College Personnel Association. His book, *Compelling Interest: Examining the Evidence on Racial Dynamics in Higher Education* (Stanford University Press), examines the body of empirical evidence related to the affirmative action debates in higher education.

**Jack K. Chung** is a graduate student in the Rossier School of Education at the University of Southern California. His research interests pertain to issues of equity and the definition of merit.

**Dolores Delgado Bernal,** Ph.D., is a former elementary school teacher and community educator. She earned her Ph.D. and bilingual and cross-cultural teaching credential from UCLA. She has completed a Ford Postdoctoral Fellowship at the Center for Latino Policy Research at the University of California, Berkeley. She is an Assistant Professor at the University of Utah in the Department of Education, Culture and Society and the Ethnic Studies Program. Her research and teaching are in the area of social foundations and draw from critical race theory and Chicana feminist theories to examine and improve the educational experiences of Chicanas/os and other students of color. She has presented her work at numerous national conferences and is author of "Using a Chicana Feminist Epistemology in Educational Research," *Harvard Educational Review,* 68, no. 4 (1998). Address queries to her at Department of Education, Culture, and Society, University of Utah, 1705 E. Campus Center Dr., Rm 307, Salt Lake City, UT, 84112-9256; telephone: (801) 587-7814; e-mail: bernal_d@ed.utah.edu.

**Edgar G. Epps,** Ph.D., is a Professor of Educational Policy and Community Studies at the University of Wisconsin-Milwaukee (since 1999), and the Marshall Field IV Professor of Urban Education Emeritus at the University of Chicago, where he served on the faculty from 1970 to 1998. He has held faculty positions at Tuskegee University, the University of Michigan, Florida A&M University, and Tennessee State University. Dr. Epps was educated at Talladega College (Alabama), Atlanta University, and Washington State University, where he earned a Ph.D. in sociology. His books include *Black Students in White Schools*; *Cultural Pluralism*; *College in Black and White*; and *Black Consciousness, Identity, and Achievement*. Recent articles include "Race, Class, and Educational Opportunity," *Socological Forum* 10 (1995): 593–60 and "Affirmative Action and Minority Access to Faculty Positions," *Ohio State Law Journal,* 59, no. 3 (1998): 755–74. Dr. Epps has served as consultant to foundations and government agencies, and as an expert witness in the *Knight v. Alabama* higher education desegregation case. In 1996 he served as a member of the American Sociological Association's expert panel on Social Science Perspectives on Affirmative Action. Among other honors he has received a Mentor Award from the Spencer Foundation, and the DuBois, Johnson, Frazier Award of the American Sociological Association. Address queries to him at University of Wisconsin-Milwaukee, Department of Educational Policy and Community Studies, School of Education, P.O. Box 413, Milwaukee, WI 53201.

**Joe R. Feagin,** Ph.D., is currently the Graduate Research Professor in Sociology at the University of Florida. His research interests focus on racism and sexism issues. Recent publications include *Racial and Ethnic Relations* (6th ed. 1999, with Clairece Booher Feagin); *Living with Racism: The Black Middle Class Experience* (1994, with Mel Sikes); *White Racism: The Basics* (1995; with Hernán Vera); *Double Burden: Black Women and Everyday Racism* (1998, with Yanick St. Jean); *The Agony of Education: Black Students at White Colleges and Universities* (1996, with Hernán Vera and Nikitah Imani); and *The New Urban Paradigm* (1998). An earlier book, *Ghetto Revolts* (1973), was nominated for a Pulitzer Prize, and *Living with Racism* and *White Racism* have won the Gustavus Myers Center's Outstanding Human Rights Book Award. He is Past President of the American Sociological Association.

**John A. Freeman,** Ph.D., is Assistant Professor of Educational Leadership in the College of Education at the University of Alabama. A former K-12 administrator and State Department official, his teaching and research areas include the study of principalship, desegregation, economics of education, and school effectiveness and improvement. Address queries to him at University of Alabama, Area of Professional Studies, Box 870302, Tuscaloosa, AL 35487-0302; e-mail: jfreeman@bamaed.ua.edu.

**Elizabeth A. Guillory,** M.A., is a doctoral student in the Department of Sociology at the University of California, Los Angeles. Research interests include issues of race and gender in higher education with a focus on African American faculty and students. Current research includes a large-scale project on college choice, access, and attainment, incorporating both quantitative and qualitative analysis of various Los Angeles high schools. Future publications include a coauthored paper on the influence of race and gender on faculty status and satisfaction. Address queries to her at Department of Sociology, 2201 Hershey Hall, 610 Charles E. Young Drive, Los Angeles, CA 90095-1551.

**Sylvia Hurtado,** Ph.D., is Associate Professor and Director of the Center for the Study of Higher and Postsecondary Education at the University of Michigan. She is coauthor of *Enacting Diverse Learning Environments: Improving the Climate for Racial/Ethnic Diversity in Higher Education* (Ashe-Eric Report Series, 1999, with J. F. Milem, A. Clayton-Pederson, and W. Allen) and *Intergroup Dialogue: Deliberative Democracy in School, College, Workplace and Community* (forthcoming, University of Michigan Press) with D. Schoem. She has written numerous articles on student transition to college, access, and creating campus climates for learning among diverse peers. Dr. Hurtado has directed several national research projects including the National Study of Hispanic College Students, studying longitudinal cohorts of Latino students entering college in the 1990s. More recently, she directs a national project on how colleges are preparing college students to acquire the cognitive, social, and democratic skills necessary to participate in a diverse democracy. Address queries to her at: Center for the Study of Higher and Postsecondary Education, 610 E. University Ave, 2117 SEB, Ann Arbor, MI 48109–1259; telephone: 734-647-1647; fax: 734-754-2510; e-mail: hurtados@umich.edu.

**Nikitah Okembe-RA Imani,** Ph.D., is Assistant Professor of Sociology at James Madison University in Harrisonburg, Virginia, and Chief Minister of the Reapalife Ministries. His scholarly and personal interests focus on patterns of continuity between African traditional society and the diaspora with an eye toward using such research for the social, political, and economic advancement of all members of that collective. He coauthored *The Agony of Education* (1996), a study of African American students at predominantly Euro-American institutions. Dr. Imani received a BSFS degree in international politics from Georgetown University in 1989 and completed graduate work at the University of Florida where he received a master's degree in political science (1991), and master's and Ph.D. degrees in sociology (1992, 1995). He has published articles on the role of Eurocentric psychological assumptions in the *Brown v. Board of Education* decision, Eurocentrism in psychotherapy, the African griot origins of hip-hop culture, Africentric methodology, the social and psychological behavior of African American students in higher education, the Eurosupremacist elements of the vampire mythology, the inattention of environmental management officials to environmental justice issues, and Afrikan spiritual essentialism.

**Peter Nien-chu Kiang,** Ph.D., is Associate Professor at the University of Massachusetts at Boston where he teaches graduate courses in social studies curriculum design and directs the university's Asian American Studies Program. Professor Kiang's research, teaching, and advocacy related to Asian Americans in both K-12 and higher education have been honored or supported by the National Academy of Education, the National Endowment for the Humanities, the Massachusetts Teachers Association, the Massachusetts Association for Bilingual Education, the NAACP, the Anti-Defamation League, and others. He holds a B.A., Ed.M., and Ed.D. from Harvard University and is a former Community Fellow in the Department of Urban Studies and Planning at MIT.

**Shariba Rivers** is a doctoral candidate in the Educational Leadership Department at Louisiana State University in Baton Rouge. Her research interests include mentoring African American high school students for college attendance and independent African-centered schools. She has written and cowritten several articles and book chapters. Currently, she is the Principal of Sankofa Shule in Lansing, Michigan.

**James Joseph Scheurich**, Ph.D., is an Associate Professor in Educational Administration at the University of Texas at Austin, Coordinator of its Public School Executive Leadership Program, and Director of its Principalship Program. He is also the editor of the *International Journal of Qualitative Studies in Education*. He is the author of *Research Method in the Postmodern* and a coeditor of *The Knowledge Base in Educational Administration: Multiple Perspectives*. He is the author of articles in *Educational Researcher, Educational Administration Quarterly, Urban Education,* the *Journal of Education Policy,* and the *International Journal of Leadership in Education,* among others. His academic areas of focus are educational equity, particularly issues of white racism, and research methodology and epistemology. Address inquiries to him at Educational Administration, Sanchez 310, University of Texas at Austin, Austin, Texas 78712; telephone: (512) 475-8583; e-mail: jjs@ccwf.cc.utexas.edu.

**Tamara W. Schiff**, Ph.D., is a Research Associate at the Milken Family Foundation.

**Lewis C. Solmon**, Ph.D., is Senior Vice President and Senior Scholar at the Milken Family Foundation. He can be reached at 1250 Fourth Street, Santa Monica, CA 90401-1353; telephone: (310) 998-2800.

**Matthew S. Solmon** received his B. A. in economics from the University of Pennsylvania and is a law student at Arizona State University.

**Martha L. A. Stassen**, Ph.D., is Director of Assessment at the University of Massachusetts at Amherst and Adjunct Assistant Professor in the School of Education. Her research focuses on institutional and individual responses to racial diversity in higher education and on the evaluation of programmatic and pedagogical innovations. She was awarded the Dissertation of the Year from the Association for the Study of Higher Education (ASHE) for "White Faculty Members' Responses to Racial Diversity." Her publications include "White Faculty Members and Racial Diversity: A Theory and Its Implications," *Review of Higher Education* 18, no. 4 (1995): 361–91 and "It's Hard Work! Faculty Development in a Program for First-Year Students," *To Improve the Academy* 18 (1999): 254–77. Dr. Stassen received her Ph.D. in Higher Education from the University of Michigan. Address queries to her at Office of Academic Planning and Assessment, 237 Whitmore Administration Building, University of Massachusetts, Amherst, MA 01003.

**Susan A. Suh,** M.A., is a doctoral student in the Department of Sociology, University of California, Los Angeles. She received her M.A. from the department in 1996. Her thesis, "Impacts of Gender, Racial Group, and Class in Perceptions of Workplace Discrimination," will be published in an edited volume by the Russell Sage Foundation. Ms. Suh has collaborated with Lawrence Bobo and Walter R. Allen on articles about racial attitudes and higher education experiences of African Americans and Whites. Her research interests include the sociology of higher education, race/ethnicity theory, workplace experiences, and race/class/gender perspectives. Ms. Suh's dissertation will explore Asian Pacific American academics in higher education. Prior to her interests in academia, she worked as an engineer after receiving a B.S. from Columbia University. Address queries to her at Department of Sociology, 2201 Hershey Hall, 610 Charles E. Young Drive, Los Angeles, CA 90095-1551.

**Charles Teddlie,** Ph.D., is Professor of Educational Research Methodology in the College of Education at Louisiana State University. He has also served on the faculties of the University of New Orleans and the University of Newcastle (UK) and was Assistant Superintendent for Research and Development at the Louisiana Department of Education. He has authored over seventy-five chapters and articles and has coauthored or coedited six books, including *The International Handbook of School Effectiveness Research* (2000) and *Mixed Methodology: Combining Qualitative and Quantitative Approaches* (1998). He serves as the series editor for Readings on Equal Education. Address queries to him at Louisiana State University, College of Education, 111 Peabody Hall, Baton Rouge, LA 70803-4721; telephone: (225) 388-6840; e-mail: edtedd@unix1.sncc.lsu.edu.

**William G. Tierney,** Ph.D., is Wilbur-Kieffer Professor of Higher Education and Director of the Center for Higher Education Policy Analysis at the University of Southern California. He has written extensively on affirmative action and issues of access in higher education. The results of his work have appeared in the *Review of Educational Research, Educational Researcher,* and the *Journal of Negro Education.* He is currently involved in a project on increasing access to college for low-income urban youth, and a campus-based study about ways to diversify the faculty.

**Hernán Vera, Ph.D.,** is Professor of Sociology at the University of Florida. An award-winning teacher, he is also the author of six dozen articles and several books among which is *White Racism: The Basics,* which he coauthored with Joe R. Feagin (1995). He is currently working with Andrew Gordon, a literary and cinema critic, on *Sincere Fictions of the White Self in the American Cinema, 1915–2000.*

**Octavio Villalpando,** is Assistant Professor of Educational Leadership and Policy at the University of Utah and Co-director of the Center for the Study of Race and Diversity in Higher Education. His research contributes to the field of higher education around questions of how structural and racial inequality in colleges and universities shape the experiences of Chicana/o students and Chicano/a faculty, as well as other students and faculty of color. He employs Critical Race Theory and Latina/o Critical Theory as conceptual lenses in his research and utilizes both quantitative and qualitative research methods. He has worked as a research analyst at the UCLA Higher Education Research Institute, received a major doctoral research grant by the Spencer Foundation and AERA, and was recently awarded a postdoctoral research fellowship by the Ford Foundation. He has worked as an educator for over 15 years, including holding several leadership positions in higher education institutions, most recently serving on the staff of the president of California State University, Monterey Bay as Senior Research Scholar and founding Director of University Planning & Assessment.

**Charles V. Willie, Ph.D.,** is the Charles William Eliot Professor of Education Emeritus at the Harvard University Graduate School of Education. Dr. Willie was formerly chair of the Department of Sociology and Vice President of Syracuse University. He is a sociologist, Vice President of the American Sociological Association and a former member of its governing council, and Past President of the Eastern Sociological Society. He was appointed by President Jimmy Carter to the President's Commission on Mental Health and has been a member of the Board of Directors of the Social Science Research Council and an overseer of the Boston Science Museum. Among his areas of research, he includes school desegregation, higher education, health, race relations, urban community problems, and the family.

**Michelle D. Young, Ph.D.,** earned her Ph.D. from the University of Texas at Austin in Educational Policy and Planning. While at the University of Texas, she served as the Research Coordinator for the Effective Border Schools Research and Development Initiative and served as the managing editor of the *International Journal of Qualitative Studies in Education.* Dr. Young is presently executive director of the University Council for Educational Administration and a faculty member at the University of Missouri. Her scholarship focuses on how school leaders and school policies can ensure that students are well educated and treated equitably. Her work has been published in the *Review of Educational Research,* the *Educational Researcher,* the *American Educational Research Journal,* and the *International Journal of Qualitative Studies in Education,* among other publications.

# Index

Aaron, Charles, 154

academic rank. *See* "faculty of color" *and* "faculty" *subheadings under individual racial groups.*

activism, student, 32, 37, 105

*Adams v. Bell* (1982), 82

*Adams v. Califano* (1977), 82–83, 88–89, 93

*Adams v. Richardson* (1973), 82–83, 86

*Adams v. Weinberger* (1975), 82

admissions. *See* "enrollments" *subheading under individual racial groups and individual states.*

advising. *See* "faculty, advising" *subheading under individual racial groups,* "faculty of color," *and* "women faculty."

affirmative action

and Asian Americans, 145–47

as "moral imperative," 89, 96

backlash, xvi, 15–19, 24, 28, 30–31, 35–36, 60, 64, 83, 89, 104–6, 110–12, 138, 271–81

contributions, 14–15, 280–81

history, 11

legal challenges to, 16–17, 23, 82–86, 95, 146, 271–76, 280–81

and selective institutions, 62

support for, 60, 272, 276

and White women, 215–16

AAUP. *See* American Association of University Professors.

African Americans. *See* Blacks.

African Methodist Episcopal Zion church, 6

African Methodist Episcopal (AME) church, 6

Agassiz, Louis, 3

*Agony of Education: Black Students at White Colleges and University, The,* 289

Alabama A&M, 8

Alabama, enrollments, 7, 9, 58

Alabama State Teachers College, 8

Alaska, enrollments, 58, 60

Alaskan Natives, 13–14, 72–73. *See also* "students of color" *and* "Native Americans."

Alcorn College, 9

Alger, Jon, 271

alien (nonresident) faculty, 73

Allen University, 6

Allen, Walter R., 10, 194, 217, 247, 286, 290, 292

Altbach, Philip G., 138, 285, 243

American Association of University Professors (AAUP), 275–76

American Baptist Home Mission Society, 6–7

American Civil Liberties Union, 276

American College Personnel Association, 288

American Council on Education (ACE), 72, 90, 138, 143

American Educational Research Association (AERA), 293

*American Educational Research Journal,* 294

American Indian Survey, 253

American Indians. *See* "Alaskan Natives," "Native Americans," "students of color," *and* "faculty of color."

American Missionary Association, 6

# SUNY series, Frontiers in Education
Philip G. Altbach, Editor

**List of Titles**

*College in Black and White: African American Students in Predominantly White and in Historically Black Public Universities*—Walter R. Allen, Edgar G. Epps, and Nesha Z. Haniff (eds.)

*Critical Perspectives on Early Childhood Education*—Lois Weis, Philip G. Altbach, Gail P. Kelly, and Hugh G. Petrie (eds.)

*Textbooks in American Society: Politics, Policy, and Pedagogy*—Philip G. Altbach, Gail P. Kelly, Hugh G. Petrie, and Lois Weis (eds.)

*Black Resistance in High School: Forging a Separatist Culture*—R. Patrick Solomon

*Emergent Issues in Education: Comparative Perspectives*—Robert F. Arnove, Philip G. Altbach, and Gail P. Kelly (eds.)

*Creating Community on College Campuses*—Irving J. Spitzberg Jr. and Virginia V. Thorndike

*Teacher Education Policy: Narratives, Stories, and Cases*—Hendrik D. Gideonse (ed.)

*Beyond Silenced Voices: Class, Race, and Gender in United States Schools*—Lois Weis and Michelle Fine (eds.)

*The Cold War and Academic Governance: The Lattimore Case at Johns Hopkins*—Lionel S. Lewis

*Troubled Times for American Higher Education: The 1990s and Beyond*—Clark Kerr

*Higher Education Cannot Escape History: Issues for the Twenty-first Century*—Clark Kerr

*Multiculturalism and Education: Diversity and Its Impact on Schools and Society*—Thomas J. LaBelle and Christopher R. Ward

*The Contradictory College: The Conflicting Origins, Impacts, and Futures of the Community College*—Kevin J. Dougherty

*Race and Educational Reform in the American Metropolis: A Study of School Decentralization*—Dan A. Lewis and Kathryn Nakagawa

*Professionalization, Partnership, and Power: Building Professional Development Schools*—Hugh G. Petrie (ed.)

*Ethnic Studies and Multiculturalism*—Thomas J. LaBelle and Christopher R. Ward

*Promotion and Tenure: Community and Socialization in Academe*—William G. Tierney and Estela Mara Bensimon

*Sailing Against the Wind: African Americans and Women in U.S. Education*—Kofi Lomotey (ed.)

*The Challenge of Eastern Asian Education: Implications for America*—William K. Cummings and Philip G. Altbach (eds.)

*Conversations with Educational Leaders: Contemporary Viewpoints on Education in America*—Anne Turnbaugh Lockwood

*Managed Professionals: Unionized Faculty and Restructuring Academic Labor*—Gary Rhoades

*The Curriculum: Problems, Politics, and Possibilities* (2nd ed.)—Landon E. Beyer and Michael W. Apple (eds.)

*Education/Technology/Power: Educational Computing as a Social Practice*—Hank Bromley and Michael W. Apple (eds.)

*Capitalizing Knowledge: New Intersections of Industry and Academia*—Henry Etzkowitz, Andrew Webster, and Peter Healey (eds.)

*The Academic Kitchen: A Social History of Gender Stratification at the University of California, Berkeley*—Maresi Nerad

*Grass Roots and Glass Ceilings: African American Administrators in Predominantly White Colleges and Universities*—William B. Harvey (ed.)

*Community Colleges as Cultural Texts: Qualitative Explorations of Organizational and Student Culture*—Kathleen M. Shaw, James R. Valadez, and Robert A. Rhoads (eds.)

*Educational Knowledge: Changing Relationships between the State, Civil Society, and the Educational Community*—Thomas S. Popkewitz (ed.)

*Transnational Competence: Rethinking the U.S.-Japan Educational Relationship*—John N. Hawkins and William K. Cummings (eds.)

*Women Administrators in Higher Education: Historical and Contemporary Perspectives*—Jana Nidiffer and Carolyn Terry Bashaw (eds.)

*Faculty Work in Schools of Education: Rethinking Roles and Rewards for the Twenty-First Century*—William G. Tierney (ed.)

*The Quest for Equity in Higher Education: Towards New Paradigms in an Evolving Affirmative Action Era*—Beverly Lindsay and Manuel J. Justiz (eds.)